Clemson
christologies priest/laos — (49)

issue for me
- difference between "a priestly people"
  and "a community of priests"
  (Clemson seems to go for the former? — (contra p.53?)
   so - actually - does Hebrews)

focus in Clemson still priest/laity (with some
                                    discuss. of laities
(see also Pholo, p.68)              with priests)

Sic as Hebrews it's Christ/people (with full inclusion)

p.124 - it's High-priestly access - not priestly! (contra
                                                  Schütz)
p.90 - seems a weird error?

# JOURNAL FOR THE STUDY OF THE NEW TESTAMENT
## SUPPLEMENT SERIES
## 49

*Executive Editor, Supplement Series*
David Hill

*Publishing Editor*
David E Orton

JSOT Press
Sheffield

# PROLEPTIC PRIESTS

Priesthood in the
Epistle to the Hebrews

John M. Scholer

Journal for the Study of the New Testament
Supplement Series 49

Copyright © 1991 Sheffield Academic Press

Published by JSOT Press
JSOT Press is an imprint of
Sheffield Academic Press Ltd
The University of Sheffield
343 Fulwood Road
Sheffield S10 3BP
England

Typeset by Sheffield Academic Press
and
Printed on acid-free paper in Great Britain
by Billing & Sons Ltd
Worcester

British Library Cataloguing in Publication Data
Scholer, John M.
　Proleptic Priests.
　1. Bible. N.T. Hebrews
　I. Title II. Series
　222

ISSN 0143-5108
ISBN 1-85075-266-4

CONTENTS

Abbreviations 7

INTRODUCTION 9

Chapter 1
THE PRIESTHOOD IN THE EXTRA-NEW TESTAMENT LITERATURE 13
1. The Priesthood in the Old Testament 13
2. The Priesthood in Pseudepigraphical Literature 23
3. The Priesthood in Rabbinic Literature 29
4. The Priesthood in the Qumran Literature 35
5. The Priesthood in Philo 63
6. The Priesthood in the Mystery Religions 71

Chapter 2
THE HIGH PRIEST CHRISTOLOGY IN HEBREWS 82
1. The Heavenly High Priesthood 83
2. The Earthly High Priest 85
3. The Son and Sons 89

Chapter 3
ΠΡΟΣΕΡΧΕΣΘΑΙ AND HEBREWS 91
1. Προσέρχεσθαι in the LXX 91
2. Προσέρχεσθαι in Hebrews 95

Chapter 4
ΕΙΣΕΡΧΕΣΘΑΙ AND HEBREWS 150
1. Εἰσέρχεσθαι in the LXX 150
2. Εἰσέρχεσθαι in Hebrews 153

| | |
|---|---|
| Chapter 5 | |
| ΤΕΛΕΙΟΥΝ AND HEBREWS | 185 |
|   1. Τελειοῦν and its Meaning | 187 |
|   2. Τελειοῦν in Hebrews | 195 |
| CONCLUSION | 201 |
| Bibliography | 208 |
| Index of Biblical References | 221 |
| Index of Authors | 239 |

## ABBREVIATIONS

| | |
|---|---|
| AI | R. de Vaux, *Ancient Israel* |
| ALGHJ | Arbeiten zur Literatur und Geschichte des hellenistischen Judentums |
| AnBib | Analecta Biblica |
| BA | *Biblical Archaeologist* |
| BAG | (W. Bauer), W.F. Arndt and F.W. Gingrich, *A Greek–English Lexicon of the New Testament* |
| BARev | *Biblical Archaeology Review* |
| BASOR | *Bulletin of the American Schools of Oriental Research* |
| BBB | Bonner Biblische Beiträge |
| BDB | F. Brown, S.R. Driver and C.A. Briggs, *A Hebrew and English Lexicon of the Old Testament* |
| BDF | F. Blass, A. Debrunner and R. Funk, *A Greek Grammar of the New Testament and Other Early Christian Literature* |
| BJRL | *Bulletin of the John Rylands University Library of Manchester* |
| BZ | *Biblische Zeitschrift* |
| BZNW | Beihefte zur Zeitschrift für die neutestamentliche Wissenschaft |
| CBQ | *Catholic Biblical Quarterly* |
| CBQMS | *Catholic Biblical Quarterly* Monograph Series |
| EPROER | Etudes préliminaires aux religions orientales dans l'empire Romain |
| EvQ | *Evangelical Quarterly* |
| EWzNT | *Exegetisches Wörterbuch zum Neuen Testament* |
| ExpTim | *Expository Times* |
| FRLANT | Forschungen zur Religion und Literatur des Alten und Neuen Testaments |
| Heb. | The Epistle to the Hebrews |
| HNT | Handbuch zum Neuen Testament |
| HTR | *Harvard Theological Review* |
| IBSt | *Irish Biblical Studies* |
| ICC | International Critical Commentary |
| IDB | *Interpreter's Dictionary of the Bible* |
| Int | *Interpretation* |
| ISBE | *International Standard Bible Encyclopedia* |
| JBL | *Journal of Biblical Literature* |
| JJS | *Journal of Jewish Studies* |
| JQR | *Jewish Quarterly Review* |

| | |
|---|---|
| *JSNT* | *Journal for the Study of the New Testament* |
| JSOTSup | *Journal for the Study of the Old Testament* Supplement Series |
| LCL | Loeb Classical Library |
| LXX | The Septuagint |
| MeyerK | H.A.W. Meyer, *Kritisch-exegetischer Kommentar über das Neue Testament* |
| MT | The Masoretic Text |
| *MTZ* | *Münchener Theologische Zeitschrift* |
| *Neot* | *Neotestamentica* |
| NICNT | New International Commentary on the New Testament |
| NICOT | New International Commentary on the Old Testament |
| *NIDNTT* | *New International Dictionary of New Testament Theology* |
| *NovT* | *Novum Testamentum* |
| NTAbh | Neutestamentliche Abhandlungen |
| NTD | Das Neue Testament Deutsch |
| *NTS* | *New Testament Studies* |
| *Numen* | *Numen: International Review for the History of Religions* |
| OTL | Old Testament Library |
| *OTPseud* | *Old Testament Pseudepigrapha* |
| *RB* | *Revue Biblique* |
| *RevQ* | *Revue de Qumran* |
| *RGG* | *Religion in Geschichte und Gegenwart* |
| RSV | The Revised Standard Version |
| SBLDS | Society of Biblical Literature Dissertation Series |
| SNT | Studien zum Neuen Testament |
| SNTSMS | Society for New Testament Studies Monograph Series |
| Str–B | H. Strack and P. Billerbeck, *Kommentar zum Neuen Testament aus Talmud und Midrasch* |
| SUNT | Studien zur Umwelt des Neuen Testaments |
| *TD* | *Theology Digest* |
| *TDNT* | *Theological Dictionary of the New Testament* |
| *TDOT* | *Theological Dictionary of the Old Testament* |
| *THAT* | *Theologisches Handwörterbuch zum Alten Testament* |
| *TRu* | *Theologische Rundschau* |
| *TWAT* | *Theologisches Wörterbuch zum Alten Testament* |
| *TZ* | *Theologische Zeitschrift* |
| *VT* | *Vetus Testamentum* |
| *WTJ* | *Westminster Theological Journal* |
| WMANT | Wissenschaftliche Monographien zum Alten und Neuen Testament |
| WUNT | Wissenschaftliche Untersuchungen zum Neuen Testament |
| *ZNW* | *Zeitschrift für die neutestamentliche Wissenschaft* |

INTRODUCTION

Scholarly investigation in the Epistle to the Hebrews (hereafter cited as Heb.) has preoccupied itself with the high priesthood of Christ.[1] This is certainly understandable in light of the central importance of the high priestly motif throughout Heb. In fact, it would not be incorrect to affirm that all other cultic references and allusions in Heb. are ancillary to the high priestly category. Were Jesus Christ not high priest, there would be no reason for any further consideration of things cultic, much less any purpose in depicting the recipients of the Epistle as priests.

A cursory perusal of the literature reveals the near complete dearth of works dealing with the priestly status of the readership in Heb. To our knowledge, only three articles have been written in this century that concern themselves with any extended investigation of the priesthood. The articles by Olaf Moe,[2] Ernest Best,[3] and L. Floor[4] are all very general and introductory in nature. On the one hand, not a single monograph on the subject of the priesthood of the readers of Heb. has appeared. On the other hand, works of all sorts dealing with every imaginable aspect of the nature of Christ's priesthood have appeared.

The reason for this situation is, of course, clear enough. The high priesthood of Christ is explicit in Heb. and the author goes to great

---

1. For a good review of introductory matters in Heb. refer to C. Spicq, *L'Epître aux Hébreux* (2 vols.; Paris: Libraire Lecoffre, J. Gabalda, 1952), especially vol. 1 (hereafter cited as Spicq, *L'Epître*); E. Grässer, 'Der Hebräerbrief 1938–1963', *TRu* (N.F.) 30 (1964), pp. 138-236 (hereafter cited as Grässer, 'Der Hebräerbrief'); J.C. McCullough, 'Some Recent Developments in Research on the Epistle to the Hebrews', *IBSt* 2 (1980), pp. 141-65, and 'Some Recent Developments in Research on the Epistle to the Hebrews: II', *IBSt* 3 (1981), pp. 28-45.

2. O. Moe, 'Der Gedanke des allgemeinen Priestertums im Hebräerbrief', *TZ* 5 (1949), pp. 161-69.

3. E. Best, 'Spiritual Sacrifice: General Priesthood in the New Testament', *Int* 14 (1960), pp. 273-99.

4. L. Floor, 'The General Priesthood of Believers in the Epistle to the Hebrews', *Neot* 5 (1971), pp. 72-82.

lengths to portray this high priesthood in a unique fashion. But, in contrast, the priestly status of the readership is never once mentioned or considered explicitly. The readers are not designated 'priests' as is the practice in certain other works of the New Testament.[1] Instead, the priesthood remains an implicit assertion. As will be seen, we believe that the application of cultic language (προσέρχεσθαι, εἰσέρχεσθαι, and τελειοῦν) is convincing evidence that betrays the intention of the author regarding his readers. From where the author derived his notion of priesthood, and why he applied it specifically to the recipients of his letter, are matters to be investigated in this book.

Chapter 1 will examine the role and function of the priesthood as portrayed in various extra-New Testament sources: Old Testament, Pseudepigraphical literature, Rabbinic literature, Qumran, Philo, and Mystery Religions. We shall observe that Heb. most probably constructs its argument for the priesthood of the readers already on the basis of the form and function of the priesthood in the Old Testament. To be sure, similarities to Heb. may be found in all of the above traditions (e.g. Ceslas Spicq,[2] Ronald Williamson,[3] Herbert Braun,[4] Otto Michel,[5] Otfried Hofius,[6] and Ernst Käsemann[7]), but even the

---

1. 1 Pet. 2.5, 9; Rev. 1.5; 5.10; 20.6. See the important work, E.S. Fiorenza, *Priester für Gott: Studien zum Herrschafts- und Priestermotiv in der Apokalypse* (NTAbh, 7; Münster: Aschendorff, 1972), hereafter cited as Fiorenza, *Priester*, which although primarily concerned with the Revelation of John makes frequent reference to the verses in 1 Pet. Also see A. Vanhoye, *Old Testament Priests and the New Priest: According to the New Testament* (trans. J.B. Orchard Petersham, MA: St Bede's, 1986).
2. Spicq, *L'Épître*.
3. R. Williamson, *Philo and the Epistle to the Hebrews* (ALGHJ, 4; Leiden: Brill, 1970), hereafter cited as Williamson, *Philo*.
4. H. Braun, *Qumran und das Neue Testament* (2 vols.; Tübingen: Mohr [Paul Siebeck], 1966), hereafter cited as Braun, *Qumran*; and *An die Hebräer* (HNT, 14; Tübingen: Mohr [Paul Siebeck], 1984), hereafter cited as Braun, *Hebräer*.
5. O. Michel, *Der Brief an die Hebräer* (MeyerK, 13; 14th edn; Göttingen: Vandenhoeck & Ruprecht, 1984), hereafter cited as Michel, *Kommentar*.
6. O. Hofius, *Katapausis. Die Vorstellung vom endzeitlichen Ruheort im Hebräerbrief* (WUNT, 11; Tübingen: Mohr [Paul Siebeck], 1970), hereafter cited as Hofius, *Katapausis*; and *Der Vorhang vor dem Thron Gottes: Eine exegetisch-religionsgeschichtliche Untersuchung zu Hebräer 6,19f. und 10,19f.* (WUNT, 14; Tübingen: Mohr [Paul Siebeck], 1972), hereafter cited as Hofius, *Der Vorhang*.
7. E. Käsemann, *The Wandering People of God: An Investigation of the Letter to the Hebrews* (trans. R.A. Harrisville and I.L. Sandberg; Minneapolis: Augsburg, 1984), hereafter cited as Käsemann, *The Wandering People*.

background of these traditions finds a common foundation in the Old Testament.

Since Heb. never addresses the readers as priests, but rather with cultic allusions, our task will differ somewhat from studies of 1 Peter and Revelation where 'priests' is expressly applied, and where the use of Exod. 19.6 or Isa. 61.6 may be discerned. Therefore, Chapter 2 will initiate our look into the reasons why Heb. refers to the readers using cultic terminology. Here, we shall observe the rationale for any cultic imagery in the Epistle—it is inextricably related to the early ὁμολογία with which the author and his readers were quite familiar. It appears that the liturgical faith-profession of Christ as high priest was a central tenet in the community's faith. Precisely because this high priest was a 'Son' and also a 'brother' (e.g. 2.10-18), his high priestly lineage also had a bearing on his 'brothers'. By virtue of their relatedness to the high priest, they are entitled to be 'priests' also. Our further investigation will help to establish this point.

In Chapter 3 the term used exclusively of the readership, προσέρχεσθαι (4.16; 7.25; 10.1, 22; 11.6; 12.18, 22), will be investigated. The tendency of most scholars to cite certain occurrences as cultic while demurring on others, will be shown to be unwarranted. Every occurrence of προσέρχεσθαι has its setting within the cultic context (including the single occurrence of ἐγγίζειν at 7.19). Furthermore, a correspondence between the cultic usages of προσέρχεσθαι in the LXX and in Heb. will lead us to conclude that the term refers to a preliminary access into the holy of holies, into the direct presence of God through inner spiritual service such as worship and prayer, to be superseded by a still future and greater access.

At the same time, we shall observe that Heb. employs εἰσέρχεσθαι at times in a manner synonymous with προσέρχεσθαι, but at other times in the aorist tense, in order to emphasize the prerequisite death of the person who enters. In Chapter 4, then, the cultic occurrences of εἰσέρχεσθαι (6.19-20; 9.12, 24, 25; 10.19) are shown also to express the access available to believers, although it primarily describes an access afforded those who have died, and who now reside in the presence of God (e.g. 12.22-24). This corresponds with the characteristic differentiation made in the LXX with the occasional usage of εἰσέρχεσθαι cultically. But regardless of any inherent distinctions between 'drawing near' and 'entering', both describe the situation of Christians prior to the Day of Judgment, the Parousia, the End of Time. So then, the use of Old Testament typology in Heb. appears much more suggestive than any Hellenistic, spatial typology. This is readily discernible from the apocalyptic and eschatological references scattered throughout the Epistle.

τελειοῦν will be considered in Chapter 5. There it is observed that Heb. employs the term with a consistency of meaning throughout.[1] When occurring with respect to the readers it mirrors the Epistle's cultic usage of προσέρχεσθαι. When concerned with those deceased it parallels the cultic εἰσέρχεσθαι in Heb. Yet, because the goal is not yet reached, and in light of what must yet take place, τελειοῦν is seen to characterize a preliminary stage in the chronology of the eschatological age, i.e. the age of salvation. At the End, when 'rest' comes, the final state of 'perfection' will be attained. Then access to God in perpetuity will be realized.

In our Conclusion, we shall further establish the importance of the eschatological dimension for Heb.,[2] by suggesting precisely why 'perfection' is not κατάπαυσις. We argue that the author of Heb. had a very sound reason for distinguishing between the 'rest' and 'perfection' in his missive to this specific circle of readers. Our work here is but a small step in the advance toward the ascertaining of the situation of the readership of Heb. The relevance of Heb. as a 'word of exhortation' for a church gone awry, not only in the first century but in every age, bespeaks the importance of our endeavor and the necessity of our task.

---

1. See D. Peterson, *Hebrews and Perfection: An Examination of the Concept of Perfection in the 'Epistle to the Hebrews'* (SNTSMS, 47; Cambridge: Cambridge University Press, 1982).
2. H.W. Attridge, 'New Covenant Christology in an Early Christian Homily', *Quarterly Review* 8 (1988), p. 99 (hereafter cited as Attridge, 'New Covenant'), too readily dismisses the eschatological emphasis in Heb. saying, 'He is not engaged in an analysis or theological critique of his own or his community's eschatology, which is apparently a somewhat Hellenized or philosophically interpreted version of apocalyptic hopes for deliverance from the world of change, decay, and oppression'. This ignores the eschatological allusions that occur throughout Heb. Also see H.W. Attridge, *The Epistle to the Hebrews* (Hermeneia; Philadelphia: Fortress, 1989), pp. 27-28, hereafter cited as Attridge, *Hebrews*.

Chapter 1

THE PRIESTHOOD IN THE EXTRA-NEW TESTAMENT LITERATURE

The idea of believers in Christ comprising a priesthood was not a creation from nothing. Studies in the history of religions have shown the inadvisability of ignoring the interplay and influence which other traditions and cultures exerted upon peoples existing at the same time or at a later period. It is with this self-evident assumption that we introduce our study of the priesthood in Heb., by looking initially at the priesthood in other traditions either antecedent to or simultaneous with the earliest Christian literary writings.

This first chapter will examine the priesthood in several different traditions with a particular interest in points of contact regarding priestly roles and functions.

### 1. *The Priesthood in the Old Testament*

It is beyond the scope of this preliminary investigation to occupy ourselves with the historical development of the Israelite priesthood— a virtually inscrutable problem. First, many such works on the subject are already available.[1] Second, we shall be concerned more properly

---

1. See especially A. Cody, *A History of the Old Testament Priesthood* (AnBib, 35; Rome: Pontifical Biblical Institute, 1969), hereafter cited as Cody, *A History*; R. de Vaux, *Ancient Israel* (2 vols.; New York: McGraw-Hill, 1961), 2.345-405 (hereafter cited as de Vaux, *AI*); L. Sabourin, *Priesthood: A Comparative Study* (Studies in the History of Religions [Supplements to *Numen*], 25; Leiden: E.J. Brill, 1973), pp. 98-157; W.G. Baudissin, 'Priests and Levites', *A Dictionary of the Bible: Dealing with its Language, Literature and Contents including the Biblical Theology* (ed. J. Hastings and J.A. Selbie; New York: Charles Scribner's Sons, 1899–1904), 4.667-97, and *Die Geschichte des alttestamentlichen Priesterthums* (Leipzig: Hirzel, 1889). Other helpful investigations include: J. Wellhausen, *Prolegomena to the History of Ancient Israel: with a Reprint of the Article Israel from the Encyclopaedia Britannica* (trans. J. Sutherland Black and A. Menzies; Edinburgh: A. & C. Black, 1885), pp. 121-51; J. Pedersen, *Israel: Its Life and Culture* (London: Oxford

with the role, character and function of the priesthood which can be discerned from the Old Testament scriptures and which served as a possible background and influence for the succeeding intertestamental and New Testament periods.

The irreconcilable inconsistencies in the historical origin of priests and the priesthood, according to the Old Testament picture, find at least a common thread in the priests' relationship to the tribe of Levi. Priesthood in the Old Testament was a hereditary office. The levite priest in Judges 17–18 was succeeded by his sons (Judg. 18.30), Eli and his sons served as priests at Shiloh (1 Sam. 1–2), and Aaron and his sons were depicted as priests, as was the Zadokite line. The special role of the tribe of Levi was seen in its having been set aside for divine service.[1] The importance of this Levite ancestry for priests is seen by the genealogical connection to the family of Levi of any personage who may appear priestly in the Old Testament.[2] Therefore, however muddled the historical picture, the hereditary lineage of priests remains fairly consistent: only descendants of the tribe of Levi possess legitimate access to the priesthood throughout the history of Israel,[3] excluding those barred from service because of physical or other defect (Lev. 21.16-24).

University Press, 1926–40), 2.150-97; G.B. Gray, *Sacrifice in the Old Testament: Its Theory and Practice* (Oxford: Clarendon, 1925), pp. 179-270; W. Eichrodt, *Theology of the Old Testament* (trans. J.A. Baker; Philadelphia: Westminster, 1961), 1.392-436; A.H.J. Gunneweg, *Leviten und Priester: Hauptlinien der Traditionsbildung und Geschichte des israelitisch-jüdischen Kultpersonals* (FRLANT, 89; Göttingen: Vandenhoeck & Ruprecht, 1965); H.-J. Kraus, *Worship in Israel* (Richmond: John Knox, 1966), pp. 93-112; G. Schrenk, 'ἱερεύς, ἀρχιερεύς', *TDNT* (ed. G. Kittel and G. Friedrich; trans. G.W. Bromiley; Grand Rapids: Eerdmans, 1964–1976), 3.257-283; M. Noth, 'Office and Vocation in the Old Testament', in *The Laws in the Pentateuch and Other Studies* (trans. D.R. Ap-Thomas; Edinburgh: Oliver & Boyd, 1966), pp. 229-48; R. Abba, 'Priests and Levites', *IDB* (New York and Nashville: Abingdon, 1962–76), 3.876-89; and M. Haran, 'Priests and Priesthood', *Encyclopaedia Judaica* (New York: Macmillan, 1972), 13.1065-76.

1. Num. 3.11-13, 41; 8.16; Exod. 13.2; 22.29b-30; 34.19-20. Num. 8.16 relates how the members of the tribe of Levi became representatives of all the firstborn of Israel; hence the relevance of the above mentioned passages from Exodus.

2. Moses: Exod. 2.1; 6.19-25; Aaron: Exod. 4.14; 6.19-25; 28.1; Samuel: 1 Chron. 6.7-13, 18-23, 33-38 (although Cody [*A History*, p. 78], does not see Samuel as a priest, but as a temple servant); Eli: 1 Sam. 1.3; 2.27; 4.4, 11, 17; Zadok: 2 Sam. 6.7-13; 15.2-4; 1 Chron. 24.3.

3. We ought not to confuse the right to priesthood with priestly activities themselves. It is evident that the Old Testament depicts assorted non-levites performing

# 1. The Priesthood in the Extra-NT Literature 15

The procedure for installation to the priestly office is described as 'filling the hand' of the priest, *millē' yād*. The LXX takes over this Hebrew expression and renders it with πληροῦν τὰς χεῖρας, ἐμπιμπλάναι τὰς χεῖρας,[1] and τελειοῦν τὰς χεῖρας.[2] To 'fill one's hand' was the rite by which one became a priest; the victims for sacrifice were placed in the prospective priest's hands and he then proceeded to minister at the altar. This ritual initiation into the cultus conferred upon a man the priestly prerogative.[3]

The feature most characteristic of the priest was his holiness. The fact that a man possessed priestly power which permitted him access to the sacred domain and to the most holy objects presupposed his own holiness. This priestly holiness was required of the priests because Yahweh's very presence, his 'Shekinah', rested on the holy of holies, and spread out with a diminishing intensity in concentric rings from there, necessitating comparable degrees of holiness and purity from any person entering into the holy spheres.[4] Eleazar was made holy (*qiddēš*; ἅγιος [LXX]) for his care of the Ark (1 Sam. 7.1). The headdress of Aaron had engraved upon it 'sanctified for Yahweh', ἁγίασμα κυρίου (Exod. 28.36). Priestly consecration went hand in hand with the prerogative of service to God, who was holy.[5] This is similarly expressed by *bādal* (διαστέλλειν [LXX]), to 'separate' or 'set apart for God'.[6] The concept of anointing is also related to holiness,

---

sacrificial functions, for instance: Gen. 22.31, 54; 46.1; Judg. 6.20-28; 1 Sam. 6.14-15; 1 Kgs 1.9; 18.30-38. M. Haran (pp. 1071-73) ties this discrepancy to the distinction between an altar and a temple structure. Priests could offer sacrifices at temples, but anyone was free to sacrifice without a mediating priest at an open-air altar. However, before the cultic centralization under Josiah, the role of the priest and just who constituted a priest was not so clearly defined, in light of the plethora of sanctuaries in Israel. See Exod. 28.1; 29.9; 32.25-29; 40.15.

1. Judg. 17.5,12; 1 Kgs 13.33; 1 Chron. 29.5; 2 Chron. 13.9; 29.31; Ezek. 32.29; 43.26.
2. Exod. 29.9, 29, 33, 35; Lev. 4.5; 8.33; 16.32; Num. 3.3.
3. The original meaning of *millē' yād* is much disputed. See details in de Vaux, *AI*, 2.346-48; Sabourin, pp. 137-38; Cody, *A History*, pp. 153-54; Gray, pp. 249-50; and other works. However, the meaning seems to have been understood to be the investing of men with the priestly prerogative at the time of the LXX. At Ezek. 43.26 (LXX), καὶ πλήσουσι χεῖρας αὐτῶν ('and they shall consecrate themselves') occurs, while in the Hebrew text the term is describing their consecrating of the altar.
4. Pedersen, *Israel*, 3–4.257-58.
5. Exod. 21.15; 28.41; 29.1, 44; 40.13; Lev. 21.6.
6. Deut. 10.8; Lev. 8; Num. 8.5-7; 16.9; 1 Chron. 23.13.

holiness, for the Priestly Document describes the anointing of both the priests and the high priest,[1] and this results in their separation from the non-priest and their special status.[2]

Priests were those men who were holy, who had separated themselves or been separated from things profane, and this separation permitted them approach to divine service within the sacred realm and with the holy objects.[3] The priests were called 'ministers' of God[4] and were also described as ministering to and serving God.[5] They also 'stand before Yahweh' (Deut. 18.5, 7).

The priestly holiness was contingent upon the priest's own constant purity: therefore special proscriptions applied to priests and the high priests.[6] Until his uncleanness was purged, a priest was prohibited from all holy service. Thus the sanctity of God's sanctuary was maintained.

The service and function of a priest was linked to his attachment to a particular sanctuary. This was not only obvious at the time of the centralized cultus in the Temple at Jerusalem, but from the earliest traditions. At Judges 17 Micah installs his own son as priest of his sanctuary but later employs the sojourning Levite as attendant priest. This same Levite eventually became the sanctuary attendant at Dan (Judg. 18.30). The wilderness account in the Pentateuch shows the close connection the priestly personnel had to the tent of meeting and its accoutrements. Priests were always in the nearest proximity to the tent, and were responsible for the transporting of it and the Ark.[7] In fact, it appears that the presence of the Ark or tent implied a priestly attendant. Such was the case at Shiloh (1 Sam. 1–2), at Kiriath-jearim (1 Sam. 7.1), and at Jerusalem.[8]

---

1. Exod. 28.41; 29.7, 21; 40.12-15; Lev. 8.12, 30; and others.
2. Noth ('Office and Vocation', p. 239) observes that the conception of anointing implied the transfer or bestowal of a 'vital energy' that placed the priest above other persons.
3. Exod. 28.2, 38; 29.34, 37; 30.10, 35; Lev. 24.9; Num. 4.15.
4. Isa. 61.6; Jer. 31.21-22; Joel 1.9, 13; 2.17.
5. Deut. 10.8; 17.12; 18.5, 7; 21.5; Num. 4.4; 8.11; Josh. 22.27; 1 Chron. 24.3; 2 Chron. 35.16; Ezek. 40.40; 43.19; 44.15, 16.
6. Exod. 28.43; 30.17-21; 40.31-32; Lev. 8.6; 10.8-11; 21.1-6, 7; Num. 8.7.
7. Num. 1.50-53; 3.9, 21-26, 31, 32, 38; 4.5-15, 22-23; Deut. 10.8; 31.9, 25-26. See also in Josh. 3.3, 14; 4.10-14; 8.33; 1 Chron. 15.2; 16.4, 41; 13.25-32; 2 Chron. 5.4-5; Ezek. 45.4.
8. 2 Sam. 15.24-29; 1 Kgs 2.26-27, 35; 4.1; 12.31. See de Vaux, *AI*, 2.348-49.

## 1. The Priesthood in the Extra-NT Literature

Moses, son of Levi (Exod. 2.1), is characterized as a priestly sanctuary attendant insofar as he appears to exercise authority over the holy tent, and he performs cultic ritual acts which can only be described as priestly functions.[1] It was therefore in the context of their sanctuary attendance that the priests exercised specific and specialized functions.

The most basic functions are mentioned in the Blessing of Moses (Deut. 33.8-10). These functions are: oracular consultation (33.8a), instruction in the rights and law of God (33.10a), and the cultic ritual service (33.10b).[2] We will see that there are other lesser functions performed by the priests, for instance giving blessings (Deut. 10.8) and the sounding of trumpets, but predominant are those mentioned at Deut. 33.8-10.

*Oracular consultation*
It is generally agreed that the earliest and exclusive function of the priest was the dispensing of oracles.[3] In Judges 18, the Danites enquire of Jonathan the Levite to 'ask' (*šā'al*) God about their resettlement plans. Such consultation at a sanctuary was commonly practiced through a priest. Moses retained the consultation of oracles for himself (Exod. 18.15, 19) so that when consultation with God was necessary the person would come to the tent of meeting with the request, and Moses would then enter and confer directly with God (Exod. 33.7, 11). This unmediated contact by Moses with God was his privilege alone (Num. 12.6-8), for elsewhere the practice of oracular consultation appears to be connected with the ephod and the urim and thummim. The precise description of these articles is 'an intricate and obscure question',[4] which need not detain us here. It will suffice to say that the terms are intimately related to the oracular consultation of

---

1. Exod. 24.6; 32.26-29; 33.7-11; Lev. 8.14, 18, 22. See Baudissin, 'Priests', p. 69; Cody, *A History*, p. 41. Gray (p. 196) terms Moses' activity as a 'priesthood for a week'. Also see Sabourin, p. 121.
2. M. Haran (pp. 1079-80) groups the functions into four categories, by considering the treatment of impurity and purification, found at Lev. 11.13-14; 15; Num. 19, as separate from the instruction in God's law. His categories are: (1) cultic, (2) mantic, (3) treatment of impurity and purification, and (4) judging and instructing of people.
3. Schrenk, 'ἱερεύς', *TDNT*, 3.260; Eichrodt, pp. 395-96; Cody, *A History*, pp. 58, 81; Baudissin, 'Priests', pp. 67, 71.
4. De Vaux, *AI*, 2.349.

God, and are the possessions of the priests.[1] Precise knowledge of how the ephod, urim and thummim were used eludes us, although glimpses of their practice are seen in 1 Sam. 14.41-42; 23.9-12; 30.7-8, and perhaps at Prov. 16.33. God's consultation appears to have been received or mediated through the urim and thummim.

The priest's role as oracular consultant evolved quite early in Israel, and appears to have been taken over by the prophetic class. On occasions similar to those on which David and Saul would have consulted with a priest the later monarchs consult God through a prophet.[2] By the time of the return from the exile, there appears to have been no priest to handle the urim and thummim (e.g. Ezra 2.63; Neh. 7.65).

Therefore, the priest's role as a mediating spokesman for God was eventually taken over by the prophets who had no use for the ephod and urim and thummim. This resulted in the diminished importance of the priest's function as oracular practitioner.

*Instruction*

The Old Testament also depicts the priest in another role: that of instructor. According to Lev. 10.10-11, the priest's role is 'to distinguish between the sacred and the profane, the impure and the pure, and teach the children of Israel the statutes which Yahweh has dictated'. Instruction by priests, therefore, was to educate the Israelite concerning what is pleasing to God. As the domain of the priests, instruction is referred to frequently in the prophetical books.[3] The book of Deuteronomy places the priest's role with regard to the instructing in the divine law above the sacrificial practice. This role as teacher was carried out within the sanctuary[4] and, according to Deuteronomy, occupied the priest in proclaiming apodictic law (Deut. 27.14-26), propounding the law (Deut. 31.9), guarding the law (Deut. 27.18), settling legal disputes (Deut. 17.8-9; 21.5), performing ministry before the Ark (Deut. 10.8), and proclaiming to Israel (Deut. 27.9).[5] What had therefore originally centered on ritual and cultic

1. Num. 27.21; Deut. 33.8.
2. The Hebrew *dāraš* is used in connection with the prophet, therefore replacing *šā'al*. See 1 Kgs 14.5; 22.5-28; 2 Kgs 3.11; 8.7-13; 22.11-20.
3. Mic. 3.11; Jer. 18.18; Ezek. 7.26; 22.26; 44.23; Hag. 2.11-13; Zech. 7.3; Mal. 2.7-9; Isa. 2.3. But also 2 Kgs 17.27; Ezra 7.10.
4. Exod. 18.15-20; Isa. 2.3; Mic. 4.2; Deut. 31.10-11.
5. Kraus, p. 97.

## 1. The Priesthood in the Extra-NT Literature 19

instruction burgeoned into the realm of the moral and ethical[1] under the auspices of the priesthood.

It is safe to say that the priests performed a judicial role as instructors, although judicial matters were not exclusively in the priests' domain. At Exod. 18.13-26 Moses divides the judging of cases between himself and the elders. The juridical task is the major priestly role in Deuteronomy. Both levites and priests serve as judges at 2 Chron. 19.8. In this role the priest was seen as speaking for God.[2]

Following the exile, the priests shared with others the task of instruction in torah. The subordinate officials, the levites, were also teachers and men with understanding.[3] Thus the unique and primary role of the priest became his cultic functioning at worship and sacrifice, by which means he could serve God as mediator. To this third and major function of the priesthood we now turn.

*Sacrifice*

We have seen how the roles of oracular consultant and religious instructor eventually gave away as the prerogatives of the priests alone. However, the offering of sacrifice became more and more a specifically priestly act, though it was only gradually that the offering of sacrifice became the function of the priests alone. Non-priests received God's sanction to offer sacrifices in the time of the judges.[4] During the monarchy, kings offered sacrifices on special occasions.[5]

At least by the time of Deuteronomy, however, sacrifice was recognized as the prerogative of the priesthood (Deut. 33.10b). It is precisely this biblical picture of the priest as an altar functionary that predominates and influences the Old Testament.[6] Exodus, Leviticus, Numbers, and Deuteronomy all betray a great interest in things cultic and, logically, in the priest's function in the cult. The priestly action in offering sacrifice involved his approaching the altar or entering the

---

1. De Vaux, *AI*, 2.354; Cody, *A History*, p. 117.
2. Cody (*A History*, p. 121) citing the monograph of A. Alt, *Die Ursprünge des israelitischen Rechts* (BVSAWL, Phil.–hist. Kl., 86; Leipzig: S. Hirzel, 1934), pp. 16-17, 33, 61-62.
3. 2 Chron. 17.8-9; 35.3; Neh. 8.7, 9.
4. Judg. 6.25-26; 13.16-23; 1 Sam. 1.3, 4, 21; 2.19.
5. 1 Sam. 13.9-10; 2 Sam. 6.13, 17-18; 24.25; 1 Kgs 3.4, 15; 8.5, 62-64; 9.25; 2 Kgs 16.12-15.
6. Jer. 33.18 (MT); 2 Chron. 5.14; 29.16, 21; 30.16; 35.11.

tent of meeting,[1] pouring or sprinkling the blood of the victim upon the altar or curtain, or placing its flesh upon the altar. Contact with the altar, as we have seen, was the priestly privilege (Lev. 1–7; 16). Therefore, the priest's obligation did not include immolation. This was performed by the person presenting the victim for sacrifice, or by a substitute.[2]

The reason for the priestly prerogative of approaching the altar was based on the idea of holiness. As one who was 'set apart', 'consecrated', 'made holy', the priest could approach the sacred and holy realm of the sanctuary and altar. Because he was holy, he alone could bring the blood (Lev. 17.11, 14) into contact with the altar and sanctuary. This is also the reason why the incensing of the tent was the sole privilege of the priests. Incense was burnt upon the altar situated within the tent of meeting which only the priests could enter.[3] The priests also had charge of the table of shewbread and the candlestick which were positioned within the tent as well (Num. 17.5; Exod. 27.1).

The value of the priestly function of sacrifice was in its mediatorial role. The priest's offerings effected forgiveness. They made atonement for sins unwittingly committed.[4] The offering of sacrifices purged the Temple of the 'miasmic' impurity accumulating within it because of the sins of the people.[5]

There is little wonder that the sacrificial function of the priest became so prominent. This was particularly true by the time of Josiah's reform, when he abolished all of the cultic centers except the Temple in Jerusalem and its priesthood. The priests were so busy meeting the daily-offering demands that 'the earlier proportion between sacrificial worship and the imparting of torah was consequently inverted'.[6] Of course, this function also provided the sole

---

1. In Deuteronomy the role of the priests is expressed as 'to serve Yahweh' or 'to stand before Yahweh' (Deut. 17.12; 18.5, 7; 21.5).
2. Exod. 24.3-8; Lev. 1.5; 3.2, 8, 13; 4.14, 29, 33; 2 Chron. 30.17; Ezek. 44.11. An exception to this rule was when the victim was a bird. In such a case, the priest killed the bird upon the altar, which explains why the layman was excluded (Lev. 1.14-15; 5.8).
3. Exod. 30.7-10; Num. 17.5; 1 Chron. 23.13; 2 Chron. 26.16-18.
4. Lev. 4.20, 26, 31, 35; 5.6, 10, 13, 16, 18; 6.7.
5. J. Milgrom, 'Atonement in the Old Testament', *IDB Supplement*, pp. 78-80.
6. Eichrodt, 1.400. Cody (*A History*, p. 113) comments that the larger sanctuaries were so busy that they were 'bogged down in clerical routine', which would

means of income for priests (1 Sam. 2.36), which could further explain its growth, and suggest a reason why the priests permitted their role as oracular consultants and instructors to fall into the hands of lesser functionaries.

The abuse of this altar service, which came to be regarded as automatically effecting forgiveness, was well attested by the prophets.[1] It created the growth in importance and prestige of the Temple and priesthood, but it also portended the disappearance of priestly influence once the Temple fell. The priesthood had become so identified with the sacrificial role that with the Temple's destruction, law not based on cultic ritual replaced the Temple activity as central to Israelite life, and rabbis supplanted the priests.[2]

Secondary functions of the priests include offering prayer (intercession) and blessings, and the sounding of trumpets. The mediatorial character of these tasks is evident. Prayer was making intercession to God on behalf of the people (1 Sam. 2.25; Ezra 9.6-15), and blessing normally occurred in the context of sacrifice,[3] as did the sounding of trumpets.[4]

*The high priesthood*
The title *hakkōhēn haggādôl*, or 'high priest', occurs rarely in the Old Testament.[5] The frequent designation for the priestly characters Aaron, Eleazer, and Phineas is 'the priest', or 'the anointed priest'.[6] Here, the Old Testament reveals its composite character, for on the one hand, the high priest alone is anointed,[7] but on the other hand, all

---

leave little time for other priestly tasks, such as instruction. Also see Vanhoye, *Old Testament Priests*, p. 24.
1. 1 Sam. 15.22; Hos. 4.6-9; 5.6; 6.6; Jer. 29.13; Mic. 6.6-8; Isa. 1.11-17.
2. De Vaux, *AI*, 2.356.
3. Exod. 17.8-16; Lev. 9.22-24; Num. 6.22-27; Deut. 10.8; 21.5; 1 Chron. 23.13; Ps. 3.8.
4. Num. 10.1, 2, 10; 1 Chron. 16.6; 2 Chron. 5.15; 7.16; 13.14; 29.26-28; Ezra 3.10; Neh. 12.35, 41.
5. Lev. 21.10; Num. 35.25, 28, 32; 2 Chron. 3.49; Neh. 3.1, 20; 13.28; Hag. 1.1, 12, 14; 2.2, 4; Zech. 3.1, 8; 6.11.
6. The term 'anointed priest' appears in the cultic regulations at Lev. 4.3, 5, 16. There the high priest (Aaron) appears to have sole authority to offer the *ḥaṭṭā't* for the people and himself. In the same chapter, the mention is frequently to 'the priest', which points to some uncertainty or inconsistency in the cultic practice, or at least in the designation of titles for the offerant.
7. Exod. 29.4-9; Lev. 4.3, 5, 16; 6.13.

priests are anointed as well.[1] The anointing of priests found in the Priestly tradition was introduced after the eclipse of the monarchy.[2] The high priest as anointed clearly comes to be seen as the chief representative of all the community (Zech. 3.2; 6.13), so that by the close of the Old Testament period the high priest had appropriated the king's role, as seen in his anointing and his wardrobe.[3] However, prior to the exile, a priest was always a priest 'to ($l^e$-, inseparable preposition)' someone or some group,[4] whereas the king was not a 'priest', because he would then be in service 'to' himself, and not to other men.

The distinguishing trait of the high priest in the practice of the cultus was his greater degree of holiness. Of all the priests only he was permitted to enter behind the second curtain on the Day of Atonement and perform the ritual activities within the holy of holies (Lev. 16). The high priest's greater degree of holiness also required a greater measure of care be taken to maintain this holiness. Harsher restrictions were therefore applied to the high priest regarding matters of impurity and marriage (Lev. 21.10-15), his installation (Exod. 29.4; Lev. 8.6; 16.4), and his clothing (Exod. 28; 39). Hence, the high priest's characteristic activity was one of access and mediation, whereby he made atonement for the holy place because of the people's transgressions (Lev. 16.16.).[5]

These priestly functions, therefore, have a common basis, which was mediational. The priest stood as an intermediary between God and human beings, whether at oracular consultation, instruction, or sacrifice. The prominent interest in sacrifice and the cult in the Old Testament points particularly to the special access the priests enjoyed as mediators (and supremely the high priest with access to the holy of holies). Priests nearing the altar or entering the holy place were approaching the hearth in the house of God which was to be perpe-

---

1. Exod. 28.41; 30.30; 40.12, 15; Lev. 7.35-36; 10.7; Num. 3.3.
2. De Vaux (*AI*, 1.105) writes that 'after the disappearance of the monarchy, the royal anointing was transferred to the high priest as head of the people, and later extended to all priests'.
3. *Ibid.*, 2.400; Baudissin, 'Priests', p. 80.
4. Cody, *A History*, p. 102. Such was the case with Micah (Judg. 17.5, 10, 12); Danites (Judg. 18.4, 19); Tribe of Danites (Judg. 18.19, 30); David (2 Sam. 20.26).
5. This mediatorial role is depicted by the high priest's breastplate which bore the names of the children of Israel. This breastplate was worn when entering the sanctuary. See Baudissin, 'Priests', p. 84.

tually lit.¹ Therefore, priests had unparalleled access to God, for the altar was a sign of God's presence, indicated by its especial holiness,² and upon it the offerings were given to God, which then resulted in the bestowal of the divine blessing (Exod. 20.24).³ But the high priest alone possessed the highest degree of access. He could pass into the most holy place where the Ark resided, the very seat of God's presence (Lev. 16).

## 2. The Priesthood in Pseudepigraphical Literature

We now turn to the role of the priesthood in the literature of the period between the Old and New Testaments.⁴ This literature does not necessarily limit itself to works dating from after the composition of the entire Old Testament, nor does it antedate all of the New Testament literature. These materials represent 'a reflection upon the Old Testament marked by tendencies characteristic of the later period (apocalyptic, Hellenistic, etc.), providing at the same time a contemporary thought background to the writings of the New Testament'.⁵ The most probable dating is between 200 BC and 100 AD, although a precise determination of the dates of composition of the works seems, in most cases, elusive.

According to Aelred Cody, 'the nature and structure of priesthood established earlier in the course of the post-exilic period prevails' into the intertestamental period.⁶ This statement will be supported by our investigation of the priestly role and function in the intertestamental

---

1. Lev. 6.5-6; 2 Macc. 1.18-36. See de Vaux, *AI*, 2.413.
2. Exod. 29.36, 37; 30.10; Lev. 8.15; 10.18-19.
3. De Vaux, *AI*, 2.414.
4. For translations of the intertestamental literature see: P. Riessler, *Altjüdisches Schrifttum ausserhalb der Bibel* (Augsburg: Filser, 1928); *The Apocrypha and Pseudepigrapha of the Old Testament in English, with Introductions and Critical and Explanatory Notes to the Several Books* (ed. R.H. Charles; 2 vols.; Oxford: Clarendon, 1913); *The Old Testament Pseudepigrapha* (ed. J.H. Charlesworth; 2 vols.; Garden City, NY: Doubleday, 1985), hereafter cited as Charlesworth, *OTPseud*. A useful concordance to the apocryphal works is *A Concordance to the Septuagint and the Other Greek Versions of the Old Testament (Including the Apocryphal Books)* (ed. E. Hatch and H.A. Redpath; 2 vols.; Oxford: Clarendon, 1897–1906; repr. edn, Grand Rapids: Baker, 1983).
5. B. Byrne, *'Sons of God'—'Seed of Abraham': A Study of the Idea of the Sonship of God of All Christians in Paul against the Jewish Background* (AnBib, 83; Rome: Pontifical Biblical Institute, 1979), p. 19.
6. Cody, *A History*, p. 194.

writings. Such an investigation is hindered somewhat since no writing in this period affords the reader a thoroughgoing presentation of the priesthood. Rather, we must rely on allusions and brief references to priests mentioned in contexts frequently secondary to the central meaning and message of a specific writing.

*Sacrifice*

As was seen above in our examination of the Old Testament priesthood, the attachment of the priest to a sanctuary and his ritual role before the altar came to predominate over all other functions of the priesthood. Clearly this is still the case in the pseudepigraphical literature. The preponderance of text references find the priesthood attached to the sanctuary and performing ritual and cultic functions. Characteristically the priests are portrayed as operating within the Temple precincts.

Priests are therefore considered mediators between the people and God, possessing a special access to God. This access is realized at the altar and within the Temple, and is based on their own special holiness.[1] The high priest is also defined by his access to God and sacrifical role in the cult, seen by his presence within the Temple sanctuary.[2]

The background for this picture of the priests and high priests is clearly the Old Testament, which served as the source and influence. Even the eschatological priest of the *Testament of Levi* 18 finds his origin in Psalm 110, with allusion to the Maccabean priest-kings.[3] The role of the priest in the intertestamental period logically finds its basis in the history and tradition in which it exists. Therefore the priesthood portrayed (both in terms of the priest and the high priest) is intimately connected with the sanctuary. The role centers on the performing of

---

1. 1 Esdr. 1.18; 5.46, 48-49, 50-53, 59; 7.9; 8.46, 58, 60; Tob. 1.6; 1 Macc. 1.46; 3.49, 51; 4.36-61; 7.33, 36; 10.42; 14.42; 2 Macc. 1.21, 23, 30; 3.15; 4.14; 14.31, 34; 15.31; Jdt. 4.14, 15; 11.3; Sir. 7.29-31; 45.6-22, 23-36; 50.12; *3 Macc.* 1.11, 16; 2.1-20; *4 Macc.* 4.9; *T. Levi* 4.2; 5.2; 8.1-19; 9.6, 7; 14.5-8; 17.1-11; *T. Isaac* 4.32-42; *T. Moses* 7.1-10; 10.2; *T. Sol.* 6.4; *T. Adam* 1.12; *Ep. Arist.* 87, 92–93, 95; *Jub.* 21.7-18; 30.18-20; 31.14, 16; 32.3-9; *Bib. Ant.* 13.1-2; 63.1-5; *Pss. Sol.* 2.3; *Odes Sol.* 20.1-10; *Ps.-Hec.* 187-88, 199.

2. 1 Esdr. 5.48-49; 1 Macc. 2.54; 14.41, 44, 47; Jdt. 4.14; Sir. 45.23-26; 50.1-24; *3 Macc.* 1.11 (here, only the high priest is permitted εἰσέρχεσθαι the holy of holies); 2.1-20; *2 En.* 69–71; *Ep. Arist.* 96–99; *Ps.-Hec.* 187.

3. H.C. Kee, 'Testaments of the Twelve Patriarchs', in Charlesworth, *OTPseud*, Vol. 1: *Apocalyptic Literature and Testaments*, p. 794 n. 18a.

## 1. The Priesthood in the Extra-NT Literature 25

ritual service upon the altar (and also the immolation before the sacrifice in *2 En.* 70.21), the offering of incense (*T. Adam* 1.12), and the care and construction of the altar and sanctuary (restricted to priests because of their holiness). Therefore, within the realm of the sanctuary, the cult, and the practice of sacrifice and offering, nothing is out of character with the priestly activities already portrayed in the Old Testament literature.

*Prayer and blessing*
The priestly functions of prayer and blessing are found occasionally in the Old Testament, but they are noticeably more pronounced in the pseudepigraphical literature.[1] Such priestly prayer typically occurs within the sanctuary and during the performance of the cultic duties, though not exclusively so.[2] Blessing, as praise to God, is not solely a priestly prerogative, for on occasions it is simultaneously offered by the priest and the people.[3]

We observe, therefore, that although priestly prayer is more prominent in the intertestamental literature, in the sacrificial milieu it was already known and practiced in the Old Testament (e.g. Ezra 9.6-15). Hence prayer, as a mediating communication with God, indicating access to him, broadens its pervasiveness in the intertestamental texts to the point where it takes on the character of a sacrificial offering in its own right.[4]

*Instruction*
A 'curious' feature of the intertestamental literature is the frequent characterization of the priests as instructors of the people and as

---

1. 'Blessing' is included here because frequently the blessing is a prayer to God. See H.W. Beyer, 'εὐλογέω', *TDNT*, 2.758; H-G. Link, 'Blessing', *NIDNTT* (ed. C. Brown; 3 vols.; Exeter: Paternoster, 1975–1978), 1.211.
2. 1 Esdr. 8.74-90; *Jub.* 32.2; 1 Macc. 7.36; 2 Macc. 1.23, 3.15; 14.34; Jdt. 4.15; 15.9-10; *3 Macc.* 1.16; 2.1-20; 6.1; *4 Macc.* 4.9; *2 En.* 70.16-19; *T. Isaac* 4.32-42.
3. 1 Esdr. 9.46; Pr. Azar. 2; *3 Macc.* 7.13; *2 En.* 71.18, 30-31.
4. T. Gaster ('Sacrifices and Offerings', *IDB*, 4.147-59) notes that prayer after 70 AD became a legitimate substitute for sacrifice. G. Bornkamm ('Lobpreis, Bekenntnis und Opfer', in *Apophoreta: Festschrift für Ernst Haenchen zu seinem siebzigsten Geburtstag am 10. Dezember 1964* [BZNW, 30; ed. W. Eltester and F.H. Kettler; Berlin: Töpelmann, 1964], pp. 46-63) however, finds prayer as a substitute for sacrifice already in Old Testament materials.

empowered with judicial functions.¹ For as Cody suggests, 'it seems to show a new direction opposite to that seen by those who hold that with the Maccabean period the scribe (and levites) in Judah began to take over ordinary concern with the law (and instruction), while the priests were relegated more exclusively to matters of liturgy'.²

This new feature is best seen, not only in the frequent occurrences of priestly instruction of the law, but in Sirach, where the Greek text differs from the Hebrew text and grants to the priests a specific judicial role. According to Cody, 'the Hebrew text of Sir. 45.17 simply restates the tradition of the priests as guardians of Israel's sacral law, but the corresponding Greek text expands this in a judicial direction, saying that God gave Aaron "authority in legal decisions (ἐξουσίαν ἐν διαθήκαις κριμάτων) for teaching Jacob the testimonies and enlightening Israel with his law"'.³

An insertion was also made in the Greek text at Sir. 45.26, κρίνειν τὸν λαὸν αὐτοῦ ἐν δικαιοσύνῃ, which is absent in the Hebrew text. Reconciliation of this problem of reinvesting the priesthood with judicial powers need not concern us here, since our primary interest is with cultic matters. Perhaps we may say, however, (1) that the priesthood never relinquished all of its authority with regard to law and instruction, (2) that as time passed the distinctions between priests and their subordinates such as levites became blurred and ambiguous, particularly in the Hellenistic culture,⁴ or (3) that the priestly function of instructor or judge in the Old Testament is being depicted in the pseudepigraphical literature, dependent as such literature was upon the Old Testament for much of its source material.

*Oracular consultation*

The Old Testament priestly role of oracular consultant is lacking in the intertestamental materials, except in the *Lives of the Prophets*,

---

1. 1 Esdr. 8.3, 7, 8, 9; 9.16, 39, 40, 42, 48; Sir. 45.17, 26; *4 Macc.* 5.35; *T. Levi* 4.3, 5; 9.6; 13.2, 9; 14.4, 6; 18.1-14 (eschatological); *Jub.* 31.12-17; 45.16.
2. Cody, *A History*, p. 195. See his mention of H. Wenschkewitz, 'Die Spiritualisierung der Kultusbegriffe Tempel, Priester und Opfer im Neuen Testament', *ΑΓΓΕΛΟΣ* 4 (1932). That the two traditions exist side by side is seen in 1 Esdras, where at 9.48, 49 the levites explain the law to the people and instruct the multitudes.
3. Cody, *A History*, p. 195.
4. R. Doran, 'Pseudo-Hecataeus', in Charlesworth, *OTPseud*, Vol. 2: *Expansions of the 'Old Testament' and Legends, Wisdom and Philosophical Literature, Prayers, Psalms and Odes, Fragments of Lost Judeo-Hellenistic Works*, p. 915.

which is a midrash on particular Old Testament passages (*Liv. Pr.* 22.2 and 1 Kgs 19.16; *Liv. Pr.* 23.1-2 and 2 Chron. 24.20-22). The absence of the consultant role seems in keeping both with the disappearance of this function from the priestly sphere, and with its transfer to the prophetic school already early in the Old Testament.

*Healing*
That the priest was gifted with healing power is seen in *T. Adam* 1.7 and 2.10. Such a function on the part of the priest betrays the late date of the composition of this writing, and the Christian influence on it.[1]

*Warrior*
One role of the priesthood not attributed to priests in the Old Testament is that of military warrior. In the Old Testament, the tribe of Levi is linked with the tribe of Simeon as the avengers upon Shechem for the rape of Dinah (Gen. 34; 49), but priests are never characterized as a warrior class (though Exod. 32.25-29 is perhaps an exception).[2] In two texts (*T. Levi* 5.3; *Jub.* 30.18-20) the zeal of Levi against Shechem (Gen. 34) is specifically recalled, and the text in Jubilees suggests that the reason for the descendants of Levi being chosen for the priesthood and the levitical orders for ministry to the Lord is precisely this zealous militarism.

The military aspect found in the intertestamental caricature of the priesthood[3] has its plausible origin in the historical personages of the Maccabean revolt. The Hasmonean dynasty of rulers had a lineage from Levi, although an obscure one, so that Mattathias (1 Macc. 2.1-48) and his sons, Simon (1 Macc. 14.29) and Judas Maccabaeus (1 Macc. 2.66; 3.1; 4.42-51), are both depicted as priests as well as zealous defenders of Yahwism. What compels the priesthood to take up arms appears to be their zeal for the godly holiness, whereby any defilement of the Temple merits immediate and deliberate retribution (e.g. *3 Macc.* 7.13). The type of the warrior-priest clearly finds its

---

1. S.E. Robinson, 'Testament of Adam', in Charlesworth, *OTPseud*, 1.990.
2. For a convincing look at the role of the Tribe of Levi with regard to the purging of covenant-threatening crimes (e.g. Judg. 19–20), see Robert B. Robinson, 'The Levites in the Pre-Monarchic Period', *Studia Biblica et Theologica* 8 (1978), pp. 3-24.
3. 1 Macc. 2.1, 6; 3.1; 4.42-51; 5.67; 14.29; Jdt. 4.6; *3 Macc.* 7.13; *T. Levi* 5.3; *T. Moses* 10.2 (here the cultic designation 'to fill one's hands' is for the avenger of enemies); *Jub.* 30.18-20; 31.17; *Jos. Asen.* 27.6.

origin in the extra-Old Testament circumstances of the second century BC, and as we shall see, it will also be found at Qumran in the War Scroll.

*Leader*
The special dual role of the high priest as leader and priest has its origin in the post-exilic period in the Old Testament material. This role of the high priest as priest and ethnarch is also prominent in the intertestamental literature, based again on the historical development in the Hasmonean period. Simon is declared both eternal high priest and ethnarch (1 Macc. 14.41, 47; 15.1). Also at *2 Enoch* 69–71, a midrash on Gen. 5.21-32, the personages are characterized as prince and leader (*2 En.* 70.14; 71.18-23). *Jub.* 31.12-17 foretells that the descendants of Levi (i.e. priests) will become judges, rulers, and leaders. *T. Judah* 21.2, 4 clearly shows the priesthood superseding the monarchy.

However, we may see this high-priestly and royal feature already in the Old Testament: in the anointing of the high priests, and in the adorning of the high priest in kingly attire. It need not be understood as a development of the intertestamental period.

*Spiritual sacrifice*
Thus far, we have seen priests characterized cultically when offering sacrifices and prayers. In one late first-century AD work, *Odes of Solomon*,[1] the priest offers spiritual righteousness manifested by ethical behavior (*Odes Sol.* 20.1-10). While the prophets of the Old Testament exhorted the people of God to spiritual sacrifices, here the early Christian interest in spiritual sacrifice appears to be applied to the priesthood, although particular influence of this passage upon the New Testament is not likely, since it post-dates much, if not all, of the writings of the New Testament.

It serves to show, however, that priests and spiritual sacrifices were already linked in the later-dated pseudepigraphical material.

---

1. See J.H. Charlesworth, 'Odes of Solomon', in Charlesworth, *OTPseud*, 2.725-34; R. Harris and A. Mingana (eds.), *The Odes and Psalms of Solomon*, Vol. 2: *The Translation with Introduction and Notes* (Manchester: Manchester University Press, 1920), pp. 312-19.

## Conclusion

What we have observed is that where the priest is portrayed in the pseudepigraphical literature, he is characterized chiefly by functions directly dependent on or influenced by the Old Testament priestly picture. Most prominent is the role of the priest busy with cultic activities at the altar and sanctuary. The intertestamental period seems to suggest further that such sacrifice exceeds the merely material offerings and involves the presentation of prayers and spiritual sacrifice on the part of the priest.

Where the literature presents the priest as warrior, this characterization does not appear to be drawn from the Old Testament,[1] but is based upon the history of the Maccabean period. At any rate, the priest as warrior seems to exercise no influence at all on the idea of priesthood in the New Testament writings.

As in the Old Testament, so here also, the priests as cultic officials with a special holiness permitting them access to God within his holy realm of the Temple is the prevailing view portrayed and disseminated.

## 3. The Priesthood in Rabbinic Literature

The attempt to unravel the problematical and complex historical problem concerning the state of Rabbinic literature that occupies and divides current scholarship is a matter far beyond the realm of a preliminary and quite general investigation.[2] However, a brief glance at the role and function of priesthood in its Jewish background ought to prove valuable as a means of establishing the origin of its tradition. Our investigation will center on the work of the Tannaim (in particular, as found in the Mishnah), but this does not preclude the

---

1. F.M. Cross ('The Priestly Houses of Early Israel', in *Canaanite Myth and Hebrew Epic: Essays in the History of the Religion of Israel* [Cambridge, MA: Harvard University Press, 1973], p. 214) connects the priest Zadok with the character Zadok, the aide to the commander of the Aaronide forces with David at Hebron (1 Chron. 12.27-28).

2. One need only recall the criticism by Jacob Neusner of E.P. Sanders's works or the frequent depreciation by certain scholars of the value to be found in Hermann L. Strack and Paul Billerbeck, *Kommentar zum Neuen Testament aus Talmud und Midrasch* (5 vols.; München: C.H. Beck [Oskar Beck], 1922–28), hereafter cited as Str–B, *Kommentar*.

idea that even later traditions may yield information and evidence that were actually grounded in an earlier, formative period.

We shall see that at least with regard to the priesthood itself, the priestly traditions formulated in the rabbinical writings appear manageable, since the Temple and cult ceased their functioning after 70 AD. Accordingly, there was little reinterpretation of cultic traditions continuing. The predominant reference to the priesthood in the pentateuchal portion of scripture also served to retard any large-scale additions or alterations.[1]

Certainly, the occurrence of cultic material in the Rabbinic literature is not without its problems. Foremost is the problem of understanding the possible reason for retaining materials recounting pre-70 AD practices in post-70 AD documents.[2] However, there is a persistent hope for a restored Jerusalem and Temple that would again serve as the focus of national and religious life, and this makes the interpretation, preservation and dissemination of such traditional material comprehensible.[3]

Much of the Mishnaic material relating to the Temple and cult appears to predate the fall of Jerusalem. For instance, Eliezer ben Jacob and Simeon of Mizpah are credited with composing the *Middoth* and *Yoma*, respectively.[4] What becomes obvious is that the Rabbinic tradition of the priest's role and function does not differ markedly from that already characterized in the Old Testament. Even later works which contain descriptions of priestly functions (e.g. Baby-

---

1. H. Danby, *The Mishnah: Translated from the Hebrew with Introduction and Brief Explanatory Notes* (London: Oxford University Press, 1933), p. xiv. Danby remarks that 'the Mishnah's minute treatment of the Temple cultus and its portrayal of Jewish religious and secular life as though the nation still enjoyed privileges lost to it generations earlier, constitute the Mishnah's chief value as well as the chief problem in its study'.

2. *Ibid.*, p. xv. According to Danby, since some traditions (e.g. *Yoma, Middot, Tamid, Bikkurim*, and *Seqalim*), did not apply to quotidian Jewish life, these traditions have encountered fewer interpretations and interpolations imposed upon them that could result from the influence of 'later fashions of interpretation'.

3. *Ibid.*, p. xv. Such appears to have been the reason for the presence of the Temple Scroll at Qumran, which appears to have had no practical relevance to the daily life in that Dead Sea community.

4. *B. Yom.* 16a. See Danby, pp. xxi-xxii. Both men lived at the time when the Temple was still standing. Other pre-destruction texts are the *Tamid* (credited to Simeon of Mizpah) and portions of the *Shekalim* and the *Bikkurim*. So also H.L. Strack, *Introduction to the Talmud and Midrash* (New York: Jewish Publication Society of America, 1931; repr. edn, New York: Atheneum, 1969), pp. 21-22.

1. *The Priesthood in the Extra-NT Literature* 31

Ionian Talmud, Tosefta, etc.) and which contain early traditions as well as later ones, do not have any roles and functions additional to those already practiced by priests in the Old Testament and Mishnah. Granted, certain details may vary, but the roles and functions of the priests remain substantially the same.[1]

The priestly role and function revolved around the Temple and its prescribed cultic practice. The priests and their attendants, according to an established and developed hierarchy, were the functionaries in every task involved in the ritual ceremony.[2] At *m. Tam.* 3.1, lots are cast to determine the function each priest in service to God for the day will perform—whether it be the immolation, the sprinkling of blood, the cleaning of the altar of ashes (also at *m. Yom.* 1.8; 5.5), the trimming of the candlesticks, or the approaching of the ramp with sacrifices.

The featured function of the priest and high priest, therefore, related to the sacrifice. As we have already seen, priests were responsible not only for the preliminary preparations, but for the act of the offering itself.[3] Thus, priests are characterized as persons with access to the 'most holy things' and to the altar (*m. Kidd.* 4.5).

Most significant is the special role of the high priest in the sacrificial service.[4] The high priest, possessing a 'lifelong sanctity' that granted him the ability to atone for the sins of the whole country,[5] had the

---

1. Here, in fact, is where Str–B, *Kommentar* can be most instructive despite its being a compilation of differently dated traditions. Str–B, *Kommentar* illustrates the continuity of priestly role and function being maintained in Rabbinic literature from pre-destruction to very late periods. For example, refer to the Index in Str–B, *Kommentar*, 4.2, under the listings 'Tempeldienst' or 'Priester' for further illustration of this.

2. Such is the general point made by George Foot Moore, *Judaism: In the First Centuries of the Christian Era, The Age of the Tannaim* (Cambridge, MA: Harvard University Press, 1927–30), 2.10. Joachim Jeremias (*Jerusalem in the Time of Jesus: An Investigation into Economic and Social Conditions during the New Testament Period* [Philadelphia: Fortress, 1969], p. 160) lists the hierarchical order under the high priest as: the Captain of the Temple, the director of the weekly course, the director of the daily course, the Temple overseer, the treasurer, the ordinary priest, and the Levite.

3. E.g. *m. Ter.* 8.1; *m. Pes.* 1.6; *m. Kidd.* 4.5; *m. Tem.* 3.4; *m. Mid.* 5.4.

4. The daily offerings that the high priest did not perform himself, he was obligated to finance (*m. Šeqal.* 7.6), and the daily course would then perform the offering (e.g. *m. Yom.* 2.3-5; *m. Tam.* 3.1; 4.3).

5. *M. Naz.* 7.1 is cited by Jeremias, *Jerusalem*, p. 148. The sanctity of the high priest's office was conveyed by the eight-part high priestly vestments with which he

prerogative to offer the sacrifices whenever he desired, but he was explicitly mandated to do so on the seven days preceding the Day of Atonement and on the Day of Atonement itself.[1] He was constantly accompanied by two helpers, one at his left and one at his right, as he performed his cultic duties. However, on the Day of Atonement, the special role of the high priest is characterized by his entering alone into the holy of holies, four times on that single day.[2] The superior role of the high priest is characterized by his access into the holy of holies because this access represents the highest degree of holiness. Holiness, in Rabbinic literature, extended outward in a concentric manner from the holy of holies all the way to the land (*m. Kel.* 1.6-9). Into this 'most holy' domain the high priest enters and brings both incense to be burned and blood to be sprinkled.

Such access to God on the part of the priests and the high priest required that they also scrutinize and maintain their own purity as well as the purity of the people, lest any unacceptable sacrifice profane the altar and thereby endanger all of Israel. Hence, there was a strict code of purity on the part of the priests, as found already in the Old Testament, with special notice paid to descent, marriage, and physical defect.[3] Priests also performed purification rites for Jews rendered impure, by using the sprinkled oil for leprosy contact and the ashes of the red heifer for those defiled by contact with a corpse.[4] The high

---

was invested, since the anointing was no longer practiced in Herodian-Roman times (*b. Yom.* 52b), according to Jeremias (*Jerusalem*, p. 158).

1. See *m. Yoma*, in particular, 1.2 ('Throughout the seven days he must toss the blood and burn the incense and trim the lamps and offer the head and the hind leg'); 3.9; 4.1; *m. Tam.* 7.3. Also see Str–B, *Kommentar*, 3.698, 700. Josephus (*Ant.* XV.408) says that the custom of the high priest was to officiate also on Sabbaths, the Feast of the New Moon, pilgrim festivals, and gatherings of the people. See Jeremias, *Jerusalem*, p. 151.

2. See *m. Yoma* and *b. Yoma* Observe that at *m. Yom.* 5.1 the division between the Holy Place and the Holy of Holies is partitioned by two curtains that are one cubit apart. Access into the Holy of Holies was restricted to the high priest alone. However, at *m. Mid.* 4.5, 7, we read where there were openings above the Holy of Holies in order to permit workers to lower themselves into it in boxes so that they should not feast their eyes on the Holy of Holies. Therefore, the high priest remains the sole personage who enters into the Holy of Holies through the curtains for cultic purposes.

3. *M. Kidd.* 4.4, 6; *m. Yeb.* 9.1, 2; *m. Ḥul.* 1.6; *m. Bek.* 7.1-7. In *m. Yom.* 1.1-8, the high priest is isolated and protected in order to maintain the necessary purity.

4. *M. Neg.* 14.10; *m. Par.* 3.5, 9.

## 1. The Priesthood in the Extra-NT Literature

premium placed on purity resulted from the special and holy proximity the priest entered into with respect to God.[1] The purity of the Temple proper was also maintained by the Temple guard which was comprised of three priests and twenty-one levites, who would sleep in the Temple at night.[2]

A further function of the high priest was to read the scripture. On the Day of Atonement he read to the people from Leviticus 16. The prefect carried the scroll of the Law and handed it to the high priest on the necessary occasions.[3] Priests also pronounced blessings and uttered prayers. This was done according to the prescribed ritual purity, with the sandals removed, while standing erect, and in a loud voice in the Hebrew tongue.[4] The prayer offered by the high priest in the holy place after entering the holy of holies with the incense was to be brief in order that the people should not be terrified by his delay (*m. Yom.* 5.1).

The priesthood was also the recipient of the first fruits as well as any dedicatory gifts brought to the temple by the people. This suggests the existence of a developed administrative organization to oversee and maintain records of Temple transactions, as well as to expend and distribute such revenues.[5]

---

1. The priest functions as a representative of God at the burning of the sacrifice. See Str-B, *Kommentar*, 3.4, and *b. Yom.* 19a. Also see *b. Kidd.* 23b.
2. This watch was also determined by the casting of lots; e.g. *m. Tam.* 1.1; *m. Mid.* 1.1.
3. *M. Yom.* 7.1; *m. Soṭ.* 7.7, 8. So Schrenk, 'ἱερεύς', *TDNT*, 3.262.
4. *M. Ber.* 5.4; *m. Meg.* 4.3-10; *m. Tam.* 5.1; 7.2; *m. Yom.* 7.1. Str-B, *Kommentar*, 2.76; 3.458, 645; and 4.6, 23, mention *b. Soṭ.* 39a and 39b, 40a, and also *Sifre Num.* 6.23. Schrenk ('ἱερεύς', *TDNT*, 3.263) notes also *m. Ber.* 4.5, 6; *m. Ta'an.* 4.2. According to Moore (*Judaism*, 2.57), *m. Yoma* introduces to the Day of Atonement the general confession of sin for the high priest, the priesthood, and the people (*m. Yom.* 3.8; 4.2; 6.2).
5. Schrenk ('ἱερεύς', *TDNT*, 3.263) cites in particular Str-B, *Kommentar*, 4.646-50. Other texts include: *m. Bik.* 3.12; *m. Yeb.* 11.7; *m. Ber.* 1.1; *m. Soṭ.* 3.7; *m. 'Arak.* 8.5-7; *m. Ḥal.* 4.11; *m. Beṣ.* 1.6; *m. Ned.* 11.3; *m. Ḥul.* 10.1-4; *m. Šeq.* 5.2. Jeremias (*Jerusalem*, p. 166) comments that 'the financial affairs of the Temple—landed property, wealth and treasure, administration of the flood of tribute money and votive offerings as well as private capital deposited at the Temple; responsibility for the produce and materials needed for the cultus; supervision of the Temple monopoly in the sale of birds and other produce for sacrifice; concern for the maintenance and repair of the full complement of gold and silver vessels, of which no less than ninety-three were needed for each daily ritual—all this provided the treasurers with ample scope for activity and demanded a staff of officials whom they employed'.

In other instances, the priests appear to serve in a judicial capacity by levying fines (*m. Ket.* 1.5), decreeing the eligibility of one attending a feast (*m. Roš Haš.* 1.7), and determining what women may eat at the heave-offering (*m. Yeb.* 7.6). The high priest further held the privileged office of president of the Sanhedrin and therefore was involved in decisions of civil law, including cases of capital offenses involving the high priest himself.[1]

Lesser functions of the priests include their continuing to blow the trumpets before, during, and after the offering is made.[2] Finally, the priest appears as the exhorter of the people entering into battle, on the basis of Deut. 20.2-7.[3]

As we have illustrated, the role and function of the priest and the high priest do not differ in essence from the similar roles already prescribed in the Old Testament literature. It is to be expected that specific details would vary, since the very nature of Rabbinic literature was to interpret and apply the scripture to contemporary Jewish life. Hence we have Judaism's gross elaboration of the details originally mentioned in the Old Testament. For example, this is seen in the comparative consideration of the Day of Atonement at Leviticus 16 and in the *m. Yoma* (even more so in *b. Yoma*), where the details in the latter are extensive and elaborate, yet rooted solidly in the Old Testament.

Conspicuously absent as a function of the priesthood in Rabbinic literature is the specific role of instruction. This absence evolved with the destruction of the Temple, when the scribe became the center of the community, because being an expert in the law was more important at that point for the life of Judaism.[4] The saying of the fourth generation Tannaite, Rabbi Meir, that 'a non-Jew who occupies himself with the Torah is a high priest', speaks in a metaphorical manner of the total replacement of the cultus by the Torah.[5] Thus, the

---

1. *M. Sanh.* 1.5 is cited in Jeremias (*Jerusalem*, p. 151). At p. 159, he remarks that in fact, 'the importance of the high priest greatly increased during the first century AD because, as president of the Sanhedrin and principal agent of the people at a time when there was no king, he represented the Jewish people in all dealings with Rome'. Jeremias also mentions *m. Ket.* 13.1-2 in *Jerusalem*, p. 177.
2. *M. Suk.* 5.6-8; *m. Tam.* 7.3. There were never to be fewer than 21 blasts in a day.
3. *M. Soṭ.* 7.2; 8.1.
4. Schrenk, 'ἱερεύς', *TDNT*, 3.262-63.
5. *Ibid.*, p. 263, notes the citation by Rabbi Meir at *b. Sanh.* 59a; *b. B. Bat.* 38a; *b. 'Abod. Zar.* 3a. Also, see *m. Ab.* 5.5 which suggests that the Torah itself was

Torah's place in Judaism had superseded that of the Temple, its cult, and the priesthood itself. The disappearance of the priest's role as instructor was also observed in our study of the Old Testament priesthood. Following the exile, the importance of the scribe in pedagogical and didactic matters increased as the priesthood busied itself more and more with the cult.

What then may be said about the notion of the ordinary Jew as priest? Despite the developing view that the 'study of the Torah is as meritorious as offering sacrifices' (*Lev. R.* 7.3), there appears to be no indication that a Jew considered himself as adopting the priestly role, except in a metaphorical sense.[1] In fact, the anticipated re-establishment of the Temple and its cult precludes the people viewing themselves in any way as actual priests.[2] It is plausible, however, that they saw their role, in relation to the law, as empowered with the identical efficacy that the priest wielded through his exercise of the cultic ritual.

## 4. *The Priesthood in the Qumran Literature*

Whatever conclusion may be reached concerning the origins of this Dead Sea community, what is quite unmistakable is the pervasive interest in the Temple cult and priesthood held by the sectarians at Qumran. Nearly every document of substantial length betrays some connections with or content relevant to Temple and priestly concerns.

---

more than either the priesthood or the monarchy. Hence, for Moore (*Judaism*, 2.13-15) the collapse of the cultus did not spell catastrophe for Judaism since the Torah and synagogue worship filled this void with the notion of an imputed sacrifice (*b. Ta'an.* 27b; *b. Meg.* 31b).

1. Cited by Danby, p. xv. Moore (*Judaism*, 1.498) notes, however, that already at *m. Yom.* 8.8 repentance is the 'conditio sine qua non' for the forgiveness of sins, which is in accord with the statements of the Old Testament prophets. Again at *Judaism*, 1.506, Moore repeats that 'for the sacrificial expiations of the law, repentance, with its fruit, good works, was the equivalent'. This however is far from understanding the people as priests.

2. Even the constituted twenty-four courses that were comprised of priests, levites, and laity betray that distinction maintained between the priesthood and the laity. Moore (*Judaism*, 2.13) states that just how the 'lay deputation' was made up is not known, but their presence seems to have been included in order to ensure a 'public' sacrifice (*m. Bikk.* 3.2). Apparently they did not fill some sort of priestly or levitical role or function.

The recently published Temple Scroll attests to this sacerdotal interest.[1]

It appears that the origins of the community may be traced to a conflict between the powers that were currently operating the Temple at Jerusalem. This is implied by the numerous criticisms of those priests serving in the Temple (CD 4.18-19; 1QpHab 8.8-13; 9.4-5; 11.12-15; 12.7-9). The harsh criticism was not without foundation. The Qumran sectarians accused the present Temple workers of profaning the Temple and of failing to observe the Law and its regulations for service in the Temple (CD 5.6; 6.12–7.6).[2] Underlying this animus was the doctrinal issue of the proper cultic calendar. Apparently, the Qumranites and the Temple leadership disagreed on which calendar was the legitimate authority.[3] Even the Temple design was of improper dimensions.[4] Precisely those differences that arose within the priestly hierarchy at Jerusalem led to this irreconcilable rift. F.M. Cross views the struggle for the Temple arising between rival priestly factions: the then regnant Hasmonean priestly family, and the formerly official priesthood of the Zadokite line.[5] When these priests of orthodoxy[6] realized that their ideal theocratic community

---

1. English translations, commentary, and introductory materials are found in Y. Yadin, *The Temple Scroll* (3 vols.; Jerusalem: The Israel Exploration Society, 1983); J. Maier, *The Temple Scroll: An Introduction, Translation & Commentary* (JSOTSup, 34; Sheffield: JSOT, 1985).

2. B. Gärtner, *The Temple and the Community in Qumran and the New Testament: A Comparative Study in the Temple Symbolism of the Qumran Texts and the New Testament* (SNTSMS, 1; Cambridge: Cambridge University Press, 1965), p. 19. A brief but insightful article is: Elisabeth Schüssler Fiorenza, 'Cultic Language in Qumran and in the NT', *CBQ* 38 (1976), pp. 159-77.

3. Gärtner, p. 14. Also see C. Newsom, *Songs of the Sabbath Sacrifice: A Critical Edition* (Harvard Semitic Studies, 27; Atlanta: Scholars Press, 1985), p. 62; B.A. Levine, 'The Temple Scroll: Aspects of its Historical Provenance and Literary Character', *BASOR* (1978), pp. 7-11.

4. Y. Yadin, 'The Temple Scroll, the Longest and Most Recently Discovered Dead Sea Scroll', *BARev* 10 (1984), p. 49.

5. See F.M. Cross, *The Ancient Library of Qumran and Modern Biblical Studies* (rev. edn; Garden City, NY: Doubleday, 1958), pp. 127-60; L. Sabourin, p. 172; Gärtner, p. 14.

6. Determining the nature of orthodox Judaism is a different task. With the Temple Scroll, the entire question of texts and canon has again been raised. So, Yadin, *The Temple Scroll*, 1.390-92 and Levine, 'The Temple Scroll', pp. 5-23, in his review of the Hebrew edition of Yadin's three-volume work. Also J.A. Sanders, 'Cave 11 Surprises and the Question of Canon', in *New Directions in Biblical Archaeology* (ed. D.N. Freedman and J.C. Greenfield; Garden City, New York: Doubleday,

## 1. The Priesthood in the Extra-NT Literature 37

would not occur under the reigning priesthood, they departed Jerusalem, separating themselves in order to assure maintenance of the requisite degree of holiness. They then sought realization of their Temple ideal within an apocalyptic spiritual community.[1]

There seems no question that the Qumran leadership was comprised of priests. Bertil Gärtner observes that the hierarchical arrangement at Qumran is so similar to that of the Temple that the Qumran sectarians ought to be regarded as those who broke away from the Jerusalem Temple.[2] In fact, what was once speculation has now been confirmed by other texts found amid the Qumran library: the dominant personality, the Teacher of Righteousness, was a priest (4QpPs37 3.5), and so was his adversary the Wicked Priest (e.g. 1QpHab 7.8, 16; 9.9).[3] The priestly organization of the Qumran community also indicated the group's former background. The institutional structures (1QS 4.7; 6.3-4) and the ordered hierarchy, with each member in his proper role as priest, levite, or 'member' with his own responsibilities (1QS 2.19-22; 6.4-8; 7.2-3; 1QSa 1.16-18, 23; 2.14, 21) betrays a sacerdotal influence,[4] where increased holiness was prized and attained only by deliberate practice and maintained by evaluation on an annual basis. That the idea of priestly cultic holiness should be of interest to the people of Qumran was based, as we shall see, on their understanding that they had taken over the atoning function which had been the work of the Temple (1QS 5.1-7).[5] This is illustrated by their calling themselves the 'holy place' and even the 'holy of holies' (1QS 8.5-6, 8; 9.6; 10.4).[6]

The Qumran community, then, arose out of the turmoil within the Temple itself. Priestly members of the Temple separated themselves from the profanation occurring in Jerusalem and set up a temporary substitute in the 1QS desert. This exile was to continue, however, only until they again came into the congregation in Jerusalem (1QM 3.10).

1969), pp. 101-16. It appears that to speak of Qumran 'orthodoxy' is to refer to the doctrine considered by this particular community to be legitimate and authoritative, while leaving its relationship to other 'orthodox' forms of Judaism an open question.
   1. Sabourin, p. 172
   2. Gärtner, pp. 8, 14
   3. Cross, *The Ancient Library*, pp. 128-29; Newsom, p. 62.
   4. Newsom, p. 62; Gärtner, p. 8.
   5. R.J. Daly, *Christian Sacrifice: The Judaeo-Christian Background before Origen* (CUASCA, 18; Washington, DC: Catholic University of America Press, 1978), pp. 163-64.
   6. Gärtner, p. 15.

Obviously, the Qumran leadership was not intrinsically opposed to the Temple cult, only to the impure and perverted forms of it which were then being practiced. They therefore departed to Qumran 'in the hope of creating a new spiritual center to replace the desecrated Temple until the day when God would finally reveal himself and confirm Israel's victory'.[1]

It is precisely the tension between the present activity at Qumran and their hopes for future restoration that compels us to look briefly at the eschatology of the sect before we address the specific portrayal of priestly functions, both current and anticipated.[2]

Qumran did not see itself as an eternal replacement for the Temple cultus. Rather, it held the expectation that the Temple cult would one day be re-established in Jerusalem.[3] Texts with eschatological indications were 1QS 4.20-22; CD 6.11–7.6; 1QM 2.1-6; 1QSb 3.1-5; 4QFlor 1.5-7; and 1QSa. Gärtner, however, questions whether such a future restoration would be in the form of an actual physical Temple. Rather, he views any future establishment entirely in spiritual terms.[4]

The claim that a realized eschatology pervaded the community's thought has been most forcefully argued by H.-W. Kuhn in relation to the Psalms at Qumran.[5] G. Klinzing also agrees in principle with Kuhn, although he sees only the period of exile from the Temple as the time for sacrifices of a 'blameless walk' and 'praise' to God. This situation would lead (or, was leading) to a restored Temple cult, in

---

1. *Ibid.*, p. 14.
2. This problem will also be addressed in the section below concerning the Temple Scroll, where the issue of present and future practice of the cult is problematical for the understanding of the place of 11QTemple within the Qumran community.
3. G. Klinzing, *Die Umdeutung des Kultus in der Qumrangemeinde und im Neuen Testament* (SUNT, 7; Göttingen: Vandenhoeck & Ruprecht, 1971), p. 224; Daly, p. 159; M. Burrows, *More Light on the Dead Sea Scrolls* (New York: Viking, 1958), pp. 355-56.
4. Gärtner, p. 121. This is also the position held by J. Carmignac, 'L'utilité ou l'inutilité des sacrifices sanglants dans la "Règle de la Communauté" de Qumrân', *RB* 63 (1956), pp. 524-32, especially pp. 529-31, where he observes that the texts at Qumran (1QS and 1QM) clearly point to the restored cultus, although the erection of a cultic edifice in this time of restoration is doubtful because of the silence of any such mention in 1QS.
5. Heinz-Wolfgang Kuhn, *Enderwartung und gegenwärtiges Heil: Untersuchungen zu den Gemeindeliedern von Qumran mit einem Anhang über Eschatologie und Gegenwart in der Verkündigung Jesu* (SUNT, 4; Göttingen: Vandenhoeck & Ruprecht, 1966). For a critique of this position see the review by K.-H. Müller, *BZ* 12 (1968), pp. 303-306.

## 1. The Priesthood in the Extra-NT Literature

accord with God's plan.[1] Such a view is not a thoroughgoing realized eschatology, which J. Chamberlin also maintains was not held at Qumran.[2] The anticipation of an actual eschatological intervention is most clearly seen in both the War Scroll and in 1QSa.[3] M. Burrows and R.E. Brown have both convincingly shown that 1QSa contemplates the time of the last days (also at CD 6.2; 8.10; 1QpHab 2.5-6; 9.6). Brown persuasively refutes T. Gaster's claim against the eschatological outlook in 1QSa 1, with an analysis of *b'ḥryt hymym* ('in the last days')—a clear eschatological expression.[4]

Clearly the laws at Qumran are appropriate for their day. Burrows notes that CD refers to the use of the law and other ordinances as 'for the period of wickedness' (CD 6.10, 14; 15.7, 10), and that 1QS dictates repeated covenant renewal ceremonies annually 'all the days of the dominion of Belial' (1QS 2.19). In accordance with the eschatological expectation of the Qumran community, in the coming age these laws would be replaced by a new law.[5] Fragments of what appear to be descriptions of the restored Temple found in Caves 1, 4, and 5 may have contained regulations for worship in the new Temple (which is

---

1. Klinzing, p. 223. Here he argues that the Temple is a 'self-realizing, eschatological means of salvation', but does not contradict the fact of a divine future eschatological fulfillment in the last days, p. 224. He writes, 'Wie im Neuen Testament ist dieser Tempel ein sich schon verwirklichendes, eschatologisches Heilsgut'. This future restoration found in Klinzing's exposition of Qumran thought is ignored by Fiorenza ('Cultic Language', pp. 163-64), e.g. where she asks, 'Why did this apocalyptic-eschatological understanding of history lead in only some of the Qumran writings to the re-interpretation of the cultic institutions, but not in others? Why did apocalyptic traditions such as those found for example in the War Scroll not develop the notion of the community as eschatological temple, even though these traditions contain a strong apocalyptic-eschatological outlook and evidence the hope for a new temple and a new cult in the Jerusalem of the endtime? Moreover, why did Qumran theology not reinterpret and transfer the notion of "priest" explicitly to all members of the community, but retain a hierarchical, priestly order and leadership despite its belief that the community itself was the new temple of the endtime?'

2. J.V. Chamberlin, 'Toward a Qumran Soteriology', *NovT* 3 (1959), 305-13; Klinzing, p. 224.

3. However, the nature of the eschatological intervention is disputed. L.H. Silberman ('The Two "Messiahs" of the Manual of Discipline', *VT* 5 [1955], p. 81) sees no evidence of any cosmic catastrophe occurring in 1QM, but rather sees the coming kingdom upon the earth. R.E. Brown ('The Messianism of Qumran" *CBQ* 19 [1957], p. 62 [hereafter cited as Brown, 'The Messianism']), finds 1QH 3.19-36 an episode of cosmic upheaval relating to the defeat of Belial.

4. Burrows, p. 356; Brown, 'The Messianism', p. 79.

5. Burrows, pp. 342-43.

also suggested by the recent publication of the Temple Scroll, in which such directions could indeed be considered applicable for the eschatological age).

There is no denying that the Qumran group held to an eschatological belief. Burrows concludes in this regard: 'Presumably, the sect, like many other Jews, expected the New Jerusalem with its Temple to be built on earth, but on earth miraculously renewed' (1QS 4.25).[1]

In this period of time, therefore, the community of the New Covenant found it necessary to consider the priestly activity as both a present and a future concern. Hence we shall find the roles of priests as practiced at Qumran determined by the required present regulations, as well as by their anticipated function in the restored Temple.

*Composition of the Qumran community*

The composition of the community at Qumran suggests a stratified distinction between two major divisions: priesthood and laity. According to relevant texts, this two-fold division into 'Aaron and Israel' (e.g. 1QS 5.6; 8.6; 9.6, 7, 11; 1QSa 1.16, 23; 2.13; CD 1.7; 5.18; 10.5) may be further broken down into 'priests', levites', and 'all the people' (1QS 2.19-21), or 'Israel, and Levi and Aaron' (1QM 5.1), or 'priests, levites, sons of Israel, and proselytes' (CD 14.3-6).[2] However, the basic two-fold division between priest and laity remains intact. Further allusion to this two-fold structure is found at 4QpIsa$^a$ frg. 1; 1QpHab 12.1-10; 1QS 8.1-10; 9.5-7.[3]

Members within the 'ruling' division were termed 'priests', 'sons of Aaron', and 'sons of Zadok',[4] with 'priests' occurring as the over-

---

1. *Ibid.*, p. 351.
2. W.S. LaSor, 'Dead Sea Scrolls', *ISBE* (ed. G.W. Bromiley; rev. edn; 3 vols.; Grand Rapids: Eerdmans, 1979–1986), 1.890; Gärtner, p. 23; Burrows, p. 358.
3. Gärtner (p. 42) sees the allusion to 'priests' and 'people' as comprising the House of God at 4QpIsa$^a$ where the foundation of the building represents the priests, and the 'stones' or superstructure of the building characterize the people. At 1QpHab 12.1-5, the contrast between Lebanon and beasts serves as allusion to the council of the community and the members of the sect; so Gärtner, p. 43. The division of the Temple into the holy place and the holy of holies corresponds to the people and the priests (Gärtner, p. 29). LaSor (p. 890) is careful to note that any such expression rules out the possibility that the community considered itself a community of priests. Our study, however, will show otherwise.
4. See Klinzing, p. 132, for a thorough detailing of the frequency of occurrences and usages of these terms for 'priests' at Qumran. For his conclusion that there is

whelming common usage. The inclusion of the levites (or sons of Levi) within the upper division is based on the fact that they were assistants to the priests, with an access superior to the laity at large (1QSa 1.15-16; 2.13).[1] The significance of classifying the priests as the 'sons of Zadok', is still a much discussed area of research, but it is generally considered to have been adopted by the sectarians because of the connection of the legitimacy of the high priest with the Zadokite lineage, and therefore, the locating of the 'true' high priesthood away from Jerusalem, and at Qumran.[2] This polemical title served to enhance the legitimacy of the Qumran settlement, whether or not it was actually true that the leading priests at Qumran were of Zadokite origin.[3]

Despite this hierarchical arrangement at Qumran, the thought persists in some circles that Qumran considered all of its members 'priests'.[4] Yet this is not consistently borne out in the texts. Most frequently considered universal in application is CD 3.18–4.4, but the present or eschatological meaning of this specific text remains problematical:

> Der Gedanke, dass alle Gemeindeglieder Priester sind, ist in der Qumrangemeinde vorbereitet, aber in den erhaltenen Texten nicht konsequent durchgeführt. Wie oben ausführlich dargestellt, leben zwar alle in priesterlicher Reinheit, vollziehen alle das Opfer des untadeligen Wandels und des Lobpreises und wirken alle Sühne, aber der Priesterbegriff bleibt denen vorbehalten, die ihrer Abstammung nach Priester sind.[5]

We shall look at the community as priests again, shortly.

The composition of the 'Gemeinde' as priestly is illustrated not only by the designations bestowed upon the priests, but also by the character of their penchant for purity. Gärtner notes the priestly relevance of Josephus' remarks about the Essenes: that they underwent

---

absolutely no difference in the two titles, Sons of Aaron and Sons of Zadok, see Klinzing, p. 136.

1. Sabourin, p. 169; Gärtner, p. 4. Even more striking are the enhanced levitical privileges in 11QTemple. See Jacob Milgrom, 'Studies in the Temple Scroll', *JBL* 97 (1978), pp. 501-506.
2. Gärtner, p. 4; Klinzing, p. 133.
3. Sabourin, p. 169. Klinzing (p. 136) rejects the idea that the titles were used in a polemic against a non-Zadokite and non-Aaronide high priesthood, on the grounds of insufficient textual evidence.
4. Contra: Fiorenza, 'Cultic Language', p. 168.
5. Klinzing, p. 217.

rites of purification before partaking of the meal, the putting on of special garments of white linen, the strictly private character of their meal, the conclusion of the meal with purifications, and the taking off of the white garments (*War* II.8.5).[1] There were also physical requirements and age restrictions lest any possibility for defilement occur (1QS 2.7-9; CD 10.6-7; 15.15-17; 4QFlor 1.3-4) and the Qumran community be deemed unacceptable for God's favor at the end of the age. Qumran therefore relied upon the regulations from the Old Testament relating to priests and purity (e.g. Ezek. 44.9; Lev. 21.17-22), in order to establish their own standards of perfection and sanctity.[2] Such concerns point to the priestly composition of the Qumran sectarians.

One other area that connects Qumran with priests is the close relation between the then current understanding of angels as quasi-priestly and the priesthood itself. At 1QSb we find explicit statements that associate the Qumranic priests with the angelic priestly service. What is ambiguous at 1QSb 3.25-26 is unequivocally related to angels in 4.24-26.[3] Even should 1QSb be oriented to the eschatological epoch, the fact that at Qumran angels and priests were co-participants in the cultus informs us about the nature of the present membership at Qumran.[4] Precisely because the company of angels is understood as a priestly group, since they 'serve before God', this imagery would be of significance for Qumran.[5] Hence the scrolls suggest that when a person enters the community he at the same time enters into company with the angels, i.e. he is priestly himself.[6] So 1QS 11.8 and 1QH 11.10-14 may describe the person as being at the place of the angels when he is brought into the community,[7] or into the future eschatological Temple (4QFlor 1.4; 1QSb 4.25).[8]

1. Cited in Gärtner, p. 12.
2. *Ibid.*, pp. 4, 6, 31-32.
3. Newsom, p. 63.
4. Klinzing, p. 126.
5. *Ibid.*, p. 128. The context of 1QH shows clearly that the company with the angels is thought of as a priestly community. Also see Klinzing, p. 125.
6. H.-W. Kuhn, p. 161.
7. Klinzing, p. 125. Such communion is not some mystical experience (see J. Maier, *Die Texte vom Toten Meer* [München: Reinhardt, 1960], 2.12) by which the members participate in the heavenly cult. It is, rather, actual communion in the eschatological future as in Jewish literature when the righteous are united with angels (*1 En.* 39.4-8; 104.6; Wis. 5.5; *T. Isaac* 4.8). See Klinzing, p. 128.
8. Klinzing, p. 129.

## 1. The Priesthood in the Extra-NT Literature 43

The actual participation by Qumran members in cultic activity accompanying the angelic host of priests is attested to in 4QShirShabb. This is a cycle of thirteen Sabbath liturgies 'designed to evoke a sense of being present in the heavenly Temple'.[1] Therefore the Sabbath Shirot possess the same interest in cult and priestly concerns as does the rest of Qumran literature, but 4QShirShabb, by expressing the communion with the angels, provides 'a primary vehicle for the experience of "standing before [God] with the everlasting host . . . in common rejoicing with those who have knowledge"'.[2] Hence the praise of angels in the heavenly Temple is existentially experienced by the Qumran sectarians, and this indicates the priestly character and interest of the community.

*Role of the priest at Qumran*
The evidence from the Old Testament and the intertestamental literature showed the predominant function of the priest to be in the realm of sacrifice. However, in the literature from Qumran there is no evidence for active sacrificial ritual being practiced by the community.[3] Even the archaeological evidence does not support the claim that sacrifice was practiced by the sectarians. The celebrated cache of bones found stored in jars does not suggest a thoroughgoing sacrificial system, but rather, at best, an annual meal with meat that was not offered in the prescribed sacrificial manner.[4]

The apparent cessation of cultic sacrifices at Qumran is seen in 1QS 9.4-5; CD 9.14-16; 16.13-16, and is also attested to by Josephus (*Ant.* XVIII.1.5) and Philo (*Quod omn. prob.* 75). The single text that may speak of a sacrificial cult, CD 11.17–12.2, because it appears to suggest the presence of an altar at Qumran, is best seen as dealing with purification regulations for prayer worship. Klinzing admits that the verses 'erwähnen zwar einen anderen Kultraum als den Jerusalemer Tempel, setzen aber das Gebet an die Stelle des Opfers und sprechen vom Gebetsgottesdienst'.[5] We observe, therefore, that Qumran has

---

1. Newsom, p. 59.
2. *Ibid.*, p. 64.
3. This is disputed by Cross (*The Ancient Library*, pp. 100-103, 129 n. 37) and by many others. Best (p. 273) argues for the prominence of the teaching function at Qumran, yet this is to ignore the cultic character of Qumran literature.
4. Klinzing, pp. 41-43. A contrary position is argued by Cross (*The Ancient Library*, p. 102) who sees sacrifices occurring at Qumran. See also Gärtner, p. 13.
5. Klinzing, p. 27.

apparently replaced the active cultic ritual as performed in a polluted manner at Jerusalem with its own sacrificial substitute, that is, the practice of praise offering and the proper walk.[1]

It is generally agreed, however, that the absence of sacrificial ritual activity at Qumran was merely a temporary feature. At the end of the evil age, the Temple and its pure cultus would again be established.[2] Therefore the texts of Qumran have a fundamentally high regard for the Temple cult practice, and many see it as being re-established as the eschatological cultus (e.g. 4QFlor 1; 1QM 2.5-6; 2Q24.5–8; 1QapGen 21.1-4, 20; 1Q22 3.11–4.3; 4QTestim 18).

The initial concern for the Qumran community, therefore, was the role and function of the priest within the interim, since animal sacrifice was rejected because of the impurity at Jerusalem and the legal requirement that all sacrifice take place there. It is to the role and function of the priest at Qumran that we now turn.

That the priests were the leaders within the community is beyond dispute. The council of the community consists of twelve laymen and three priests (1QS 8.1).[3] At the head of the divisions of the camps of ten men is to be a priest and an overseer who was also a priest (CD 12.22–14.12; 1QS 6.3-5).[4] This superior role of the priest is illustrated by his pre-eminence in all functions, as we shall see. Within the council his leadership is acknowledged by the fact that the priest is the first to be seated, and he is followed by others according to their status (1QS 6.8-9). That the 'Overseer' or 'Guardian of the Camp' held a leadership role is seen in his divers functions. He admits new members, instructs the community, is involved in decision-making, determines proper conduct, and deals with practical and financial matters (CD 13.7-13). As leaders, the priests were entrusted with the proper maintenance of the community's life.[5]

---

1. *Ibid.*, p. 41. See also the section on spiritual sacrifices below.
2. Gärtner (p. 21) seems to see the future, restored Temple as being represented by the community and its life. How sacrificial cultus would emerge from such a 'spiritual' edifice is entirely unclear.
3. At CD 10.5 a variation occurs: 6 laity and 4 priests.
4. The implication, at least, is that he is a priest. This is evidenced by his role as teacher and overseer. Burrows, p. 359; A. Dupont-Sommer, *The Essene Writings from Qumran* (trans. G. Vermes; Cleveland: World, 1962; Meridian Books, 1962), p. 157 n. 1.
5. Gärtner, p. 9. To 'preserve' or to 'watch over' is used in 1QS 5.2-4 to describe the task of the priests.

Inherent in this leadership capacity was both legislative and judicial authority. Priests had jurisdiction over matters of justice, property and doctrine, as is seen in their role as interpreters of the law (1QS 5.1-3; 6.2-8; 9.7; CD 10.5-6).[1]

Priests also enjoyed the most prominent position in the table-fellowship within the community. At the meal that may have anticipated the eschatological messianic banquet[2] the priest presided and also blessed the bread and the wine, and was the first to partake of them (1QS 6.2-8; 1QSa 2.11-12, 19, 20). At this meal the strict hierarchical structure of Qumran was maintained in order to ensure the requisite purity.

Priests continued to exercise functions of prayer and worship in the community (CD 11.20-22; 1QM 13.1–14.16; 1QS 1.18–2.25; 9.3-5), activities which replaced the actual sacrifices within the community's life.[3] The priest was also the primary instructor or teacher within the community. He had to bring to mind the iniquities of the children of Israel (1QS 12.18-23; 1QM 10.2-5; 15.6-11), as well as to explain the relevance of particular texts for his time (1QpHab 2.8-9).[4] This instructional role is also inherent in the leadership position of the priest and the guardian of the community.

Finally, the role of the levites in the Qumran material appears to coincide with their role in the Temple services. They are of an inferior standing and perform the less important tasks (1QS 2.20; 1QSa 2.1; CD 14.3-6), although a levite may occasionally be given a higher status if he is well versed in the Torah (CD 13.3-4).[5]

---

1. Sabourin (p. 170) seeks to distinguish between the roles of priests as Sons of Zadok and those of the Sons of Aaron, by suggesting that perhaps the Sons of Zadok represent the supreme governing body of the community, while the Sons of Aaron are all the other priests. Without any evidence, this remains only a hypothesis, however.

2. Cross (*The Ancient Library*, p. 90); Gärtner (p. 11), where the priest and the lay leader represented the types of Messiahs to come, in the same order of significance, the Messiah of Aaron and the Messiah of Israel. To the contrary, see Burrows, p. 370, who argues that the present meals had nothing to do with the Messiah.

3. Burrows, p. 363. See J.M. Baumgarten, 'Sacrifice and Worship among the Jewish Sectarians of the Dead Sea (Qumran) Scrolls', *HTR* 46 (1953), pp. 158-59.

4. J.L. Teicher, 'Priests and Sacrifices in the Dead Sea Scrolls', *JJS* 5 (1954), p. 97. In a rather extreme argument against the priest as sacrificer, Teicher notes that 1QpHab refers to the priest as spiritual leader of the sect. The mentions of cult and sacrifice are purely metaphorical language, e.g. pp. 93-95.

5. Gärtner, p. 5.

We have seen therefore that at Qumran, the role and functions of the priest do not differ from those we have seen in our previous enquiries. Significant, however, is the fact that the priest does not participate in any sacrificial cultus, which was so prominent in the Old Testament. What appears to have happened is that this sacrificial role has become spiritualized, on the basis that the law requires cultic sacrifice only to be practiced at the Temple proper. Insofar as Qumran formed itself as a new Temple, the new form of sacrifice took on a spiritual character.

Qumran's priestly origin and concern is also seen in the eschatological texts such as 1QM, which show a marked interest in the divisions and hierachy of the priesthood, in the allocation of their duties within the Temple and in their dress (e.g. 1QM 7.10-13).[1]

In the eschatological text of 1QM we see most clearly the role of priest in relation to military encounters.[2] Here our earlier consideration of the angels as priests finds a point of contact, because not only do the angels perform cultic service, but also they provide a divine military service.[3]

The priestly role in the eschatological conflict is diverse.[4] The chief priest plays the central role as director and leader of the battle (1QM 2.1; 15.4; 16.13; 18.5) by compiling the plan for the battle and also setting the battle array. Lesser priests also serve as encouragers of the soldiers before battle; they assist in drawing up the battle order, they sound trumpets for the various maneuvers, and under the directions of the chief priest they are led in blessing God and the victory thanksgiving (1QM 7.9-13; 9.1-9; 13.1-3; 14.2-5; 15.4-15; 16.11-13;

---

1. *Ibid.*, p. 9. Gärtner, however, questions whether all of 1QM looks to the future time, or simply employs symbolic description of the actual cultus of the community.

2. K.G. Kuhn ('Qumran', *RGG* [ed. K. Galling; 3rd edn; Tübingen: Mohr (Siebeck), 1957–62], 5.750) sees the origin of this idea in the Old Testament holy war concept. According to Klinzing (p. 124 n. 79), 'Das kultische Verständnis des heiligen Krieges im Alten Testament wird die Voraussetzung für die Verbindung gewesen sein'.

3. Klinzing, p. 125.

4. For a cogent and clear argument that maintains that the chief protagonist in the eschatological battle is the priestly Messiah, see Brown ('The Messianism', pp. 57-58). Here he clearly establishes the Aaronide pre-eminence (contrary to Cross, Vermes, Yadin, and others). What becomes evident is that the Messiah of Israel, notable by his absence from the writing, should not be read into the document, as is so frequently done.

## 1. The Priesthood in the Extra-NT Literature 47

17.10-15; 18.3-6; 19.9-13). At Qumran we see that trumpets were cultic as well as war-time instruments (CD 9.22).[1] The role of the priests in the battle confrontation itself is disputed. It is understood that the priesthood placed a high premium upon cultic purity and that they would not therefore risk defiling themselves by coming into contact with a corpse. K. Schubert comments: 'Der Priestermessias nimmt am eschatologischen Krieg also nicht direkt und nicht unmittelbar teil, er ist als Priester zu heilig, um sich mit der Unreinheit des Schlachtengetümmels... einzulassen'.[2] R.E. Brown disagrees, however, and presumes that there were many possibilities for participation in the battle short of actually coming into contact with the dead. Hence we should not rule out even the participation by priests in the battle itself.[3]

The eschatological nature of this battle picture is further characterized by the worship of blessing and thanksgiving participated in by the priests. The universal praise of God is often a 'staple' in apocalyptic descriptions, as evidenced from relevant literature.[4]

The other function of the priest in the eschatological age is his role at the revived Temple cultus. This is seen particularly in 1QM 2.1-6; 7.11;[5] but also at 4QpPs37 2.10-13, where the community was expected to possess Zion and the sanctuary in the future. Depending on the significance of the Temple Scroll, the prescriptions contained therein may also point to the future, restored, legitimate practice at the Temple.

It is clear that the aversion at Qumran to the cultic practice was only operative until the end of the age. The restoration of the proper practice was anticipated. According to Klinzing,

> aber nicht um den gegenwärtig geübten Kult und die Teilnahme an ihm geht es hier. Ebenso wie der in der Kriegsrolle beschriebene Kampf in der Endzeit

---

1. Gärtner, p. 10; G. Friedrich, 'σαλπίζω', *TDNT*, 7.71-88.
2. K. Schubert, 'Zwei Messiasse aus dem Regelbuch vom Chirbet Qumran', *Judaica* 11 (1955), p. 232.
3. Brown, 'The Messianism', p. 58.
4. E.g. *T. Levi* 3.8; *1 En.* 39–40; *2 En.* 20.21; *Apoc. Abr.* 17–18; Isa. 7–9; Rev. 4–5. See Newsom, pp. 59-60.
5. Here it is stipulated that the priest is not to enter the sanctuary wearing his 'garments for battle'. Cultic activity requires a different attire.

stattfinden wird, betreffen auch die Anordnungen in 1QM 2.1ff. den Kultus der zukünftigen Endzeit.¹

The attitude of Qumran toward ritual sacrifice was, in principle, favorable. No passage suggests a hostility toward ritual sacrifice, but only an antipathy to the contemporary practice in Jerusalem.²

The role of the priestly Messiah (or for that matter even his presence in the texts) as the leader in the eschatological community with precedence over the royal Messiah remains controversial, although most evidence now favors the notion of two Messiahs, with the priestly one possessing a superior dignity.³ K.G. Kuhn correctly points out that the two Messiahs concept was not a creation *ex nihilo* by the Qumran sectarians. Already the *Testament of the Twelve Patriarchs* (e.g. *T. Judah* 21.2-5) presented the concept of a higher-ranking priestly Messiah.⁴

In our investigation of the role of the priests in Qumran literature we have seen that the functions are similar to those of the Old Testament and the intertestamental writings. Conspicuous, however, is the spiritualized character of the sacrifice offered by priests in the contemporary activity at Qumran. That this spiritualized sacrifice replaced the material cult, while being alienated from Jerusalem, illustrates the current feeling among the sectarians that they represented the Temple and place of God's dwelling, as long as the Temple was being profaned.⁵ To the matter of access to God by means

---

1. Klinzing, p. 35. Also see Y. Yadin, *The Message of the Scrolls* (London: Weidenfeld and Nicolson, 1957), p. 135; Burrows, p. 363; Maier, *Die Texte*, 2.116; Daly, pp. 170-71.
2. Daly, p. 171.
3. CD 12.23; 14.19; 19.10; 20.1; 1QS 9.10-11; 1QSa 2.11-16, 18-21. K.G. Kuhn ('The Two Messiahs of Aaron and Israel', in *The Scrolls and the New Testament* [ed. K. Stendahl; New York: Harper and Row, 1957], pp. 54-64; Brown, 'The Messianism', pp. 57-82) present convincing evidence for the existence of two Messiahs that has become widely accepted by scholars.
4. K.G. Kuhn, 'The Two Messiahs', p. 58; Sabourin, p. 174.
5. This, however, is never explicitly stated in the literature. Cf. e.g. Klinzing, p. 91: 'Vom Jerusalemer Heiligtum wird nicht gesagt, dass Gott dort wohne oder dass die Herrlichkeit Gottes es um der Unreinheit willen verlassen habe [only at CD 3.1—author]. Auffallender ist noch, dass im Zusammenhang mit der Vorstellung von der Gemeinde als Tempel fast nie vom Wohnen Gottes, von seiner Herrlichkeit oder sonst von seiner Gegenwart in der Gemeinde die Rede ist. Nur ein einziges Mal begegnet "Wohnung" als Bezeichnung für diesen neuen Tempel (1QS 8.8), aber ohne jeden Akzent und als ein Tempelbegriff unter anderen. Von einer Wohnung

## 1. The Priesthood in the Extra-NT Literature 49

of such spiritual offerings we will turn shortly. But first we must examine the portrayal at Qumran of the entire community as priests.

*Community as Temple and priests*
There is little doubt that the Qumran community perceived itself as a new Temple.[1] But most scholars understand that the Temple community would at the end of the age be replaced by the re-established cultus in Jerusalem.[2] This provides evidence of the strong priestly influence and understanding at Qumran. Klinzing seems to suggest a marked division between the priests and laity on this matter, for nowhere do the concepts of the future restored Temple in Jerusalem and of the community of the Temple appear together. It would appear, then, that among the priestly circles the expectation continued for a return to the cultic service of the Jerusalem Temple, while the lay element concentrated on the present Temple idea.[3]

The origin of the concept of the entire community as priests is beyond the scope of this investigation. What we may say is that while a division existed between the priestly and lay elements at Qumran, there was also the belief that the entire community was priestly. This is implied in particular texts by the atonement effected by the community, by the strict concern for community purity, and by a

Gottes wird im übrigen nur beim himmlischen Heiligtum gesprochen.' However, it is implicit from the conception of the Temple that this is so.

1. Klinzing, p. 74: 'Das Selbstverständnis als Tempel gehört zu den Grundlagen der Gemeinde'. This explains the passion for 'holiness' at Qumran, e.g. Gärtner, p. 13.

2. Maier, *Die Texte*, 2.116; H. Braun, 'Qumran und das Neue Testament: Ein Bericht über 10 Jahre Forschung (1950–1959)', *TRu* 28 (1962), p. 132; Gärtner, pp. 21, 53. A different view however, is taken by Klinzing (p. 92), who sees this reconciling of two contradictory ideas (Qumran as Temple and the expectation of the future temple) as too simple a solution by harmonizing. The texts contain no evidence for the thought of a temporary Temple; no interim motif is found with this Temple idea. He therefore sees the community as the realization of the eschatological Temple. However, this seems to ignore the contrast between present and eschatological terminology found in the documents themselves: e.g. 1QM 2.3; 7.11; 4QpPs37 3.11; 4QFlor 1.2, 3, 6; 4QSb 4.25.

3. Klinzing, pp. 93, 143. It is interesting to note that the evidence of Qumran as Temple occurs only in particular texts (1QS, CD and 1QpHab), while other writings which betray a more priestly outlook (1QH, 1QM, 4QpPs37) do not have this concept. This was the partial result of different sources, but was also due to the fact that the idea of Temple was not held at the beginning of the community, but grew out of the competing beliefs at Qumran over its two hundred year history. So Klinzing, p. 89.

terminology that is perceptively sacerdotal.¹ Nevertheless, while priestly prescriptions are applied to the entire community, the 'priestly idea' remains the reserve of those who were genealogically priests.² As such, any priestly concept of the lay members appears to have been of a relative degree. For instance, the fully initiated lay members who could participate in the activities of the community were labeled 'the many' by the priestly leaders. But to the novitiates and the other candidates these same lay members were know as 'masters'. Hence there was also a stratification of leadership within the lay portion of the community, whereby the more advanced laity was esteemed more highly and deemed more priestly by its peers, although not received as bona fide priests by the priestly element.³

We shall see that certain characteristics of the Temple priests are therefore applied to the entire community. Gärtner comments about this apparent tension between priests and laity and the community as priests: 'This is not to say that the entire community was made up of priests, but certain aspects of the priests' ideal of sanctification were elevated into general conditions of membership of the community—a phenomenon also to be found in Pharisaism'.⁴ The members of the community appear to have been priests at least in terms of purity, but contrary to Gärtner, also in terms of practice and access—since they effect atonement and offer spiritual sacrifices.

The primary text that depicts the community as priests is CD 3.21–4.4, where CD has altered Ezek. 44.15 by the addition of an 'and'. Here, 'Priester und Heiligtum werden im folgenden auf die Gemeindeglieder und die Gemeinde gedeutet',⁵ although Klinzing himself sees this as a first step, at best, in the presentation of a general priesthood.⁶

---

1. Newsom, p. 62; Klinzing, p. 106: 'Aber wenn auch eine direkte Bezeichnung aller Gemeindeangehörigen als Priester fehlt, so sind doch priesterliche Vorschriften, Gebräuche, und Vorrechte auf das Leben der ganzen Gemeinschaft bezogen, sind Vorstellungen und Terminologie in den Texten vom priesterlichen Denken geprägt'.
2. Klinzing, p. 217. Hence, even though we are more positive about the 'priestly' character of its members, we are nevertheless in general agreement with Fiorenza, 'Cultic Language', pp. 166-68.
3. Burrows, p. 362.
4. Gärtner (p. 5) Klinzing and (pp. 142-43) both note that at Qumran we come close to a general priesthood idea.
5. Klinzing, pp. 130, 142. For further information on CD 3.21–4.4, see Klinzing, pp. 75-80, 130-43; Daly, pp. 169-70; Maier, Die Texte, 2.47; Sabourin, pp. 168-72.
6. Klinzing, p. 143.

Problematical is the use of 'sons of Zadok' at CD 3.21–4.1 which, as we have seen, is usually applied in apposition to 'priests'. But here in this passage it designates the community.[1] This is most readily seen in the use of the term 'Chosen' at CD 4.3, which is used to refer to the entire community eighteen times in writings from Qumran, but only twice with reference to priests chosen by God.[2] 'Chosen' also occurs with 'righteousness' at 1QS 9.14 and 1QH 2.14.[3] 'Called by name' in its context at CD 4.4 also points to the community, as at CD 2.11 and 1QM 3.2; 4.10.[4] Finally, the special use of the verb '*āmad* (4.4) in CD directs us to see the passage applied to the community and to the circle of priests.[5]

Therefore, CD 3.21–4.4 has ignored the original meaning of Ezek. 44.15 and has reinterpreted it in terms of the situation in the Qumran community. The titles 'priests and levites and sons of Zadok' are applied to the members at Qumran, so that we come very close to the concept of universal priesthood.[6]

The 'hypnotic' ability of 4QShirShabb to transport the reciter to the heavenly realms and to create a sense of presence in the heavenly Temple seems to apply more to the consecration to the priesthood and does not pertain to the community as a whole.[7] As C. Newsom explains, 'To the extent that the worshiper experienced himself as present in the heavenly temple through the recitation of the Shabbath Shirot, his status as a faithful and legitimate priest would have been

---

1. See Klinzing, pp. 135-36. He notes that Dupont-Sommer sees the application based on the fact that most members were of Zadokite origin. However, already at this time, the distinctions between the designation of Aaronite and Zadokite was blurred. Gärtner (p. 5) and Klinzing (p. 131) see this applied to the community by means of a word-play, whereby the 'sons of Zadok', and the 'sons of Righteousness', refer to the whole community (1QS 3.20, 22; 9.14; 1QH 8.1). Also see Daly, p. 170; Sabourin, p. 169.
2. Klinzing, p. 139 n. 72, where a complete list of references is presented.
3. *Ibid.*, pp. 131-32.
4. *Ibid.*, p. 139.
5. *Ibid.*, p. 140. Klinzing notes the peculiarity of '*āmad* in CD, where its eight occurrences are always applied to historical persons.
6. Daly, p. 170; Klinzing, p. 142.
7. Newsom, pp. 82-83 n. 22: 'One cannot say, of course, whether the recitation of the Sabbath Shirot was restricted to those members of the Qumran community who were priests. Certainly the strong priestly focus of the document would make this a plausible supposition. Even if the document were recited for a mixed lay and priestly group, it is the function of the document for the community's understanding of its priestly leadership that is most important.'

convincingly confirmed in spite of persistent contradictions of his claims in the world'.¹

The priestly character of the community is further illustrated by the strict rules of purity which the members observed. Josephus' account of the Essenes is often presented as evidence for the priestly self-understanding at Qumran,² although his account is often not corroborated by any extant Qumran documents.³

A priestly purity is witnessed to in the documents, however, with regard to other areas of Qumran's life. Entry into the community was characterized by strict regulations ensuring purity (e.g. 1QSa 2.3-10).⁴ Central to the maintenance of purity were regular washings (1QS 5.13; 6.16-17), which also effected atonement, replacing the cult of sacrifice (1QS 3.4-11). Connected with the washings were the fellowship meals, which also were of strictest purity since they too represented the offering (1QS 5.14-17).⁵ Such purity necessarily led to the reinforced importance of 'separation' (1QS 5.10), which found its basis in the Old Testament where it refers to both the separation of Israel from other peoples, and the separation of priests and levites for the cultic service.⁶

---

1. *Ibid.*, p. 72.
2. Klinzing, pp. 107-14. Klinzing is convinced of the factual reliability of Josephus' account.
3. For instance, the mention of white gowns (*War* II.123, 137; V.229; *Ant.* XIII.151, 158) is nowhere confirmed at Qumran, although evidence is found for such in the Old Testament (Exod. 28.42; Lev. 16.4; Ezek. 44.17). Again, there is no information regarding celibacy or marriage among the sectarians. At certain texts, women and children are presumed (CD 7.7-9; 19.2-5; 1QSa 1.4; 1QM 7.3). There are indeed purity laws connected with sexual intercourse, laws which would be adhered to closely at Qumran. J. Milgrom ('Further Studies in the Temple Scroll [cont.]', *JQR* 71 [1980], pp. 100-101) rightly points out that even in the Temple Scroll, this interest in purity did not exclude marriage entirely, since the priestly course of service was but two weeks in the year. Hence, afterward the priest could easily return to his home, no longer under the strict obligations of Temple purity regulations.
4. See Klinzing, p. 107; J.T. Milik, *Ten Years of Discovery in the Wilderness of Judaea* (Studies in Biblical Theology, 26; trans. J. Strugnell; London: SCM, 1959), p. 114.
5. Qumran follows the strictures of the Old Testament regarding offerings and requisite purity (Lev. 10.12-20; 22.1-33; Num. 18.11; Deut. 18.1; Ezek. 44.29. Cf. also *Jub.* 31.16; *T. Levi* 8; *T. Judah* 21). See Klinzing, pp. 114-15.
6. Klinzing, p. 109. See Lev. 20.24, 26; 1 Kgs 8.53; Ezra 6.21; 9.1; 10.11; Neh. 9.2; 10.29; Num. 8.14; 16.19; Deut. 10.8; 1 Chron. 23.13.

## 1. *The Priesthood in the Extra-NT Literature* 53

'Separation' as a means of maintaining ritual purity is also the reason for the practice of common ownership. This served to ensure that the profanation of goods from outside the community would not occur (CD 6.14-16; 1QS 1.12; 3.2; 5.2-3, 14-20; 6.17, 19, 22, 25; 7.6; 8.23; 9.7-9).[1]

At Qumran Old Testament priestly tasks have become the task of the entire community (CD 6.11–7.6). In this sense, therefore, the purity of the community characterizes it as a priestly one, in stark contrast to the profaned cultic officials at the Jerusalem Temple (e.g. CD 5.6-15).

*Cultic terminology for the community*
Despite the fact that no actual sacrificial cult was in place at Qumran, the cultic terminology applied to the community members suggests that they were considered (or at least were intended to be considered) 'priests'. Cultic language reminiscent of the Old Testament priesthood describes the members at Qumran.[2]

*Gôrāl* at 1QSa 1.9, 20 and 1QH 11.11 is a term of the priesthood in the Old Testament (1 Chron. 24.5, 7, 31; 25.8, 9; 26.13-14), encompassing the notions of both casting lots and dividing into lots (sections).[3]

The action of the community represented by its standing before God with the purpose of serving him is common in the literature. *'āmad (lipnê)* refers to the Qumran community frequently, particularly in 1QH at 3.21; 4.21; 7.30-31; 11.10-11, 13; 12.22-24; 16.13; 18.10, 28.[4] However, the purpose for the 'standing' in the Old Testament texts is made clear in the cited texts which read 'stand to minister' or 'stand and minister'.[5] Therefore the value of *'āmad*, without the 'to minister', leaves the true nature of the community ambiguous. We may agree that *'āmad* refers to the cultic practice of the priests, but this is usually clarified with 'to minister'. Such a clarification is absent at Qumran.

---

1. *Ibid.*, p. 113.
2. See K.G. Kuhn (ed.), *Konkordanz zu den Qumrantexten* (Göttingen: Vandenhoeck & Ruprecht, 1960); the supplement, K.G. Kuhn (ed.), 'Nachträge zur Konkordanz zu den Qumrantexten', *RevQ* 4 (1963), pp. 163-234.
3. See Klinzing, p. 123.
4. *Ibid.*, p. 117. Klinzing considers the Old Testament references, Deut. 10.8; 17.17; 18.5, 7; Ezek. 44.11, 15; 2 Chron. 29.11.
5. See previous note.

The priestly connection of *'āmad* is affirmed by Klinzing.[1] This is evident from the occurrences of the term in the Old Testament where the majority of the instances relate to the service of priests and levites. However, in the Qumran documents, the closest parallel to the action involved in the 'service' at the altar or in the cult, as in the Old Testament, is found in the few allusions where *'āmad* means 'to worship' (1QH 16.7, 18; 17.14; CD 20.21). At Qumran the cultic terminology has been used in order to describe the contemporary practices as 'spiritual' sacrifice.

The second most frequent word for the priestly service at Qumran is *šārat* (1QM 2.1, 2, 3; 1QSb 4.25).[2] It is applied to the community, which as the 'chosen' will 'serve him perpetually' (1QH 12.23; 15.24). The occurrences of the verb *šārat* give evidence of a priestly allusion, although any precise cultic context regarding the community is absent. The term is used generally to describe the priestly community, but any specific activity by that community goes unmentioned.

*Kipper* in the Old Testament is practically a technical term which has the priest as the subject. However, in 1QS and 1QSa the subject (either expressed or implied) is either Aaron and Israel, or Zadokites and laity (1QS 8.6, 10; 9.3-5; 1QSa 1.2-3).[3] Hence it appears that the entire community effected atonement. It is to be noted, however, that the community consists of both the priests and the laity. Nothing explicit is said about the laity's ability to atone apart from the priests, although the stipulations applied to priests would have to be adhered to by the laity as well. However, insofar as spiritual sacrifices applied to all the community, the lay members may be seen as priests effecting atonement also (e.g. 1QS 9.3-5).

In the Old Testament, the verbs *bô'*, *niggaš*, and *qārêb* are technical terms for the priestly approach and entry into the cultic sphere. We are able, also, to differentiate qualities of access between *bô'*, *niggaš* and *qārêb*. Such a distinction presents itself also in the Qumran writings, although not so much in terms of meaning, as in terms of the object of each verb.

Klinzing suggests that both *niggaš* and *qārêb* are cultic terms reapplied at Qumran to refer to 'entry into the community'.[4] However,

1. Klinzing, pp. 122-23.
2. *Ibid.*, p. 117.
3. *Ibid.*, p. 116.
4. *Ibid.*, pp. 117-18. Here, Klinzing cites Gerhard von Rad, *Old Testament Theology* (trans. D.M.G. Stalker; 2 vols.; New York: Harper & Row, 1962-65),

## 1. The Priesthood in the Extra-NT Literature 55

of the fifteen occurrences of *niggaš* it appears that only three have any specific and stated purpose for 'entry' (1QM 19.11, 'to praise God'; 1QH 12.23 and CD 4.2, 'to serve') into the community. *Qārêb* is ambiguous in the seven (of twenty-one) occurrences where it approaches the meaning of 'entering the community' (1QS 6.16, 19, 22; 7.21; 8.18; 9.15; 1QH 14.14),[1] and not a single citation spells out the purpose for the 'entry', which is commonplace in the Old Testament passages. Therefore, if it be the case that certain passages do suggest 'entry into the community', at the same time there is seldom any mention of the purpose of entry that implies the replacement at Qumran of the altar sacrifices by spiritual ones.[2]

*Bô'* occurs frequently in the Qumran writings, but, as in the Old Testament, the vast majority of its more than one hundred occurrences have no priestly relevance. This has led Klinzing to admit, 'Ihr isoliertes Vorkommen würde deshalb keine Sicherheit dafür bieten, dass sich wirklich eine priesterliche Vorstellung mit ihnen verbindet'.[3]

Whereas the object of *niggaš* and *qārêb* was the 'community', the most frequent object of *bô'* is 'covenant', and more seldom, 'community'.[4] Again, however, it is to be noted that only very infrequently does the purpose of 'entry' find itself expressed (1QM 12.14; 1QH 7.30; 18.28; 1QSa 1.12; 1QS 1.7; CD 6.12; 11.22; 20.2, 28).[5]

---

2.219. Refer to K.G. Kuhn (*Konkordanz*, and 'Nachträge zur Konkordanz') for the appropriate text references, and Maier (*Die Texte*, 2.27, 107).

1. 'To approach the council' (1QS 6.16; 8.18) or even 'to approach the community' appears to us to be ambiguous phraseology, since the 'purpose' for the approach is not explicitly stated.

2. At the conclusion of his book, Klinzing (pp. 219-20) expresses doubt as to the influence of Qumran on the New Testament understanding of 'to draw near', on the basis that Qumran used the term 'nearing God' to signal 'entering into the "Gemeinde"'. We would suggest that Qumran influence is lacking here, because its concern is with spiritual sacrifice rather than the altar sacrifice that is crucial to the context in the New Testament, e.g. Heb.

3. Klinzing, p. 119. Although he notes that certain passages in 1QH 'appear' to point to a priestly usage, and at p. 108 n. 13, he nonetheless considers *bô'* a 'terminus technicus für den Eintritt in die Gemeinde!'

4. K.G. Kuhn, *Konkordanz*, pp. 28-30; Klinzing, p. 118 n. 42. Klinzing has inadvertently omitted 4QFlor 1.3 from his list. He suggests that to 'enter into the covenant' is a circumlocution for 'to enter into community', and that therefore the two phrases are identical.

5. These contain even the vaguest references to purpose. Those explicitly stating the purpose of the entry are 1QS 1.7; 1QM 12.14; 1QH 18.28.

Klinzing further observes that 1QH contains passages which characterize the purification before the service as evidence of the priestly motif (1QH 3.21; 7.30; 11.10; 16.12). Such cleansing presumes that the result will be 'entry into the community' in accordance with the Old Testament cultic practice of ritual purity. But at Qumran this purity pertains to entry into the community.[1]

One final consideration is the few occurrences where the entrance into the community is linked with the entrance into the company of angels (1QH 3.22; 11.12, 13; 16.12-14; 1QSa). We have already noted the priestly composition of the company of angels, and so entry into the company with the angels may suggest entry into the priesthood and offering praise to God (1QH 3.23; 11.14).[2]

From this survey of cultic terminology which serves to identify the community as priests, it is certain that such was the belief held by the Qumran sectarians. However, we ought not to build upon association of words used cultically in the Old Testament to conclude that their appearance at Qumran signifies synonymity. Such a conclusion belies the context of the surrounding material. For instance, the use of *bô'*, *niggaš*, and *qārêb* is clearly cultic in the Old Testament, but not exclusively so. Such terms derive their full significance only when their purpose and object are elaborated as in the Old Testament; for example, to enter the sanctuary in order 'to bring', or to approach the altar in order 'to offer'. Such purpose clauses are lacking at Qumran to a large extent, and this ought to prompt the question, Why, if such clauses were included in the Old Testament passages, are they generally omitted at Qumran?

Perhaps the purpose of entering the community was understood to be in order to offer spiritual sacrifices. But the purpose in the Old Testament was similarly obvious, yet it was stated nonetheless. At any rate, we may conclude that the practice of linking *bô'*, *niggaš* and *qārêb* as unequivocally priestly terms to their usage at Qumran may be justified, but not definitive. 'Entry into the community' remains ambiguous unless the reason is advanced, and that occurs only infrequently in Qumran literature.

---

1. Klinzing, p. 121: 'Man muss gereinigt sein wie ein Priester, der in das Heiligtum "hineingeht" und sich den heiligen Dingen bzw. Gott "naht", um seinen Dienst auszuüben'. A caveat, however, is that Klinzing does not consider the rarity of instances where 'nahen' is actually linked with 'Dienst' in the texts.
2. *Ibid.*, pp. 121-22; H.-W. Kuhn, *Enderwartung*, pp. 66-70.

## 1. The Priesthood in the Extra-NT Literature 57

*Spiritual sacrifice*

Qumran anticipated the re-establishment of actual sacrifice in the restored Jerusalem Temple (e.g. 1QSb 3.1-3; 4QDibHam 4.9-11; CD 11.17–12.2; 16.13-19; 1QM 2.1-6).[1] However, in the interim period between the sectarians' dislocation from Jerusalem and their triumphal return to the Temple, they replaced the actual sacrificial services permitted only in Jerusalem with 'a general *'abôdāh* (service)', a life according to the law, the basis for which was found already in the Old Testament.[2]

It was this spiritual sacrifice that led the Qumran community to understand itself as representing the Temple (1QH 6.25-34). Since acceptable sacrifice was occurring in the community's life they readily began to see themselves as the suitable cultic realm and to describe themselves as a Temple.[3] In this community, as at the Temple, effective atonement for members is made.[4]

The replacement offerings, in lieu of the material sacrifices, are chiefly: praise to God ('Lobpreis'), blameless walk, and prayer. At Qumran such spiritual sacrifices effected atonement for the membership,[5] and in view of the profane conditions at Jerusalem, Qumran

---

1. Daly, p. 170, where he cites Gärtner, p. 45 n. 2.
2. Gärtner (p. 46) sees the same critical attitude toward the cult in the Old Testament prophets and psalms as among the Qumran sectarians; i.e. both placed the doing of righteousness above the ritual of sacrifice. The criticism at Qumran finds its parallel in Old Testament texts:

| | |
|---|---|
| 1QS 9.3-5 | = Hos. 2.19-20; 6.6 |
| 1QS 8.2-4 | = Mic. 6.6-8; Ps. 51.19; Dan. 3.38 (LXX) |
| CD 11.20-22 | = Prov. 15.8 |
| 1QS 10.22, 26–11.1 | = Hos. 14.3; Ps. 51.19 |
| 1QS 5.3 | = Isa. 56.1 |
| 1QS 1.24 | = Mic. 6.6-8 |

Already in the prophets *ṣedeq* was no longer associated with the cult, e.g. Amos 5.21; Isa. 41.2; 45.13. See Daly, p. 160; Klinzing, p. 105.

3. Klinzing, pp. 41 and 105-106. This was an easy comparison to make in light of the priestly self-consciousness of the community.

4. Gärtner (p. 25) writes that 'the life of the community makes atonement, after the fashion of a "sacrifice", for those who belong to its number; in the same way the sacrifice made in the Temple was in some cases regarded as making a similar atonement'.

5. E.g. 1QS 2.26–3.12; 5.1-7; 8.1-10; 9.3-6; CD 3.21–4.4; 4QFlor 1.6-7. See Klinzing, p. 95; Gärtner, p. 30; Daly, pp. 161-71.

saw itself as the sole means for maintaining the holiness of Israel by effectively atoning for the sin accumulating in the Temple.

One means of atonement was the blameless walk.[1] This was closely related to living according to the law, which in turn was an expression of the life of humility and repentance (1QS 3.4-12).[2] At 1QS 8.3-4 the relation between atonement and the blameless life is clear from the expression of atonement that occurs in the midst of four regulations concerning the behavior of the community.[3] 4QFlor 1.6-7 also relates this required lifestyle to doing the works of the law, where the works of law are likened to sacrifices.[4]

The praise of God also serves as a replacement for sacrifice (1QS 9.4-5, 26; 10.6-8, 14, 22)[5] and possesses the atoning efficacy of valid cultic sacrifice. In fact, 'Lobpreis' is seen as occurring in a cultic manner (1QS 10; 1QH 12.3-11) and is specified to be done regularly (1QS 10.23; 1QH 11.6; 12.4, 7).[6]

Atoning efficacy was also accomplished by prayer. At CD 11.20-21 two forms of sacrifice are contrasted in the conclusion that 'the prayer of the righteous is a pleasing offering'. Here 'an offering' has been deliberately added to Prov. 15.18.[7]

We may therefore conclude that at Qumran the community perceived itself as priestly: it offered the true sacrifices and effected atonement in the time of defilement at the Temple. Yet they also

---

1. 1QS 4.22; 8.10; 9.2, 5, 9; 10.21; 1QM 14.7; 1QH 1.36; 1QSa 1.28; 4QM$^a$ 5. Also at Sir. 35(32).1, 'Whoever does the law, makes many sacrifices'. See Klinzing, p. 99. There is a high regard for 'Lobpreis' in the Old Testament, e.g. Prov. 15.8; Hos. 14.3; Pss. 19.15; 40.10; 51.17; 56.14; 119.108; 141.2. See Klinzing, p. 97.

2. That humility characterized the Qumran community is seen at 1QS 2.24; 4.3; 5.3, 25; 9.22; 1QH 5.21; 11.1; 14.3; 17.12; 18.14; 1QM 14.7. So Klinzing, p. 101. Daly (p. 163) notes the importance of the 'internal disposition of the worshiper' for atonement.

3. That the text in question refers to the entire community and not merely to the Council of the Community is seen at 1QS 3.4-12; 5.6; 8.6, 10; 9.5-7. Qumran is seen to have an atoning function according to Klinzing, pp. 102-104.

4. Daly, p. 169; Gärtner, p. 45.

5. Klinzing (pp. 96-97) considers sacrifice and praise as identical, saying, 'Lobpreis ist Opfer!' Such is the case at Qumran. However, in the Old Testament, it appears that the existing cult is seen less favorably than the 'Lobpreis' (e.g. Pss. 40.7; 51.19; 69.31). Hence, in the Old Testament, we see a depreciation in cult, but at Qumran the value of cult sacrifices was not denied, except that they had to be pure sacrifices, which was certainly not considered to be the case at Jerusalem.

6. *Ibid.*, p. 96.

7. *Ibid.*, p. 94; Gärtner, p. 46.

## 1. The Priesthood in the Extra-NT Literature

looked forward to the day when the priestly task of cultic sacrifice would again be the Zadokite function. Hence they saw themselves as priests, but they were fully aware that the genealogical priesthood possessed the foremost place in the eschatological Temple.[1]

*The Temple Scroll*

The discovery of the Temple Scroll (11QTemple) has served to illustrate further the priestly interest at Qumran.[2] J. Maier's cursory outline of the document clearly reflects its pervasive cultic character:

| | |
|---|---|
| Part I | Introduction: Incorporation in the Sinai Covenant, col. 2 |
| Part II | The Sanctuary in the Holy City and its Cult, cols. 3–48? |
| | A. The Building and the Altar, 3–13.7 |
| | B. The Cycle of Feasts and their Sacrifices, 13.8–30.? |
| | C. The Temple Court Construction, 30.?–45.7 |
| | D. The Ritual Protection of the Sanctuary and the Holy City, 45.7–48.? |
| Part III | Laws of General Application, cols. 48.?–66.17f.[3] |

The question of the origin of this document is yet unsolved and any solution appears to be tied to the confusing state of scholarship regarding canonicity, authority, and sectarianism in the early centuries. However, Y. Yadin suggests that 'the Temple Scroll is above all a book of the law, laws for the community both for the present and for the future time when the true heirs of the Zadokite priesthood would again reign in Jerusalem'.[4] Whether this Temple Torah was to be considered a second Torah given to Moses along with the Sinai

---

1. Cf. Klinzing, p. 217.
2. The most thorough work on the Temple Scroll at the present time is Yadin's three-volume work, *The Temple Scroll*. Also helpful is J. Maier, *The Temple Scroll*. Other articles include: J. Milgrom, 'Studies in the Temple Scroll', pp. 501-23; 'The Temple Scroll', *BA* 41 (1978), pp. 105-20; 'Further Studies in the Temple Scroll', *JQR* 71 (1980), pp. 1-17 and 'Further Studies (cont.)', pp. 89-106; W.O. McCready, 'The Sectarian Status of Qumran: The Temple Scroll', *RevQ* 11 (1983), pp. 183-91; Y. Yadin, 'The Temple Scroll', *BA* 30 (1967), pp. 135-39; 'The Temple Scroll, the Longest and Most Recently Discovered Dead Sea Scroll', *BAR* 10 (1984), pp. 32-49; B. Levine, 'The Temple Scroll: Aspects', *BASOR* 232 (1978), pp. 5-23. Also the monograph by B.Z. Wacholder, *The Dawn of Qumran: The Sectarian Torah and the Teacher of Righteousness* (Cincinnati: Hebrew Union College Press, 1983).
3. Cf. Maier (*Temple Scroll*, pp. 8-19), where he gives a detailed outline based on Yadin's extensive work. See also Milgrom, 'The Temple Scroll', pp. 107-14.
4. Yadin, 'The Temple Scroll, the Longest', p. 44.

Torah,¹ or was understood as a polemical document composed or edited by the Teacher of Righteousness against the rival Wicked Priest in the time of John Hyrcanus,² is still an open question. But what provided the incentive for 11QTemple seems to have been some opposition to laws that were considered contrary to those which God had spoken.³

Yadin has ventured to state that perhaps the creation of this document was guided by the fact that no description of the Temple's architectural plan is given in the Old Testament, although it is explicitly alluded to in 2 Chron. 28.11. Based on this reference, the author (or editor) seized the opportunity to present a picture of the Temple as it should have been at the then present time, and in the future.⁴

The authority of 11QTemple was as 'canonical' scripture for the sectarians;⁵ but the state of the canon at that time, in the light of modern scholarship, does not show that the Old Testament Torah was held in any lesser degree of authority. There may very well have been a multiplicity of 'canonical' Torahs or 'pentateuchs'.⁶

There is no question that 11QTemple presents a different version of the Old Testament Torah, in particular Deuteronomy 12–26. Yet the setting of the document, its importance, and the meaning of its words, are matters not yet dealt with by scholars in any great detail. Perhaps Yadin, Flusser, Levine and Maier⁷ propose the most viable view that there is described in 11QTemple a non-eschatological ideal Temple

---

1. Wacholder (p. 27) finds evidence for this at col. 59.
2. Milgrom ('The Temple Scroll', pp. 115-19) considers polemic occurring whenever a law is emphasized either by alteration or repetition, and so contrasting with the establishment position. Yadin (*The Temple Scroll*, 1.389) finds such polemic in the statements of the king and in the laws for Deuteronomy.
3. Yadin, *Temple Scroll*, 1.87. The unique first person address found in 11QTemple and the appearance of the tetragrammaton characterize this writing as the very word of God. Also, Yadin, 'The Temple Scroll, the Longest', pp. 40-41.
4. Yadin, 'The Temple Scroll, the Longest', p. 41.
5. Yadin, *Temple Scroll*, 1.390-92.
6. *Ibid.*, 1.390-91. Yadin recognizes this question of canon raised in articles by J. Sanders and B. Levine. Wacholder (pp. 18-21), however, sees '11QTorah' [sic] as the authoritative alternative to Old Testament Torah, citing col. 59 where he claims that redemption is said to come only where the king observes the royal charter in '11QTorah'.
7. Levine, p. 21; Maier, *Temple Scroll*, p. 6; Wacholder, pp. 22-24; D. Flusser, 'Review of Y. Yadin, *The Temple Scroll* (Hebrew)', *Numen* 26 (1979), pp. 271-74.

## 1. The Priesthood in the Extra-NT Literature

which the Israelites should build and maintain until such time as God establishes his own future Temple,[1] and this serves to distinguish the views of the sectarians on the 'days of Belial' (the present age) and the 'days to come' or 'day of blessing' (the end of the age).

The priestly character and interest of 11QTemple is seen not only by its obvious cultic context, but also by the perspective from which it was written. Maier rightly observes that the cultic program described was written from the inside outward, that is, from the priest's perspective. The writing begins at the most holy area of the holy of holies and, by concentric rings circumscribing areas of holiness, it proceeds outward, extending to cover the holy land, with laws of general application.[2] The picture in Ezekiel 40–48 also resembles 11QTemple, again indicating the priestly content and context of the latter document.[3]

---

1. The eschatology of 11QTemple is closely tied to one's translation of col. 29.8-10, and in particular the *'ad* in 29.9. Wacholder (pp. 21-22) translates it to mean 'during', while others translate as 'until'. Such a translation makes the difference between a present eschatology and a future eschatology (e.g. Maier, *Temple Scroll*, p. 86; Milgrom, 'The Temple Scroll', p. 114; Yadin, *Temple Scroll*, 1.182-87), but with a future Temple that will not differ in character from the one in 11QTemple. The only 'difference' will be that the Lord himself will build it (19.10). See Yadin, *Temple Scroll*, 1.187. This argues against Gärtner, who foresees the future Temple as a 'spiritual' one (as at 4QFlor 1.10; 2.2-3).

2. Maier, *Temple Scroll*, pp. 5-6. In ascending order:

1. Holy Land
2. Area around holy city—within a 3 days' journey
3. A zone of 3 *ris* (4 miles) around holy city
4. Holy City
5. Temple mount
6. Outer Temple court—open to male and female
7. The area for cultically qualified males
8. Priests' area
9. Outer area for cult worship around the altar for burnt offerings and the Temple building
10. Inner area for cult worship—Hall of Temple, with incense altar, etc.
11. Innermost area for cult worship, the Holy of Holies, the place of God's presence.

Milgrom, 'Further Studies (cont.)', p. 96, also considers the degrees of holiness.

3. See Milgrom, 'The Temple Scroll', p. 114. Also see S. Niditch ('Ezekiel 40–48 in a Visionary Context', *CBQ* 48 [1986], pp. 208-24), for her investigation of the meaning of the Temple depiction in Ezekiel.

The role and function of the priests do not differ to any degree from the Old Testament Torah's characterization. In matters of specific detail, the duty and role may be altered but the principal tasks are identical. We will not concern ourselves with the minor variations from the Old Testament practices evinced by the priestly role in 11QTemple.[1]

Most striking is the presupposition in 11QTemple of animal sacrifices at the Temple. Interest is focused not on spiritual sacrifices, but rather on matters cultic.[2] Indeed, the real Temple and actual sacrifice have become the salient features in 11QTemple.

11QTemple 13.8–30 deals explicitly with cultic ritual offerings at the Temple by which atonement is achieved (25.14; 26.7, 9). Even in the section dealing with the construction of the Temple courts mention is made of the cultic and sacrificial activity of the priests. For example, cf. 32.12: '[when] they come to serve in the sanctuary'; 34.13: 'shall cause everything to rise in smoke'; 35.1-9: only those whose 'hands are filled' have entrance into the cultic areas for cult worship; 36.1–38.11: sacrifices for priests; 60.10-11; 63.3-4: priests are to stand before God to serve him.

Further functions of the priests consist of blessing (60.10-11; 63.3-4), a judicial role (57.11-15;[3] 61.8; 63.3-4), and a military role (57.1-3 [census taker];[4] 58.18-21 [adviser];[5] 61.15–62.16 [exhorter of the army]).

1. Milgrom ('Studies in the Temple Scroll', p. 510) notes that much of the detail of the Old Testament is absent in 11QTemple, which suggests that 'the author of the scroll wrote down only the parts of the ceremony which were at variance with the accepted interpretations of the ritual in his own time'.

2. This would argue either for a polemical view toward the current cultic practice at the Temple, or for an eschatological picture of the anticipated Temple and cultus established by God. Yadin (*Temple Scroll*, 1.401) writes: 'Until the discovery of the Temple Scroll, many could still assume that the members of the sect and the early Christians shared an approach that found expression in a disavowal of the Temple, of sacrifices, and so forth, and in the developing of new concepts in their place (e.g. Gärtner)'.

3. In the Temple Scroll, the judicial council has swollen to thirty-six members, of which twelve are priests and twelve are Levites, who sit with the king for judgment and declaration of legal decisions. See Yadin, *Temple Scroll*, 1.349; Maier, *Temple Scroll*, p. 126.

4. It is unclear just who takes the census, but it appears to be a priestly task. See Yadin, *Temple Scroll*, 1.346-47; Maier, *Temple Scroll*, p. 125.

5. The military offensive action appears to be under the control of the high priest's oracular use of the urim and thummim (e.g. 1QM 8.8-14), to which the king was

11QTemple shows a particular enhancement of the levitical office, whereby what were distinctively priestly activities have become functions of the Levites, for example, they have restored to them the role as sacrificial slaughterers (22.4) and also have acquired the priestly function of blessing (35.4-9).[1]

We observed already that the writings of Qumran gave evidence of the priestly character of the entire community. There is no explicit designation of the community members as priests, but the allusion does present itself. The concern for the maintenance of holiness was extended beyond the priests and the Temple precincts to the entire people, since it appears that the whole Temple City is to be ritually pure (45.7–48.?).[2] Hence the entire community was envisioned as exercising a regimen identical to that of the priests.[3]

*Conclusion*

A definitive conclusion regarding the role of the community as priests remains elusive. With some equivocation we may safely say with M. McNamara that 'the Qumran Community... it would appear, regarded their community as the Temple and themselves in some way as priests'.[4] This much at least is suggested by the endemic concern for holiness among the sectarians.

### 5. *The Priesthood in Philo*

Any investigation of the priesthood in Philo must consider its role and function at two levels: first, the actual description of the cultic ritual

---

subject. Maier (*Temple Scroll*, p. 128) notes that 'this whole section is a mosaic of biblical motifs'. Also see the relevant sections in Yadin, *Temple Scroll*, and Milgrom, 'The Temple Scroll' (p. 117).

1. Milgrom, 'Studies in the Temple Scroll', pp. 501-504. However, Milgrom ('Further Studies [cont.]', pp. 103-104) determines that at 60.14 (from Deut. 18.7) the meaning of 'to serve' does not entail any officiating role, but rather that of 'assisting' those in attendance. Therefore, although 'the scroll has greatly enhanced the powers of the Levites even to the extent of their assuming the priestly function of blessing the people, they in no way usurp the priestly role of officiating at the altar'.

2. For a different view on the meaning of 'Temple City', see Levine, pp. 13-17.

3. Milgrom, 'The Temple Scroll', p. 117; Martin McNamara, *Palestinian Judaism and the New Testament* (Good News Studies, 4; Wilmington, DE: M. Glazier, 1983), p. 142.

4. McNamara, p. 142. However, Klinzing (p. 218) remarks that Qumran makes no use of Exod. 19.6.

taken from the Old Testament itself, and second, the allegorical or representational symbolism employed by Philo regarding these roles and functions.[1] Sowers sees Philo postulating the Platonic concept that 'every sense-perceptible likeness has [as] its origin an intelligible pattern in nature', citing as examples *Qu. in Exod.* II.52; cf. I.19; *De op. m.* 13, 34, 130; *De spec. leg.* III.207; *De somn.* I.206.[2] Such different levels correspond to the sensible and intelligible realms, between which Philo constantly distinguishes, and into the latter of which a person is to strive to enter.[3]

*The literal priesthood in Philo*

In speaking of the ordinary priest and also the high priest Philo does not diverge significantly from the Old Testament tradition on which his writings are based. The priestly function appears to be largely two-fold: first and more prominently, the priestly role is for sacrificial and cultic matters; second, the priests concern themselves also with the interpretation of the law.[4]

The most thoroughgoing priestly and cultic portions of Philo are found in *De spec. leg.* I and II. There the priest and high priest are characterized by the Old Testament levitical legislation having to do with sacrifices, ritual purity, and cultic festivals.[5] What is significant

---

1. The two meanings of scripture, the literal and the allegorical, exist side by side. This idea is particularly frequent in *Qu. in Gen. and Exod.* (so also at *De spec. leg.* I.200), where Philo elaborates the 'deeper meaning' after having first presented the 'literal meaning'. See S. Sowers, *The Hermeneutics of Philo and Hebrews: A Comparison of the Interpretation of the Old Testament in Philo Judaeus and the Epistle to the Hebrews* (Basel Studies of Theology, 1; Richmond, VA: John Knox, 1965), p. 28. It appears that Philo's primary interest, however, is with the allegorical (e.g. *De Ios.* 28: 'all or most of the law-book is an allegory'). E. Schürer, *The History of the Jewish People in the Age of Jesus Christ (175 B.C.–A.D. 135)* (rev. edn. G. Vermes, F. Millar, M. Goodman; Edinburgh: T. & T. Clark, 1987), vol. III.2, p. 875 observes that Philo's allegorical commentary is a method of Palestinian midrash transferred to the realm of Hellenism, in order to show that his philosophical doctrine already exists in the Old Testament.

2. Sowers, p. 106. Philo also considered the Torah as mirroring the eternal law of Nature, according to Sowers, p. 97.

3. S. Sandmel (*Philo of Alexandria: An Introduction* [New York: Oxford University Press, 1979], p. 80) sees the overarching message of Philo as: 'Train yourself to rise up into the intelligible world, the world of concepts.'

4. Philo seems to place a disproportionate amount of interest on the cult. In *De spec. leg.* I and II he discusses cultic matters under the elaboration of the first commandment, and then again when discussing the fourth commandment.

5. See *De spec. leg.* I.66-298 and II.39-222; also, *De vit. M.* II.66-186.

for Philo is neither that the priests are literally servitors and ministers to God, nor that they perform sacrifices or maintain ritual purity, but as we shall see, that these functions symbolize a higher reality in the intelligible realm.

Philo is not particularly careful in his use of ὁ ἱερεύς as distinguished from ὁ ἀρχιερεύς. Many times when the high priest is being referred to, the mention will be of ὁ ἱερεύς (occasionally ὁ μέγας ἱερεύς).[1] What most distinguishes the high priest from the ordinary priest is not only his special access into the holy of holies once a year and his special attire, but also the stricter ritual purity standards by which he must abide. *De spec. leg.* I.113 notes that the priest can always be replaced by a deputy, but the high priest has no such substitute.[2]

A minor, and indeed insignificant, function of the priest is that of judge and interpreter of the law. This role too is grounded in the Old Testament where the priests are already depicted as such. Thus, *De vit. M.* I.214 is taken from Num. 15.32-36, *De spec. leg.* III.56-60 is from Num. 5.12-31, and *De spec. leg.* IV.190 from Deut. 17.8-9.

Therefore on the literal level, Philo has characterized the priesthood, with minor variations, according to the Old Testament. The

1. For example, Moses, Aaron and Phinehas are each often termed 'priest' rather than 'high priest'. In accordance with the Old Testament, when Philo deals with the entrance into the holy of holies by the high priest (Lev. 16), he most frequently uses only ὁ ἱερεύς, as in the LXX (e.g. *Quis rer.* 84; *Leg. ad G.* 307). At *De spec. leg.* I.72, Philo appears to be mistaken as to the access to holy place being limited only to the high priest (see also *De ebr.* 136; *De gig.* 52), for the priests had such access as well; see *Philo* (LCL; trans. and ed. F.H. Colson, G.H. Whitaker and Ralph Marcus; London: William Heinemann, 1929–53), 7.141, in particular, n. *d*.

High priest and priest are mentioned as mediators of their respective 'temples' of God in *De somn.* I.215. The high priest of the universe is also said to be the divine Logos, and in the same sentence, the priest of the rational soul is the true man. The description of the 'priest' parallels that of the high priest, for Philo says of the priest, 'the outward and visible image of whom [the logos] is he who offers the prayers and sacrifices handed down from the fathers, to whom has been committed to wear the aforesaid tunic, which is a copy and replica of the whole universe'. It appears that in *De somn.* I.215 the use of the term priest is simply a synonym for high priest. See Daly, pp. 415-16.

2. Passages from Philo that depict the sacrificial role of the priest are: *De Abr.* 198: *De ebr.* 2, 126; *Quis rer.* 84, 174; *De cong.* 89, 103, 105; *De somn.* II.74; *De vit. M.* II.138, 141, 150-52, 153, 174, 224; *De dec.* 159; *De spec. leg.* I.72, 82, 96, 98, 122, 125, 131, 151, 168-256 (*passim*); II.39-222 (*passim*); *De ebr.* 129, 136; *Quis rer.* 82-85; *De vit. contemp.* 82; *Leg. ad G.* 234, 307; *De praem.* 56; *Leg. All.* III.135; *De fug.* 93.

sacrificial function of the priest and high priesthood is overwhelmingly pervasive, and therefore so are all the prerequisites for the proper, holy performance of the cultic ritual. The superiority of the high priest is evident from his entering into the holy of holies, whereas the priests proceed only as far as the holy place.

## The allegorical role of the priesthood in Philo

According to Wilhelm Bousset, Philo found 'a deep and secret wisdom' in every letter of Moses' writings.[1] Therefore the priestly role which Philo adopted from the Pentateuch, whereby priests and the high priest served as mediators with access to God via sacrificial rites, betrays a symbolism beyond the literal. For Philo, the priest symbolizes the 'logos' or 'reason'.[2] It would be more accurate to say that the 'high priest' in Philo symbolizes the 'logos'. Philo is not explicit regarding the allegorical role of the 'ordinary' priests, for he seems to concentrate on the high priestly symbolism. However, insofar as the priest approaches and serves at the altar, this symbolizes that the priest is one who has 'virtue' in view. Therefore, this true priest, 'conviction' or 'conscience', illumines one's soul by bringing the divine reason (virtue) to him like a light.[3] As such, anyone who knows virtue, and therefore is pure and walking in the sinless way, is a priest.[4]

The allegorical meaning of the high priest is similar to that of the priest, but on a grander and more elaborate plan. The high priest in his mediatorial role with special access into the holiest partition of the Temple has, as his symbolism, the logos, which served as the mediator between God and man. What man could know of God, how he could approach God, was by a knowledge mediated by the logos. Thus, as we have said, to write about the high priest and sacrifices is actually to

---

1. W. Bousset, *Die Religion des Judentums im späthellenistischen Zeitalter* (HNT, 21; ed. H. Gressmann; 3rd edn; Tübingen: Mohr [Siebeck], 1966), p. 439. Also see Schürer, 5.366. Williamson, *Philo*, p. 171, comments that 'what the Old Testament says about sacrifices is symbolic of a deeper, spiritual meaning'. For example, *De spec. leg.* I.205 reads, 'So, then, he teaches in this symbol'. Sowers (p. 56) considers the earthly priest and Temple as a 'peg for allegorization'.

2. Schrenk, 'ἱερεύς', *TDNT*, 3.259-60. Schrenk gives several text references where the priest (or high priest) is mentioned with 'logos'.

3. *De somn.* I.81-84; *Quod Deus* 132-35.

4. *De spec. leg.* I.243. Schrenk ('ἱερεύς', *TDNT*, 3.260) observes that Philo regards the wise (virtuous) man, or sage, rather than the Jew is the true priest, citing *Quis rer.* 82-83; cf. 303.

## 1. The Priesthood in the Extra-NT Literature

be representing something higher than the sensible, in the intelligible world: the logos seen in its function as mediator through which the world approaches God. It appears that 'Philo sees in the High Priest entering the Holy of Holies a symbol of the Logos as a means of access for the human mind into the world of ideas'.[1] This finds support in Philo's peculiar interpretation of Lev. 16.17, for whenever the high priest enters the holy of holies, he is no longer a man, but the divine logos.[2] This is also apparent in the parallel sinlessness of the high priest, as in the logos.[3]

A further development of the logos/mediator concept is seen in the allegorical significance of the high priestly vestments, which Philo creates into a 'soteriological universalism'.[4] Such garments reflect the cosmos, so that the high priest does the bidding and praising for the entire cosmos, since he enters the sanctuary with the universe (his vestments),[5] and therefore has figuratively been transformed from a man into the nature of the world.

The developed allegorical interpretation in Philo ought not, however, to lead us to conclude that the sensible world serves only to illumine the intelligible reality. For 'the basic idea must not be lost sight of: the cult observances are the medium by which the loyal and observant Jew can be united with the Divine Logos'.[6] Therefore, the sensible Temple and cult at Jerusalem were still important for Philo.[7]

Hence, insofar as the human language could express matters numinous, the high priest symbolized the logos as the highest possible mediator toward the ultimate goal of the 'unfathomable Being of

---

1. Williamson, *Philo*, p. 419. According to *De migr. Abr.* 174, only through the assistance of the Divine Word does one achieve 'full understanding'.
2. *Quis rer.* 84; *De somn.* II.189, 231; *De fug.* 108; *De gig.* 52. Sowers (p. 61) sees the high priest as having become a 'quasi-divine figure'.
3. Schrenk, 'ἀρχιερεύς', *TDNT*, 3.273.
4. Daly, pp. 408-409. This is best expressed in *De spec. leg.* I.84-97. Also see Shrenk, 'ἀρχιερεύς', *TDNT*, 3.274. Occurrences in Philo include: *De vit. M.* II.109-135; *Qu. in Exod.* 107-124; *De fug.* 110; *De somn.* I.215. At *De vit. M.* II.131, the 'turban' and not a 'diadem' shows the superiority of the high priest over the people and even over the king.
5. Schrenk, 'ἀρχιερεύς', *TDNT*, 3.274. This is seen particularly at *De spec. leg.* I.96-97.
6. Sandmel, p. 96.
7. Daly (pp. 413-14) points to the extensive descriptions of the temple at *De vit. M.* II.71-108; *De spec. leg.* I.66-75; *Qu. in Exod.* II.51-106; *Leg. ad G.* 307f. It was also given a prominent place in the Passover (*Qu. in Exod.* I.10, 12).

God'. Along the way to this goal, the logos serves as the guide, until the soul is perfected. God remains known only indirectly through the logos. In like manner, mediation is indirectly accomplished for the people through the high priest.[1]

*Universal priesthood and spiritual sacrifice*

Philo associates his understanding of the universal priesthood with the Passover.[2] The Passover festival is the one occasion when the people of Israel are explicitly characterized as functioning priests.[3] At the Passover the 'entire nation acts as priests' and God bestows on them the honor and dignity of the priesthood. Philo's own most comprehensive explanation of this general priesthood is found at *Qu. in Exod.* I.10. There Philo tells why the whole people together were honored with the priesthood. First, 'it was the beginning of this kind of sacrifice' before the establishment of the cult. Second, 'the Savior and Liberator... deemed them [all] equally worthy of sharing the priesthood.' Third, 'because a temple had not yet been built, he showed that the dwelling together of several good persons in the home was a temple and altar'. Fourth,

> he (i.e. God) thought it just and fitting that before choosing the particular priests he should grant priesthood to the whole nation... And he permitted the nation, as the very first thing to be done, to prepare with their own hands and to slaughter the sacrifice of the so-called Passover [as] the beginning of the good things. And he decided that there is nothing more beautiful than that the divine cult should be performed by all in harmony. And also that the nation might be an archetypal example to the temple-wardens and priests and those who exercise the high-priesthood in carrying out the sacred rites.

---

1. Bousset, *Die Religion des Judentums*, p. 457; Williamson, *Philo*, p. 415. Philo, from Greek philosophy, would suggest that perfection is attained only through instruction, intuition, or practice.

2. Daly (p. 395 n. 10) observes that 'regardless of whether or to what extent the Passover was or was not regarded to be a sacrifice in its origins, the Jewish tradition by the time of Philo had long looked upon the rite as sacrificial—indeed as one of the foundation sacrifices of Judaism. Thus, what Philo says of the Passover is generally also applicable to sacrifice as such.'

3. Philo deals with the Passover at *De vit. M.* II.224f.; *De spec. leg.* II.145f.; *Qu. in Exod.* I.4f.; *De dec.* 159f. The single other context in which the Jewish nation also is priest, is at the sheaf festival: *De spec. Leg.* II.163. However, we shall see that the significance of the literal festival is transcended by the allegorical symbolism attached to such priestly representation.

## 1. The Priesthood in the Extra-NT Literature

Fifth, it was to enable those offering this sacrifice 'to act worthily and not incur any profanation'.[1]

We discover, however, that the literal explanation such as that offered above pales in significance before the allegorical interpretation of the Passover and its priesthood. Symbolically, the Passover 'expresses the soul's crossing from passion and all that is sensible to the noetic and divine'.[2] Philo writes in *Qu. in Exod.* I.8 that the Passover signifies the good soul desiring perfection. First, it is necessary to eradicate the sins, but then, when these have been expunged, to carry out and practice daily virtues. Hence, the literal actions in the Passover feast have their corresponding 'deeper meaning', the end of which is 'a happy, fortunate, and immortal life'.[3]

We observe therefore that the Old Testament account of the Passover in Exodus 12 is used by Philo to further his allegorical portrayal of the soul's progress toward God. That the Jewish nation appears here as priests is contingent upon its presence in the Old Testament narrative and it must be remembered that the major point Philo desires to make is the allegorical, not the literal. At the sheaf festival, in *De spec. leg.* II.163-64, the Jewish nation is also depicted as priests, again on the basis of the reference in the Old Testament. The point Philo most wishes to make is not the literal one—that the Jewish nation is literally composed entirely of priests—but the allegorical one, that whoever abandons the life of the senses and progresses towards God is a priest. For this is precisely what we have observed priests to be: those with virtue in view. Hence, the wise man, or the sage, rather than the ethnic Jew per se, is actually the true priest.[4] What appears to be suggestive of universal priesthood, then, is really stating in allegorical terms the path to immortal life.

That the priesthood belongs to those who concentrate on the spiritual sacrifices shows that it does not encompass the Jewish people

---

1. See Daly (pp. 410-11) for these five points.
2. Williamson (*Philo*, p. 171), who cites *De cong. quaer.* 106; *De sac. A. et C.* 63; *De spec. leg.* II.147. E.R. Goodenough (*By Light, Light: The Mystic Gospel of Hellenistic Judaism* [New Haven: Yale University Press, 1935], p. 204) agrees, saying 'the passover is a constant symbol with Philo for the abandoning of the life of the passions and the beginning of the journey to ὁ σωτὴρ θεός'. In addition, he cites *Quis rer.* 192 and *De migr. Abr.* 25.
3. *Qu. in Exod.* I.15. At *Qu. in Exod.* I.22, the migration leads to the vision of the incorporeals. So Goodenough, p. 205.
4. E.g. *Quis rer.* 82f. See Schrenk, 'ἱερεύς', *TDNT*, 3.260.

alone. At most of the occurrences where the spiritual sacrifice is considered, it is mentioned in conjunction with an actual cultic offering.[1] It is posited that the state of the worshiper's heart and mind is just as important as the purity of the sacrificial victim. In fact, the unblemished offering symbolizes that the worshiper needs also to live virtuously.[2] Thus, if the offering is to be efficacious, individual purity is the foremost criterion.[3]

Evidence of this spiritual purity is seen in the approach to sacrifice. If it is performed along with prayer, then this appears to please God. S. Sandmel comments that 'Philo does not disdain animal sacrifice, for it is prescribed in Leviticus, but he does not hesitate to commend prayer, if it is earnest, as a completely adequate way of worship'.[4] Prayer, for Philo, comes to be regarded as superior to sacrifice.[5]

Even beyond the offering of prayer, Philo states that the best offering of all is the offering of the worshipers themselves.[6] Such devotion to God is sacrifice enough. *De Plant.* 126 characterizes this as 'inaudible' hymns of praise, since the strains are raised and re-echoed by the mind, too pure for 'the eye' (sic) to discern.[7] It appears in

1. For a thorough examination of spiritual sacrifice in Philo, see Williamson, *Philo*, pp. 160-83.
2. Williamson, *Philo*, p. 172. See *De spec. leg.* I.191; *Quod Deus* 8. At *De spec. leg.* I.257f., the motive of the sacrificer is what determines the value of the sacrifice, according to Williamson (*Philo*, p. 167). The question to ask oneself is whether his mind is free from all imperfection and blemish (e.g. *De spec. leg.* I.287).
3. *De vit. M.* II.107-108.
4. Sandmel, p. 115. For Philo's personal favorable attitude toward sacrifice, see *De prov.* II.64: 'when I was on my way to our ancestral temple to offer up prayers and sacrifices'. Cited by Williamson, *Philo*, p. 164.
5. *De plant.* 126-29; *De cher.* 99-100; *De vit. M.* II.24. See Sandmel, p. 115 and H.A. Wolfson, *Philo: Foundations of Religious Philosophy in Judaism, Christianity, and Islam* (2 vols.; Cambridge, MA: Harvard University Press, 1947), 2.243, who says that 'inasmuch as divine worship by sacrifices was unaccessible to the great number of Jews living outside Palestine, there must have gradually arisen the view that prayer can serve as a substitute for sacrifices and that it is even better than sacrifices'. See also, Williamson, *Philo*, p. 165. Of course, prayer has already taken on a priestly importance in the Old Testament, first occurring simultaneously with sacrifice, but with the prophets being seen as superseding actual sacrifices in importance.
6. *De spec. leg.* I.272; *De plant.* 108; *De vit. M.* II.107f.; *Quod det.* 20-21.
7. Williamson, *Philo*, p. 165. He quotes J. Drummond, *Philo Judaeus: or, The Jewish-Alexandrian Philosophy in its Development and Completion* (London: Williams & Norgate, 1888), 2.319: 'so closely did Philo approach the view that spiritual sacrifices might replace the ritual of the altar'.

keeping with Philo's works on the whole that spiritual sacrifices should be held up here as the replacement for material ones. Since Philo's theological concern was outside the realm of the sensible, priests on the path to God would practice a sacrifice more closely mirroring the intelligible.

### 6. *The Priesthood in the Mystery Religions*

In *The Greek Mysteries* Bianchi defines a mystery religion as

> a mythic–ritual complex, implying an annual festival not without connection with the theme of seasonal fertility and the welfare of the city, but including very prominently the individual initiation of groups of citizens, and later on of men and women from all over the Greek and Hellenistic–Roman world. This initiation—protected by secrecy—conferred special personal privileges already in this life, but particularly in the afterlife.[1]

The very word 'mystery' hints at the secretive and hidden character of the religions, which has meant that our knowledge of their ritual and practice is either vague, incidental, or based on polemical sources.

What is at least generally clear, however, is that both a cultic drama and an initiation procedure were central components in these religions. The cult-drama visibly re-enacted before the gathered congregation the entire mythic story of the deliverance wrought for humanity, and the initiations, reserved for those deemed worthy of higher things, afforded a select few the chance to enter an incrementally advancing spiritual state and relationship to the gods. The approach to the gods and goddesses through the usual channels (such as procession, sacrifice, offerings, hymns, and prayers) no doubt continued, but the cult-drama was probably performed only wherever a temple's size permitted such a re-enactment. At the same time we

---

1. U. Bianchi, *The Greek Mysteries*, IR17.3 (Leiden: Brill, 1976), p. 4. H. Koester (*Introduction to the New Testament*, Vol. 1: *History, Culture, and Religion in the Hellenistic Age* [Philadelphia: Fortress, 1982], p. 198) lists seven characteristic features of a mystery religion. These are: (1) a firm organization in each congregation to which all members are subject; (2) membership obtained through rites of initiation; (3) participation in regular meetings in which sacramental ceremonies (such as meals) are celebrated according to fixed rites; (4) obligation to observe certain moral, sometimes also ascetic, precepts; (5) mutual support of all members; (6) obedience to the leader of the cult or community; (7) cultivation of traditions which were subject to arcane discipline.

need not presume that initiations occurred at every single temple, but only in particular locations.[1]

By participating in the mythic drama the observer and the initiate vicariously took part in the narrative of the deities. Bianchi notes that 'participation in the adventures of the goddess through "vision" and "sympathy", in the etymological sense of the term, implies a familiarity with these events which is enough to ensure for him a different fate, in the Nether world, from that of those who have not seen'.[2]

The appeal of the mysteries to adherents rested precisely in their ability to affect and alter the human destiny by means of their special rites of initiation. Although each of the different mysteries had its own particular initiation practices, they were all related in the significance of such rites: through them a person was 'reborn to immortality', so that the initiated believed that the mysteries would continue to be celebrated in the underworld.[3] The mysteries touched the 'deepest longings of the human soul'.[4] According to F. Cumont,

> Oriental religions had to appeal to the passions of the individual in order to make proselytes. They attracted men first by the disturbing seductiveness of their mysteries, where terror and hope were evoked in turn, and charmed them by the pomp of their festivities and the magnificence of their procession. Men were fascinated by the languishing songs and intoxicating melodies. Above all these religions taught men how to reach that blissful state in which the soul was freed from the tyranny of the body and of suffering, and lost itself in raptures.[5]

---

1. A.D. Nock, 'The Genius of Mithraism', in *Arthur Darby Nock: Essays on Religions and the Ancient World* (ed. Z. Stewart; Oxford: Clarendon, 1972), 1.455. Here Nock contrasts the later Mithraism with the other oriental religions in the period of Roman paganism.
2. Bianchi, pp. 5-6. Bianchi is careful to establish that the observer did not assume a divine nature through this dramatic portrayal, but that one's life was nonetheless existentially altered.
3. E. Lohse, *The New Testament Environment* (trans. J.E. Steely; Nashville: Abingdon, 1976), p. 234. Also see M.P. Nilsson, *Greek Popular Religion* (New York: Columbia University Press, 1940), p. 59. Nilsson (p. 58) cites the *Homeric Hymn to Demeter* (480ff.) as distinguishing the fate of the initiated from that of the uninitiated: 'Happy is he who has seen this. Who has not taken part in the intiation will not have the same lot after death in the gloomy darkness.'
4. Nilsson, *Greek Popular Religion*, pp. 63-64.
5. F. Cumont, *Oriental Religions in Roman Paganism* (London: G. Routledge & Sons, 1911; repr. edn, New York: Dover, 1956), pp. 29-30.

The satisfying of these longings resulted from the cultic experience in which only the initiated *mystae* were permitted to participate. Although some instruction was involved in the procedure toward initiation, no sophisticated indoctrination was first required of the candidates. Therefore, in light of the 'experiential' character of the mysteries, and the absence of systematic teachings, it is no wonder that the secretive mystery rites remain obscure, for any original doctrines were not compiled for distribution. This, plus the fact that the 'secret of Greek Mystery rites is always substantially respected in the literary sources available to us, [and] even more closely guarded in iconographical sources', serves to explain the elusive nature of the mysteries.[1] We shall proceed, however, to investigate something of the character, role, and function of the priesthood that operated within the mystery religions.

*The character of the priesthood*
The mystery cults were operated under the auspices of both permanent and temporary priesthoods. The Eleusinian Mysteries were originally controlled by descendants from the single family of Eumolpos, with chief decision-making power wielded by the head of the family. This explains not only how the cult remained secretive, but also the unusual assortment of citizens, strangers and slaves among its devotees.[2] Even after the mysteries became more or less state cults, charge of the rites was left in the hands of the priests or priestesses who descended from the original lineage of caretakers.[3] This does not preclude the occasional practice of purchasing the priesthood, and thereby changing the privilege of cultic control to another family.[4] But despite the changing of hands, the permanency of the priesthood was retained. A.D. Nock sees a permanent clergy as an intrinsic necessity for the

---

1. Bianchi, p. 1. Also see Lohse, pp. 241-42.
2. M.P. Nilsson, *Geschichte der griechischen Religion* (Handbuch der Altertumswissenschaft, 5.2; 2 vols.; München: C.H. Beck, 1941–50), 2.90, hereafter cited as Nilsson, *Geschichte*. Also see Nilsson, *Greek Popular Religion*, p. 46.
3. M.P. Nilsson, *A History of Greek Religion* (Oxford: Clarendon Press, 1925), p. 247. Nilsson (*Geschichte*, 2.332) finds inscriptional evidence for both priests and priestesses active in the Eleusinian mysteries, dated at 100 AD.
4. Nilsson, *Geschichte*, 2.95 and *A History*, p. 247. This appears to have been the case at Erythrai and in several Ionian cities. The practice provided further income to the state.

mysteries lest they become something less than 'secret' mysteries due to their association with innumerable priesthoods.[1]

Some of the oriental cults did operate with a temporary and changing clergy. This was characteristic of the Sarapis cult at Athens already in 166 BC, and appears particularly evident of Mithraism as it spread westward. In fact, in Mithraism there was no sign of a priestly family or caste, only ordinary men (women were excluded from Mithraism) performing as priests for a year or longer.[2]

Among the priesthoods themselves, there appears to have been a hierarchical organization. In the Osiris–Isis cult we know of four levels of priestly activity. Pre-eminent was the high priest, followed by the prophets who were skilled in the sacred science, followed by the stolists who dressed the statuary, and last, the elevated laymen who were the porters of the sacred shrine and its objects. The highest order of the priesthood, however, remained in the hands of the priestly caste from Egypt.[3]

As was the case with the other priesthoods we have already examined, purity is considered a prerequisite for all of the priests. The strict regulations under which the priests and other officials operated were intended to ensure that all uncleanness was removed, so that when the priest performed the sacrifice the expected result would occur. Such purifications were effected by ablutions, fumigations, anointings, abstention from food and sexual activity.[4] The gruesome

---

1. A.D. Nock, *Conversion: The Old and the New in Religion from Alexander the Great to Augustine of Hippo* (Oxford: Clarendon, 1933), p. 56. He recalls also that the Sarapis cult at Termessus was operated by a priest for life.
2. Nilsson, *Geschichte*, 2.116. Nock, 'The Genius of Mithraism', p. 454. Nilsson (*Geschichte*, 2.124) comments with regard to the Sarapis cult that such foreign cults purposely changed priests annually from among the leading families of the vicinity in order that the cult not be viewed as a phenomenon of the lower classes. Nock (*Conversion*, p. 53) notes that the Sarapis cult consisted of priests holding office for one year already in 180 BC. Nock specifically mentions, however, that the Mystery Religions did not subscribe to this annual arrangement. Mithraism appears to have allowed initiates of various grades to serve in the priestly capacity, according to scanty inscriptional records. See further Nock, 'The Genius of Mithraism', p. 453.
3. Cumont, p. 94. See J.E. Stambaugh, 'The Functions of Roman Temples', in *Aufstieg und Niedergang der römischen Welt: Geschichte und Kultur Roms im Spiegel der neueren Forschung II* (ed. H. Temporini and W. Haase; Berlin: W. Gruyter, 1978), 16.1, *Principat* (ed. W. Haase), p. 592.
4. Cumont, p. 91. See Nilsson, *A History*, pp. 84-86, where at p. 85, he describes uncleanness as an 'infection', a material substance which could be elimi-

## 1. The Priesthood in the Extra-NT Literature 75

practice of castration found in the Magna Mater cult gives further evidence of the importance of priestly 'Reinheit'. Eunuchism is best explained as the attempt to secure oneself as pure, since sexual impurity would no longer prove a hindrance for such men. Thus, the eunuch/priest was pure, like 'ein Kind' or 'eine reine Jungfrau'.[1]

The priests were also the educated and the scholars whose task it was to 'solve the problem of the destiny of man and matter, and of relations of heaven and earth'.[2]

Priests may be further characterized by their capacity for clairvoyance. Gods and goddesses gave oracles to priests and potential initiates which were mediated through sleep and which designated those who were permitted entry into the holy place at the temple or into the community of the initiated.[3]

Finally, we see that the priests were sworn to a secrecy regarding the mysteries. This same oath of silence also held for the initiates. To violate this secrecy meant death to any transgressor.[4] This further

---

nated by washing with water or blood, could be rubbed off, burned away, or smoked out with sulfur. The most popular sacrificial animal was the pig (p. 86).

1. Nilsson, *Geschichte*, 2.628. For a thorough examination of this understanding of cultic castration, see A.D. Nock, 'Eunuchs in Ancient Religion', in *A.D. Nock: Essays on Religion and the Ancient World* (ed. Z. Stewart; 2 vols. Oxford: Clarendon, 1972), 1.7-15.

2. Cumont (p. 32) cites the priests of Asia and Egypt in particular as being scholars.

3. Nock (*Conversion*, p. 50), who describes the Isis cult at Tithorea. This practice is also seen in the ancient texts of the first Sarapeum of Delos and the writings of Apuleius. See H. Engelmann, *The Delian Aretalogy of Sarapis: With a Frontispiece and 1 Figure* (EPROER, 44; Leiden: Brill, 1975), for a Greek edition of text and commentary. Also quoted by Nock, *Conversion*, p. 51. An extensive volume containing Book XI of *The Golden Ass* is *Apuleius of Madauros: The Isis-Book (Metamorphoses, Book XI)* (ed. J.G. Griffiths; EPROER, 39; Leiden: Brill, 1975). The familiar translation is *Apuleius: The Golden Ass, being the Metamorphoses of Lucius Apuleius* (LCL; trans. W. Adlington; rev. by S. Gaselee; London: W. Heinemann, 1922), hereafter cited as Apuleius, *Metamorphoses*. It is in Apuleius (*Metamorphoses*, XI.19) that the word from the goddess comes to Lucius Apuleius leading to his initiation.

4. Nilsson (*Geschichte*, 2.86) relates one memorable illustration of this: 'Wie streng das Geheimnis der Mysterien gehüttet wurde, zeigt die Erzählung von den beiden akarnanischen Jünglingen, die unwissentlich in das Weihefest hineingeraten waren, sich durch alberne Fragen als Nicht-Eingeweihte verrieten und, zu "den Vorstehern des Tempels" geführt, wie wegen "eines scheusslichen Verbrechens" getötet wurden; der Vorfall ereignete sich im J. 200 und veranlasste einen Krieg zwischen Athen und den Akarnanen, in den Philip V. hineingezogen wurde'.

explains why we know so little about what transpired during these mystery rites. However, despite the dearth of information, we will now investigate the role and function of the priesthood.

*The role and function of the priesthood*
The primary role of the priesthood was the care and oversight of the mystery rituals, beginning with the public events and concluding with the highest degree of initiation, the *epopteia*.[1] This priestly oversight ran the gamut of public and private acts. The two public acts were the *catharsis* (the initial purification) and the *sustasis* (the ritual and sacrifices preceding the private activities), and the two secret acts were the *myesis* (the initiation) and the *epopteia* (the highest degree of initiation). Inherent in the priestly prerogative lay an authority in the priest to call upon the name of the divinity, and to have the god or goddess obey as a slave.[2]

The mystery rites were marked by processions participated in and led by priests. During these processions the festive atmosphere was characterized by the priests' carrying of statuary, ritual ornaments and symbols, and pictures of gods or animals. The procession in the Magna Mater cult was marked by its frenetic and bloody celebration of self-flagellation, self-laceration and self-emasculation on the part of the priests and candidates moved by enthusiastic intoxication. So macabre was this frenzied display by the Cybelian priests, that Roman citizens were forbidden access into its priesthood, and therefore, Phrygian priests were its sole performing clergy.[3] *The Delian Aretalogy* of Sarapis (dating from 200 BC) shows that the priestly role was

---

1. Nilsson (*Geschichte*, 2.597) comments, 'Als Vorbild schweben den Alten und noch uns die eleusinischen Mysterien vor, die erste Einweihung in die kleinen Mysterien, die zweite, die zur Epoptie führte, d.h. die Aufteilung der Mysten in Eingeweihte zweiten und ersten Grades, die von der Priesterschaft geleitete Feier, an der alle Mysterien teilnahmen'.
2. Cumont, p. 96. Cumont (p. 93) notes the power of the ritual, in that with the proper words from the priest the superior powers were compelled to obedience. Hence, oversight and care of the ritual (and knowledge of the liturgy) placed man in a dominant position over the world of spirits.
3. Cumont, pp. 52-53; Nilsson, *Geschichte*, 2.92-94, 599, 614, 616; Stambaugh, p. 592; Lohse, p. 240. Also see Apuleius, *Metamorphoses*, XI.8-16. We shall see that the differentiation between priests and initiates is a fine line, and not only in relation to the procession.

## 1. The Priesthood in the Extra-NT Literature 77

to 'bring' his god with him in accordance to tradition, i.e. to care for the statue of Sarapis and also to continue to serve the gods.[1]

In connection with the rites of Osiris and Isis, the priest was responsible for opening the temple and making all the necessary preparations. This involved uncovering the statue, awakening the god by calling his name, reviving him through sacrifice, and cleansing the statue daily and adorning him with spectacular clothes. Sacrifice was also offered at the closing of the sanctuary's daily services.[2] Sacrifice was the jurisdiction of the priests, but it was not their primary function. At best, it served as a preliminary for the highest level of ritual, the *epopteia*. Nilsson clarifies such sacrifices by stating that they were

> not sacrifices in the ordinary sense in which the victim is handed over to the gods or serves as a medium of communication with them. These so-called sacrifices are nothing but a means of purification designed to take away the impurity attaching itself to a town or country. As such, sacrifice absorbs impurities and is destroyed, and therefore it does not matter if a sacrificial victim was without blemish or defect.[3]

By such sacrifices the priest purified the candidates, although water purification was also performed.[4] Other preliminary functions of the priests include prayer, preparation of a communion meal to be participated in by the candidates, and the collecting of money for their goddess.[5]

The central role of the priests appears to have been instructional. This involved the necessary preliminary teachings, dramatic re-enactment of the cult narrative, and the initiation rites, all leading up to the divulging of the highest mystery and secret objects.

---

1. *The Delian Aretalogy* of Sarapis is quoted in Nock, *Conversion*, p. 51; Engelmann, *The Delian Aretalogy*, p. 7; Nilsson, *Geschichte*, 2.115; R.M. Grant, *Gods and the One God* (Library of Early Christianity, 1; Philadelphia: Westminster, 1986), pp. 38-39.

2. Cumont, pp. 95-96; Nock, *Conversion*, pp. 80-81.

3. Nilsson, *A History*, p. 87. Hence, dogs and even common criminals could be sacrificed. The priestly task of sacrifice is considered by Nock, *Conversion*, pp. 55, 57.

4. Apuleius, *Metamorphoses*, XI.23; Nilsson, *Geschichte*, 2.606. Purification in the mysteries washed away the impurities of the soul: see Cumont, p. 39.

5. Nock (*Conversion*, p. 52) considers prayer by the priest to Sarapis. Apuleius (*Metamorphoses*, XI.23) mentions prayer to gods in relation to the purification of Lucius. Nilsson (*Geschichte*, 2.124, 620) considers the Magna Mater meal and the Isis collection on Samos, respectively.

We are left somewhat in the dark regarding the instruction that the priests afforded the candidates. Whether the instruction dealt with the nature of the gods and the cultic rituals, or whether it taught obligations and restrictions necessary for the *mystae* to avert attacks by evil spirits, it is clear that the initiates did first receive some sort of instruction.[1]

That instruction was a part of the higher rites and therefore dispensed to initiates, but not to the non-initiates, is seen by the lack of information we have about such instruction. This is also the case involving the rites of the mystery, the sacred drama, and the symbols and 'pronouncements' of the priests.[2]

The role and importance of the sacred drama are seen by some scholars to have embraced the very heart of the mystery event. Thus some see the drama, in which both priests and initiates took part, as the event whereby the initiates were filled with divine power, receiving the promise that they would henceforth know salvation and a superior fate in the world beyond.[3] Nilsson, however, does not believe that the drama was the central focus of the mysteries. He prefers to understand the *epopteia*, which certainly dealt with the reconciliation of Demeter with Kore, as involving something other than the observed drama.[4]

Far more certain was the place of the *taurobolium* within the initiation rites of the Magna Mater mystery and the later Mithraism. Although the *taurobolium* is attested to only once in the century before Christ, and our best attestation comes from Prudentius in the third century AD, its repugnance to the Greeks seems to indicate its earlier practice.[5] The recipient of the *taurobolium* shower appears to

---

1. Lohse, p. 238. Nilsson (*Geschichte*, 2.612) finds the evidence ambiguous regarding the dissemination of instruction in the Isis cult. However, Apuleius (*Metamorphoses*, XI.23) describes the priest confiding 'secret orders' to Lucius. Cumont (p. 41) considers the priesthood versed in 'sacred knowledge' which it transmitted to the candidates.
2. G. Bornkamm, 'μυστήριον', *TDNT*, 4.806. So also Lohse, p. 233. The vow of silence characterized not only the priests, but also the initiates into the mysteries. Thus we see in Apuleius (*Metamorphoses*, XI) that Lucius is very careful to state that he is not telling any more than he is permitted.
3. See Bornkamm, 'μυστήριον', *TDNT*, 4.805, and Lohse, pp. 234, 236.
4. Nilsson, *Geschichte*, 1.628.
5. Nilsson, *Geschichte*, 2.624-25. Also see Prudentius, *Peristephanon*, X.1011-1050. For a complete translation of Prudentius' works see *Prudentius* (LCL; trans. H.J. Thomson; 2 vols. Cambridge, MA: Harvard University Press, 1949–53).

## 1. The Priesthood in the Extra-NT Literature

be either the priest ('Oberpriester') or an initiate. Hence, the evidence suggests that initiation into the mystery required a certain level of economic means on the part of the initiate.[1] But with regard to the priest, at least, this rite appears to have marked his purification and consecration into a new life, whereby he received something of the divine power itself.[2]

In the Eleusinian mysteries the initiation was adopted from the fast of Demeter found in the mythic narrative, and is found portrayed on monuments dating from the Roman age. Elements incorporated appear to be sacrifice, fasting, regal attire, and the drinking of the cup.[3] Many of these same elements are depicted in the Isis-cult by Apuleius, *Metamorphoses*, XI.23-30.

Having now arrived at the highest mystery, the *epopteia*, there is little to consider since the mystery has been quite successfully concealed. At Eleusis,

> the silence imposed upon the *mystae* has been well kept. We possess a knowledge of certain preliminary rites which were not so important that it was forbidden to speak of them. In regard to the central rites belonging to the grade of the *epopteia*, our knowledge extends only to the general outlines. We know that there were things said, things done, and things shown, but we do not know what these things were.[4]

We do know, however, that the very name of the high priest, *hierophant*, tells us that his major function was to 'reveal' some sacred things. This 'showing' may have been accompanied by words, but the revealing of the object(s) was the climactic act. This visible wonder was further heightened by the torch-light used to illumine the proceedings.[5]

---

1. Nock (*Conversion*, pp. 57-58) correctly points out that such rites were restricted to a very few, and therefore seem to represent some additional act of piety on the part of the individual, rather than the rite of baptism. Nock, aware of the disparity of incomes among the initiates, further remarks that it was Christianity that 'democratized' mystery.
2. Nilsson, *Geschichte*, 2.628.
3. Nilsson, *Greek Popular Religion*, pp. 49-50. Of course, the fact that such rites are portrayed and even mentioned, suggests that initiation was still a preliminary stage anticipating the highest mystery.
4. *Ibid.*, p. 42.
5. *Ibid.*, p. 43. Also see Koester, *Introduction*, p. 178.

Just what was shown is not known. Most would suggest that the *hierophant* held up a reaped ear of corn in silence before the initiates.[1] We may, therefore, say that the highest mystery did not rest upon any elevated or secret didactic instruction by the priest, but rather occurred when the initiate observed the visible object presented by the *hierophant*.

The priest of the mystery religions in his maintenance and performance of the ritual was at the same time the initiate's 'spiritual guide'.[2] Lucius refers to Mithras, the high priest of Isis, as his 'father' whom he could never repay for his imparting of the mystery to him.[3] As such, the priest was revealed to be more than a cultic functionary mediating between the worshiper and the gods, but one who effects the higher state of the initiate. He was therefore an instructor extraordinary, using both the auditory and the visual media.

The extent to which the initiates also embodied the priesthood is not clear. Initiates are viewed as having offered sacrifices prior to their full initiation. But this by itself does not imply a priestly status. Initiates, on the other hand, are also admitted into the *adyton*, which, with rare exceptions, was the domain of the priests.[4] It seems that in the Isis cult the *mystae* who received the initiation would also be taken up into the priesthood.[5] This priesthood, however, was always a lesser and subordinate priestly role, and might just as easily be considered a priestly attendant status.[6] As we have already seen, the pre-eminent priesthood resided with the permanent or appointed clergy. Hence the Magna Mater cult was presided over by a priesthood that did not

---

1. Koester, *Introduction*, p. 178. Nilsson (*Greek Popular Religion*, p. 55) accepts Hippolytus' statement in *Ref. omn. haer.* V.8.39, that the priest held up an ear of corn, commenting that 'this statement may be more trustworthy than others, for it agrees exactly with the simple old agrarian character of the Eleusinian cult'. Also see Nilsson, *Geschichte*, 1.626-27. Bianchi (p. 6) however, finds a more interesting and more guarded secret than the revealing of a sacred object. This was a 'mysteriosophy' that imparted to man the proper conception of life and the universe, and the soul's place within this divine world. But this notion certainly ignores the significance of the 'visible', as seen in the meaning of the words *epopteia* and *hierophant*.
2. Cumont, p. 41.
3. Apuleius, *Metamorphoses*, XI.25.
4. Nock (*Conversion*, p. 39) cites Apuleius, *Metamorphoses*, IX.
5. Nilsson, *Geschichte*, 2.618.
6. For instance, the *pastophori* in Roman and Greek territories often served as surrogates for the native priests of Egypt. So Stambaugh, p. 592.

## 1. The Priesthood in the Extra-NT Literature

practice castration, since the priestly office was passed down through the family from father to son. Nevertheless the ecstatic dervishes are also depicted as priests, but it is clear that they are 'priests' of a far different level and function than the highest priesthood.[1]

There is, therefore, no conception of a general atoning priesthood such as we encountered in our previous investigations. Nor are the initiates as priests ever elevated to a status equal to that of the entrenched and established priesthoods.

---

1. Nilsson, *Geschichte*, 2.619.

Chapter 2

THE HIGH PRIEST CHRISTOLOGY IN HEBREWS

Prior to our investigation of cultic-priestly terminology in Heb., the characterization of Jesus as high priest (unique here in the entire New Testament) demands a brief summary. Because Jesus is high priest, this reality is by implication not only crucial for Christians, but definitive of their very character and function in the world. That the high priest is described in terms borrowed from the Old Testament ought to provide fuller illustration of the cultic-priestly language employed in Heb.

The high priesthood of Jesus Christ occupies a central place in Heb. The sudden introduction of ὁ ἀρχιερεύς at Heb. 2.17, its connection to the familiar ὁμολογία (3.1; 4.14; 10.23), and the continued frequent occurrence of both the term and the concept throughout Heb. all argue in favor of prior familiarity with the high priesthood of Christ among Heb.'s readers. But familiarity with the concept does not imply a convergence of opinion as to its meaning. The investigation of the high priesthood as it is used in Heb. has elicited conclusions identifying the confused and paradoxical character of its presentation by the author, particularly with regard to the chronological confusion about Christ's high priestly activity.[1] Here general disagreement

---

1. Braun (*Hebraër*, p. 32) refers to the 'chronologische Aporie' of Heb. Others use different words to express the identical conclusion: e.g. 'die Unheitlichkeit der Aussagen' (H. Zimmermann, *Die Hohepriester-christologie des Hebräerbriefes* [Paderborn: Ferdinand Schöningh, 1964], p. 18), and in Zimmermann's expansion of this work, *Das Bekenntnis der Hoffnung: Tradition und Redaktion im Hebräerbrief* (BBB, 47; Köln: Peter Hanstein, 1977), pp. 36-43; 'eine Reihe von Inkongruenzen' (O. Kuss, 'Der theologische Grundgedanke des Hebräerbriefes. Zur Deutung des Todes Jesu im Neuen Testament', in *Auslegung und Verkündigung I: Aufsätze zur Exegese des Neuen Testamentes* [Regensburg: Friedrich Pustet, 1963], p. 317); 'Spannungen und Unausgeglichenheiten' (F. Hahn, *Christologische Hoheitstitel: Ihre Geschichte im frühen Christentum* [FRLANT, 83; Göttingen: Vandenhoeck & Ruprecht, 1963], p. 233); 'Spannung' (W.R.G. Loader, *Sohn und*

## 2. The High Priest Christology in Hebrews

reigns as to precisely when Jesus became high priest, with suggestions ranging from the time of his exaltation, to his death on the cross, to already during his earthly life.[1] Most recent scholars do not propose an 'either/or' situation (i.e. Jesus was 'either' a high priest in heaven, 'or' he was an earthly high priest, exclusively), but instead see the strange paradox of his earthly high priest activity being mentioned simultaneously and even immediately adjacent to the heavenly high priest role.[2]

### 1. The Heavenly High Priesthood

The confusion created by Heb.'s varied use of ὁ ἀρχιερεύς and ὁ ἱερεύς is readily clarified by the observation that the author used ἱερεύς when citing or alluding to Psalm 110 (e.g. 5.6; 7.11, 15, 17, 21, 24; 10.21) and ἀρχιερεύς when referring to the cultic type and antitype.[3] Except at Heb. 2.17, the use of these specific terms is applied to the heavenly high priest (and his earthly counterpart), thus offering explicit and convincing evidence for the heavenly priesthood

---

*Hohepriester: Eine traditionsgeschichtliche Untersuchung zur Christologie des Hebräerbriefes* (WMANT, 53; Neukirchen-Vluyn: Neukirchener Verlag, 1981], p. 203).

1. Those who argue for a high priesthood initiated at Christ's exaltation include H. Windisch, *Der Hebräerbrief* (HNT, 14; 2nd edn; Tübingen: Mohr [Paul Siebeck], 1931), p. 42; E. Käsemann, *The Wandering People*, pp. 219-23; U. Luck, 'Himmlisches und irdisches Geschehen im Hebräerbrief: Ein Beitrag zum Problem des historischen Jesus im Urchristentum', *NovT* 6 (1963), p. 205. For an earthly high priesthood: E. Riggenbach, *Der Brief an die Hebräer*, 2/3 edn (Kommentar zum Neuen Testament, 14; Leipzig: A. Deichert [Dr. W. Scholl], 1922), p. 63, (and see the others whom he cites at n. 60, pp. 62-63); Schrenk, 'ἀρχιερεύς', *TDNT*, 3.276, 279-80; Loader, *Sohn*, pp. 245-47; Mathias Rissi, *Die Theologie des Hebräerbriefs: Ihre Verankerung in der Situation des Verfassers und seiner Leser* (WUNT, 1.41; Tübingen: Mohr [Paul Siebeck], 1987), pp. 61-78. O. Michel (*Kommentar*, p. 106) likens the high priesthood 'enthronization' to the crucifixion event, which can be understood as part of Christ's earthly life, though he stops far short of the position held by those advocating that Jesus was already a high priest during his earthly life.

2. Zimmermann, *Die Hohepriester-christologie*, pp. 18-25; Braun, *Hebräer*, pp. 32, 71-74; Attridge, *Hebrews*, pp. 146-47.

3. Rissi, *Die Theologie*, p. 55; Braun, *Hebräer*, pp. 71-72. To the contrary is G. Schille, 'Erwägungen zur Hohepriesterlehre des Hebräerbriefes', *ZNW* 46 (1955), pp. 81-84; and Zimmermann, *Die Hohepriester-christologie*, p. 26, both of whom find different traditions used by the author to account for the intermingling of terms.

of Christ.[1] So, consonant with the Epistle's careful use of the Day of Atonement ritual (Leviticus 16), Heb. depicts Jesus Christ as having entered ἐφάπαξ not only into heaven, where the true sanctuary stands established, but even into the heavenly holy of holies (4.14; 6.19-20; 8.2; 9.11-12, 24; 10.19-20; 12.24). Having entered into the heavenly holy of holies, Christ the high priest remains within the second tent seated at the right hand of God (1.3, 13; 8.1; 10.12; 12.2). The fact that we have here a clear utilization of an early Christian confession based on Ps. 110.1 is evidenced by its New Testament presence at Rom. 8.34, Col. 3.1, Eph. 1.20, and 1 Pet. 3.22.[2] Heb. thereby establishes the unsurpassable access to God enjoyed by Christ as high priest since he continues there 'forever'.[3]

The position of glory at God's right hand clarifies the meaning of τελειοῦν when used of Christ (2.10; 5.9; 7.28). At 2.9, βλέπομεν Ἰησοῦν... δόξῃ καὶ τιμῇ ἐστεφανωμένον has its synonym in τελειῶσαι (2.10). Thus, for God to make Jesus 'perfect' was to 'crown him with glory and honor', i.e. to bring him into his direct presence at his right hand.[4] Further, God's perfection of the high priest is simultaneous with his designation of Jesus as ἀρχιερεὺς κατὰ τὴν τάξιν Μελχισεδέκ (5.9-10; 7.15, 28).[5] Jesus as *heavenly* high priest did not possess his status from all eternity, but was accorded direct access to God only at his perfection, at the time of his designation as a priest κατὰ τὴν τάξιν Μελχισεδέκ, which occurred when he entered (εἰσῆλθεν) and sat down at the right hand of the throne of God.[6]

---

1. Most see Heb. 2.17 as also referring to the heavenly high priestly office of Christ. Yet as we shall see, it is clearly a reference to his earthly priesthood. Hence, the first mention of ἀρχιερεύς in Heb. is an earthly reference.
2. Michel, *Kommentar*, p. 277.
3. εἰς τὸν αἰῶνα does not mean 'eternally'. In the Psalms it refers to the time frame involved with the sovereign's rule. Hence, Christ continues at the right hand of God until the time his enemies are made a footstool (1.13; 10.12). Therefore, the period of Christ's heavenly priesthood is temporally bounded.
4. See Rissi, *Die Theologie*, p. 79. In the LXX, the consecration of the priests is described with τελειοῦν (τὰς χεῖρας). The terminology in Heb. is therefore cultic, although it is used with a different meaning, 'to enjoy the direct access to God'. Also see below in Chapter 5.
5. Heb. 7.28b, read in the light of v. 28a, is an obvious reference to Ps. 110.4.
6. It has been observed that εἰσέρχεσθαι, when appearing in the cultic contexts of Heb., always points to the high priestly function. When used cultically with reference to Christ, it refers to his entering into the heavenly holy of holies, i.e. into direct access with God.

## 2. The High Priest Christology in Hebrews

As the heavenly high priest, Jesus' function is no longer that of 'offering' or of 'sprinkling blood', since that has been accomplished ἐφάπαξ. He does function, however, as intercessor ὑπὲρ ἡμῶν (6.20; 7.25; 9.24; cf. 2.18; 4.14; Rom. 8.27, 34; 1 Jn 2.1), just as he has already done on earth (5.7-8). His current heavenly role, although not actively involved with the manipulation of blood, is still inseparable from it; thus he remains mediator of the new covenant, far superior to the priests of the old covenant, and his prayers are heard in the light of his atoning sacrifice and offering (12.24).

Intercession as the heavenly high priest's activity will persist only between the time of his designation as high priest κατὰ τὴν τάξιν Μελχισεδέκ and the parousia, which is not only a temporal reality (1.6, 10, 12, 13; 2.5, 8; 3.1–4.13), but an imminent one (10.25, 37-39; 12.25-29). For by Christ's appearing ἐκ δευτέρου, all who eagerly await him will be saved (9.28).

Concerning Jesus Christ's heavenly high priesthood: in order to maintain a typology congruent with the high priestly activity according to the Old Testament, it is necessary to recognize that no high priest was consecrated a high priest simply upon his entry into the holy of holies. High priestly installation and rules of purity always preceded any form of entry on the part of the priest. Therefore the heavenly high priesthood of Christ ought not to be understood as his initial moment of priesthood. Furthermore, the earthly high priest's ability to sympathize with others (e.g. 5.2) does not mean that as the high priest, he once was beset by weakness, but is no longer. Rather, it is because the high priest himself is *still* burdened by sin that he is able to sympathize. Similarly then, Jesus the high priest, who was made like his brothers in every respect (2.17; 4.15), had to have been a high priest beset by weakness while on earth, although he was uniquely without sin. We would assume him to have been a high priest already during his earthly existence—a high priest who subsequently entered into the holy of holies.

### 2. The Earthly High Priest

The importance of the earthly life of Jesus Christ, the heavenly high priest, is evidenced by the inclusion of his name, Ἰησοῦς, in what appear to be pre-formulated confessional statements (e.g. 3.1; 4.14; 6.20; 7.22; 12.2). The author of Heb. has thereby carefully linked the earthly Jesus to the confessional titles of apostle, high priest, Son of

God, forerunner, surety, great priest, and pioneer and perfecter of the faith. Thus 'der Hohepriester im Himmel ist der durch seine Erdengeschichte bestimmte Jesus aus dem Stamm Juda (7.14)'.[1] The author of Heb. can assert this because it is clear that Jesus already in his earthly life performed a priestly function: one in which he was uniquely both the offering and the offerant.

Distinctive in Jesus' earthly priestly activity was the once-for-all character (ἅπαξ, ἐφάπαξ: 7.27; 9.12, 26, 28; 10.10) of his offering, whereas the former priests had to offer sacrifices repeatedly year after year.[2] This single sacrifice proved efficacious because it was capable of removing guilt and atoning for the sins of the people, a purely high priestly cultic activity (1.3; 2.9, 17; 7.27; 9.26, 28; 13.12).[3] Jesus, as a high priest, is further implied in the frequent occurrence of θυσία to describe his earthly sacrifice which he himself presented (7.27-28; 9.22, 23, 26, 28; 10.10, 12), in the mention of the 'cross' (i.e. his death) at 12.2, and in the consideration of αἷμα which, while referring to the substance carried into the holy sanctuary for sprinkling, at the same time evokes Jesus' own death (9.12, 14; 10.19; 12.24; 13.12, 20). προσφέρειν (5.1, 7) provides a further parallel to Christ's earthly priesthood and that of the old covenant high priest. Even ἐν ταῖς ἡμέραις τῆς σαρκὸς αὐτοῦ Jesus performed priestly offering consisting of prayers of loud cries and tears.[4] The term σάρξ in Heb.

---

1. See Rissi, *Die Theologie*, pp. 59-60. Two other occurrences of Ἰησοῦς appear in conjunction with his 'blood', thereby referring to his sacrificial death as a human (10.19; 13.12; cf. 2.9). Also see B.L. Melbourne, 'An Examination of the Historical-Jesus Motif in the Epistle to the Hebrews', *Andrews University Seminary Studies* 26 (1988), pp. 285-86, 292.

2. προσφέρειν is the cultic term typically employed to refer to the action of bringing sacrificial offerings to the altar.

3. The sacrifice of the high priest on the Day of Atonement atoned for the sins of the people (Lev. 16.6, 11, 17, 19). This is reminiscent of Isa. 53.12, ὑπὲρ ἡμῶν (Heb. 9.28). The efficacy of Christ's one-time offering is captured by A.B. Davidson (*The Epistle to the Hebrews: With Introduction and Notes* [Edinburgh: T. & T. Clark], pp. 193-94): 'Christ's offering was not of value because it was one of obedience and hence spiritual, but rather because it was the sacrifice prophesied according to the divine will'.

4. For a thorough analysis of Heb. 5.1-10, see Michel, *Kommentar*, p. 220; Martin Dibelius, 'Der himmlische Kultus nach dem Hebräerbrief', in *Botschaft und Geschichte: Gesammelte Aufsätze von Martin Dibelius*, 2: *Zum Urchristentum und zur hellenistischen Religionsgeschichte* (ed. G. Bornkamm and H. Kraft; Tübingen: Mohr [Paul Siebeck], 1956), pp. 171-72; J. Moffatt, *A Critical and Exegetical Commentary on the Epistle to the Hebrews* (ICC; New York: Scribner's, 1924), p. 64;

## 2. The High Priest Christology in Hebrews

encompasses Jesus' entire earthly existence (5.7; 10.20),[1] so that his whole earthly life attained to that high priestly objective which had forever evaded the former priests: access through the curtain into the heavenly holy of holies. Thus, the chiastic parallel in 5.1-10 shows that a correspondence is described which relates the earthly high priest's repeated activity (5.1-3) with that of Jesus the high priest while on earth.[2]

Therefore the prevalent understanding that Heb. 5.7-8 reiterates the Gethsemane experience of Jesus, as found in Mt. 26.36-46, Mk 14.32-42, and Lk. 22.39-46,[3] is deemed deficient. Already M. Dibelius and others have argued against a specific dependence on the Gethsemane tradition in view of the apparent utilization of texts from the Psalter which speak of the Lord's humiliation and passion; i.e. 'sie stellt nur

---

K. Weiss, 'προσφέρω', *TDNT*, 9.67; Christian Maurer, '"Erhört wegen der Gottesfurcht", Heb. 5,7', in *Neues Testament und Geschichte: Historisches Geschehen und Deutung im Neuen Testament. O. Cullmann zum 70. Geburtstag* (ed. Heinrich Baltensweiler and Bo Reicke; Zürich: Theologischer Verlag, 1972), p. 280; Rissi, *Die Theologie*, pp. 58-65.

1. See B.F. Westcott, *The Epistle to the Hebrews: The Greek Text with Notes and Essays* (2nd edn; London: Macmillan, 1902; repr. edn; Grand Rapids: Eerdmans, 1950), p. 125; Windisch, *Hebräerbrief*, pp. 43-44; T. Boman, 'Der Gebetskampf Jesu', *NTS* 10 (1964), pp. 264, 268; M. Rissi, 'Die Menschlichkeit Jesu nach Heb. 5.7-8', *TZ* 11 (1955), p. 39; Rissi, *Die Theologie*, p. 43. Braun (Hebräer, p. 141) draws attention to Heb. 3.8 and ἡμέρα in W.F. Arndt and F.W. Gingrich, *A Greek-English Lexicon of the New Testament and Other Early Christian Literature* (Chicago: University of Chicago Press, 1957), p. 348 (hereafter cited as BAG); and G. Delling, 'ἡμέρα', 2.950, where the time-frame intended is one's entire lifetime. Attridge (*Hebrews*, p. 149) admits that 'flesh' in Heb. 'connotes the sphere of weakness and suffering to which Christ was subject', but he does not see this as incorporating Christ's entire earthly life, despite Heb. 2.17 and 4.15.

2. See, for instance, the consideration of this in our discussion of Heb. 10.1, below. Also see J. Jeremias, 'Hebräer 5.7-10', in *ABBA: Studien zur neutestamentlichen Theologie und Zeitgeschichte* (Göttingen: Vandenhoeck & Ruprecht, 1966), p. 322, and M.C. Parsons, 'Son and High Priest: A Study in the Christology of Hebrews', *EvQ* 60 (1988), pp. 209-10.

3. Despite the admitted problems, the Gethsemane tradition in Heb. is accepted by most commentators. For specific references, see Braun, *Hebräer*, pp. 140-41. For example, see O. Cullmann, *The Christology of the New Testament* (trans. S.C. Guthrie and C.A.M. Hall; rev. edn; Philadelphia: Westminster, 1963), pp. 95-96; Theodor Lescow, 'Jesus in Gethsemane bei Lukas und im Hebräerbrief', *ZNW* 58 (1967), p. 238; J. Smith, *A Priest for Ever: A Study of Typology and Eschatology in Hebrews* (London: Sheed and Ward, 1969), p. 81.

eine Parallele zu ihr (the Gethsemane scene) dar'.[1] Furthermore, the occurrence of σάρξ at 10.20 underscores the entire earthly existence of Jesus[2] as the efficacious high priestly ministry.

The author of Heb. went to great effort to avoid any hint of 'chronologische Aporie'.[3] This he did within the already mentioned texts which dealt with the heavenly high priesthood of Jesus Christ. Time and again, the author connects his statements about the perfected, 'after the order of Melchizedek' high priest with the life, sacrifice and death of Jesus (1.3; 2.9-10; 4.14-16; 5.7-10; 7.26-28; 8.1–10.18; 10.19-20; 12.2), thereby illustrating the indivisibility of the earthly and heavenly high priesthood of Christ.[4] Christ's heavenly priesthood presupposes his earthly priesthood so that as a perfected priest in heaven he still is able to be a sympathetic high priest (4.15) and help those who are suffering, by interceding at the right hand of God. Hence, Christ's heavenly service is dependent upon his completed earthly work, something which has apparently been disregarded by the readers enthralled with a spiritualistic-enthusiastic realized eschatology as found in their confession in 8.1-12. This is corrected by the author in Heb. 9–10.[5]

---

1. Dibelius, 'Der himmlische Kultus', pp. 171-72. See also, Michel, *Kommentar*, p. 221; Maurer, 'Erhört', pp. 279-80; F.F. Bruce, *The Epistle to the Hebrews: The English Text with Introduction, Exposition and Notes* (NICNT; Grand Rapids: Eerdmans, 1964), p. 100. Robert McL. Wilson, *Hebrews* (New Century Bible; Grand Rapids: Eerdmans, 1987), pp. 97-98. Again, refer to Braun, *Hebräer*, pp. 140-41; August Strobel, 'Die Psalmengrundlage der Gethsemane-Parallele Heb. 5.7ff.', *ZNW* 45 (1954), pp. 252-66. Also see H.W. Attridge, 'Heard Because of His Reverence', *JBL* 98 (1973), p. 91.

2. O. Hofius, 'Inkarnation und Opfertod Jesu nach Heb. 10,19f.', in *Der Ruf Jesu und die Antwort der Gemeinde: Festschrift für Joachim Jeremias* (ed. Eduard Lohse; Göttingen: Vandenhoeck & Ruprecht, 1970), pp. 138-39; Hofius, *Der Vorhang*, p. 82. Also see Rissi, *Die Theologie*, p. 43; Wilson, p. 98.

3. Braun's understanding of the 'chronologische Aporie' in Heb. is repeatedly rejected by Rissi, *Die Theologie*, e.g. pp. 52, 62, 69.

4. Rissi, *Die Theologie*, p. 81. He cites H. Bietenhard, *Die himmlische Welt im Urchristentum und Spätjudentum* (WUNT, 2; Tübingen: Mohr [Paul Siebeck], 1951), p. 126: 'Sein [Jesus] Werk auf Erden und sein Walten im Himmel sind eine Einheit'. Also see G.L. Cockerill, 'The Melchizedek Christology in Heb. 7.1-28' (ThD dissertation, Union Theological Seminary in Virginia, 1976), p. 183.

5. For a brief consideration of the situation of the readers, see our Conclusion. That this is also illustrated in Heb. 8.1-12 is argued by Rissi (*Die Theologie*, pp. 56-59). The author of Heb. proceeds to refute the readers' overly exalted doctrine of 8.1-12 most emphatically in 9.11-14.

## 2. The High Priest Christology in Hebrews

Finally, Heb. 2.17 connects the term ἀρχιερεύς, otherwise used only to designate the heavenly high priest, with Jesus' earthly life.[1] This first occurrence of ἀρχιερεύς in Heb. serves to identify the earthly high priest, who became like his brothers, as the very same heavenly high priest. Thus 'der grosse Hohepriester im Himmel ist derjenige, der durch sein Leben und Sterben auf Erden charakterisiert ist'.[2]

### 3. The Son and Sons

Jesus the pre-existent (1.2) and exalted Son and high priest (1.4; 5.5) chose to become human (2.14) and a member of a specific community ἐκκλησία (2.12) and covenant people. So the Epistle's message circumscribes a particular segment of the human sphere. Heb. may therefore say that both the sanctifier and those being sanctified are ἐξ ἑνός (2.11). More specifically, Jesus chose to become one of the sons of God by becoming a descendant of Abraham (2.11, 16), recipient of the promise (6.13-15; 11.12).[3] Therefore, when Jesus became human, taking the form of blood and flesh (2.14), he also became a brother among the sons of God.[4] This was the only means by which Christ could become a merciful and faithful high priest for his brothers, in order to effect the forgiveness of sins (2.17). Had he never been tempted and suffered, or had he not died, he would have been unable to help those brothers who were being tempted (2.18), since according to 2.14-15, the one with power over death, the διάβολος, would not have been destroyed. In fact, Christ became so much like his brothers that he too put all his trust in God (2.13b).

---

1. The aorist subjunctive γένηται ought to be seen as a present (not future) reference, as in its other occurrence at 6.12. It has already been seen that Jesus the high priest made expiation for the sins of the people by his death on the cross.
2. Rissi, *Die Theologie*, p. 62.
3. Recent works that attribute the ἐξ ἑνός to Abraham (not God, or Adam) are F. Laubach, *Der Brief an die Hebräer* (Wuppertaler Studienbibel; Wuppertal: R. Brockhaus, 1967), pp. 65-67; G.W. Buchanan, *To the Hebrews: Translation, Comment and Conclusions* (Anchor Bible, 36; Garden City, NY: Doubleday, 1972), p. 32; J. Swetnam, *Jesus and Isaac: A Study of the Epistle to the Hebrews in the Light of the Aqedah* (AnBib, 94; Rome: Biblical Institute, 1981), pp. 132-34, 168-69 (he sees it as the 'spiritual seed of Abraham'); and Rissi, *Die Theologie*, pp. 60, 120.
4. Rissi, *Die Theologie*, p. 60.

The author establishes very early in Heb. that the brother who sacrificed himself as a priest did so in order to sanctify his brothers (2.10-18; 9.13-14; 10.10, 14, 29; 13.12).[1] And just as the prerogative of claiming the sons as 'brothers' was accepted by the 'author of salvation', so the πρόδρομος enters ὑπὲρ ἡμῶν (6.19-20).[2] Thus the very notion of 'forerunner' anticipates the accessibility of the holy of holies to the sons, his brothers, the people of God.

Heb., in accordance with the Old Testament, sees the brothers and παιδία of the high priest as also entitled to hold the priestly office. As the result of Christ's efficacious sacrifice he has set apart his brothers from the rest of the world for God's service. Already the christology of Heb. introduces the 'sons' as those with a special access to God. We must now undertake an investigation of this access afforded the readers of Heb. in order to discover whether the textual evidence bears out the impression that believers are themselves 'priests'.

---

1. *Ibid.*, pp. 59-61, 120-21.
2. It is to be observed that 'forerunner' is used in close proximity to other Abraham material in Heb. 6.13-15.

Chapter 3

ΠΡΟΣΕΡΧΕΣΘΑΙ AND HEBREWS

Our initial investigation will center on the term προσέρχεσθαι (and the single use of ἐγγίζειν) which occurs frequently in Heb. with reference to the readership (e.g. 4.16; 7.25; 10.1, 22; 11.6; 12.18-24; 7.19) and which in the LXX regularly connotes cultic activity.

1. Προσέρχεσθαι *in the* LXX

One prevalent function of the multi-dimensional προσέρχεσθαι as 'cultic' becomes evident in its frequent usage (along with its synonyms) to describe the activity of the Old Testament priests. The Hebrew *qārêb* and *niggaš* are most often rendered in the LXX: προσέρχεσθαι, προσπορεύεσθαι ἐγγίζειν, προσάγειν, and προσεγγίζειν. These terms translate the related word *bô'*: εἰσέρχεσθαι, εἰσπορεύεσθαι, and εἰσιέναι. Prior to our investigation of προσέρχεσθαι in Heb., we shall look at its use in the LXX, and its particular application in describing the cultic function of both the priesthood and the laity.

In their sacerdotal context, *qārêb* and *niggaš* refer to the approach by the priest to the alter, or the approach of the non-priests for worship. The stated purpose of this priestly approach to the altar is (either implicitly or explicitly) 'to offer' or 'to minister' at the θυσιαστήριον: the terms are used synonymously in the LXX (e.g. προσφέρειν, λειτουργεῖν, λατρεύειν).[1] Typically, προσέρχεσθαι (or its synonyms) is followed by the preposition πρός and an object at the cult center (e.g. Exod. 40.32 [38.27(LXX)]; Lev. 9.7-8; 10.9;

---

1. Exod. 28.43; 30.20; 40.32; Lev. 2.9; 9.7-8; 10.9; 21.18, 21, 23; 22.3; Num. 18.3, 7; Deut. 21.5; 2 Chron. 13.9; 29.31; Ezek. 40.46; 42.13; 43.19; 44.8, 13; 45.14. The following is considered briefly by Cockerill (pp. 136-38) and Peterson (p. 230 n. 33).

21.23; 22.3; Num. 4.19; 18.3; Ezek. 44.16), or by an infinitive denoting worship or offering. Occasionally προσέρχεσθαι (or its synonyms) appears without an object (e.g. Lev. 21.18 [pertaining to priests]; Lev. 9.5; Deut. 4.11 [pertaining to people]), or followed by the dative case (Exod. 19.22; Lev. 10.3 [priests]; Ps. 148.14; Isa. 29.13; 58.2; Jdt. 8.27 [people]). In at least one instance προσέρχεσθαι is used for worshipers, where it is followed by ἐναντίον and then the divine designation, τοῦ θεοῦ (Exod. 16.9).

The LXX use of ἐναντίον and ἔναντι generally translates the Hebrew *lipnê*, but the other renderings of *lipnê* in the LXX seem to follow no systematic rule for their translation from Hebrew into Greek. Thus the 'verb' plus the preposition *'el* and its object, or the preposition *l-* prefixed to the 'infinitive construct' in the Hebrew, may be rendered in several different ways in Greek: either by a πρός or absolutely or by a dative (e.g. Exod. 19.5 [although not a cultic use]) or by an infinitive, according to no apparent system.[1] We are reminded therefore of the many hands involved in the composition of the LXX and need not too hastily separate one LXX usage from another usage, or seek parallels in other traditions, since already the variety of usages in the LXX may provide the appropriate background for Heb.[2]

In several passages the LXX appears to maintain a careful distinction between the priestly approach to the altar and the entry into the tent itself. At Exod. 28.43; 30.20; 40.32 (38.27[LXX]) εἰσπορεύεσθαι is juxtaposed with προσπορεύεσθαι, each with a different object: the tent of meeting and the altar, respectively. At Lev. 10.9 the LXX has added to the Hebrew text ἢ προσπορευομένων ὑμῶν πρὸς τὸ θυσιαστήριον, so that εἰσπορεύεσθαι is juxtaposed by this additional clarification.[3] We observe therefore that the majority of the

---

1. For instance, at Isa. 29.13 the Hebrew absolute has had the dative pronoun, μοί, added in the LXX.
2. According to R. Jewett (*Letter to Pilgrims: A Commentary on the Epistle to the Hebrews* [New York: Pilgrim, 1981], pp. 79-80) the number of occurrences of προσέρχεσθαι used cultically, as well as the absolute uses, 'confirms the judgment that the author derives the technical use of approach from the Septuagint'. See also J. Schneider, 'προσέρχομαι', *TDNT*, 2.683-84. J. Swetnam ('Christology and the Eucharist in the Epistle to the Hebrews', *Biblica* 70 [1989], p. 91) observes that a liturgical setting is implied throughout Heb.
3. The altar at Exod. 28.42 is the altar of burnt offerings within the greater sanctuary, occasionally referred to as 'the holy place' in Exodus (e.g. Exod. 36.1, 3, 4, 6). See S.R. Driver, *The Book of Exodus* (Cambridge: Cambridge University Press, 1911), p. 312.

occurrences of the cultic προσέρχεσθαι (or its synonyms) appear with reference to the priestly approach to the altar of burnt offerings which was located outside the tent proper.

Less frequent are LXX renderings of *qārêb* and *niggaš* for the priestly approach, within the tent, to the table of shewbread[1] and to the altar of incense.[2] In these few instances the priest is described as offering either the bread as a thanksgiving offering, or the incense as an incense offering.

To 'draw near' is descriptive therefore of the ministering, sacrificing, and offering function of the priest. For this reason the common priest is never characterized as drawing near to the 'mercy seat' (τὸ ἱλαστήριον) within the holy of holies, because priestly sacrifices and offerings are not made within the second tent.[3] This careful distinction is borne out in the LXX where on at least two occasions *bô'* is rendered by προσέρχεσθαι and προσπορεύεσθαι (rather than the anticipated εἰσέρχεσθαι or εἰσπορεύεσθαι).[4] That the LXX used these verbs in translation of *bô'*, instead of 'to enter', suggests that the LXX translator wished to clarify any possible ambiguity which may have left the reader thinking that the priests mentioned had entered within the holy of holies which was solely the domain of the high priest. Accordingly the LXX at Lev. 21.23 reads that the priest does not enter into the curtain (as in the Hebrew text), but rather, he 'approaches or draws near' to the curtain; that is, he only enters within the first tent, the holy place.[5] At Num. 4.19-20 the LXX clarifies any ambiguity by stating that Aaron and his sons 'draw near' to the holy of holies but do not 'enter' it, since such entry is the unique prerogative of the high priest. Furthermore, at Lev. 16.1, the death of Abihu and Nadab (cf. Lev. 10.1-3) took place because they 'drew near' (*qrb*) to the Lord, according to the Hebrew text. But the LXX at 16.1 has replaced *qrb* with 'brought strange fire' (ἐν τῷ

1. Lev. 21.17, 21; Ezek. 44.16.
2. Lev. 10.3, 4-5; 16.1; Num. 16.40.
3. It is to be observed that in Leviticus the word 'offer' (*hqryb*) suggests the immolation and sacrifice at the altar, as it occurs before the death of the sacrificial animals. But the manipulation of the blood at the altar or at the 'mercy seat' occurs with the words 'take' (*lqḥ*) and 'bring' (*hby'*). For the occurrence of these words in relation to the Day of Atonement, see W. Stott, 'The Conception of "Offering" in the Epistle to the Hebrews', *NTS* 9 (1962), pp. 62-67 (especially, pp. 63-64).
4. Lev. 21.23; Num. 4.19.
5. The καταπέτασμα is the curtain dividing the first and second tent. See C. Schneider, 'καταπέτασμα', *TDNT*, 3.628-30.

προσάγειν αὐτοὺς πῦρ ἀλλότριον), thereby suggesting that the two sons had actually entered into the holy of holies with the fire, which would seem most probably based on the content of what follows immediately at Lev. 16.2.

To our knowledge προσέρχεσθαι (or its synonyms) never occurs in conjunction with the ἱλαστήριον or κιβωτός which are situated in the holy of holies. As has been seen, in the few passages where ambiguities appeared (e.g. Lev. 16.1; 21.23; Num. 4.19) the LXX deftly resolves any incongruity.

The cultic approach to God or his holiness by the people has already been broached, and it occurs frequently in the drawing near to God's presence,[1] or in the posture of worship,[2] and prayer.[3] The use of 'draw near' may also have no immediately discernible cultic or ritual content, as when it refers to witnessing an occurrence, or as a warning not to approach either intentionally or inadvertently what is holy; for instance, the tabernacle, the maintenance of which was reserved for the Levites.[4]

We may conclude, therefore, that the cultic use of *qārēb* and *niggaš* in the LXX makes reference to the priestly access to the sanctuary, altar and first tent, in order to minister for the people by making offerings. At the same time the LXX applies 'to draw near' to the people and thus depicts their approach to God, their worship and prayer; i.e. sacerdotal circumstances.

The differences between προσέρχεσθαι (or its synonyms) and εἰσέρχεσθαι (or its synonyms) will again be considered at the outset of Chapter 4.[5]

---

1. Exod. 3.5; 22.8; Num. 16.5; Deut. 4.11; 5.27.
2. Exod. 16.9; 24.2; Lev. 9.5; Num. 3.38; 4.19.
3. Jer. 7.16; Zeph. 3.2; Pss. 31.9(LXX); 118.169(LXX).
4. Num. 1.51; 3.38; 8.19; Josh. 3.4.
5. The investigation of the verbs considered here and at Chapter 4 is dependent on the following resources: Hatch and Redpath, *A Concordance*; E. Jenni, '*bô*' ', *Theologisches Handwörterbuch zum Alten Testament*, 2 (ed. E. Jenni with C. Westermann; München: Chr. Kaiser, 1971–76), 1.264-69 (hereafter cited as *THAT*); H.D. Preuss, '*bô*'', *Theological Dictionary of the Old Testament* (ed. G. Botterweck and H. Ringgren; trans. J.T. Willis, G.W. Bromiley, and D.E. Green; 5 vols.; Grand Rapids: Eerdmans, 1974–86), 2.20-25 (hereafter cited as *TDOT*); H. Ringgren, '*nāgaš*', *Theologisches Wörterbuch des alten Testaments* (ed. G. Johannes Botterweck, H. Ringgren, and H.-J. Fabry; Stuttgart: Kohlhammer, 1973–86), 5.232-37 (hereafter cited as *TWaT*); J. Kühlewein, '*qrb*', *THAT*, 2.674-81; J. Schneider, 'προσέρχομαι', *TDNT*, 2.683-84; J. Schneider, 'εἰσέρχομαι', *TDNT*,

## 2. Προσέρχεσθαι in Hebrews

After this brief introductory review we now come to our examination of προσέρχεσθαι in Heb. We shall begin our undertaking with Heb. 10.1 where the cultic meaning of προσέρχεσθαι, already familiar in the LXX, is readily discerned from its context and content. The other occurrences will then follow according to their sequential arrangement throughout the Epistle.

### Heb. 10.1

The meaning of οἱ προσερχόμενοι (10.1) cannot be separated from its context within the larger unit in which it finds itself, Heb. 7.1–10.18, where Heb. develops the presentation of Christ's heavenly high priesthood.[1] The cultic context of 10.1 is even more narrowly delimited by reason of the progression of the sacerdotal argument begun at 9.1 and climaxing with 10.1-8, which uses the Day of Atonement ritual as the obvious paradigm.[2] Thus, the similarity of content, even the parallel character of thought, argue for a unified continuity from 9.1 through 10.18.[3] Heb. 10.1 logically follows Heb. 9 by illustrating the insufficiency of the old covenant practice. Westcott comments that 'that which seemed to give [the work of the high priests] special attractiveness and power, as appealing sensibly to the

---

2.676-78; H. Preisker, 'ἐγγίζω, προσεγγίζω', *TDNT*, 2.330-32; F. Hauck, S. Schulz, 'εἰσπορεύομαι', *TDNT*, 6.578; K.L. Schmidt, 'προσάγω', *TDNT*, 1.131-33. In the recent article, 'The Use of Προσέρχεσθαι in the Gospel of Matthew' (*JBL* 106 [1987], pp. 65-67), J.R. Edwards has observed that most references to προσέρχεσθαι in the LXX occur either in the P material or Holiness Code (Lev. 17–26), 'both of which were concerned with establishing cultic practices'.

1. So Dibelius ('Der himmlische Kultus', p. 164) can call the content of Heb. 7.1–10.18, the 'Leitidee des Hebräerbriefes'.

2. Peterson, p. 144. Moffatt (*Commentary*, p. 135) sees what follows 10.1 as 'the author's final verdict on the levitical cultus'. Windisch (*Hebräerbrief*, p. 87) describes this as follows: 'Das einmalige wirksame Opfer Christi hat die nutzlosen Häufungen von Tieropfern zum Stillstand gebracht'.

3. Michel (*Kommentar*, p. 329) writes: 'Auffallend ist allerdings, dass unser Brief keine Spannung zwischen Kap. 9 und 10.1-18 empfunden hat'. He states prior to this that 'Kapitel 10.1-18 ist also ein formal selbstständiger, inhaltlich aber angehängter exegetischer Midrasch zur Verstärkung von Kap. 9'. This is also cited in Zimmermann, *Das Bekenntnis*, p. 117. The interconnectedness between Heb. 9 and 10.1-18 is seen by the parallel use. See W.G. Johnsson, 'Defilement and Purgation in the Book of Hebrews' (PhD dissertation, Vanderbilt University, 1973), p. 339 (Heb. 9.11); and J. Swetnam, *Jesus and Isaac*, p. 120 n. 191 (Heb. 9.9).

worshiper year by year by a visible and impressive service, was a sign of its inefficacy and transitoriness to those who looked deeper'.[1]

The causal particle γάρ serves to link the argument beginning at 10.1 with what has been said antecedent to it by establishing the reason why the unique and single offering of Christ (9.27-28) opens the future salvation.[2] This is further accentuated by the emphatic position of ἔχων, so that the nature of the law is contrasted pejoratively with the nature of Christ's work.[3] That ὁ νόμος (with the exception of 10.28) means the Old Testament 'Kultgesetz' (e.g. 7.5, 16; 8.8; 9.19, 22; 10.8) which has been superseded by Christ is plain from the cultic character of Heb. and the occurrences of νόμος within this central section, 7.1–10.18.[4] This law merely represents the future benefits and does not effect the reality of their appearance, as is evident from Heb. 8–9.[5]

The insufficiency of the old covenant ritual is described by the contrast between σκιά and εἰκών (10.1a). The cultic law is only a shadow

---

1. Westcott, *Hebrews*, p. 303. So also Windisch, *Hebräerbrief*, pp. 90-91; Riggenbach, *Der Brief*, p. 295. Michel (*Kommentar*, p. 329) notes the conspicuous contrast being made between old and new, and many and once-for-all, in 10.1-18 (but already considered in Heb. 9): e.g. κατ' ἐνιαυτόν (10.1, 3); καθ' ἡμέραν (10.11); πολλάκις (10.11); but also εἰς τὸ διηνεκές (10.1, 12, 14); ἅπαξ-ἐφάπαξ (10.2, 10); μία θυσία, μία προσφορά (10.12, 14).

2. Braun, *Hebräer*, p. 288. The reason is 'weil das Kultgesetz es nur mit der Kopie des himmlischen Kultus, nicht mit dessen Original zu tun hat'. On γάρ as a 'Vorzugswort' in Heb., as well as a connective particle, see Karl-Heinz Pridik, 'γάρ', *Exegetisches Wörterbuch zum Neuen Testament* (ed. H. Balz and G. Schneider; Stuttgart: Kohlhammer, 1980–83), 1.572 (hereafter cited as *EWzNT*); F. Blass and A. Debrunner, *A Greek Grammar of the New Testament and Other Early Christian Literature* (trans. and rev. R.W. Funk, supplementary notes by A. Debrunner; Chicago: University of Chicago Press, 1961), pp. 235-36 (hereafter cited as BDF, *Grammar*); F. Delitzsch, *Commentary on the Epistle to the Hebrews* (trans. T.L. Kingsbury; 2 vols.; Edinburgh: T. & T. Clark, 1987; reprint edn, Minneapolis: Klock & Klock, 1978), 2.141.

3. Westcott, *Hebrews*, p. 304, who notes that the other rendering could have been ὁ γὰρ νόμος σκιὰν ἔχων.

4. Hans Hübner, 'τελειόω', *EWzNT*, 3.827; Hübner, 'νόμος', *EWzNT*, 2.1170-71; W. Gutbrod, 'νόμος', *TDNT*, 4.1078.

5. Riggenbach, *Der Brief*, p. 294. According to Hübner, 'νόμος', *EWzNT*, 2.1171, this is to be viewed as a positive aspect, e.g. 'Der positive Aspekt des atl. Gesetzes zeigt sich daran, dass es Gottes Gesetz war und immerhin einen Schatten der künftigen Güter besass (10.1)'. See also R.H. Smith, *Hebrews* (Augsburg Commentary on the New Testament; Minneapolis: Augsburg, 1984), p. 121. However, exactly how 'positive' the law as 'shadow' is to be seen, pales in the contrast presented by τὴν εἰκόνα τῶν πραγμάτων, as will be seen in what follows.

('copy', 'Abbild', 8.5) and not the true reality ('image', 'Urbild') itself. Here Heb. uses εἰκών in a manner peculiar within the current Hellenistic literature—in which it is usually synonymous with σκιά— as the true form itself.¹ The law as σκιά is thus the very opposite of τύπος (Exod. 25.40) or εἰκών, and 'does not deal with the essence of things'.² F.F. Bruce sees σκιά as meaning a foreshadowing, more than a platonic sense of a copy of the external idea. Therefore 'Christ and his new order are the perfect reality to which the earlier ordinances pointed forward'.³ Thus a very pointed contrast is presented by the use of σκιά and εἰκών between the old and the new covenants. The parallel genitives of apposition, τῶν μελλόντων ἀγαθῶν and τῶν πραγμάτων, further characterize this contrast between σκιά and εἰκών.⁴ The law as the 'shadow of the good things to come' is seen as future from the standpoint of the law as well as in its actualization among Christians (e.g. 13.14), but it alludes to the present eschatological reality in the fact of the heavenly high priesthood of Christ: e.g. 6.5, γευσαμένους . . . δυνάμεις τε μέλλοντος αἰῶνος; 9.11, ἀρχιερεὺς τῶν γενομένων ἀγαθῶν.⁵ Therefore the law at best

1. Michel, *Kommentar*, p. 330; Windisch, *Hebräerbrief*, p. 88; F.F. Bruce, *Hebrews*, p. 225 n. 1; A.E. Gowie, 'Shadow and Substance', *ExpTim* 28 (1916–17), p. 398; Peterson, p. 145; H. Kleinknecht, 'εἰκών', *TDNT*, 2.388-89; Riggenbach, *Der Brief*, p. 294; Delitzsch, 2.143-44. See especially the thorough examination of εἰκών in concurrent traditions by Braun, *Hebräer*, p. 289, G. Kittel, 'εἰκών', *TDNT*, 2.395-97 (e.g. to the contrary is Philo, *Leg. All.* III.96: σκιά = εἰκών). Westcott (*Hebrews*, p. 304) and Moffatt (*Commentary*, p. 135) qualify εἰκών as a 'complete representation', yet inferior to the archetype.
2. G. Kittel, 'εἰκών', *TDNT*, 2.395; S. Schulz, 'σκιά', *TDNT*, 7.394. Riggenbach, *Der Brief*, p. 294, likens the σκιά to the 'simple outline sketch', contrasting the 'full color painting' (as Chrysostom). Also see Spicq, *L'Epître*, 1.75; Braun, *Hebräer*, p. 289.
3. F.F. Bruce, *Hebrews*, p. 226; Peterson, pp. 144-45. However, Moffatt (*Commentary*, p. 135) and Spicq (*L'Epître*, 1.75; 2.301-302) both stress the platonic character of the phraseology.
4. So Delitzsch, 2.144; Braun, *Hebräer*, p. 289. Michel (*Kommentar*, p. 331) writes, 'Dass beide Begriffe . . . identisch sind, ist wohl anzunehmen' (9.11; 6.18; 11.1). Also, Westcott, *Hebrews*, p. 305; Moffatt, *Commentary*, p. 135; Riggenbach, *Der Brief*, p. 295.
5. Delitzsch, 2.142; Westcott, *Hebrews*, p. 305; F.F. Bruce, *Hebrews*, p. 226. The eschatological dimension (i.e. internal evidence) argues for the acceptance of γενομένων rather than μελλόντων at 9.11. As such, these are benefits which belong to the future world, but which are already present in Christ; e.g. W. Grundmann, 'ἀγαθός', *TDNT*, 1.15; Hugh Montefiore, *A Commentary on the Epistle to the Hebrews*, (London: A. & C. Black, 1964), p. 164.

foreshadowed what is accessible through the new covenant by hope (6.19-20), but it could not itself accomplish such benefits.[1] This point is further clarified in the remainder of 10.1, by reference to the inability of the Day of Atonement ritual to transcend the shadows.

The repetition of animal sacrifices was ordained by the νόμος. The particular sacrifices in mind at 10.1 are those presented annually at the Day of Atonement, a subject which has already been broached in the preceding chapters of the Epistle. κατ' ἐνιαυτόν has a special place of emphasis, as seen in its separation from προσφέρουσιν.[2] Its usage clearly refers to the Day of Atonement ritual (e.g. 10.4, the bull and goat offerings) and not to the multifarious and manifold daily offerings, for which Heb. elsewhere utilizes καθ' ἡμέραν (3.13; 7.27; 10.11), but not in the present context.[3] Hence αἱ αὐταὶ θυσίαι are indeed the identical offerings stipulated by the Day of Atonement in Leviticus 16. The intensive pronoun, αὐταὶ confirms that the allusion is to the repetition of the Day of Atonement ritual, and not to the offerings of the priests, which varied according to the persons bringing the offerings to be immolated and presented.[4] Inherent in the

---

1. Peterson, p. 145; Riggenbach, *Der Brief*, p. 295; Christian Maurer, 'πρᾶγμα', *TDNT*, 6.638-40; Attridge, *Hebrews*, pp. 270-71.

2. Westcott, *Hebrews*, p. 303; Riggenbach, *Der Brief*, p. 295 n. 7; Windisch, *Hebräerbrief*, p. 88; Michel, *Kommentar*, p. 331; Moffatt, *Commentary*, p. 136; Braun, *Hebräer*, p. 255.

3. Most scholars see 10.1 as making reference to the Day of Atonement; e.g. Michel, *Kommentar*, p. 331; Windisch, *Hebräerbrief*, p. 88; F.F. Bruce, *Hebrews*, p. 226; Peterson, pp. 146, 265-66 n. 128; Zimmermann, *Das Bekenntnis*, p. 119; Delitzsch, 2.144; Moffatt, *Commentary*, p. 136; Braun, *Hebräer*, p. 255; Riggenbach, *Der Brief*, pp. 295-96. The 'annual' character of κατ' ἐνιαυτόν is seen often in pertinent literature and is mentioned by Braun, *Hebräer*, p. 255: Lev. 16.34; *3 Macc.* 1.11; Philo, *Leg. ad G.* 306; *De ebr.* 136; *De spec. leg.* I.72; *De gig.* 52; Josephus, *War* V.236; as well as in Heb. itself: 9.7, 25; 10.3-4. The insistence by some on linking the sacrifices with the daily offerings (based on 10.11) ignores, it seems, the context of Heb. 7.1–10.18, as well as the singular usage of κατ' ἐνιαυτόν, according to Spicq (*L'Epître*, 2.302, citing Ephraem and Chrysostom); Westcott, *Hebrews*, p. 307. At p. 305, Westcott mitigates his position by proposing that the Day of Atonement serves as representative of the long line of ritual activities centered around the tent throughout the year. This view of the Day of Atonement as all-incorporating paradigm is, however, presented without evidence, and it is not necessary for the meaning at 10.1. Consonant with the bull and goat offering is Lev. 16: e.g. 16.6, 11-14 (bull); 16.7-10, 15-16, 20-22 (goat).

4. Peterson, p. 146. The day of Atonement accords well with the considerations in Heb. 10.2-3 also. The Day of Atonement served as a reminder of sins because the people annually 'afflicted themselves' (Lev. 23.26-32) and 'confessed sins' (Lev.

offering of these same sacrifices κατ' ἐνιαυτόν is the repeated character of the practice. Thus we shall see the redundancy involved if εἰς τὸ διηνεκές were to be connected with προσφέρουσιν.[1] The sacrifices are offered by the high priests.[2] The plural προσφέρουσιν further suggests the succession of high priests who have served as offerants on the Day of Atonement.[3]

In order to avoid the unnecessary redundancy it is best to link εἰς τὸ διηνεκές with τελειῶσαι and not with προσφέρουσιν. Such a connection also agrees with the usage elsewhere in Heb., and would be parallel to the emphatic separation of κατ' ἐνιαυτόν from its verb.[4] Accordingly, the difficulty rests with the meaning of εἰς τὸ διηνεκές either expressing a result, e.g. 'into the future, forever', or simply as a further suggestion of repetition, i.e. 'repeatedly, continually'. The restricted occurrence of εἰς τὸ διηνεκές (Heb. 7.3; 10.1, 12, 14) in the New Testament causes interpretive difficulty.[5] It is, however, used in place of εἰς τὸν αἰῶνα from Ps. 110.4 at Heb. 7.3, and appears to

16.20-22). The curtain into the holy of holies also perpetually reminded the people of the rift between God and humanity.

1. To call something an 'annual' event obviously refers to an event repeated once every year.
2. Michel, *Kommentar*, p. 331; Westcott, *Hebrews*, p. 305 (the appointed ministers of the system); Delitzsch, 2.144.
3. K. Weiss ('προσφέρω', *TDNT*, 9.65-68) observes that the twenty occurrences in Heb. of προσφέρω betray a LXX influence, where it is a sacrificial term used for the offering of gifts. Hence, προσφέρειν is to accomplish the sacrifice. It is to be observed that Philo never uses προσφέρειν in a cultic sense.

Moffatt (*Commentary*, p. 136) suggests that the idiomatic use of the plural is in order to emphasize the action, rather than the subject (citing J.H. Moulton, W.F. Howard, and N. Turner, *A Grammar of New Testament Greek* [4 vols.; Edinburgh: T. & T. Clark, 1908-76], 1.58). This may be true, but the subject was nonetheless known by any person familiar with the Day of Atonement ritual practice.
4. E.g. Westcott, *Hebrews*, p. 303. Those who link εἰς τὸ διηνεκές with τελειῶσαι include: Westcott, *Hebrews*, pp. 303-304; Michel, *Kommentar*, p. 331; Windisch, *Hebräerbrief*, p. 88 (with some reservation); Montefiore, p. 164; Johnsson, 'Defilement and Purgation', p. 452; and the *New English Bible*. Those with contrary opinions include: Delitzsch, 2.145 (where he comments further that 'Tholuck observes with striking truth, that this three-fold κατ' ἐνιαυτόν, ταῖς αὐταῖς, εἰς τὸ διηνεκές, represents almost pictorially the ever self-repeating cycle of those annual acts of atonement'); Riggenbach, *Der Brief*, p. 296, esp. n. 9; Moffatt, *Commentary*, p. 136; Braun, *Hebräer*, p. 290; R.H. Smith, p. 121; Peterson, pp. 146, 265 n. 128.
5. Moffatt (*Commentary*, p. 93) notes that this classical phrase is used only by Heb. in the entire New Testament.

designate an extended or uninterrupted time into the future, or future eternity itself.¹ That εἰς τὸ διηνεκές replaces εἰς τὸν αἰῶνα at 7.3 in traditional material, argues for their synonymity.² εἰς τὸ διηνεκές ought to be regarded, therefore, as referring to time in the future, i.e. forever (1.8; 5.6; 6.20; 7.17, 21, 24, 28; 13.8, 21; also 7.3; 10.12, 14), and not as a repetitive process, i.e. 'continually' or 'repeatedly'. Heb. is already amply familiar with terms to describe the latter feature (e.g. διαπαντός—6.19; 13.15; πολλάκις—6.7; 9.25, 26; 10.11). Therefore, the law was absolutely unable (οὐδέποτε) to make perfect 'into the future', 'forever', τοὺς προσερχομένους, recalling, of course the Son made perfect forever (7.28).³ ὁ νόμος appears to be the subject of 10.1, hence the preferred text reading is δύναται, despite the better attested plural δύνανται. Not to accept δύναται is to entangle oneself in an unbearable anacoluthon.⁴ Thus, indeed, it is the νόμος, the old covenant 'Kultgesetz', that cannot make perfect those who 'draw near'.

We have seen previously in our study of the use of προσέρχεσθαι in the LXX that its cultic occurrences either depict the priestly approach to God (e.g. Lev. 9.7-8; 21.17-24; 22.3) or the approach of non-priests for worship (Exod. 16.9; Lev. 9.5; Num. 18.4). When descriptive of the priestly ritual service, προσέρχεσθαι (or its synonyms) is typically followed by πρός and a cultic object, or by an infinitive verb denoting worship, offering, or service. Exceptions appear to be the uses of προσέρχεσθαι without an object (e.g. Lev.

---

1. H. Sasse, 'αἰών', *TDNT*, 1.198-200. That Delitzsch (1.335-36) and Westcott (*Hebrews*, pp. 174, 305) attempt to distinguish a difference between εἰς τὸν αἰῶνα and εἰς τὸ διηνεκές, does not seem justified by the contexts in which they are situated. See Cockerill, pp. 60-62.
2. εἰς τὸ διηνεκές is present at 7.3 based upon the traditional *Vorlage* used by the author: e.g. Zimmermann, *Das Bekenntnis*, pp. 79-99; Rissi, *Die Theologie*, pp. 81-90; G. Theissen, *Untersuchungen zum Hebräerbrief* (SNT, 2; Gütersloh: Gütersloher Verlagshaus [Mohn], 1969), pp. 20-28; Michel, *Kommentar*, p. 263.
3. J. Héring, *The Epistle to the Hebrews* (trans. A.W. Heathcote and P.J. Allcock; London: Epworth, 1970), p. 64 (on 7.28) connects the understood καθίστησιν with εἰς τὸν αἰῶνα, for which he finds little support among scholars.
4. Delitzsch, 2.142; Riggenbach, *Der Brief*, p. 293; Windisch, *Hebräerbrief*, p. 88; Michel, *Kommentar*, p. 332; Moffatt, *Commentary*, pp. 135-36; B.M. Metzger, *A Textual Commentary on the Greek New Testament: A Companion Volume to the United Bible Societies' Greek New Testament* (3rd edn [corrected]; New York: United Bible Societies, 1975), p. 669; Peterson, p. 265 n. 25; F.F. Bruce, *Hebrews*, p. 225 n. 2; Braun, *Hebräer*, p. 290. To my knowledge, no recent commentator accepts the better-attested δύνανται.

21.18), although there the object is obvious from the immediate context at Lev. 21.17, and when ἐγγίζειν is followed immediately by the dative case (Exod. 19.22). At Exod. 16.9, προσέρχεσθαι occurs with ἐναντίον and a genitive designation for God, i.e. τοῦ θεοῦ, and depicts non-priests as worshipers. In the writings of Philo and in other Hellenistic occurrences of the cultic προσέρχεσθαι,[1] the verb appears with the dative designation for God (e.g. τῷ θεῷ) and characterizes the participants as worshipers.[2]

The Day of Atonement context already has characterized Heb. 10.1 as cultic.[3] That the object of προσέρχεσθαι is omitted causes no difficulty because it is perfectly clear from the context of the other occurrences of the word: to God (7.9, 25; 11.6); to the throne of grace (4.16); to Mt Zion (12.22)—the latter two being circumlocutions for God's very presence. Hence, a scene of cultic approach (i.e. worship), as operative under the old covenant law, is being characterized. That the entire gathered community is included in this approach is seen by the representative nature of the high priest's act. The high priest offers 'for himself and his house' and then 'for the people' (Lev. 16.11, 15, 19). Heb. frequently reiterates the same understanding (Heb. 5.1, 3; 7.27-28; 8.3; 9.7; 10.11). Accordingly οἱ προσερχόμενοι are the high priests, who approach God κατ' ἐνιαυτὸν ταῖς αὐταῖς θυσίαις, but also the people represented by them.[4] A parallel phrase at 10.2, οἱ λατρεύοντες, also seems to

---

1. For relevant texts, see J. Schneider, 'προσέρχομαι', *TDNT*, 2.683.
2. This general use with the dative may suggest that this is the sense applied by Heb. (4.16; 7.25; 10.1, 22; 11.6; 12.18, 22). See Cockerill, pp. 136-38. But also see our comments above on προσέρχεσθαι in the LXX.
3. W. Thüsing, '"Lasst uns hinzutreten..."' (Heb. 10.22)', *BZ* (n.F.) 9 (1965), p. 6; though O. Kuss ('Der Brief an die Hebräer', in *Der Brief an die Hebräer und die Katholischen Briefe* [Das Neue Testament, 8; Regensburg: Friedrich Pustet, 1953], p. 90) is slow to regard προσέρχεσθαι as a cultic term absolutely. But see J. Schneider, 'προσέρχομαι', *TDNT*, 2.684, who considers it 'purely cultic'.
4. Michel (*Kommentar*, p. 332) sees προσέρχεσθαι as designating the 'weitere Kreis der Gemeindeglieder... denen das Opfer gilt'. But clearly at the Day of Atonement the victims atone for the high priest as well as the people. Cf. also Delitzsch, 2.144; Peterson, p. 145 (citing Exod. 16.9; 34.32; Lev. 9.5; Num. 10.3-10); Riggenbach, *Der Brief*, p. 297, though he qualifies his understanding by including priests in this term, 'Natürlich aber sind die Priester, sofern es sich wie am Versöhnungstag um Gemeindeopfer handelt, in die προσερχόμενοι miteingeschlossen'. In agreement with this position are Westcott, *Hebrews*, p. 305;

embrace both the priests and the laity (8.5; 9.9; 13.10),[1] since the repetition of the Day of Atonement sacrifices obviously indicates that the consciousness of sin has been removed neither on the part of the high priest nor on the part of the people. Hence, οἱ προσερχόμενοι at 10.1 refers to the old covenant practice of drawing near to God, of coming into his very presence, through the prescribed cultic ritual.

The term τελειοῦν will be investigated in some detail later in this study. We have already adduced from the meaning of προσέρχεσθαι, however, the fact that τοὺς προσερχομένους is the object of the sentence ὁ νόμος . . οὐδέποτε δύναται τοὺς προσερχομένους τελειῶσαι εἰς τὸ διηνεκές, thereby connecting τελειοῦν with προσέρχεσθαι. This is already borne out by the cultic character of τελειοῦν.[2] By maintaining in the latter half of 10.1 the identical σκιά/εἰκών paradigm found already in 10.1a, the προσέρχεσθαι is contrasted with τελειοῦν. The 'drawing near' practiced in the cult was always a shadow of the real access—evident most cogently in its frequency of repetition: the 'real' drawing near, the entrance into the heavenly—not earthly—holy of holies, is 'perfection'. We may say then that the law was unable to give 'real' access forever to those who drew near on the Day of Atonement.

The intimate connection between 'drawing near' and 'perfection' is similarly contrasted elsewhere in Heb. At 7.18-19 the law's inability to make perfect has its parallel in the actual drawing near to God through the introduction of a better hope.[3] At 7.27-28 the repeated cultic activity of the high priests involving 'drawing near' (implied

---

Windisch, *Hebräerbrief*, p. 88; Braun, *Hebräer*, pp. 290-91 (who notes the use for lay access in Plutarch, *E. Delph.* 2. 385c).

1. Windisch, *Hebräerbrief*, p. 88; Braun, *Hebräer*, p. 291. However, H. Strathmann ('λατρεύω', *TDNT*, 4.63-64) sees it as a technical term for priestly ministry on the basis of Heb. 8.5 and 13.10.

2. E.g. Käsemann, *The Wandering People*, pp. 132-44; Delling, 'τελειοῦν', *TDNT*, 8.79-86. Cf. also Rissi, 'Die Menschlichkeit Jesu', pp. 28-45; Rissi, *Die Theologie*, pp. 79, 102-103; Moe, pp. 161-69; Dibelius, 'Der himmlische Kultus', p. 165. For H. Hübner ('τελειοῦν', *EWzNT*, 3.827-28) τελειοῦν is 'in den Zustand versetzen, den sie vor Gott haben sollten'.

3. See Cockerill, p. 121. According to Rissi (*Die Theologie*, p. 103), 'Der Unmöglichkeit der alten Heilsordnung, zur Vollendung zu führen, steht die Einführung einer besseren Hoffnung gegenüber, "durch welche wir zu Gott hinzutreten". Es ist die Hoffnung, die schon 6.18-20 genannt wurde, die mit dem Allerheiligsten verbindet. Das Nahen zu Gott als priesterliches Vorrecht ist also selbst die Vollendung.' This will be examined more fully when we turn to ἐγγίζειν at 7.19.

from the knowledge of the cultic procedure) is sharply contrasted with the Son who has been made perfect forever. Thus the old covenant προσέρχεσθαι is devalued in light of the 'real' access (i.e. 'perfection') belonging to the Son. In the same way, at 9.9, the drawing near with gifts and sacrifices cannot effect the 'real' access to God (perfection), hence the inadequacy of the old covenant cultic practices. A final example is 5.1-10, where the functions of the high priest are chiastically contrasted with those of Jesus Christ. The earthly high priest is appointed to 'draw near' to no real avail (5.1-3), but Christ has 'really' drawn near (τελειωθείς, 5.9) to God. So προσέρχεσθαι and τελειοῦν appear to be words of similar meaning in Heb., but of a wholly different soteriological order depending on whether they are used in a context to contrast the old covenant 'Kultgesetz' or in the context of the new covenant reality accessible through hope.[1]

## Heb. 4.16

Cultic allusion predominates in and around Heb. 4.16. The author's initial use of προσέρχεσθαι is a hortatory (present subjunctive) call situated in the central section of the Epistle which expounds the theme of the high priesthood of Jesus (4.14–10.39).[2] Following the paraenesis at 3.1–4.13 the author resumes the consideration of the high priesthood of Jesus that was already mentioned in 2.17-18.[3] This in no way, however, suggests that 3.1–4.13, as an originally independent midrash on Ps. 95.7-11, is not integral to the argument of Heb. It is precisely the high priest mentioned in 2.17-18 who leads the people of God in a typological comparison to the leadership of Moses. Heb. 3.1–4.13 does not therefore interrupt the train of thought of the author, but succeeds in emphasizing the point of the Epistle.[4]

---

1. Peterson, pp. 145-47; Bruce, *Hebrews*, pp. 227-28; R.H. Smith, p. 121.
2. The inclusion by parallel structures at 4.14-16 and 10.19-25 defines the limits of this section. E.g. F.J. Schierse, *Verheissung und Heilsvollendung: Zur theologischen Grundfrage des Hebräerbriefes* (Münchener Theologische Studien, 9; München: Karl Zink, 1955), pp. 199-203; W. Nauck, 'Zum Aufbau des Hebräerbriefes', in *Judentum, Urchristentum, Kirche: Festschrift für Joachim Jeremias* (ed. W. Eltester; BZNW, 26; Berlin: Töpelmann, 1960), pp. 203-204. The placement of 10.32-39 need not concern us here. See Spicq, *L'Epître*, 2.315; Thüsing, p. 5.
3. Jeremias, 'Hebräer 5.7-10', p. 322.
4. This point is made by Rissi (*Die Theologie*, pp. 14-16) in his discussion of 3.1–4.13. Hofius (*Katapausis*, p. 54) argues for a continuity based on the cultic consideration of the heavenly holy of holies in which the high priest resides, which

The particularly cultic interest at 4.16 is best discerned from its present context. The inferential consecutive conjunction οὖν links 4.16 to what immediately precedes it. Thus the grounds for the Christians' approach are presented in 4.14-15 (and 2.17-18). The very same Jesus (the 'great high priest, ἀρχιερεὺς μέγας), who has 'entered through the heavens' (διεληλυθότα τοὺς οὐρανούς) into the very presence of God in the heavenly holy of holies, was none other than the earthly high priest who knew man's weakness and temptations κατὰ πάντα.[1] Jesus can (whereas the old covenant priest could not), therefore, truly effect authentic atonement for man since he not only has the ability to sympathize with man's weakness (without having sinned) but has also entered into the one true sanctuary (not the earthly) with his own blood (not the blood of others). On the other side of 4.16, Heb. 5.1-10 introduces the readers to the earthly high priesthood (5.1-4) and to Jesus' own priesthood (5.5-10). Thus Westcott is correct to say, 'the minds of writer and readers are full of the imagery of the Levitical system, and of the ceremonial High-priestly atonement'.[2]

In light of the effectiveness of Jesus' earthly and heavenly high priesthood the author exhorts his readers: προσερχώμεθα οὖν μετὰ παρρησίας τῷ θρόνῳ τῆς χάριτος. The readers are admonished to draw near to God's heavenly throne, now characterized by the grace that proceeds from it.[3] This has led some scholars to see Heb. depicting the throne as a heavenly 'antitype' to the mercy seat (9.5) of the earthly sanctuary, which was situated in the holy of holies.[4] God's

for Hofius is the same as the κατάπαυσις. This, however, is not likely in light of the present access to the heavenly holy of holies and the future expectation of the 'rest'. This will be considered further in our Conclusion.

1. For a cogent analysis of this act of 'passing through the heavens', see Rissi, *Die Theologie*, p. 39. See, in particular, Heb. 8.1-2; 9.11-12; 10.19-21. This view successfully avoids the stumbling block encountered by others who are at a loss to explain the author's complete reticence to discuss the ascension elsewhere in Heb. or the absence of such spatial speculation of graduated heavenly spheres in the Epistle.

2. Westcott, *Hebrews*, p. 108.

3. This is the meaning of the genitive of quality. So Riggenbach, *Der Brief*, p. 122; Delitzsch, 1.223.

4. Windisch (*Hebräerbrief*, p. 40) observes that already in the Old Testament sanctuary, the place of God's presence was compared to a throne, citing Isa. 6. W. Eichrodt (*Theology of the Old Testament*, 2.193) remarks that 'the earthly counterpart to the heavenly throne, however, is the ark of Yahweh with the cherubim'. See also Otto Schmitz ('θρόνος', *TDNT*, 3.161 n. 13) who notes that Yahweh bears the name 'he who is seated between the cherubim' (e.g. 1 Sam. 4.4; 2 Sam. 6.2; 2 Kgs

throne, therefore, was located in its corresponding holy of holies in heaven.[1] This would certainly be in keeping with the cultic interest of Heb., for such a scheme would pose the same contrast (i.e. κρείττων) between the old covenant and new covenant order as shown elsewhere (e.g. 10.1). Thus, the futile acts of propitiation before the earthly mercy seat on the annual Day of Atonement by the high priest have their superior counterpart in the completed act in heaven, since Christ has passed into the heavenly sanctuary with his own blood (4.14).

On the other hand, O. Michel argues that ὁ θρόνος is an Hebraic periphrasis for God himself, so that by drawing near to the 'throne', it is access to God to which reference is being made, and to the risen Christ.[2] It appears to me that both of these options are 'much the same',[3] inasmuch as both center on the fact of God's presence and man's access to it.

According to the Old Testament the conception of the throne of God takes its imagery from the earthly, royal throne. This is particularly in evidence at 1 Kgs 22.10, 19 where the earthly and heavenly are juxtaposed.[4] Typically, God's throne is portrayed as being in heaven, or as being heaven itself, which expresses 'the overwhelming majesty of the divine Ruler'.[5] The eschatological Temple (which will be earthly) will contain the seat of the throne of God and be his abiding presence, but until that time God is portrayed as ruler in heaven.[6] Most striking is the tradition in Rabbinic Judaism of the double thrones—the throne of Justice and the throne of Grace, where special petitions were necessary in order to move God from his throne of

---

19.15; Ps. 80.1). Schmitz, at p. 162 n. 17, cites G. von Rad, that 'in earlier times especially the ark was regarded as the throne of Yahweh invisibly present'.

1. F.F. Bruce, *Hebrews*, p. 86; R.H. Smith, p. 70; D.A. Hagner, *Hebrews* (Good News Commentaries; San Francisco: Harper & Row, 1983), p. 60; G. Buchanan, *To the Hebrews*, p. 82; Westcott, *Hebrews*, p. 109. However, Delitzsch (1.222-23) finds no basis for this within the text itself.

2. Michel, *Kommentar*, p. 209. This is of course true, but one ought not ignore the pregnant royal imagery in such a phrase.

3. Peterson, p. 79.

4. O. Schmitz, 'θρόνος', *TDNT*, 3.162.

5. *Ibid.* For instance, 1 Kgs 22.19; Isa. 66.1; Ezek. 1.26; 10.1; Job 26.9; Pss. 11.4; 103.19. At Isa. 6.1-13, God is enthroned in majesty in the Temple. In Hellenistic Judaism, the throne of God is synonymous with heaven, e.g. *4 Macc.* 17.18. There are no occurrences of the throne in Philo and few references in Josephus. See O. Schmitz, 'θρόνος', *TDNT*, 3.163.

6. Jer. 3.17; 14.21; 17.12-13; Ezek. 43.7.

Justice onto his throne of Grace.[1] Whereas in the Rabbinic tradition there were two thrones, with the throne of Justice being occupied most frequently by the Deity, in Heb. there is now only one throne, the throne of Grace, from which proceed mercy, forgiveness, and help.[2]

In Heb. the throne is now the θρόνος τῆς χάριτος since the Son, Jesus, is enthroned at the right hand of God (1.3, 13; 8.1; 10.12; 12.2). This Jesus has entered into the heavenly holy of holies (4.14; 8.2) and has sat down at the right hand of God (8.1; 12.2).[3] God's throne has therefore now become a gracious reign, because Jesus, the embodiment of grace, the agent of redemption, now resides with God in the heavenly holy of holies,[4] so that, 'pardoning grace rather than pitiless judgment now streams forth from it'.[5] That the throne of God is also the throne of Christ is seen explicitly by the application of Psalm 45 to Jesus Christ at Heb. 1.8.

Therefore, according to Heb., Jesus' passing through the heavenly sanctuary (4.14) finds its correlate at 4.16, where the readers are exhorted to draw near to the throne of grace. Heb. 8.1-2 locates this throne of God within the heavenly holy of holies. Thus the readers are called to 'draw near' to this throne, to the heavenly holy of holies, as Jesus did: access has been made possible because the throne is now characterized by his grace. But just how do living, breathing, corporeal entities draw near to the throne, or enter into the heavenly holy of holies, or stand in God's very presence—especially since such access is already a present enjoyment, as seen by the προσεληλύθατε in 12.22?

The present subjunctive προσερχώμεθα exhorts that this practice not be initiated, but that it continue. Already the context in which 4.16 is located suggests a cultic application. The 'great high priest' has

---

1. For a listing of these writings, see Str–B, *Kommentar*, 2.112; Riggenbach, *Der Brief*, p. 122 n. 21; Michel, *Kommentar*, p. 209 n. 2; or Héring, p. 36 n. 23.
2. C. Blendinger ('θρόνος', *NIDNTT*, 2.614) calls this an 'implicit antithesis'. However, he does not show that the author of Heb. was in conversation with any such Rabbinical traditions.
3. On μεγαλωσύνη as a circumlocution for the divine name, see O. Schmitz, 'θρόνος', *TDNT*, 3.161 n. 7, and Riggenbach, *Der Brief*, p. 219 n. 7.
4. The throne of God and of Jesus appear to be one and the same. God and Christ are on the throne, e.g. Spicq, *L'Epître*, 2.94. At Rev. 3.21b and 22.1, 3, both thrones are expressed identically, e.g. Braun, *Hebräer*, p. 39.
5. Riggenbach, *Der Brief*, p. 122; Michel, *Kommentar*, pp. 209-10. The effectiveness of Jesus' high priestly work and office to effect 'grace' is seen in the δι' αὐτοῦ of 7.25, according to Delitzsch (1.223).

## 3. Προσέρχεσθαι *and Hebrews*

entered into the heavenly holy of holies (4.14), and the exhortation seems to provide a parallel: *now* the readers are encouraged to 'draw near to the throne of grace', or to enter into the same holy of holies. Heb. 5.1-10 also concerns high priestly, cultic practices. Thus, it would certainly be an anomaly for 4.16 not to be cultic-ritually oriented as well.[1]

However, as will be seen at 12.22, προσέρχεσθαι cannot refer to a re-enactment of the same cultic ritual performed earlier by the old covenant priests. The Christians are still on earth, suffering the human foibles that accompany worldly existence, so that they can not enter, physically, into the heavenly holy of holies.[2] At 12.22-24 Heb. presents the parallel between the heavenly 'worshipers' and the earthly Christians, whose access to God appeared to be through a similar 'worship'.[3] Such an application of προσέρχεσθαι to worship, particularly in the posture of prayer, is not unfamiliar to the LXX. At Jer. 7.16, προσέρχεσθαι as 'prayer' is used, and at Jer. 42.1-6 (49.1-6[LXX]) and Ps. 34.5 (33.6 [LXX]) the context of the verb's use prescribes that prayer be practiced. Thus, 'such prayer is to be

---

1. Such a non-cultic interpretation is maintained by Moffatt (*Commentary*, p. 60) and Montefiore (p. 92) who see προσέρχεσθαι as an approach to the highest authority, who is empowered to favor the request made to him. Most commentators, however, observe the cultic character of 4.16; e.g. Delitzsch, 1.223 n. 1; Westcott, *Hebrews*, p. 108; Windisch, *Hebräerbrief*, p. 95; Michel, *Kommentar*, p. 209; Käsemann, *The Wandering People*, p. 54; Schierse, *Verheissung*, pp. 167, 200; Best, p. 282; Spicq, *L'Epître*, 2.94; N.A. Dahl, 'A New and Living Way: The Approach to God According to Hebrews 10.19-25', *Int* 5 (1951), p. 408; and Braun, *Hebräer*, p. 127. Riggenbach (*Der Brief*, pp. 121-22) seems to equivocate by arguing that it cannot here be called a 'priestly act', but it is nonetheless cultic. F. Schröger ('Der Gottesdienst der Hebräerbriefgemeinde', *MTZ* 19 [1968], pp. 177-78) appears satisfied with his distinction between the 'theological' and the 'cultic' uses of προσέρχεσθαι, based on the past priestly practice or the current exhortation to draw near in the 'Gottesdienst der Gemeinde'. However, the cultic character of the προσέρχεσθαι cannot be overlooked, whether or not it is now being seen as making a general theological statement about the Christian 'hinzutreten' to God. All uses of προσέρχεσθαι are clearly grounded in the high priestly saving event of Jesus.

2. Michel (*Kommentar*, p. 209) observes that they approach not in priestly service, but as a 'company of sinners' hoping for mercy and grace. They have nothing to give—only to receive.

3. Dahl, 'A New', p. 409: 'Through worship they participate in the heavenly worship of the angels, and perfected saints, 12.22-29; 13.10-16; 1.6. Thus, having in prayer access to God, they already have a share in the life of the new, eschatological world, i.e. proleptically.'

understood as the means of expressing the reality of a relationship already existing through the mediatorial work of Christ'.[1]

Heb. has transformed cultic terminology and applied it to the Christian community in such a manner that the work of Jesus Christ can have an efficacy for them, not only in the future, but in the present. Thus, to 'draw near' bespeaks an access to God (although not a physical access) within the heavenly sanctuary made possible by the high priestly activity of Jesus Christ.[2] 'The idea (behind προσέρχεσθαι) is not that we should ascend to heaven—for example, in mystical experiences—but that we should come before God who is in heaven. This means prayer. Worship through thanksgiving and prayer is the sacerdotal service to which the "consecrated" of the new covenant are exhorted.'[3] By applying προσέρχεσθαι within the already cultic context of 4.14–5.10 the author has transformed cultic terminology to encompass activity beyond the sacerdotal activity at the altar. Prayer and worship are characterized as cultic and priestly functions. The importance of prayer is seen further in the close connection with 4.16 at 5.7 where Jesus' prayers describe his entire earthly high priestly activity preceding his death. Hence, the true cultic activity (προσφέρειν) on earth is characterized as prayer and worship, as embodied by Christ, and as commended as such to the Christian readers.

The readers are not only exhorted to draw near to the throne of grace. They are also called to do so in a certain manner, namely μετὰ παρρησίας. According to H. Schlier, what was originally a term from the political sphere for freedom of speech, an openness to truth, and a candor or boldness in address, developed and took on divers and

---

1. Peterson, p. 79.
2. Thus, Michel (*Kommentar*, p. 209) calls this approach a 'real and concrete occurrence that is attained in worship'. See Schierse, *Verheissung*, p. 167; Rissi, *Die Theologie*, p. 98.
3. Dahl, 'A New', p. 408, citing Heb. 7.25; 9.14; 12.28; 13.16. Also see Riggenbach, *Der Brief*, p. 122, and Moffatt, *Commentary*, p. 60. The mention of 'imploring aid' by Delitzsch (1.223) suggests the posture of prayer. Attridge (*Hebrews*, p. 141) sees the 'drawing near' as metaphorical rather than as having cultic overtones. It therefore expresses the 'image for entering into a covenantal relationship with God'. Elsewhere (pp. 204, 318, 400-401), however, Attridge does see this manifested by Christian worship practices.

3. Προσέρχεσθαι *and Hebrews* 109

diverse meanings.[1] In the LXX and later Jewish Hellenistic literature παρρησία appears as something God gives to the individual, but it is also used of the person's παρρησία towards God, so that the objective (freedom, permission, authority) as well as the subjective (boldness, confidence) character of παρρησία become common uses.[2]

The dual understanding of παρρησία is evident in LXX occurrences when individuals interact with God.[3] At Job 22.26-27 and 27.9-10 the relation of Job to God is depicted by his freedom to speak out and address God with boldness. But whatever boldness or joy may be brought into this relationship, it always appears to have its basis in an initiating action by God (e.g. Lev. 26.13) or a prior knowledge of God's graciousness (Job 27.9-10; 22.26-27). Hence, with regard to Heb., Käsemann is correct to assert that παρρησία is not purely subjective joy.[4]

> [The] purely subjective interpretation requires a supplement. We concede that it is justified to the extent παρρησία describes a Christian attitude (cf. 4.16; 10.35). One 'has' (10.19) παρρησία, not merely as a subjective attitude, but as an appropriation of something already given. One holds it fast, not merely by holding on as a believer, but by clinging to the presupposition of faith in the promise. As ἐπαγγελία is more than mere promise, so also παρρησία is more than mere subjective trust. *That is, it is the joyful enlistment in a cause already guaranteed by God in an objective* ἔλεγχος.[5]

Subjective 'confidence' always possesses its prior guarantee. Thus the παρρησία of 4.16, typically translated by 'confidence, boldness', has a parallel in 10.22 where, immediately following the hortatory

---

1. Heinrich Schlier ('παρρησία, παρρησιάζομαι', *TDNT*, 5.871-86) presents a valuable compendium of the uses of παρρησία in both biblical and extra-biblical texts.
2. *Ibid.*, pp. 875-79. Texts include: Job 22.23-27; 27.9-10; Josephus, *Ant.* II.52, 131; V.38; Philo, *Quis rer.* 5-29; *1 En.* 47.2-4; 48.8; 51.5; 61.1-13; 62.3-5; 63.1-12; 69.26; 104.1-5; *4 Ezra* 7.87, 98-101. Schlier ('παρρησία, παρρησιάζομαι', *TDNT*, 5.879) writes that 'the meaning of παρρησία found in Job (i.e. the LXX) is thus continued' into later Jewish Hellenistic literature.
3. Schlier, 'παρρησία, παρρησιάζομαι', *TDNT*, 5.875-76.
4. Käsemann, *The Wandering People*, pp. 42-43. For instance, Moffatt (*Commentary*, p. 60), 'a resolute confidence'; Delitzsch (1.223), 'a joyous confidence'; Schierse (*Verheissung*, p. 200) sees a 'subjective' use at 4.16; Kuss, *Der Brief*, p. 45, 'Zuversicht'. Also see Michel, *Kommentar*, pp. 178, 180-81, 209.
5. Käsemann, *The Wandering People*, p. 43. See Schlier, 'παρρησία, παρρησιάζομαι', *TDNT*, 5.884.

προσερχώμεθα, we find 'with a true heart in full assurance of faith'. Here we see the supplementary character of the subjective to the objective. Prior to any confidence or boldness, or any joyful stand before God, there needs to be the saving knowledge of Jesus Christ who has entered into heaven ('by the blood of Jesus') and so has made any approach to God thinkable and possible. This is then 'worked out' as confidence and openness.[1] Van Unnik reads Käsemann and Schlier correctly when he concludes that

> the 'freedom of speech' has two sides: the free right to approach God, given in the sacrifice of Christ, which is the essence of the Christian faith, and the open confession of this faith, which is an unshakable hope. These two sides are an inseparable unity. In the situation in which the Christians lived they had it as a gift and a task.[2]

Therefore to speak of confidence or boldness is to have appropriated already the work of Christ and God; on the other hand, to speak of the freedom or permission to enter is to presume a subjective attitude characterized by joy and confidence.[3]

The readers are exhorted to 'draw near' to the throne with a 'confidence' derived from the knowledge of their freedom to stand before, and to address God on the basis of the Christ event. This 'drawing near' was seen to be through prayer and worship. Further support for this characterization of prayer in 4.16 is found in the close connection between παρρησία and prayer in pertinent LXX texts. παρρησία, the free and lively access to stand before God and to address him, is characterized by the posture of prayer. The immediate contexts of Job 22.26-27 and 27.9-10 are those of prayer as seen by

---

1. Schlier, 'παρρησία, παρρησιάζομαι', *TDNT*, 5.884; Peterson, p. 80.
2. W.C. van Unnik, 'The Christian's Freedom of Speech in the New Testament', *BJRL* 44 (1962), p. 485. So also Dahl, 'A New', p. 403: 'the Greek word παρρησία must be assumed to imply both the God-given permission and the personal confidence and frankness arising from it'. Buchanan (*To the Hebrews*, p. 83) comments that 'in Heb., it can mean the unquestioned right to approach God (3.6; 4.16; 10.19), or the openness with which they should confess their faith'. For further comment on παρρησία in Heb. refer to Riggenbach, *Der Brief*, pp. 312-13; Schierse, pp. 166-67; E. Grässer, *Der Glaube im Hebräerbrief* (Marburger Theologische Studien, 2; Marburg: Elwert, 1965), pp. 16-17, 96-98; Peterson, pp. 79-80; Braun, *Hebräer*, p. 84; Rissi, *Die Theologie*, p. 98.
3. This is the position of Spicq, *L'Epître*, 2.315. But see Michel (*Kommentar*, p. 344) who subordinates the subjective to the objective absolutely. Also see Grässer, *Glaube*, p. 109.

the use of the verbs ἐπικαλεῖσθαι and εὔχεσθαι.¹ At 1 Jn 3.12; 4.17; 5.14 prayer may be expressed with παρρησία, on the basis of the prior faithful trust in the Son of God.² Therefore the posture of those who draw near and stand before God is one of prayer, grounded in the knowledge that God hearkens to such petitionary activity, since he has opened the way into the very holy of holies in heaven (e.g. 4.14; 10.19-21).

The reason for this 'drawing near' is then stated by a final clause, ἵνα λάβωμεν ἔλεος καὶ χάριν εὕρωμεν εἰς εὔκαιρον βοήθειαν (4.16b). This clause, too, expresses the activity of prayer.³ Windisch noted the prayerful content, stating, 'Die Aoriste λάβωμεν and εὕρωμεν weisen auf konkrete Fälle der Gebetserfahrung'.⁴

In light of the frequent occurrences of χάρις and ἔλεος together, as well as the observed chiastic structure at 4.16b, the question is often expressed regarding the synonymity of the two terms.⁵ This is seen by the frequency of such pairings elsewhere: e.g. grace and peace, grace and truth, mercy and grace. Westcott, however, carefully distinguishes between the terms, noting that 'the twofold aim corresponds with the two-fold necessity of life. Man needs mercy for past failure, and grace for present and future work.' He also observes the difference in the 'mode of attainment' between mercy and grace.⁶

---

1. Schlier, 'παρρησία, παρρησιάζομαι', *TDNT*, 5.876-77; Attridge, *Hebrews*, p. 142. παρρησία, expressed in prayer, also occurs at Philo, *Quis rer.* 21; *1 En.* 47.2-4.
2. R.E. Brown, *The Epistles of John* (Anchor Bible, 30; Garden City, NY: Doubleday, 1982), pp. 380-81.
3. Peterson (p. 79) suggests that 'the particular need expressed in 4.16—to "receive mercy" and find "timely help" for running the Christian race—indicates the activity of prayers'. Montefiore (p. 92), describes the 'sinner' as 'asking' for mercy.
4. Windisch, *Hebräerbrief*, p. 41. Braun (*Hebräer*, p. 128) lists several text references and then comments, 'Öfter in diesen Texten als Bitte um Barmherzigkeit'.
5. Peterson, p. 80; Delitzsch, 1.223; J. Moffatt, *Grace in the New Testament* (New York: Long & Smith, 1932), p. 352, Kuss, *Der Brief*, p. 45; Braun, *Hebräer*, p. 128. Michel (*Kommentar*, p. 210) writes: 'Die beiden Begriffe sind also als Eigenschaften und Gaben Gottes inhaltlich miteinander verwandt und weisen auf die hellenistische Tradition zurück'. For Riggenbach (*Der Brief*, pp. 122-23) the two terms are difficult to differentiate.
6. Westcott, *Hebrews*, p. 109. He receives support from Peterson (p. 80) and A. Strobel ('Der Brief an die Hebräer', in J. Jeremias, *Die Briefe an Timotheus und Titus, Der Brief an die Hebräer* [NTD, 9; Göttingen: Vandenhoeck & Ruprecht, 1981], p. 124). His overtly theological consideration, however, ignores the fact that

What seems clear, at any rate, is that the reception of mercy and the finding of grace are sought through prayerful activity. This is particularly true of ἔλεος and its verbal form ἐλεεῖν.[1] ἔλεος and ἐλεεῖν occur frequently in the Psalms, where the cry of prayer is for mercy, or in petitions to God to hear the cry to him.[2] Hence, in Heb. 4.16, prayer is being described as the activity of those who draw near in order to find mercy and find grace at the throne of God (Heb. 7.25).

Also in the LXX the Psalms contain βοήθεια as the desired object of the people's prayer to God.[3] At Heb. 5.7 Jesus is depicted as praying πρὸς τὸν δυνάμενον σῴζειν αὐτόν. Thus Heb. is familiar with the relationship between prayer and the need for help, which is a continuous need that must be acknowledged day after day, as is implied by the present tense of the hortatory subjunctive προσερχώμεθα.

*Conclusion*
Heb. 4.16 depicts the readers of the Epistle in cultic terminology which originally applied to old covenant priests, but which now characterizes the Christian community as those who draw near to the heavenly holy of holies through prayer and worship without human mediation, in their desire for divine help (εὔκαιρος)[4] in the face of temptation and trial. This very temptation and trial serves to remind the readers that their entry into the holy of holies is not yet fulfilled and final, but accessible now through prayer, worship and thanksgiving.

for Heb., in Jesus, humanity's past, present and future have once for all been fulfilled (13.8).
    1. H. Conzelmann ('χάρις', *TDNT*, 9.389, 391) observes that χάρις is never used in the LXX as a theological term. In the New Testament, it is used formulaically with ἔλεος at 1 Tim. 1.2; 2 Tim. 1.2; Titus 1.4; 2 Jn 3.
    2. W. Zimmerli ('χάρις', *TDNT*, 9.376-87) considers the Hebrew roots *hnn* and *hsd* in great detail, both of which are most frequently rendered by ἔλεος and its verb form in the LXX. Psalms cited are: 6.2; 9.13; 25.7; 30.10; 31.9; 41.4, 10; 44.26; 51.1; 56.1; 57.1; 86.3; 86.16; 109.26; 119.88, 149, 159; 123.3. Also see R. Bultmann, 'ἔλεος', *TDNT*, 2.477-87. He notes that in later Judaism, mercy was hoped for (Sir. 2.9), and prayed for (*Pss. Sol.* 8.33-34; 9.16). See Käsemann, *The Wandering People*, pp. 232-34.
    3. F. Büchsel, 'βοήθεια', *TDNT*, 1.628-29. These Psalms include: 19.2; 21.19; 34.2; 37.22; 59.11; 69.1; 70.12; 107.12; also *Ps. Sol.* 15.1. Michel (*Kommentar*, p. 210) is aware that 'Gebet' is a 'possibility' in one's attempt to attain help, but the fact that prayer is not mentioned at either Heb. 2.18 or 4.16 leads him to disregard it. It is significant for Michel that the first occurrence of prayer is at Heb. 5.7.
    4. Michel, *Kommentar*, p. 210.

Thus the help needed on this side of death 'besteht darin, dass ich die Verheissung des Hohenpriesters, der für mich eintritt, der für mich gelitten hat, annehme—dass ich weiss, dass dies Wort, das für mich gesprochen, dass dies Opfer, das für mich dargebracht ist, gerade in meiner Anfechtung hilft'.[1] The knowledge of what has been realized by Christ (4.14-15) provides the encouragement to draw near to God as well as the absolute assurance of divine help at his right time.

*Heb. 7.19*
The very fact that a new priesthood after the order of Melchizedek arose (7.11) gave scriptural evidence for the insufficiency of the old priesthood as well as its law (7.12). Thus to declare, 'You are a priest for ever after the order of Melchizedek' (7.17) is to proclaim a qualitatively different kind of priesthood, because this priesthood succeeds where the old could only persevere in futility, accomplishing figuratively what the new achieves actually.

It is within this larger 'Schriftauslegung' of Ps. 110.4, where the context of cult and priesthood is unmistakable (7.11-25), that Heb. 7.18-19 is situated. Heb. 7.18 reintroduces what has previously been mentioned (7.11-12), but this time it appears as the first of three consecutive antitheses between the old and the new priesthood, 7.18-19, 20-22, and 23-25.[2] This contrast is evident in the occurrence of μέν and δέ, and in each instance 'wo zwei Sätze durch μέν und δέ einander gegenübergestellt werden, liegt der Nachdruck...auf dem zweiten'.[3] What is introduced again at 7.18 does, however, receive a much more emphatic expression than in 7.12. The 'change' (μετάθεσις) of the law has now become the 'annulment' (ἀθέτησις) of the old, and later, the 'introduction' (ἐπεισαγωγή) of the new.[4] Thus the 'rechtskräftige Annullierung der levitischen Priesterordnung' is something more severe than the rather tame μετάθεσις νόμου at 7.12.[5] F.F. Bruce notes that ἀθέτησις occurs again at 9.26 in reference to the 'cancellation of sin by the self-oblation of Christ', and also

---

1. *Ibid.*, p. 210.
2. Windisch, *Hebräerbrief*, p. 65.
3. Riggenbach, *Der Brief*, p. 201. This is clearly the case in 7.19b, 21, and 24.
4. Moffatt (*Commentary*, p. 97) points out the negative and positive character of the respective terms.
5. Riggenbach, *Der Brief*, pp. 201-202. On the placement of ἀθέτησις at the beginning of the sentence see Riggenbach, *Der Brief*, p. 201.

that the corresponding verb form appears a dozen times in a similar manner to that found in Mk 7.9, speaking of those who 'set aside the commandment of God' in order to keep their own traditions.[1] Furthermore, in the papyri, the term occurs often as a 'juristischer Terminus in der Verbindung εἰς ἀθέτησιν καὶ ἀκύρωσιν' (e.g. 'for the cancellation of debts').[2] Thus, the complete 'otherness' of the old and the new is made plain by ἀθέτησις: they are different in kind, and as such, in efficacy.[3]

The former ἐντολή that has been annulled is that which dealt with the legal ordinances of the levitical priesthood, i.e. matters of physical descent (7.16) and external ritual observance.[4] This ἐντολή was not even 'leading to' or 'preparatory for' the new order.[5] As stated above, the context emphasizes the absolute inadequacy of the old, rather than its functioning positively as the shadow of the new (e.g. 10.1). The προαγούσης ἐντολῆς is therefore 'previous', 'transitory', and consequently annulled in light of something new.[6]

---

1. F.F. Bruce, *Hebrews*, p. 147 n. 56.
2. Riggenbach, *Der Brief*, p. 202 n. 60. Cf. also Michel, *Kommentar*, p. 273; BAG, p. 20; A. Deissmann, *Bible Studies: Contributions Chiefly from Papyri and Inscriptions to the History of the Language, the Literature, and the Religion of Hellenistic Judaism and Primitive Christianity* (trans. A. Grieve; 2nd edn; Edinburgh: T. & T. Clark, 1909), pp. 228-29. Braun (*Hebräer*, pp. 212-13) gives detailed references to its use in extra-biblical materials.
3. This absolute contrast is something different than the contrast of σκιά and εἰκών at 10.1. However, the point made is the same: the new accomplishes that which the old, in actuality, only portended. See Attridge, *Hebrews*, p. 203.
4. See Riggenbach, *Der Brief*, p. 202 n. 61, and Westcott, *Hebrews*, p. 186. R.H. Smith (p. 93) correctly observes that to speak of priesthood, commandment, or law is to speak about the same 'bundle'. So also Michel, *Kommentar*, p. 270. Thus the ἐντολή, while referring specifically to the commandments regarding the priesthood, also refers to the larger understanding of the law. He equates the old law with the former commandment. This then puts 7.18-19 in the very same context as 7.11 and 10.1. Peterson (p. 108) also draws attention to the close connection between priesthood and law in Heb. Braun (*Hebräer*, p. 213) observes that the context shows that Heb. has the priesthood and sacrifice in mind.
5. Delitzsch, 1.360. However, Westcott (*Hebrews*, pp. 186-87) and Peterson (p. 111) see a dual meaning as 'an earlier commandment' and also as 'a foregoing commandment'.
6. Riggenbach, *Der Brief*, p. 202 n. 63. Cockerill (p. 115) establishes correctly that the old commandment was not preparatory for the new hope, but predated it. This was because of the obsolescence and imperfection of the old law and its priesthood. See Buchanan, *To the Hebrews*, p. 126.

The cause of this annulment is then stated, διά + accusative. The ἐντολή (αὐτῆς) was weak (ἀσθενής) and useless (ἀνωφελής) and therefore it was annulled or set aside. According to Michel 'ἀσθενής und ἀνωφελής (e.g. Tit. 3.9) ist das Gesetz, weil es den Menschen in seiner eigentlichen Existenz nicht berühren und nicht umschaffen kann (συνείδησις, καρδία).[1] As seen at 9.9 and 10.2, 22, this touches on the concept of perfection, which immediately follows in a parenthesis (7.19a).[2] 'Weakness' and 'uselessness' therefore characterize the system (in Heb. it is the levitical priestly practice, e.g. 10.1) unable to fulfill its intended reason for being, which was to open real and direct access to God. Hence Heb. may add parenthetically that the 'law made nothing perfect', which is precisely the result of the ἐντολή when viewed from the light of the better hope. τελειοῦν, as can be seen (e.g. 7.25; 10.1, 14; also 7.11), refers to the real access to God, entrance into the heavenly holy of holies, which was unattainable by the law. A contrast is being established, as is typical in Heb. Here it is explicit by the μέν. . . δέ construction. We can expect to learn more about τελειοῦν (just as at 10.1 and 7.25) if the contrast is being presented with any semblance of logic and consistency by the author.

The conclusion (7.19b), characterized by δέ, contrasts ἀθέτησις to ἐπεισαγωγή, προαγούσης ἐντολῆς to κρείττονος ἐλπίδος, and οὐδὲν ἐτελείωσεν to ἐγγίζομεν τῷ θεῷ. ἐπεισαγωγή occurs only here in the New Testament and is absent from the LXX, Philo, and the Apostolic Fathers, but is found elsewhere in Hellenistic and classical Greek literature, where it means to 'introduce'.[3] The context of the ἀθέτησις of the law suggests an entirely new 'introduction', if the proper contrast is to be maintained. Since the law had been nullified, anything succeeding the law would be 'introduced' as something new.

---

1. Michel, *Kommentar*, p. 273. See Heb. 9.9, 14; 10.2, 22; 13.9, 18. Braun (*Hebräer*, p. 213) finds no evidence of the law or commandments being weak or useless in the LXX or in Philo. Against Michel, Braun sees the 'weakness' resulting from the sinfulness and inevitable death of the priests (7.23-24, 27-28), and the 'uselessness' from the inability of the animal sacrifices to make the priests cultically pure.
2. Windisch, *Hebräerbrief*, p. 65; Braun, *Hebräer*, p. 213.
3. Michel, *Kommentar*, p. 273. This understanding of ἐπεισαγωγή is seen in Josephus, *Ant.* XI.196, where it refers to the 'replacing' of Vashti by Esther; e.g. see Westcott, *Hebrews*, p. 187; Moffatt, *Commentary*, p. 98; Spicq, *L'Epître*, 2.194; Braun, *Hebräer*, p. 214. This seems far more logical than the idea of Delitzsch (1.358-59, 361, 'in addition to' [thereby either continuing the association or superseding it]) and Bruce, *Hebrews*, p. 148 n. 57.

Thus, in contrast to the 'abolished' former commandment (which proved to be no 'hope' at all) a 'better hope' is introduced. This 'better hope' is that through which believers draw near to God.

The comparative 'better' (κρείττων) is a particular favorite of Heb., used to identify the 'new order' inaugurated by Jesus, thereby contrasting the inefficacy of the old law.[1] The 'real' effectiveness of Christ's ministry, covenant, promises, sacrifice, and possession (e.g. 1.4; 7.22; 8.6; 9.23; 10.34) is described in Heb. by κρείττων. It designates, therefore, not simply an efficacy that is superior to an inferior by degree, but an entirely new reality or kind, 'a direct and lasting access to God'.[2] This 'better' means actual fulfillment, 'd.h. eine verbürgte, gewisse und zum Ziel führende'.[3] Thus Heb. is careful to emphasize that only under the 'better' does actual, certain access to God occur, of which the old was at best a 'shadow' and at worst, 'weak' and 'useless'.[4]

The contrast between the 'former commandment' and the 'better hope', while seemingly a mixing of metaphors,[5] is wholly consistent within Heb. and the context of the argument. As long as the central argument revolves around the accomplished sacrifice of Christ the high priest, the content is addressing the access or lack of access to God under the new and old covenants. 'Hope' (ἐλπίς) is the confidence of salvation based on the knowledge of the Christ-event. It thus appears to be rooted in the Old Testament understanding of hope as

1. M. Bourke, 'The Epistle to the Hebrews', in *The Jerome Biblical Commentary* (ed. R.E. Brown, J.A. Fitzmyer, and R.E. Murphy; 2 vols; Englewood Cliffs, NJ: Prentice–Hall, 1968), 2.394.
2. Moffatt, *Commentary*, p. 98; Peterson, p. 112.
3. Michel, *Kommentar*, p. 273. In this regard 11.40 is to be considered, where the believers under the old law are dependent on the 'something better', which is the actual new reality of the new covenant; e.g. see Cockerill, p. 117.
4. Riggenbach (*Der Brief*, p. 203) is therefore in error when he writes, 'Allerdings verlieh auch schon die gesetzliche Ordnung eine Hoffnung; denn die ganze Opferdarbringung war von der Erwartung getragen, dadurch die Vergebung und die Beseitigung aller Störungen im Verhältnis zu Gott zu erlangen (9,22)'. The old covenant ritual could never extend to its practitioners any semblance of real hope, and insofar as it was practiced, the hope elicited was false or futile. Michel (*Kommentar*, p. 273) says the law 'könnte eine trügerische Hoffnung erwecken'; see also Moffatt (*Commentary*, p. 98). As at 7.25, what is important is worship δι' αὐτοῦ, 'through Jesus', which is worship under the new order.
5. Riggenbach (*Der Brief*, p. 203 n. 64) notes the 'Ungleichartigkeit' of the contrast. Delitzsch (1.362) has no difficulty in seeing the 'better hope' as simply contrasting the ἐντολή and its present unsatisfying practical effect.

## 3. Προσέρχεσθαι and Hebrews

the general confidence in God's protection and help: a trust that knows that the future is in the hands of God, and that one must surrender oneself fully to God.[1] Thus Windisch is not entirely incorrect to liken 'hope' to 'Jesus', because the foundation of hope is clearly based on the Christ-event.[2] Through this hope (δι' ἧς) we have access to God already (4.16; 10.22), and yet it is also a reality extended into the future. Bultmann notes that 'Christian hope rests on the divine act of salvation accomplished in Christ, and, since this is eschatological, hope itself is an eschatological blessing; i.e. now is the time when we may have confidence'.[3] But Heb. warns against self-absorption in a present confidence to the neglect of the future and so reminds the readers to hold on to hope ἄρχι τέλους (e.g. 6.11; also 3.6, 14).

But this 'hope' is nevertheless a present reality, for confidence results from the evidence of God's faithfulness, even surpassing the faithfulness shown to Abraham (6.13-15). Christians may cling to both the oath of God and the Christ-event as grounds for their hope and confidence (6.18). In fact, this hope already affords one access into God's very presence within the heavenly holy of holies. Thus 7.19b appears to be related to or 'resuming' the thought of 6.19-20.[4] Hope enters the inner shrine like an anchor, whereby our inner person is bound to the heavenly holy of holies. Therefore, with hope and confidence, the Christian anticipates that which will be—namely full communion with God.[5] The priestly cultic understanding is made clear in Heb. 6.20 where Jesus (who was already high priest on earth, e.g. 2.17-18; 5.1-10) 'has entered for us' (ὑπὲρ ἡμῶν εἰσῆλθεν) as a forerunner and is the designated high priest after the order of Melchizedek. Thus, through this hope, whereby our inner beings are anchored within the holy of holies, we have an access to God, i.e. we 'draw near (ἐγγίζομεν) to God' (7.19). This suggests that ἐγγίζειν

---

1. Bultmann, 'ἐλπίς', *TDNT*, 2.523; Rissi, *Die Theologie*, p. 113.
2. Windisch, *Hebräerbrief*, p. 59. Michel (*Kommentar*, p. 253 n. 6) takes exception to this.
3. Bultmann, 'ἐλπίς', *TDNT*, 2.532.
4. Moffatt, *Commentary*, p. 98; cf. also Bourke, p. 394; Rissi, *Die Theologie*, p. 103.
5. Rissi, *Die Theologie*, pp. 97-98. More will be said about 6.19-20 when we look at εἰσέρχεσθαι in Chapter 4. Delitzsch (1.362) writes that since Jesus the forerunner has entered into the heavenly holy of holies, 'it has for the eye of faith no veil'.

itself points to the priestly prerogative and is characterized as 'perfection'.¹

The contrast is present again at 7.19, as at 10.1 and 7.25, between the inability to perfect (or to bring into direct access to God) and the 'drawing near to God'. Here, ἐγγίζειν is used rather than the usual προσέρχεσθαι but the terms are virtual equivalents.² As with προσέρχεσθαι, ἐγγίζειν typically renders some form of *qārêb* or *niggaš* and is frequently used of the cultic approach to God (Exod. 3.5; 24.2; Lev. 10.3; 21.3) or of priests going before God (Exod. 19.22; Lev. 21.21, 23; Ezek. 40.46; 42.13; 43.19; 44.13; 45.4). Thus the synonymity of the two words is clear.³

Apart from the frequent cultic use of ἐγγίζειν in the LXX, the context of Heb. 7.1-28 also casts a cultic light on the term. The first person plural ἐγγίζομεν serves, then, to characterize the readers (i.e.

---

1. Riggenbach (*Der Brief*, p. 203) shows that the people have now obtained what was already designated for them in the old covenant (Ps. 148.14), that is, access to God. This access by the old priests had never been attained.

2. Braun (*Hebräer*, p. 214) begins his discussion of ἐγγίζειν by likening it to 7.25 and 4.16 where προσέρχεσθαι appears, with the suggested meaning of the drawing near of people to God. Moe (p. 162) notes the synonymity of προσέρχεσθαι and ἐγγίζειν but perhaps ventures too far when he suggests that this use of ἐγγίζειν is 'bedeutungsvoll; denn ἐγγίζειν wird vorzugsweise von den Priestern gebraucht' in the LXX. Its priestly use appears no more prevalent than does προσέρχεσθαι. More interesting is his insight that the term λατρεύειν, which in the Old Testament denotes the cultic worship of the people, has been used in a similar manner as λειτουργεῖν in Heb., so that λατρεύειν refers to priestly worship at Heb. 8.5; 9.1; 10.2; 13.10: see Moe, p. 162 n. 3. Also see Floor, pp. 76-77; Strathmann, 'λατρεύω', *TDNT*, 4.63-64; and Best, p. 282.

3. For instance, at Deut. 4.11 προσέρχεσθαι occurs, but the similar context at Exod. 19.21-22 reads ἐγγίζειν. This suggests that the composition of the LXX was in fact the work of multiple hands. However, just as προσέρχεσθαι also occurred in non-priestly, even non-cultic usages, so too does ἐγγίζειν. This is logical, based on their translating *qārêb* and *niggaš*. ἐγγίζειν refers to Abraham drawing near in prayer (Gen. 18.23), which Philo uses to express the idea of drawing near to God through wisdom and partaking of life immortal (*Leg. All.* III.9; *Deus Imm.* 161; *De migr. Abr.* 132). Eccl. 4.17 uses 'to draw near to listen' and 'to draw near to sacrifice' for approaching God in his 'house'. Hos. 12.7; Zeph. 3.2; Hag. 2.15; Isa. 29.13; 58.2, point to the drawing near of all people (either in cultic worship or in prayer). Further texts are mentioned in Braun, *Hebräer*, p. 214. On this basis, Peterson (pp. 112, 246 n. 49) seems unnecessarily cautious when warning against the sacerdotal interpretation of ἐγγίζειν here, as also does Best (p. 283). The very context of Heb. 7 centers on cultic and priestly concerns.

believers) as participants in the cultic approach.¹ The effectiveness of their approach is sharply contrasted to that approach under the old covenant. What was totally ineffective with regard to affording access to God has in fact been replaced by a new order, a better hope, which does lead the believer already to perfection, to full access to God (something the law could not do, e.g. 7.19a). Through hope, this access to God, perfection, is already attainable in the present, and it is to this hope and this access that believers cling until the end (6.11).² Precisely what this access to God means for the present readership of Hebrews is found in the hortatory passages that admonish the believers to 'draw near' (4.16; 10.19-39).

### Heb. 7.25

The contrast between the former priests and the possessor of the ultimate priesthood, Jesus (7.22), provides the immediate context for the occurrence of οἱ προσερχόμενοι, which is found within the larger contextual contrast between the priesthood of Melchizedek and the levitical priesthood in Heb. 7. There is no denying, therefore, the cultic milieu in which 7.25 is situated, since it continues the *Schriftauslegung* of Ps. 110.4 begun at 7.11.³

The inferential consecutive conjunction ὅθεν intimates that 7.25 logically results from what is stated previously in 7.23-24.⁴ However, 7.25 surpasses the content of these verses by stating what Jesus is able to do (i.e. δύναται σῴζειν) without reference to what benefits the former priests were able to effect. Hence, in order to present a logically ordered argument, Heb. must have assumed or implied a certain knowledge of the old covenant cult, i.e. that the former priests

---

1. Westcott, *Hebrews*, p. 187: 'All believers are, in virtue of their Christian faith, priests. That which was before (in a figure) the privilege of a class has become (in reality) the privilege of all; and thus man is enabled to gain through fellowship with God the attainment of his destiny.' Attridge (*Hebrews*, pp. 204, 400-401) prefers the term 'metaphorical' for the same understanding. We call the present approach of the readers 'cultic', even though their offerings are 'spiritual' ones.
2. Jewett (*Letter to Pilgrims*, p. 124) correctly identifies 'hope' for Heb. as the 'sense of holding to a relationship through to the future'.
3. See especially, Zimmermann, *Das Bekenntnis*, pp. 81-182, and his attached fold-out following p. 236.
4. Michel, *Kommentar*, p. 276, where he mentions the other similar occurrences in Heb. 2.17; 3.1; 7.25; 8.3; 9.18. Spicq (*L'Epître*, 2.197) also sees it introducing 7.26-28.

were unable to save οἱ προσερχόμενοι.¹ In fact, frequently in Heb. the former priests are characterized as those who draw near, but always with the blood of others (7.27; 9.7; 10.1, 4, 11). As we have already seen in 10.1, such a practice is unable to perfect or provide authentic access for the priests and people of the old covenant.² Heb. 7.25 logically follows 7.23-24 by continuing the contrast between the old covenant and the 'better covenant' (7.22) of which Jesus is the ἔγγυος (guarantor). The former priests (7.23) were those who drew near under the old covenant, but at 7.25 there are also οἱ προσερχόμενοι under the 'better covenant'. Hence, the cultic meaning of οἱ προσερχόμενοι (7.25) appears to be established, but the certainty of this must await further investigation.

The benefit accrued by this final, ultimate (and therefore also permanent) priest is his ability σώζειν εἰς τὸ παντελές.³ The meaning of the phrase εἰς τὸ παντελές is obscured by its infrequent occurrence in the New Testament. The only other occurrence is found at Lk. 13.11. Therefore, scholars are divided between its temporal and absolute meanings ('forever' and 'completely', respectively).⁴

1. Peterson (p. 113) notes that for Heb., 'plurality is apparently a sign of incompleteness and imperfection (1.1ff.; 10.1ff.) and thus the superiority of Christ's priesthood is illustrated in the fact that he uniquely, as an individual "continues forever" (7.24)'.
2. Schröger ('Der Gottesdienst', p. 177) says that 'gemeint [sind] Priester und Volk des Alten Bundes'. Also see Kuss, 'Der Brief', p. 65.
3. Braun (*Hebräer*, p. 220) notes that this is the only explicit New Testament statement that Jesus can save.
4. Michel (*Kommentar*, p. 276) comments that 'die Kommentare zeigen die exegetische Unsicherheit an, ob die Vollständigkeit oder die Ewigkeit des Heiles gemeint ist'. Wilson (p. 127) considers either rendering 'apposite'. Interpreters accepting the temporal meaning include: Windisch, *Hebräerbrief*, p. 67; Strathmann, 'Der Brief', p. 112; Moffatt, *Commentary*, p. 100; Montefiore, p. 129; Kuss, 'Der Brief', pp. 64-65; Bruce, *Hebrews*, p. 153 (however Bruce's n. 78 and his translation on p. 152 suggest the absolute use). Braun (*Hebräer*, p. 220) notes that the majority of recent commentaries prefer the temporal sense, as he does himself. Those who argue for the absolute meaning are: Delitzsch, 1.371; Westcott, *Hebrews*, p. 191; Riggenbach, *Der Brief*, p. 208; Michel, *Kommentar*, p. 276 (although his translation suggests a temporal meaning, p. 273); T.H. Robinson, *The Epistle to the Hebrews* (Moffatt New Testament Commentary; London: Hodder & Stoughton, 1933), p. 103; R.C.H. Lenski, *The Interpretation of the Epistle to the Hebrews and of the Epistle of James* (Columbus, OH: Wartburg, 1946), pp. 239-40; Spicq, *L'Epître*, 2.197; Héring, p. 62; Strobel, 'Der Brief', p. 158. However, many scholars arguing for the absolute usage concede a certain temporal quality to εἰς τὸ παντελές also: e.g. see Michel's *Kommentar*, Delitzsch, Robinson, and Lenski.

Although the meaning of παντελής is 'absolute', 'perfect', or 'complete' and εἰς τὸ παντελές was used in later Greek for the adverb παντελῶς (completely, absolutely), other later Greek writings employ the phrase to mean 'forever'.[1] The oft quoted conclusion of O. Michel that the distinction drawn between the temporal and absolute meanings of εἰς τὸ παντελές perhaps goes too far seems to dominate current thought. The idea of complete salvation also suggests an eternal salvation, so that 'Für Heb. ist immer beides miteinander verbunden'.[2]

The ambiguity of εἰς τὸ παντελές is clarified somewhat by its context in 7.25. Already Heb.'s penchant for εἰς τὸν αἰῶνα and εἰς τὸ διηνεκές is well established.[3] In the immediately previous verse Jesus is said to continue as a priest εἰς τὸν αἰῶνα (7.24), so the parallel meaning used in the exegesis of Ps. 110.4 could be anticipated, using of course different terms.[4] And, in fact, the Hellenistic formula σωτηρία παντελής is not particularly uncommon.[5] But the parallel of εἰς τὸ παντελές is not only with the εἰς τὸν αἰῶνα of 7.24. We saw in 10.1 a similar phraseology, although τελειοῦν was used rather than σώζειν.[6] For Heb. a certain congruence is present between the verbs 'to perfect' and 'to save', not only contextually, but also interpretively. According to H. Zimmermann, the two verbs are linked in the traditional material already known and used by the author, although his own emphasis differed. Zimmermann writes,

---

1. BAG, p. 613; G. Delling, 'παντελής', *TDNT* 8.66-67; Michel, *Kommentar*, p. 276. For a thorough mention of pertinent texts refer especially to Braun, *Hebräer*, p. 220.
2. Michel, *Kommentar*, p. 276 n. 2. Braun (*Hebräer*, p. 220) concurs. Also see Peterson (pp. 114 and 248 n. 61), and Hagner (*Hebrews*, pp. 91, 94), who emphasizes the 'quality' of the salvation. Attridge, *Hebrews*, p. 210.
3. Heb. 1.8; 5.6; 6.20; 7.17, 21, 24, 28; 13.8; 7.3; 10.1, 12, 14.
4. Windisch, *Hebräerbrief*, p. 67: 'Durch seine ewige Dauer verbürgt uns das Priestertum eine bleibende Zuflucht'. Buchanan (*To the Hebrews*, pp. 127-28) sees this parallel in 7.24 and 25, meaning 'for the age'. Also see J.W. Thompson, *The Beginnings of Christian Philosophy: The Epistle to the Hebrews* (CBQMS, 13; Washington, DC: Catholic Biblical Association of America, 1982), pp. 126-27, and P.E. Hughes, *A Commentary on the Epistle to the Hebrews* (Grand Rapids: Eerdmans, 1977), pp. 268-69 n. 34.
5. So Michel, *Kommentar*, p. 276. Texts cited include: *3 Macc.* 7.16; Philo, *De agr.* 94; *De migr. Abr.* 2. Also see the occurrence of αἴτιος σωτηρίας αἰωνίου at Heb. 5.9.
6. So also at Heb. 10.14. εἰς τὸ διηνεκές is used in 10.1, and εἰς τὸν αἰῶνα at 10.14.

Hier am Abschluss des Kapitels zeigt sich noch einmal die besondere Aussageabsicht des Verfassers im Unterschied zu der ihm vorgegebenen Tradition. Nach der Auffassung der Tradition hat die Erhöhung Jesu und seine Proklamation als Hoherpriester das Heil und die Vollendung gebracht (vgl. 5.10; 10.14). Der Verfasser dagegen verbindet mit dem Opfer Christi nur die Beseitigung der Sünden. Die σωτηρία, also das endgültige Heil, steht noch aus und gilt denen, die ihn erwarten. Damit wird die Erlösung des Menschen durch Christus nicht auf das negative Moment der Beseitigung der Sünden reduziert, weil ja doch mehr geschehen ist: Christus steht als der Geopferte (vgl. 7.28) vor dem Angesichte Gottes 'für uns' (7.24).[1]

Thus the author, although he utilized a traditional *Schriftauslegung*, was well aware that the 'perfection' or 'salvation' at 7.25 was not the end of the matter, as evidenced by Heb. 9.28.

In Heb., on the one hand, σωτηρία is the imminent salvation.[2] This is seen at 1.14, 9.28, and 2.10, where salvation is about to be inherited, where Christ's second appearance will be for salvation, and where salvation is described as δόξα, respectively. On the other hand, however, salvation is also a present reality in that Christians, by drawing near to God, already experience something of the coming salvation (6.9; 7.25). Salvation was already proclaimed by Jesus (2.3), and the Christian may experience the purging of sin and receive help in time of need *now* (2.17-18; 4.16).[3] For Heb. the unique efficacy of this salvation is grounded in Christ's 'having been perfected' (5.9), i.e. in his heavenly high priestly ministry. Thus, 'this salvation removes the consequences of sin and gives a part in the divine life and majesty'.[4] In Philo σωτηρία is removed entirely from the realm of the eschatological, pointing instead to the spiritual participation in the

---

1. Zimmermann, *Das Bekenntnis*, pp. 201-202.
2. Schierse, *Verheissung*, p. 128. What follows is discussed in G. Fohrer and W. Förster, 'σώζω, σωτηρία, σωτήρ, σωτήριος', *TDNT*, 7.996.
3. This finds its antithesis in the cultic futility described in 10.11. Hofius (*Katapausis*, p. 142) notes that this is evident by the signs, wonders and powers of the new age that pervade the readership already.
4. Cockerill, p. 139. For the present and future eschatological meaning of σωτηρία in Heb., see G. Fohrer and W. Förster, 'σώζω, σωτηρία, σωτήρ, σωτήριος', *TDNT*, 7.965-1023, especially p. 996. Also see Michel, *Kommentar*, p. 276 n. 2. Cockerill (p. 139 n. 382) explains that 'in Heb. 6.9 σωτηρίας is opposite of κατάρας, but it also refers to the present state of the readers which leads to that salvation'.

divine since God has aided in 'subduing the passions'.¹ At any rate, in Heb., the meaning of σωτηρία seems to encompass both the future and the present 'access to the Divine' afforded the believer.

Our tentative evaluation of τελειοῦν (see above under Heb. 10.1), then, agrees with the meaning of σώζειν in 7.25. N. Dahl says as much, noting that 'to the unknown author of the Epistle to the Hebrews, salvation means to have free approach to God and communion with him'.² Thus it appears that σώζειν εἰς τὸ παντελές carries the same meaning as parallel phrases in 10.1 and 10.14. At 10.1 the inability of the νόμος to make perfect forever told the story of the old covenant. Therefore the former priests of 7.23, who could neither make perfect nor be made perfect themselves, are contrasted in 7.25 by the guarantor of the 'better covenant', the great high priest, who *is* able to save forever.

That Heb. describes those whom Jesus saves as οἱ προσερχόμενοι corresponds with the apparent cultic context of 7.1-28.³ As has been seen, the LXX uses προσέρχεσθαι for the approach of priests to God (Lev. 9.7-8; 21.17-24; 22.3) as well as the general approach for worship.⁴ The occurrence of προσέρχεσθαι followed by the dative designation for God, although quite rare in the LXX, is found in other Hellenistic works where this combination serves to characterize the general actions of those practicing some form of worship.⁵ It is with the meaning 'worship' that προσέρχεσθαι functions in Heb.⁶

1. See Fohrer and Förster, 'σώζω, σωτηρία, σωτήρ, σωτήριος', *TDNT*, 7.989. Also Philo, *De spec. leg.* I.252; *De agric.* 94; *De migr. Abr.* 2, 124; *De somn.* I.86; *De ebr.* 72, 111. This point is also made by Cockerill, pp. 139-40.
2. Dahl, 'A New', p. 401. Delitzsch (1.371) agrees by noting that 'this very access to free and joyous communion with God . . . is in itself the all-including commencement of that perfect σωτηρία'. Westcott (*Hebrews*, pp. 191 and 49) also recognizes the connection between σώζειν and τελειοῦν, saying 'σώζειν expresses the same idea as τελειοῦν', but his understanding of τελειοῦν as a moral category differs markedly from our understanding. But the congruence he cites is conspicuous. It is to be observed that σωτηρία also occurs alongside of τελειοῦν at Heb. 5.9; 9.12; 10.14.
3. Thüsing (pp. 5-6) remarks that with this verb we come to the heart of the 'Kulttheologie' in Heb., especially at 7.25; 10.1; 11.6; 12.18-24. Spicq (*L'Epître*, 2.197) refers the cultic sense to 4.16 also. See Cockerill, p. 136.
4. The same applies for ἐγγίζειν (e.g. 7.19), used synonymously with προσέρχεσθαι and other synonyms to translate *qārēb* and *niggaš*.
5. See J. Schneider, 'προσέρχομαι', *TDNT*, 2.683-84.
6. Dahl ('A New', p. 408) cites Heb. 7.25; 9.14; 12.28; 13.16 and 4.16 as suggesting worship through prayer. Also see the reference to Heb. 4.16 in Rissi, *Die*

The cultic sense of οἱ προσερχόμενοι is clearly seen in the contrast between the 'former' and 'better' covenants in 7.23-25 and in 10.1. The former priests, those who drew near with the blood of others (7.27; 9.7; 10.1, 4, 11), never possessed anything more than a figurative access to God, symbolized by their ritual practices of approaching the earthly altar and sanctuary. But οἱ προσερχόμενοι δι' αὐτοῦ τῷ θεῷ have full and real access to God, and so we may imagine not only a cultic, but also a priestly meaning for οἱ προσερχόμενοι in Heb.[1] Thus 'those who draw near to God through Jesus' contrasts with the former priests in 7.23, a parallelism that in itself argues for a priestly designation. That this privilege belongs to believers is represented by δι' αὐτοῦ and also by ἐγγίζομεν at 7.19. Believers may thus be called simply, 'die durch ihn zu Gott herantretenden'.[2] Cultic activity is prescribed by δι' αὐτοῦ at 13.15, 21 and 7.19 (δι' ἧς). In these texts Christ is characterized explicitly as the originator of the action.[3]

Nevertheless οἱ προσερχόμενοι remain subordinate to Jesus 'since' (ζῶν at 7.25c is a causal participle) it is he alone who functions in the high priestly role of mediator and intercessor ὑπὲρ αὐτῶν (7.25c). Thus a qualitative difference remains between the priesthood of believers and the priesthood of Jesus, and this will be examined below.[4]

---

*Theologie*, p. 97. Cockerill (p. 138) notes that the worshipers approach God through the 'great high priest', citing Riggenbach, *Der Brief*, p. 120.

1. See Moe (pp. 163-65) who rightly sees that Christians possess the high priestly privilege of access to God's very presence.
2. Rissi, *Die Theologie*, p. 97. The privilege of Christians to draw near is grounded in his death (10.19), his intercession (ἐντυγχάνειν) (7.25), and his 'Bürgschaft im Wort' (7.22), according to Michel, *Kommentar*, p. 277.
3. BAG, p. 179: διά with genitive of means, instrument, agency. Windisch (*Hebräerbrief*, p. 67) comments: 'Das bedeutet, dass alle Christen Zeit ihres Lebens sich immer an denselben Parakleten, Seelsorger und Mittler ihres Verkehrs mit Gott wenden können'.
4. Moe (pp. 163-65) sees this distinction as Jesus' right to mediatorship. Peterson (p. 113) bases the distinction on the surpassing nature of Jesus the 'surety' or 'guarantor', rather than 'mediator'. Bruce (*Hebrews*, p. 153) calls him the 'unique Mediator between God and man'. See further Michel, *Kommentar*, p. 275. Moffatt (*Commentary*, p. 100) too easily likens μεσίτης and ἔγγυος on the grounds of assonance with γέγονεν (7.22) or possibly ἐγγίζομεν (7.19).

## 3. Προσέρχεσθαι *and Hebrews* 125

*Heb. 10.22*

The hortatory προσερχώμεθα which introduced the section on the high priesthood of Christ at Heb. 4.16 reappears at the conclusion of this central section.[1] The parallels between 4.14-16 and 10.19-25 are striking.[2] Both are introduced by the causative participle ἔχοντες which not only establishes the foundation for the subsequent exhortation (as also at 12.1), but introduces some conclusions from the preceding argument as well.[3] Again, the inferential consecutive conjunction, οὖν, indicates that the author is making reference to his preceding cultic interpretation of the work of the high priest Jesus Christ in 4.14–10.18, an argument that Thüsing categorizes as 'durch und durch kultische Begrifflichkeit'.[4] The ἔχοντες οὖν of 10.19 therefore continues the sacerdotal interest of the material it follows.

Heb. 10.22 is introduced by a brief overview or summary of the priestly section in 10.19-21. These three verses 'summarize what was said earlier'[5] concerning the priesthood of the old covenant and the surpassing worth of Christ's new covenant high priesthood. Jesus has performed the ultimate sacrifice and realized what the Old Testament cult could only promise. Thus, 'what the blood offering of the High Priest who went into the Holy of Holies once a year did not achieve, Jesus accomplished when he offered once-for-all his own blood as a

---

1. Others who draw this parallelism are Spicq, *L'Epître*, 2.315; Buchanan, *To the Hebrews*, p. 170. For a brief but helpful look at the various structures proposed for Heb., refer to Grässer, 'Der Hebräerbrief', pp. 160-67; McCullough, 'Some Recent Developments', pp. 153-56; G.W. Buchanan, 'The Present State of Scholarship on Hebrews', in *Christianity, Judaism and other Greco-Roman Cults: Studies for Morton Smith at Sixty* (Studies in Judaism in Late Antiquity, 12.1; ed. J. Neusner; Leiden: Brill, 1975), pp. 311-16.
2. The parallelism is such that it establishes the fact that 'we have a high priest'. Nauck ('Zum Aufbau', pp. 203-204) finds several conspicuous correspondences with much more detail than Spicq (*L'Epître*, 2.315). Nauck (p. 204) is led to conclude: 'Diese beiden Abschnitte bilden den Rahmen, innerhalb dessen über das Hohepriestertum Christi gesprochen wird'.
3. This was already seen at 4.16, and appears to be so at 10.19-25; also at 12.1, where the 'cloud of witnesses' serves as a link between Heb. 11 and what follows in Heb. 12.
4. Thüsing, p. 1. According to Moffat (*Commentary*, p. 141), with ἔχοντες οὖν 'the writer presses the weighty arguments of 6.2–10.18, but he returns with them to reinforce the appeal of 3.1–4.16'.
5. Michel, *Kommentar*, p. 344; O. Glombitza, 'Erwägungen zum kunstvollen Ansatz der Paränese im Brief an die Hebräer—x,19-25', *NovT* 9 (1967), p. 149; Attridge, *Hebrews*, p. 288.

sacrifice, which was eternal redemption for man; his access to God'.[1] Appropriately, then, the first object of the participle ἔχοντες is παρρησίαν εἰς τὴν εἴσοδον τῶν ἁγίων. By[2] the 'blood of Jesus', i.e. his death (10.10),[3] the readers now have the 'freedom', 'prerogative', 'permission', to enter into the holy of holies.[4] It is the faithful knowledge of the high priestly ministry of Christ on earth and in heaven that gives the readers access to the heavenly holy of holies. However, as we have seen, this 'freedom to enter'[5] is accomplished 'through hope', and so is not as yet a totally fulfilled actuality in the lives of living Christians (7.19; 6.19-20).

Heb. 10.19 finds its parallel in 10.20[6] which reiterates what has already been dealt with in the preceding chapters, Heb. 8–9. However, it expands the 'entering' based on the death of Christ to include his entire earthly life which was high priestly (e.g. 2.17; 5.1-10).[7]

1. W. Nauck, 'Blut Christi', *RGG*, 1.1329-30. This is explicit at Heb. 9.6-15, 25-28; 10.1-4, 19, 22.
2. Here, the instrumental use of ἐν (see e.g. Michel, *Kommentar*, pp. 344-45).
3. The 'blood of Christ' is a synonym for his death. For instance, Nauck ('Blut Christi', 1.1329-30) points out that 'der Begriff Blut Christi spricht immer vom Tode Jesu in seiner Heilsbedeutung für die Gläubigen'.
4. The meaning of παρρησία was discussed above, in the section on 4.16 in the present chapter. There we saw that any παρρησία had its initial impetus in the Christ event, whereby Christians were 'permitted' or 'free' to draw near to God, which implicitly bespoke an attitude of confidence, based on the assurance grounded in their faith. Here at 10.19, the meaning 'freedom' or 'permission' is preferred, based on the theological material preceding 10.19 that serves as the grounding for this 'freedom of access to God'. Christians have παρρησία because their consciences are cleansed (e.g. 9.14), they have been sanctified (10.10, 14), and have forgiveness of sins (10.18). Spicq (*L'Epître*, 2.315) remarks that 'παρρησία rests on a threefold certainty: (1) the heavenly sanctuary is accessible, (2) the way is open and certain, and (3) the Christ precedes us as priest and offering and introduces us'.

We would suggest that insofar as παρρησία means 'confidence', this is nuanced by the phrase, μετὰ ἀληθινῆς καρδίας ἐν πληροφορίᾳ πίστεως (10.22) which has its parallel in 4.16 (also directly following προσερχώμεθα). 'Confidence' rightfully follows the grounding of the 'access' which is being recapitulated in 10.19-21.
5. Whether εἴσοδος occurs here infinitively or as an object does not affect us. For differing opinions see: Michel, *Kommentar*, p. 344, and Rissi, *Die Theologie*, p. 98 (infinitively); Westcott, *Hebrews*, p. 318 (objectively).
6. See the parallelism in the schema proposed by J. Jeremias, 'Hebräer 10.20: τοῦτ' ἔστιν τῆς σαρκὸς αὐτοῦ', *ZNW* 62 (1971), p. 131.
7. Jeremias's parallelism, of course, places σάρξ with the αἷμα; however, when used of Jesus, σάρξ encompasses his entire earthly life (e.g. 5.7, which has its chiastic counterpart in 5.1-3, dealing with the earthly, old covenant high priest).

The second object of ἔχοντες is ἱερεὺς μέγας (10.21). Moe attempts to find a great significance in the single occurrence of this term here in Heb., but his effort does not hold up under the scrutiny of its occurrences already in the LXX.[1] Heb. 10.21 parallels the ἀρχιερεὺς μέγας in 4.14, so that what is here depicted is the Jesus who now sits at God's right hand interceding for man, having been made 'perfect', in accord with what is explicated throughout 4.14–10.18. Heb. 10.19-21 has succinctly reiterated the central priestly section, thereby providing the legitimate foundation for the exhortation which follows. It is this high priesthood of Christ and the efficacy of his ministry (10.19-21) on which the Christian's own access to God wholly depends (hence the causative participle ἔχοντες).

In light of Christ's efficacious priesthood, therefore, the readers are exhorted to 'draw near' to the throne of grace (4.16), or to God (7.19, 25; 11.6; 12.22).[2] This approach is to be made repeatedly, as is implied by the present subjunctive (as at 4.16).[3] Since the earthly situation of the readers is in view, this would again allude not to an actual approach through the heavenly curtain by corporeal beings, but a 'drawing near' through worship,[4] prayer[5] or the eucharist.[6] By this use of cultic terminology the author 'does not mean that Christians are priests, with the right of entry in virtue of a sacrifice which they pre-

---

1. Moe (p. 163) states, 'Vielleicht erklärt sich daher auch die Wahl der eigentümlichen Bezeichnung Christi als ἱερεὺς μέγας statt ἀρχιερεύς: er ist nicht der einzige Priester des Neuen Bundes; er ist nur im Vergleich mit den andern der grosse'. However, see Michel (*Kommentar*, p. 346) who notes the references in the LXX for ὁ ἱερεὺς ὁ μέγας.
2. The only other absolute use of προσέρχεσθαι is at Heb. 10.1, which is a clear reference to cultic activity seen as approach to God under the former covenant. According to Jewett (*Letter to Pilgrims*, p. 80), the frequency of absolute occurrences in the LXX confirms a cultic, priestly, technical use of 'draw near'.
3. E.g. Braun, *Hebräer*, p. 309.
4. Montefiore, p. 174; Westcott, *Hebrews*, p. 322.
5. See B. Weiss, *A Commentary on the New Testament* (trans. G.H. Schodde and E. Wilson; 4 vols.; New York: Funk and Wagnalls, 1906), 4.198. Also see Dahl, 'A New', p. 409.
6. Thüsing (pp. 1-17) attempts to show the place of the eucharist celebration in the community of the readers. He does admit however, that 'das "Hinzutreten" meint keinesfalls nur die Teilnahme an der Eucharistiefeier' (p. 12). He sees a 'sowohl–als auch' approach in Heb: 'sowohl Eucharistiefeier als auch das ganze christliche Leben mitsamt Glaube, Gebet, Gottesdienst und Leiden' (p. 12). However, the consideration of the eucharist in Heb. is decisively refuted in a thorough study of all pertinent texts by Schröger, 'Der Gottesdienst', pp. 161-81; also see R. Williamson, 'The Eucharist and the Epistle to the Hebrews', *NTS* 21 (1975), pp. 300-12.

sent, but, as the approach to God was a priestly prerogative under the older order, he describes the Christian access to God in sacerdotal metaphors. προσερχώμεθα is one of these.'[1]

The characterization of προσέρχεσθαι to describe the readers at 'worship' is given further support by the admonitions that follow at 10.23, 25. The ὁμολογία to which the readers are exhorted to hold fast is depicted as a corporate acclamation which would be recited in worship.[2] At 10.25 the readers are admonished to continue to meet together (i.e. for worship), τὴν ἐπισυναγωγὴν ἑαυτῶν. Thus the cultic metaphors serving to characterize the unique approach that Christians have in worship and prayer are present: the realized access to God behind the curtain which the old covenant only foreshadowed but could not accomplish or enjoy.

Those who are exhorted to draw near are characterized in a fourfold manner in Heb. 10.22: (1) μετὰ ἀληθινῆς καρδίας, (2) ἐν πληροφορίᾳ πίστεως, (3) ῥεραντισμένοι, and (4) λελουσμένοι, expressing what the worshipers are and what they have received.[3] The first two phrases in 10.22a encapsulate the meaning of παρρησία, which has its parallel in 4.16. Rissi observes the synonymity of the parallel phrases at 10.22a. 'Das aufrichtige Herz', writes Rissi, 'steht im Gegensatz zum "bösen Herzen" (3.12), das bestimmt ist durch Unglauben. Darum tritt zum aufrichtigen Herzen als Parallele "die Fülle des Glaubens". Das aufrichtige Herz ist das glaubende. Glaube oder Unglaube prägt das Wesen des Herzens, d.h. das innere Wesen des Menschen, das sich in der ganzen Lebensverwirklichung äussert.'[4]

---

1. Moffatt, *Commentary*, p. 144. Windisch (*Hebräerbrief*, p. 95) says essentially the same thing by noting the once-for-all character of the heavenly high priest's offering (e.g. 10.19-25) so that 'das Handeln der Gemeinde ist daher auch nur in abgeleitetem Sinne "Kultus" zu nennen'. For Attridge (*Hebrews*, p. 288), the 'access certainly implies participation in a worshiping community'.

2. This is seen by the ἡμῶν in 3.1, and the first person plural verbs κρατῶμεν and κατέχωμεν at 4.14 and 10.23, respectively. Whether or not the author refers to a 'Taufbekenntnis', as postulated by G. Bornkamm ('Das Bekenntnis im Hebräerbrief', in *Studien zu Antike und Urchristentum: Gesammelte Aufsätze*, 2 [München: Chr. Kaiser, 1959], pp. 188-203) and accepted by countless scholars is not germane here. See below, where the allusion to baptism in 10.22 is addressed. Conspicuous, however, is the corporate and liturgical character that he observes as encapsulated in the term ὁμολογία.

3. Westcott, *Hebrews*, p. 322. Jewett (*Letter to Pilgrims*, p. 176) identifies the four parts and their correspondence in pairings, so that 10.22a contains two 'non-cultic' phrases, and 10.22b contains two 'cultic' expressions.

4. Rissi, *Die Theologie*, p. 99.

## 3. Προσέρχεσθαι and Hebrews

Hence we see the complementary meaning of the two phrases, but also the fact that they embody the παρρησία. Both the 'sincere heart' and the 'fullness of faith' depict what it means to have 'freedom to stand before God', as well as the concomitant 'confidence' or 'boldness', since this freedom is grounded in the knowledge of what Jesus the high priest has accomplished, with result that one's own approach to God will be legitimate and actual. Thus the readers are exhorted to draw near with a 'confidence' (grounded in the 'freedom' or 'permission' already mentioned at 10.19) which expresses the subjective (or inner) dimension of their disposition.

The admonition to 'draw near' is further characterized in 10.22 by Old Testament cultic ritual practice that also finds frequent consideration in the central portion of Heb. ῥεραντισμένοι and λελουσμένοι call to mind the Old Testament practices of sprinkling blood and the water-bath as means of priestly consecration and ordination, priestly and lay cleansing, and covenant-making access, e.g. Exod. 24.6-8; 29.4, 21; 30.30; 40.30-32; Lev. 8.6, 11, 23, 24, 30; 16.4; Num. 8.6-7; 19.3, 19; Heb. 9.13, 19-21.[1] But also relevant for Heb., where the high priestly sacrifice of Jesus corresponds with the earthly high priest's role at the Day of Atonement festival, are the references to the priests' sprinkling of the blood of the sin offerings on the veil and altar of incense in order to make atonement for the sanctuary, priesthood, and the people (Lev. 4.6, 17; 5.9; 16.14, 15, 34).[2] This practice appears to be the one recalled at Heb. 9.9; 10.1-4, 11. Atonement was never really achieved under the old covenant ritual, as evidenced by the repetitious character of these rites and their inability to cleanse the conscience (10.2). Similarly, the washing by the high priest on the Day of Atonement (Lev. 16.4; *m. Yoma* 3.3) proved far from perfect, since it was evidence of his being constantly reminded of his uncleanness and of the inability to extirpate sin absolutely.

We would suggest therefore, that the oft held position according to which the imagery of sprinkling the people (externally) at Heb. 9.18-22 is deemed programmatic for 10.22—that this is but one understanding wherein the old covenant access is paralleled by the superior new covenant access.[3] But the sprinkling of the ashes of the red heifer,

---

1. See Claus-Hunno Hunzinger, 'ῥαντίζω, ῥαντισμός', *TDNT*, 6.977-83; Strathmann, 'Der Brief', p. 133.
2. Westcott (*Hebrews*, p. 251) agrees.
3. E.g. see Delitzsch, pp. 175-76; Riggenbach, *Der Brief*, pp. 317-18; Michel, *Kommentar*, pp. 346-47; Strathmann, 'Der Brief', pp. 133-34; Hunzinger,

or any reference to bodily sprinkling, is not the most appropriate parallel when speaking of the 'sprinkling of the heart', or when presenting an argument for the sacrifice of Jesus.[1] It is better to see here the cultic practice of the sprinkling of the altar so pertinent to the Day of Atonement ritual, for this finds a direct correlation to the sacrifice of Jesus, characterized also as the taking of blood (cf. 'blood of sprinkling', 12.24) into the heavenly holy of holies (6.20; 9.12, 24, 25), which alone was able to atone for sin, purify the heart, and redeem one's evil conscience (9.14; 10.2; 12.24).

The author of Heb. has taken priestly-cultic language and applied it to the Christian situation. He has taken two parallel phrases and placed them beside each other. The sacrifice of Christ is that which figuratively sprinkles and washes the entire person (σῶμα) clean.[2] Thus, 'Christi Tod ist die Erfüllung und der Abschluss der Opferung von Rindern und Böcken, der Opferung der roten Kuh, der Sprengung des Blutes von Rindern und Böcken und der Sprengung des Reinigungswassers'.[3] So, where the two phrases in 10.22a spoke of one characteristic, so again at 10.22b, one reality is expressed with two phrases.[4] Thus the sprinkling of the heart or the washing of the

---

'ῥαντίζω, ῥαντισμός', *TDNT*, 6.982-83; Héring, pp. 91-92; Peterson, p. 155; Braun, *Hebräer*, pp. 309-10.

1. It is precisely this external sprinkling in Heb. 9.13, 18-22, that has led practically all scholars to find in Heb. 10.22 a clear reference to baptism. Influential as well, of course, has been Bornkamm's 'Das Bekenntnis im Hebräerbrief', which links the 'confession' to a baptismal liturgy. Among the few scholars who reject this approach are: J. Calvin, *Commentaries on the Epistle of Paul the Apostle to the Hebrews* (ed. and trans. by J. Owen; Edinburgh: Calvin Translation Society, 1853; repr. edn, Grand Rapids: Eerdmans, 1948), p. 237; M. Barth, *Die Taufe: ein Sakrament? Ein exegetischer Beitrag zum Gespräch über die kirchliche Taufe* (Zollikon-Zürich: Evangelischer Verlag, 1951), pp. 473-80; Rissi, *Die Theologie*, pp. 99-100; R.H. Smith, pp. 129-30.
2. Regarding σῶμα, see M. Barth, p. 479; Rissi, *Die Theologie*, p. 99; Delitzsch, 2.177.
3. M. Barth, p. 477.
4. Rissi, *Die Theologie*, p. 99; R.H. Smith, p. 129. The sprinkling and washing are one, for Smith can say that the 'whole person, the entire being, in deepest inwardness and in all externalities, has already been washed and purified and rendered fit for access to God by the work of Christ'. This, in our judgment, is classic Heb. doctrine. And this is the reason to reject any notion of baptism here. The cleansing has been through Christ's high priestly ministry; there is no need for any ritual baptism, as a requisite for approaching God. E.g. see R.H. Smith, p. 129: 'Neither whole oceans nor entire rivers of water, nor any ceremony or hallowed ritual can remove the deep stain of sin', or see M. Barth, p. 479: 'Der Hebräerbrief streitet

body with 'pure water' express the identical thought: the efficacious power of the death of Jesus that was worked by the 'eternal Spirit' (9.14).[1]

Heb. has used cultic terminology in order to present the contrast between the former priests, whose sprinkling and washing was ineffective, and the Christian readers. The latter are characterized by priestly language as those persons who may approach God since, in Jesus' high priestly ministry, the true sprinkling and washing was accomplished once-for-all. Hence what the old covenant priests could never attain is now a reality for Christians: the freedom and confidence actually to draw near to God in worship and prayer.

*Heb. 11.6*

The single occurrence of προσέρχεσθαι in Heb. 11 is found at 11.6. What has hitherto been seen to be an exclusively cultic term in Heb. appears in a context of a compendium of the Old Testament heroes of faith. Thus we must examine the meaning of προσέρχεσθαι in this context.

It is generally accepted that both traditional and redactional materials are joined in Heb. 11 to form one extensive '*tractatus de fide*'.[2] Accordingly Heb. gives evidence of applying a traditional Jewish method of enumerating Old Testament witnesses, as seen in

---

gegen jeden neuen Ritualismus, indem er für die Anerkennung des vollkommenen Opfers Christi und die Vollkommenheit seiner Wirkung kämpft'.

1. So Rissi (*Die Theologie*, pp. 99-100) may point with justification to the one use of 'das reine Wasser' at Ezek. 36.25 as an 'eschatological outpouring of the Spirit'. Also see Calvin, *Commentaries*, p. 237. It is all the more surprising that M. Barth (pp. 479-80) makes no reference to Ezek. 36.

2. See H. Thyen, *Der Stil der jüdisch-hellenistischen Homilie* (FRLANT, 47; Göttingen: Vandenhoeck & Ruprecht, 1955), p. 18; Theissen, *Untersuchungen*, pp. 98-99; F. Laub, *Bekenntnis und Auslegung: Die paränetische Funktion der Christologie im Hebräerbrief* (Biblische Untersuchungen, 15; Regensburg: Friedrich Pustet, 1980), p. 258 n. 233; Rissi, *Die Theologie*, pp. 105-13. Thyen (p. 18) cites F. Blass, *Die rhythmische Komposition des Hebräerbriefes*, as the early representative of this position which distinguished on rhythmic and stylistic grounds between 11.13-16 and 11.32-38 and the rest of Heb. 11. Laub (p. 258) concurs with Theissen's more detailed division of tradition and redaction. Rissi (who finds the *Vorlage* at 11.2, 4, 5, 7-9, 11-12, 17-25, 27-31) has a minor disagreement with Theissen's model regarding particular verses, e.g. 11.1 and 11.3. However, it is evident to all that 11.6 is material that has been added by the author.

Pss. 78; 105; 106; 135; 136; Ezek. 20; Sir. 44–50; Wis. 10; 1 Macc. 2.52-60; *3 Macc.* 6.4-8; *4 Macc.* 18.11-19; Neh. 9.3-31; Acts 7.[1]

The immediate context for Heb. 11.6 is derived from the preceding verse where Enoch (Gen. 5.22-24) is mentioned, in accordance with LXX translation, as 'having pleased God' (εὐηρέστησεν τῷ θεῷ), which is then carried over into 11.6a, χωρὶς δὲ πίστεως ἀδύνατον εὐαρεστῆσαι. Occasionally in extra-biblical writings Enoch appears to have been 'perfected' in a moral sense, but the word used is one familiar in Heb., τελειοῦν.[2] Enoch furthermore is depicted as an offerer of incense (a priestly function) which is acceptable to the Lord in *Jub.* 4.23-26. By taking from the traditional *Vorlage* the fact that Enoch was 'pleasing' to God, here in Heb. 11.6 the author gives his own interpretation of what 'pleasing God' means by using προσέρχεσθαι at 11.6b.[3] Hence, the author has added to the *Vorlage* a further interpretation of faith (of which nothing is said in Gen. 5.22-24), which he began in 11.1, recalling εὐαρεστῆσαι in the Enoch story from the LXX.[4]

By again taking up the definition of faith begun in 11.1, Heb. is able to make a statement about the faith of one who draws near to God which logically follows from what the *Vorlage* had expressed about Enoch. Consequently, both ἔλεγχος οὐ βλεπομένων and ἐλπιζομένων ὑπόστασις are referred to at 11.6. The presupposition for 'drawing near' is a faith which, as the ἔλεγχος οὐ βλεπομένων, is convinced of the real and personal existence of the invisible God. Parallel to this is the prerequisite faith of those who seek God who will bestow his good pleasure and the guarantee of his fellowship and

---

1. Thyen (p. 18) notes, 'Besonders das elfte Kapitel des Heb. zeigt uns die Gewandheit unseres Homileten und seine Vertrautheit mit dieser in der hellenistischen Synagoge beliebten Methode, durch Aufzählung atl. Zeugen Beweise zu führen'. At p. 76, Thyen lists further references. There he notes the frequent appearance of both Abraham and Daniel as 'beliebte Beispiele'.
2. Sir. 44.16; 49.14; Wis. 4.10; *Jub.* 10.17; Josephus, *Ant.* 1.85.
3. Heb. 11.6 is not part of the *Vorlage* as seen by the appearance of favorite words of the author's that occur only here in Heb. 11; e.g. προσέρχεσθαι and μισθαποδότης (a hapax legomenon, although its root occurs three other times in the New Testament, all in Heb.). The verb πιστεύειν occurs only here and at 4.3, in all of Heb. The author's vocabulary here is briefly mentioned in Rissi (*Die Theologie*, p. 106).
4. Riggenbach (*Der Brief*, p. 350) asserts that the author adds a sentence (11.6a) that shows that the taking up of Enoch was the result of necessary faith. Also see Delitzsch, 2.230.

3. Προσέρχεσθαι *and Hebrews* 133

eternal life as the 'reward'. Thus faith is 'the reality of things hoped for'. O. Michel concurs, saying that 'die Existenz Gottes gehört zur Unsichtbarkeit der himmlischen Dinge, während seine Vergeltung ein Teil der christlichen Hoffnung ist'.[1] The author of Heb. has therefore continued with his prior statement at 11.1 by illustrating it with exemplars of faith and, when necessary, further interpreting them (as he does in 11.6). That Heb. presumes a cultic meaning within 11.6 must now be investigated.

*Cultic meaning of* προσέρχεσθαι

A cultic understanding at 11.6 would not be without precedent in Heb. 11. Already with the mention of the first hero, Abel, at 11.4 cultic language is utilized. προσφέρειν occurs exclusively with a cultic sense throughout Heb.[2] Abel and Cain (long before the establishment of any priestly hierarchy) are characterized in Heb. as performing cultic, ritual sacrifices to God.

Enoch (11.5-6) is not described in explicitly cultic terms. In the LXX he is described as εὐηρέστησεν Ἐνὼχ τῷ θεῷ (Gen. 5.24), and Heb. uses this phraseology to speak universally (ἀδύνατον) and generally about faith in 11.6. The fact that Enoch 'pleased God' was for Heb. an indication of faith, for χωρὶς δὲ πίστεως ἀδύνατον εὐαρεστῆσαι. Thus, in the LXX, εὐαρεστῆσαι does not have a cultic meaning but serves to translate *hithalēk 'et-hā'ĕlōhîm* and to express an 'attitude' (e.g. Gen. 39.4 where εὐαρεστῆσαι translates *šrt*).[3] Hence, the Hebrew phrase 'to walk before', or 'with' God is expressive of the closest intimacy and fellowship between a human being and God (e.g. Gen. 5.22, 24; 6.9) and is rendered in the LXX as either 'to be well-pleasing to God', or 'to strive to please God'.[4] Elsewhere the Hebrew 'to walk before God' is translated by 'to be

---

1. Michel, *Kommentar*, p. 386. See also, Delitzsch, 2.230, and Rissi, *Die Theologie*, p. 105. Riggenbach (*Der Brief*, pp. 350-51) observes also that the similar reference to Heb. 11.1 in the mention of Noah at 11.7, is 'unmistakable'.
2. See Heb. 5.1, 3, 7; 7.27; 8.3, 4; 9.7, 9, 14, 25, 28; 10.1, 2, 8, 11, 12; 11.4, 27; 12.7.
3. Riggenbach, *Der Brief*, p. 350; Werner Förster, 'ἀρέσκω', *TDNT*, 1.455.
4. See Delitzsch, 2.229. Riggenbach (*Der Brief*, p. 350) finds the first expressed in Exod. 21.8, and the second at *1 Clem*. 62.2 and Gal. 1.10 (ἀρέσκειν). Also see Braun, *Hebräer*, p. 347.

well-pleasing', though the context is clearly different than at Gen. 5.22, 24 and 6.9.[1]

According to Michel, 'εὐαρεστεῖν, προσέρχεσθαι τῷ θεῷ, ἐκζητεῖν αὐτόν sind offenbar für den hellenistischen Leser miteinander verwandt'.[2] Riggenbach observes the synonymity between εὐαρεστεῖν and προσέρχεσθαι τῷ θεῷ in Heb., remarking 'ein gottgefälliges Verhalten betätigt sich vor allem in einem heilsverlangenden und gottesdienstlichen Hinzutreten zu Gott'.[3] In actuality, this appears to be less a synonymity than a necessary characteristic of one who draws near. As is seen at Heb. 10.22, the drawing near to God requires the proper inner condition of 'true hearts' and its parallel, 'full assurance of faith'. Unbelief, on the other hand, is described at Heb. 3.12 as an 'evil heart'. Hence to please God, a person must have faith, which is having a true heart, by which we draw near to God. The synonymity thus rests on both εὐαρεστεῖν and προσέρχεσθαι revealing authentic faith.[4] On the other hand, W. Förster seems to be in agreement with Riggenbach, for he writes, 'μεμαρτύρηται (Enoch) εὐαρεστηκέναι τῷ θεῷ means "to walk well-pleasing", as shown by the continuation' in 11.6, referring to the verbs προσέρχεσθαι and ἐκζητεῖν.[5]

But is there any 'cultic' allusion being made here? The aforementioned cultic references to Enoch in the extra-biblical materials seem remote possibilities when confronted by the text of Heb. itself. The only other New Testament occurrence of the verbal εὐαρεστεῖν appears in Heb. 13.16 in the context of spiritual sacrifices with which God is well pleased. This is reiterated in the benediction at 13.21 by the adjectival εὐάρεστος. The 'work to be done in us through Jesus Christ' is precisely the hortatory admonitions uttered throughout the text, but particularly those at the close, e.g. 13.16, and other exhorta-

---

1. Riggenbach, *Der Brief*, p. 350. For relevant texts see: Gen. 17.1; 24.40; 48.15; Pss. 26.3; 35.14; 56.13; 116.9; Sir. 44.16.
2. Michel, *Kommentar*, p. 386.
3. Riggenbach, *Der Brief*, p. 350. He cites Chrysostom as initially presenting this interpretation.
4. Rissi (*Die Theologie*, p. 99) describes 10.22 in connection with 11.6.
5. Förster, 'εὐάρεστος, εὐαρεστέω', *TDNT*, 1.457. Here he seems to consider the act of 'walking' to be congruous, or synonymous, with the terms 'drawing near' and 'seeking'. Thus, he agrees with both Michel and Riggenbach, by acknowledging the connection that exists between the three verbs.

## 3. Προσέρχεσθαι and Hebrews

tions from a cultic context.¹ The one final use of εὐάρεστος (adverb) at 12.28 serves to describe the sort of worship (λατρεύειν) the readers are to offer—again, a purely cultic context.² Thus, outside of 11.5-6 Heb. uses εὐαρεστεῖν only in a cultic context. It would not be unusual to consider, therefore, a cultic context at Heb. 11.6, if the author is consistent. This would suppose that 'to walk well-pleasing' (11.5) is a linking word whereby the author of Heb. launches once again into what he began at 11.1, so that 'walk well-pleasing' could indeed have an entirely different meaning than that originally intended in Gen. 5.24 (LXX). As we have shown above in discussing Heb. 10.22, the parallel between εὐαρεστεῖν and προσέρχεσθαι suggests itself.

The singular attributive participle ὁ προσερχόμενος does not refer back to Enoch but is making a general reference, supported by the plural ἐκζητοῦσιν.³ Hence, as with the other occurrences of προσέρχεσθαι in Heb., at 11.6 it has a plural meaning. Thus, the believers' 'nearing to God' constantly presupposes faith in God's existence and his reward, one of the elementary doctrines of Christ considered at Heb. 6.1. In fact, to 'draw near' would be unthinkable without faith. The verb δεῖ therefore asserts a logical necessity rather than a legal obligation.⁴ This is expressed prior to 11.6 in hortatory address at 10.22 within the obvious cultic context (10.19-25) of entering into the heavenly presence of God through worship (e.g. 4.16), based as it is on the earthly and heavenly high priestly activity of Christ. The synonymity with εὐαρεστεῖν also points to a cultic context. We may conclude, therefore, that the occurrence of προσέρχεσθαι at 11.6 is consistent with usage elsewhere in Heb. and that it is cultic in meaning.⁵

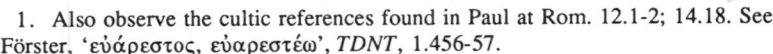

---

1. Also observe the cultic references found in Paul at Rom. 12.1-2; 14.18. See Förster, 'εὐάρεστος, εὐαρεστέω', *TDNT*, 1.456-57.
2. As has been shown previously, λατρεύειν and λειτουργεῖν are favorite cultic terms of the author.
3. Braun, *Hebräer*, p. 348; Hagner, *Hebrews*, pp. 166-67.
4. Braun, *Hebräer*, p. 348; Delitzsch, 2.230; Riggenbach, *Der Brief*, p. 350.
5. So Delitzsch, 2.230; Windisch, *Hebräerbrief*, p. 100; Käsemann, *The Wandering People*, p. 54; Braun, *Hebräer*, p. 127. Among scholars rejecting a cultic interpretation are Best (p. 282), Peterson (p. 79), and Hagner (*Hebrews*, p. 168). Peterson cautions that the other cultic occurrences of the word should not prejudice the issue at 11.6. At pp. 230-31 n. 34, Peterson argues his case for the non-cultic use: 'When προσέρχεσθαι is used to express the idea of foreigners coming to join the congregation of Israel as proselytes (e.g. Exod. 12.48f.; Lev. 19.33; Num. 9.14), the notion of entering into a relationship with the God of Israel is

Faith, then, reckons the existence of God but it also seeks God as the Rewarder.[1] This conviction that God exists is often found connected with the notion of reward, and here the stress is upon the 'rewarding by God'.[2] This 'reward' from God in Heb. is the state of being in the divine presence. μισθαποδότης and μισθαποδοσία are words peculiar to Heb., and they carry significant import. At 10.35, the 'confidence' to which the readers are exhorted has a great reward. This παρρησία points to the access believers have to God's very presence (4.16; 6.19-20; 10.22). At 11.26, the reward to which Moses looked was already delineated at 11.13-16—again, communion with and access to God. Thus it appears that H. Braun is indeed correct to state that God himself is the reward. In our text Enoch knew this reward by his being taken up by God (i.e. brought into his very presence). This 'rewarding' is something God still does, as evidenced by the present tense use of γίνεσθαι[3] and the parallel ὑπόστασις ἐλπιζομένων at 11.1.[4]

Therefore, in the context of Heb., where cultic terminology is applied to establish the access to God (e.g. προσέρχεσθαι, εἰσέρχεσθαι, τελειοῦν), ἐκζητεῖν occurring with εὐαρεστεῖν and προσέρχεσθαι also suggests a cultic meaning. Such is already the case in the Old Testament, where it is cultically oriented and established.

---

thereby implied. In Sir. 1.28, 30; 2.1, the more general sense of a relationship with God by serving him is prominent (cf. the idea of drawing near to Wisdom with all your soul in Sir. 4.15; 6.26). Philo shows a development of this concept in his assertion that "only for souls who regard it as their goal fully to be conformed to God who begat them is it lawful to draw nigh to him" (*De op. m.* 144, compare *Quod Deus* 8. 161). The "levite mind" is perfectly cleansed and purified, "renounces all the things pertaining to creation" and is acquainted with God "to whom it has drawn nigh, by whom also it has been taken to himself" (*De plant.* 64, 97; *De conf. ling.* 55, *De fug.* 41, *De mut. nom.* 13). In Hebrews 11.6, the one who would "draw near" to God is the one who seeks him in faith.' It appears to us, however, that Peterson places too little emphasis on the material as used by Heb., as well as the context in which 11.6 is found, both of which suggest a cultic, sacerdotal interest.

1. See H. Greeven, 'ἐκζητέω', *TDNT*, 2.894-95.
2. Grässer (*Der Glaube*, p. 132) mentions that there are 'viele Belege' and directs the reader to Windisch and Michel. Also see Grässer, *Der Glaube*, p. 167. For a thorough list of texts concerning the 'Existenzaussage' of God, see Braun, *Hebräer*, p. 348. For the combination of existence and reward of God under the single word ἐστίν, see Braun, *Hebräer*, p. 349; Grässer, *Der Glaube*, p. 133.
3. Braun, *Hebräer*, p. 349.
4. Moffatt, *Commentary*, p. 167.

3. Προσέρχεσθαι *and Hebrews* 137

Furthermore, the priestly community at Qumran used 'to seek' in a cultic manner in its writings.[1]
We have observed, therefore, that 11.6 characterizes the faith of the faithful by cultic terminology. O. Michel is correct to assert, 'der Glaube ist von Gott verordnete Voraussetzung für den, der am Gottesdienst der Gemeinde teilnimmt'.[2] In worship believers repeatedly (cf. the present-tense usage of 'draw near' and 'seek') have access into the heavenly holy of holies and fellowship with God.

*Heb. 12.18-24*
The cultic character of Heb. transcends its utilization of the high priestly type and antitype. In fact the centrality of the cultic terminology, particularly at the Epistle's most emphatic passages, evinces an author preoccupied with cultic categories. Thus, Käsemann suggests that 'the idea of the people of God is also culticly [*sic*] defined' since the Old Testament λαός itself is an inherently cultic community.[3] This is in particular evidence at Heb. 12.18-24.

It is generally agreed that the author of Heb. has made use of a preformulated tradition already known to the readers, which interrupts the hortatory content of 12.12-17 and 12.25-29. Käsemann finds in the writings of Philo (*De dec.* 44) a parallel which indicates a fixed tradition known in circles that extend far beyond Heb. and its readership.[4] The striking parallelism between 12.18-21 and 12.22-24,

---

1. Michel, *Kommentar*, p. 386. In the Old Testament: Pss. 33.5; 68.33; Deut. 4.29; in the New Testament: Acts 15.17. At Qumran: CD 1.10; 1QS 1.1-2. The purity of 'heart' has been seen in Heb. to refer to cultic approach to God (10.22; 3.12). Thüsing (p. 6 n. 28) concurs on the cultic use of ἐκζητεῖν, noting the parallel with προσέρχεσθαι in activity, such as is described at Heb. 4.16.
2. Michel, *Kommentar*, p. 386; Grässer, *Der Glaube*, p. 133.
3. Käsemann, *The Wandering People*, p. 48 (and see n. 82). At p. 49, Käsemann emphasizes the cultic nature of the λόγος τῆς ἀκοῆς which is the basis and foundation for cultic activity, e.g. 4.1; 12.19, 24. Johnsson ('Defilement and Purgation', p. 11), Michel (*Kommentar*, p. 461 n. 1) and Schierse (*Verheissung*, p. 200) also recognize the prominent cultic influence in Heb. On the other hand, Peterson (pp. 160-62) is careful to reject the too easy acceptance of the cultic influence in (for example) Käsemann and Michel. Peterson, however, appears to miss the predominant cultic character of Heb. which would certainly be borne out in the language and terminology employed by the author. His disagreement with those who argue for a far-reaching cultic characterization in Heb. ignores the Epistle's content, it seems.
4. Käsemann, *The Wandering People*, p. 49. Here he also quotes Michel as saying that 'lofty and solemn speech, a deliberate mode of expression and definite

consisting of two scenes comprised of a setting, participants, and mediator, the formulaic pattern of seven earthly realities (12.18-21) and eight (or seven) heavenly realities (12.22-24), the peculiar syntax of the passage in its entirety, and the extensive use of καί, argue for a *Vorlage* introduced here by the author into the text.[1]

Heb. 12.18 opens with the conjunction γάρ in its characteristic second position. What has been stated up to this point in a hortatory address, calling for the readers to 'lift hands, and to 'make straight paths' and to 'strive for peace', now finds its grounding justification in 12.18-24.[2] The striking contrast (οὐ, 12.18; ἀλλά, 12.22) serves to encourage but also to warn (e.g. 12.25-29) the readers. In language obviously taken from the Sinai covenant story in the Pentateuch (e.g. Exod. 19.9b-25; 20.18-21; Deut. 4.11-12; 5.22-27; 9.19) the author informs the readers of that place to which they have 'drawn near'. In contrast to the Old Testament people who 'drew near' (προσῆλθον) to Sinai, the readers 'have drawn near' (προσεληλύθατε) to the heavenly Zion. ἀλλά denotes the absolute contrast between the two situations under the old and new covenants.

## Heb. 12.18-21

Verses 18-21 reflect the Old Testament portrayal of the covenant-making at Sinai. There the people are said to have 'drawn near' (Deut.

---

rhythm' is found also in vv. 22-24. Rissi (*Die Theologie*, pp. 101-102) also sees the use of a traditional *Vorlage* at 12.22-24.

1. Juliana M. Casey ('Christian Assembly in Hebrews: A Fantasy Island?', *TD* 30 [1982], p. 325) gives a parallel outline of the correspondence between 12.18-21 and 22-24. For a look at the sevenfold appearance of God in vv. 18-21, and the eight (or seven) appearances at Zion in vv. 22-24, see Michel, *Kommentar*, p. 461 (who credits Bengel with this observation), and Delitzsch, 2.343-44. Käsemann (*The Wandering People*, p. 49) correctly observes the parallel portrayals in the two texts, but places too much emphasis on the epiphanic character of the pericopes, which is clearly not the intent here in Heb., where the old and new covenants are being contrasted. Commenting on the peculiar language of 12.18-24, Riggenbach (*Der Brief*, p. 411) notes, 'Die durchgängige Weglassung des Artikels bei den Substantiven v. 18f. und v. 22-24 gibt zu erkennen, dass alle Begriffe in ihrer Eigenart und besonderen Bedeutung zu werten sind'. Rissi (*Die Theologie*, p. 100) also comments on the peculiar vocabulary. The peculiarity of the location of καὶ πνεύμασι δικαίων τετελειωμένων leads Rissi (*Die Theologie*, pp. 101-102) correctly to conclude the insertion of this material into the *Vorlage*. This best explains the countless problems caused by the placement of καὶ πνεύμασι δικαίων τετελειωμένων between 'God' and 'Jesus', and which has confounded scholars (cf. most commentaries).

2. Westcott, *Hebrews*, p. 410; Delitzsch, 2.337-38; R.H. Smith, p. 163.

## 3. Προσέρχεσθαι and Hebrews

4.11, προσέρχεσθαι) to the fire, cloud, darkness, and voice (Deut. 4.11-12; 5.22) in what appears to have been a ceremonial or cultic assembly (e.g. Exod. 20.18, 'all the people'; and Deut. 5.22, συναγωγή).[1] The fear of the people led to their urging of Moses alone to draw near to God in their stead as mediator, for they said to Moses: 'Go near (πρόσελθε), and hear all that the Lord our God will say, and speak to us all that the Lord our God will speak to you; and we will hear and do it' (Deut. 5.27, RSV). Hence the access to God by the assembly of the people of God, which permitted them to perceive divine manifestations of glory (e.g. God's voice, the fire, the cloud and thick darkness) but 'no form' (Deut. 4.12), was transferred to Moses. He then mediated the events for the people: 'So Moses went down to the people and told them' (Exod. 19.25, RSV). The cultic context of this access is seen in Exod. 19.22 when, in the midst of the covenant-making, the priests are characterized as οἱ ἐγγίζοντες (niggaš) Κυρίῳ τῷ θεῷ. Furthermore, Moses' own access was not direct, but rather God manifested himself to Moses only through oral communication and an opaque darkness (Exod. 20.21). Thus a cultic activity on the part of the people of God and Moses at this covenant ceremony is evident at Exod. 19.10-12, 14-15 where consecration and purification rites (both priestly acts) are to be practiced by 'the people' as well.

Heb.'s desire to claim this cultic meaning for προσεληλύθατε at Heb. 12.18 may also be seen by its preference for the προσέρχεσθαι found at Deut. 4.11 rather than the ἐγγίζειν at Exod. 19.21, 22. Hence Heb. is careful to conform to its application of προσέρχεσθαι as a

---

1. For LXX references to the manifestations of God's holiness and the veiling of himself mentioned in 12.18-21, see Riggenbach, *Der Brief*, pp. 411-13; Michel, *Kommentar*, p. 461; Delitzsch, 2.343-44; Westcott, *Hebrews*, pp. 410-11. Braun (*Hebräer*, pp. 430-34) provides a thorough set of extra-biblical references to these manifestations in contemporary literature also. Of course, not all scholars find προσέρχεσθαι as cultic, but C.K. Barrett ('The Eschatology of the Epistle to the Hebrews', in *The Background of the New Testament and its Eschatology: Essays in Honor of Charles Harold Dodd* [ed. W.D. Davies and D. Daube; Cambridge: Cambridge University Press, 1954], p. 376) rejecting the cultic meaning, construes its use for a 'faith-approach', which in light of the content of Heb. comes very close to the cultic meaning. W.J. Dumbrell ('The Spirits of Just Men Made Perfect', *EvQ* 48 [1976], p. 155) rejects a cultic meaning, for 'what is involved is a profession of faith'.

cultic term (as has already been seen at Heb. 4.16, 7.25; 10.1, 22; 11.6).[1]

Standing as it does under the shadow of the οὐ, 12.18-21 informs the readers (second person plural verb) that they are not in the same predicament as the old covenant people of God. As has been seen elsewhere in Heb. (e.g. 7.11, 18-19; 9.8-10; 10.1), the efficacious and actual access to God was not attainable (Exod. 19.12) under the old covenant. Not only was the encounter with God mediated by a priestly Moses, but Moses himself did not have direct access to God. He too encountered a veiled and hidden God.[2] This inability to 'draw near' is further heightened by the tangible (ψηλαφωμένῳ) character of the entire old covenant scenario. The mountain to which the people were forbidden access (Exod. 19.12) was precisely that: tangible, earthly, material, devoid of the heavenly and intangible.[3] So Michel can insist that 'the intention of the law was to maintain the holiness of God and demonstrate the distance between God and man to the people'.[4] It is this merely earthly, temporal, and mediated approach that stands in contrast to what follows in 12.22-24.

*Heb. 12.22-24*

The οὐ ... ἀλλά construction depicts this latter clause as contrary to the former.[5] Thus, already the parallelism between 12.18-21 and 12.22-24 would lead us to suspect that the προσεληλύθατε is being

1. We shall also see in Chapter 5 that Heb. is consistent in its use of another cultic term, τελειοῦν.
2. It is indeed unfortunate that Casey (p. 327) transforms Heb.'s argument contrasting the old and new covenant into one that calls the actual presence of God at Sinai into question. Heb. would not deny the presence of God at Sinai: that is nowhere a central concern in the Epistle. But the author is interested in reiterating what he has said several times in Heb. already: that the people under the old covenant were unable to attain real, efficacious access to God. It is not a question of God's presence, or absence, at Sinai.
3. Friedrich Schröger (*Der Verfasser des Hebräerbriefes als Schriftausleger* [Biblische Untersuchungen, 4; Regensburg: Friedrich Pustet, 1968], p. 209) writes, 'Die Anordnung (Exod. 19.12), vom Berge fernzubleiben, ist im alttestamentlichen Bericht nebensächlich; für den Hebräerbrief ist aber diese Stelle wichtig; sie ist für ihn ein Characteristikum der alttestamentlichen Situation überhaupt'. In a remark about the inaccessibility and terror encountered by the people of God, Johnsson ('Defilement and Purgation', p. 92) notes that 'a more vivid portrayal of lack of access and lack of boldness is difficult to imagine'.
4. Michel, *Kommentar*, p. 462.
5. BDF, *Grammar*, p. 232. See paragraph 448(1).

applied in a similar, although contrasting manner (e.g. cultically) in 12.22-24. The content of 12.22-24 confirms our suspicion.

In contrast to the earthly approach, Christians (i.e. the readers) have access to heaven itself: ἀλλὰ προσεληλύθατε Σιὼν ὄρει καὶ πόλει θεοῦ ζῶντος, Ἰερουσαλὴμ ἐπουρανίῳ.[1] Here a metaphor is introduced that differs from the cultic metaphor applied up to this point in Heb. (e.g. 4.16; 10.22) that directed access to the 'heavenly sanctuary'. The 'heavenly Jerusalem' is described as the πόλις θεοῦ ζῶντος, yet elsewhere in Heb. God is characterized on his throne within the holy of holies (1.3, 13; 4.16; 7.25; 8.1; 9.24; 10.12; 12.2). Hence, it appears that Heb. is employing the 'heavenly Jerusalem' terminology in a manner synonymous with the 'heavenly sanctuary' mentioned elsewhere.[2] The 'heavenly Jerusalem' is a concept absent in the Old Testament but frequent in Jewish apocalyptic and Rabbinic literature. In Jewish apocalypticism Jerusalem variously appears as a pre-existent heavenly city which will descend to earth at the end of the age, as an eternal residence for the righteous in heaven, and as a vast and wonderful city whose center is a new Temple.[3] In Rabbinic literature the heavenly Jerusalem appears in close connection with the heavenly Temple so that they become almost inseparable.[4] Already in Jer. 3.17, in a later addition to the prophecy, the 'throne of the Lord' and 'Jerusalem' are one and the same.[5]

---

1. The Ἰερουσαλὴμ ἐπουράνιος is placed as an appositive to what precedes it. The parallelism in 12.18-21 and 22-24 is seen in the mention of Mt Zion, to contrast Mt Sinai. Both locations frequently occur together in Jewish literature (e.g. *Jub.* 4.26). See Michel, *Kommentar*, p. 463 n. 1; Attridge, *Hebrews*, p. 374.

2. This could be easily explained by the parallelism maintained in this preformulated material, and by the fact that Heb. is using a *Vorlage* here that contained the 'heavenly Jerusalem' metaphor. See e.g. Thompson, *The Beginnings*, p. 44, and our discussion below.

3. *2 Bar.* 4.2-7; *4 Ezra* 7.26; 8.52; 10.27, 54; 13.36; *2 En.* 55.2; *Tob.* 13.10-16; *Sib. Or.* 3.787; 5.250-51. In the New Testament, see Gal. 4.26; Rev. 3.12; 21.1-4. Refer to Str–B, *Kommentar*, 3.573.

4. For example, in *b. Ḥagiga* 12b the heavenly Jerusalem is in the fourth heaven with the temple and altar; see Str–B, *Kommentar*, 3.573; Bietenhard, pp. 192-204. In *T. Dan* 5.12 the heavenly Jerusalem is the abode of the righteous after death, and at *1 En.* 90.26-39 the new Temple and the new Jerusalem pass over into each other and become one; e.g. see Bietenhard, pp. 193-95. Also see Windisch, *Hebräerbrief*, p. 113; Barrett, 'The Eschatology', pp. 373-76.

5. This appears to be the case at Rev. 5.11-12, where the myriad of angels are before the throne. In Heb. 12.22, the myriad of angels are in the 'heavenly Jerusalem'.

Heb., however, does not appear to be concerned with this apocalyptic description as found in other traditions. At least Heb. makes no mention of a Jerusalem descending from heaven in order to be established at the end of the age. Absent from Heb. is any indulgence in the magnificent or fantastic description that typically accompanies apocalyptic or mystical (e.g. the *Merkabah*) presentations of heaven.[1] We therefore may not so easily dovetail the occurrences of the πόλις and 'heavenly Jerusalem' at 12.22-24 with other references to the 'city' or 'country' elsewhere in Heb. (11.10, 13-16; 13.14) as is done, with a single exception, by practically every scholar.[2] Thus, on the basis of Heb., we cannot so readily adopt the apocalyptic presentation found elsewhere to be pertinent.[3] This is not to ignore the

---

1. For instance, Hofius (*Der Vorhang*) speaks of descriptions supplying the minute details of the angelic activity in and around the 'curtain'. For a critique of Hofius's position, see W. Horbury, 'The Aaronic Priesthood in the Epistle to the Hebrews', *JSNT* 19 (1983), p. 47.
2. For instance, see Riggenbach, *Der Brief*, p. 415, and Peterson, p. 161. However, Rissi (*Die Theologie*, p. 44) remarks that the heavenly city is not simply identified with heaven, as is the sanctuary. For literary references to Zion and the heavenly Jerusalem, see Braun, *Hebräer*, pp. 435-36. The city and land appear to be more likely assumed within the eschatology of the coming, unshakeable Kingdom, and not the heavenly presence before God. Heb.'s very silence on this matter has of course led to diverse speculations by scholars seeking to determine some coherence among the uses of 'city' in the Epistle. Schierse (*Verheissung*, p. 181) argues that 'die Stadt ist deshalb weder sachlich noch räumlich verschieden von der zukünftigen Welt, der Gottesruhe, dem himmlischen Heiligtum oder dem Vaterland'. At p. 181 n. 123, Schierse rejects Windisch's suggestion that the 'wahre Zelt' is 'in' the city, since for Schierse, they are one and the same: 'Die ganze Stadt ist Gotteswohnung. Der Heb. braucht nicht wie Joh-Apok 21.22 sich um einen Ausgleich zwischen Stadt- und Tempelwarten zu mühen; Stadt und Heiligtum meinen den gleichen umfassenden Ort jenseitiger Schöpfung.' The problem is actually one of eschatology. Along with Rissi, Johnsson ('Defilement and Purgation', p. 399) recognizes this, stating: 'The "not yet" lacks specificity in the author's treatment. On the one hand, there is the strongly underlined motif of journeying, of progress toward the "city", the "better country". We wonder whether that goal is to be attained by death or by the parousia. For on the other hand, the writer clearly holds to the near prospect of the Return. Yet, nowhere does he explicitly link that Return with the wandering motif, so we are left in doubt and it would be unwarranted to strain for his intent. His point concerning the "not yet", however, is quite clear: though there is a waiting time, the future is absolutely certain.'
3. Most scholars automatically associate the 'heavenly Jerusalem' with the Jerusalem of the age to come; e.g. see Barrett, 'The Eschatology', pp. 375-76; Dumbrell, p. 159. Braun (*Hebräer*, p. 435) notes the positions of numerous scholars on this issue.

## 3. Προσέρχεσθαι *and Hebrews*

eschatological elements clearly present in Heb. 9.28, 12.25-29, and elsewhere, but only to approach with caution what is actually said by the author about the future. From the contents of the 'heavenly Jerusalem' elaborated in 12.22-24 it does appear that Heb. is clearly depicting a cultic scene to which the readers 'have drawn near'.

Support for this unusual usage of the 'heavenly Jerusalem' is found in the suggestion that behind Heb. 12.22-24 stands traditional material that has been adapted here by the author.[1] This would also explain the peculiar motifs and vocabulary found within this pericope.[2] Hence, the author has employed this tradition, which neatly paralleled 12.18-21, in order to refer to the cultic scene occurring in the heavenly holy of holies, that is, before the throne of God. This is entirely in keeping with his usage of προσέρχεσθαι in the Epistle.

At first glance the perfect indicative προσεληλύθατε seems problematical. However, the present situation of the readers is such that they are already connected with heaven, as has been seen at 6.19-20 and 7.19,[3] so that what was formerly a one-time occurrence in the past has created a continuous 'birthright'.[4]

This access to the heavenly realities requires some clarification, however, in light of the fact that the readers still reside on earth.[5] There exists no adequate explanation for the perfect tense here unless we agree, with Riggenbach, that προσέρχεσθαι refers to 'eine dauernde, innere Beziehung zu der himmlischen Welt und ihren Gütern'.[6] This explains how the access to heaven can be depicted as a

---

1. See Käsemann, *The Wandering People*, p. 54; Michel, *Kommentar*, p. 469 n. 2; Thompson, *The Beginnings*, pp. 44, 48; Rissi, *Die Theologie*, p. 101. Thompson (*The Beginnings*, p. 44) notes: 'The author has supplied his own interpretation to his tradition. To understand this pericope is, therefore, to understand the author's redaction of his tradition.'
2. E.g. Thompson, *The Beginnings*, p. 44; Rissi, *Die Theologie*, p. 101.
3. Braun, *Hebräer*, p. 435: 'Sie sind schon da: in Glauben und Sehnsucht'. Therefore it is a reality, although yet 'unsichtbar'.
4. Casey, p. 332; Braun, *Hebräer*, p. 202; Theissen, p. 103. Peterson (p. 160) comments that 'Christians have already, in a sense, reached their heavenly destination'. Wilson (p. 230) wrongly states that 'they have not yet actually arrived'.
5. Even Hofius (*Katapausis*, p. 142) recognizes the imminence of the parousia. He writes, 'Nur noch die kurze Zeitspanne zwischen der Erhöhung Christi und seiner Parusie (ἔτι μικρόν, 10.37) trennt die Gemeinde vom Eingang in das Jerusalem der Heilszeit, lebt sie doch in dem eschatologischen Kairos'.
6. Riggenbach, *Der Brief*, p. 414.

reality 'that had been experienced all along'.[1] Thus, this 'internal' approach and access to the heavenly things points to worship and prayer (e.g. 4.16; 10.22-25) as the means by which Christians may already dwell in the heavenly, with the numinous, while still living on earth.[2] The context, as well as the perfect προσεληλύθατε, precludes any attempt, therefore, to see this as a 'futuristic' vision in which the readers now participate by faith or as some sort of fully realized eschatology.[3]

In light of the situation of the readers we may best conclude that they do indeed have access, yet they are still on earth confronting all manners of vicissitudes, sufferings and temptations (e.g. 4.16; 10.32-39; 12.3-17, 25-29; 13.1-21)—irrefutable evidence of their 'not yet' being fully in the heavenly realm. The unfulfilled access of their approach is seen clearly in the preceding verses, 12.10-17. Heb. 12.10, 11, 14-17 all point to the fact that the readers are not yet in direct contact with the Lord; for instance God the Father is still disciplining us for our good, that we may share in his holiness (12.10); and, for the moment all discipline seems painful (12.11). That discipline occurs at all serves as an indication that no complete or final entrance has yet taken place. So also at 12.14, where the future tense ὄψεται occurs when exhorting the readers to peace with others and holiness: οὗ χωρὶς οὐδεὶς ὄψεται τὸν Κύριον, that is to say, God.[4] Thus, W.G. Johnsson says, that 'since the author clearly holds that it is only in the future that the 'real' order, which now exists but is invisible, will replace the present, earthly one, it seems preferable to speak of *pro-*

---

1. R. Jewett, *Letter to Pilgrims*, p. 223. Jewett, however, develops a 'realized' eschatological understanding, and so fails to see the future fulfillment of access at the end of life. See also Kuss, 'Der Brief', p. 117. Braun (*Hebräer*, p. 435) and Theissen (p. 103) both correctly argue that 'der Kult ersetzt nicht das bevorstehende Eschaton'.

2. Schierse, *Verheissung*, p. 182; Rissi, *Die Theologie*, p. 101. Michel (*Kommentar*, p. 461) describes this as participation in the 'Gottesdienst der Gemeinde', noting Heb. 4.16; 7.25; 10.1; 11.6. This seems far more plausible than the attempt by Hofius (*Katapausis*, p. 142) to reconcile the perfect verb in 12.22 with the fact that the goal is not yet reached.

3. Peterson (p. 162) sees 12.22-24 as a 'vision of the ultimate, completed company of the people of God, membership of which is now enjoyed by faith'. Jewett (*Letter to Pilgrims*, p. 223) characterizes this text as 'one of the most dramatic and radical statements of realized eschatology in the New Testament'. But can final fulfillment have already occurred when the readers are still on earth facing temptation and trial? Wilson (p. 231) reiterates Peterson.

4. Hofius, *Der Vorhang*, p. 73.

*leptic participation* [emphasis ours] of the believers on earth in the heavenly cultus... Their full (i.e. physical presence) participation lies in the future.'¹ For the present, therefore, cultic access to God takes the form of worship, as already seen at 4.16 and 10.19-25. The Christian's access to heaven is still an 'inner' or 'spiritual' approach as long as things earthly impinge upon him or her. But it is, nonetheless, real and efficacious access to God in light of Christ's high priestly ministry on earth and in heaven (12.24).²

The cultic character of this 'drawing near' at 12.22 as 'worship' is reinforced by the depiction of the heavenly worship in the delineation of the numerous heavenly realities in 12.22-24.³ Heb. first designates the myriad of angels as inhabitants in heaven. Such were already protrayed similarly in the Old Testament (e.g. Pss. 89.6; 103.21; 148.2).⁴ The angels who are in God's direct presence (e.g. Rev. 5.11-12) are gathered in a festal assembly, πανήγυρις, for worship and hymns (e.g. Heb. 1.6).⁵ That πανήγυρις denotes a festive, cultic

1. Johnsson, 'Defilement and Purgation', pp. 332-33.
2. This explains, then, why the elements in heaven that follow in 12.22b-24, may not refer to the earthly Christians of the present age, for such Christians are not yet in the full and final presence of God, if they still suffer and undergo trials on earth. Westcott (*Hebrews*, p. 412) notes that Christians 'are even now still standing in a heavenly presence, not material but *spiritual*' [our italics].
3. For an enumeration of the eightfold (four couplet) structure of the heavenly realities in 12.22-24, see Michel, *Kommentar*, p. 462; Westcott, *Hebrews*, p. 412; Delitzsch 2.344-45. Riggenbach (*Der Brief*, p. 414) criticizes attempts such as those by Westcott and Delitzsch, as 'Künstlichkeit'. Rissi (*Die Theologie*, pp. 101-102) notes a sevenfold structure to the *Vorlage*, with one addition by the author.
4. Rissi, *Die Theologie*, p. 100.
5. The problematical syntax of μυριὰς ἀγγέλων πανηγύρει, etc. is dealt with in most commentaries. See especially Delitzsch, 2.345-53; Riggenbach, *Der Brief*, p. 415 n. 21; Michel, *Kommentar*, p. 463; Héring, p. 117; H. Seesemann, 'πανήγυρις', *TDNT*, 5.722. Westcott (*Hebrews*, p. 414) observes the strong support for this by the most ancient authorities. With Seesemann, it is best to see πανήγυρις as an appositive to what precedes it. Such would parallel the appositional use of Ἰερουσαλὴμ ἐπουρανίῳ occurring immediately prior to this. So also Spicq, *L'Epître*, 2.406-407; idem, 'La panégyrie de Héb. XII, 22', *Studia Theologica* 6 (1953), pp. 32-33. Dumbrell (p. 156) claims, however, that the association of πανήγυρις with angels would be 'tautologous' since angels are always a festal gathering. But this is patently false (cf. e.g. Heb. 1.14). Others who relate πανήγυρις with ἐκκλησία are Braun, *Hebräer*, pp. 436-37 ('offenbar soll πανήγυρις die ἐκκλησία mit besonders feierlich-fröhlichem Klang füllen'); Windisch, *Hebräerbrief*, p. 112 (in his translation); Kuss, 'Der Brief', p. 117. Riggenbach (*Der Brief*, p. 415) has the last and best word, however, saying that it makes 'für das Verständnis keinen wesentlichen Unterschied'.

assembly or 'Festversammlung' is seen in Greek as well as Jewish literature.[1]

United in the goal of acclamation and worship is the ἐκκλησία πρωτοτόκων ἀπογεγραμμένων ἐν οὐρανοῖς. The first term, ἐκκλησία, not only depicts the assembling for celebration of the people of God in the Old Testament at Deut. 31.30 and Judg. 20.2 (based on *qhl*), but at Heb. 2.12 ἐκκλησία has a definite reference to Christian assembly.[2] The Christian ἐκκλησία is further defined by πρωτότοκοι. At Heb. 1.6 the 'first-born' is Jesus Christ, and therefore the 'First-born' and 'the first-born (plural)' belong together, just as 'Son' and 'sons' (e.g. Rom. 8.29; Heb. 2.10-18).[3] Furthermore, 'those whose names are written in heaven' is also another designation for those who are specifically Christian.[4] Therefore, by the phrase ἐκκλησία πρωτοτόκων ἀπογεγραμμένων ἐν οὐρανοῖς these are designated the dead Christians already worshiping in heaven (e.g. Rev. 20.4). So Rissi may write, 'Sie sind dem Erdendasein mit seinen Kämpfen durch den Tod entnommen und vereint mit Gott'.[5] The attempt by most scholars to include all Christians here, both living and

---

1. See Seesemann, 'πανήγυρις', *TDNT*, 5.722; Michel, *Kommentar*, p. 463, especially n. 4; Braun, *Hebräer*, pp. 436-37. For use of πανήγυρις in Philo, *De cher*. 91, 92; *De spec. leg*. II.176, 214, see Williamson, *Philo*, pp. 67-70. The LXX employs πανήγυρις for a 'Kultversammlung' at Hos. 2.11; 9.5; Amos 5.21; Ezek. 46.11. The angels comprise a festal assembly in apocalyptic literature at Dan. 7.10; Jude 14; Rev. 5.11; *1 En*. 1.9; 14.22; 60.1; 71.8, 13.
2. Michel, *Kommentar*, p. 464; Rissi, *Die Theologie*, p. 101. However, Michel (*Kommentar*, p. 465 n. 1) and Westcott (*Hebrews*, p. 415) see this as including the existing church on earth, which is not feasible, based on the earthly Christians' predicament. See Braun, *Hebräer*, p. 437, for a brief review of the positions of numerous scholars.
3. Michel, *Kommentar*, p. 464. He lists several other possibilities to this 'difficult task' of determining just who the 'first-born' are. Braun (*Hebräer*, p. 437) observes that the 'first-born' are not angels, but 'noch lebende Menschen' (Christians) who have now received the same status with those 'mit ranghohen schon länger zur Gemeinde zählenden führenden Christen' (pp. 437-38). However, Rissi (*Die Theologie*, p. 101) writes: 'Wie die Bezeichnung "Söhne" vom Christus auf die Seinen übertragbar ist, so auch der Titel der Erstgeborenen'.
4. See Lk. 10.20; Phil. 4.3; Rev. 3.5; 13.8; 17.8; 20.15. Michel (*Kommentar*, p. 464 n. 3) makes the reference to 'those Christians who have fallen asleep'. Spicq (*L'Épître*, 2.407) prefers 'angels' here, and others 'Old Testament worthies'. Also see Str–B, *Kommentar*, 2.169-76. Braun (*Hebräer*, p. 438) again sees here a reference to 'lebende Menschen'. Attridge (*Hebrews*, p. 375) sees a distinction being made between men and women of faith and angels.
5. Rissi, *Die Theologie*, p. 101.

3. Προσέρχεσθαι *and Hebrews* 147

dead, fails to understand that the current earthly predicament of living Christians excludes them from this festal assembly in heaven itself. The heavenly worship occurs in the presence of God, e.g. καὶ κριτῇ θεῷ πάντων. Once again the location of the worship is the place of God's throne, the holy of holies, where God sits as Judge.[1] One final group appears before this God, namely δίκαιοι τετελειωμένοι.[2] τελειοῦν, as has been seen in Heb. elsewhere, refers to the access to God in the heavenly holy of holies.[3] Hence, the 'perfected righteous' are the deceased Old Testament faithful who are now enjoying direct access to God.[4] Heb. 11.40 proves no obstacle for this interpretation, since the entrance of Old Testament worthies coincided with the access extended to believers which occurred with the sacrifice of Jesus for them all. Rissi also notes that these 'perfected righteous' are the 'called' in Heb. 9.15, those whom Jesus redeemed from the transgressions under the former (i.e. first) covenant.[5] Thus even the

1. The picture of God as the judge on his throne is frequently encountered in the Old Testament: Pss. 9.4, 7; 11.4-7; 45.6-7; 47.8; 89.14; 93.2; 97.2; 103.19; Isa. 6.1-13; 66.1-2; Jer. 14.21. Braun, *Hebräer*, p. 438, sees God as Judge mentioned here by the author in order to strike fear into the hearers, which seems highly unlikely in light of the immediate mention of Jesus as mediator and of his efficacious blood. More likely is Riggenbach's position that κριτής denotes God as 'Retter und Helfer' (*Der Brief*, pp. 417-18). See also O. Schmitz, 'θρόνος', *TDNT*, 3.103.
2. For the placement of this phrase within the structure of the pericope (a matter which need not detain us here), see Rissi, *Die Theologie*, p. 102, who convincingly locates it outside the *Vorlage*, and which has been intentionally inserted by the author between God the Judge and Jesus the mediator. A comprehensive survey of modern research on this passage is found in Spicq, *L'Epître*, 2.407-409, and 'La panégyrie', pp. 30-38. Michel (*Kommentar*, pp. 466-67) gives a good discussion of the problem, although he fails to understand the relevance and applicability of Heb. 11.40 to 12.24, as also do Dumbrell (pp. 158-59) and Käsemann (*The Wandering People*, p. 50 n. 88).
3. Riggenbach (*Der Brief*, p. 418) writes, 'Mit ihrer τελείωσις haben sie vielmehr das ihnen gesteckte Ziel erreicht und sind zur Vollendung ihres Personlebens, vor allem zur Vollendung ihrer Gemeinschaft mit Gott gekommen (cf. 10.14; 11.39f.)'.
4. This is a traditional designation for the Old Testament faithful. See Rissi, *Die Theologie*, p. 102; Delling, 'τελειόω', *TDNT*, 8.83; Bruce, *Hebrews*, p. 378. For Hofius (*Der Vorhang*, p. 77), however, his different understanding of the meaning of τελειοῦν leads him to reject the assertion that these Old Testament pious are already in heaven with God. Michel (*Kommentar*, pp. 466-67) acknowledges that these 'spirits' are those dead; so also Braun (*Hebräer*, pp. 438-49). For Westcott (*Hebrews*, p. 416) they are the 'departed saints', cited at 2 Cor. 5.4. The phrase μὴ χωρὶς ἡμῶν (11.40) establishes that those mentioned antedated the Christ event.

Old Testament faithful are characterized by the cultic terminology of 'access' to God.

The concluding phrase that speaks of the approach to Jesus the mediator of the new covenant and to the sprinkled blood brings to mind the cultic sacrifice of Jesus the high priest which pervades Heb.[1] Thus the readers are reminded at the last of the basis and grounds for their own access to God. Jesus as mediator dwells now in heaven interceding for human beings (7.25; 9.24) with his own blood which atones and purifies (9.13, 14, 23; 10.22; 13.20). Jesus' entire heavenly presence before God cannot be separated from his death and the blood he has taken into the heavenly holy of holies with him.[2] And 'laut 9.23 müssen sogar "die himmlischen Dinge" durch die "besseren Opfer", d.h. das Blut des Christus, gereinigt werden. Das ist nur verständlich, wenn wir bedenken, dass nach dem Heb. das irdische Volk Gottes schon Zutritt zum Himmel hat, dass es also schon zu den himmlischen Dingen hinzugehört, obwohl es noch auf Erden lebt.'[3] Jesus is portrayed through the use of unabashedly high priestly cultic terminology.

*Conclusion*

It is clear from the explicit cultic references in 12.22-24 that the location to which the readers 'have drawn near' is, in fact, the heavenly sanctuary. The heavenly realities describe those beings who

---

5. Rissi, *Die Theologie*, p. 102. Westcott (*Hebrews*, p. 416) agrees: 'The righteous have realized the end for which they were created in virtue of the completed work of Christ. When the Son bore humanity to the throne of God—the Father—those who were in fellowship with Him were (in this sense) perfected, but not till then: c. 11.40.'

1. Michel (*Kommentar*, p. 468) feels that the title of Jesus as mediator of the covenant may 'perhaps be an established, liturgical expression (e.g. 8.6; 9.15)'. Braun (*Hebräer*, p. 439) raises the question of whether or not mediator is applied here as a parallel to Moses as mediator in 12.18-21, citing several scholars. The parallelism is indeed striking, as at Gal. 3.19. According to Attridge (*Hebrews*, p. 376) Heb. uses the name 'Jesus' here in order to emphasize his suffering humanity.

2. The cultic use of ὁ ῥαντισμός in the Old Testament is seen at Num. 19.9; Ps. 51.7. In Heb. its cultic use is found in 9.13, 18-22; 10.22; also 1 Pet. 1.2. For a fuller discussion, see Michel, *Kommentar*, pp. 468-69. J. Smith (p. 112) sees an actual sprinkling of blood occurring in heaven.

3. Rissi, *Die Theologie*, p. 81.

3. Προσέρχεσθαι *and Hebrews*

are in the direct presence of God, as is seen most clearly by their coming to κριτῇ θεῷ πάντων.[1]

As the προσέρχεσθαι in 12.18 expressed the cultic assembly of the people of God, so does its counterpart at 12.22, albeit as a superior, better, totally new dimension and order. Under the old covenant such access into the earthly holy of holies was restricted to the high priest, one day in the year. Under the new covenant, however, high priestly access (understood as being in the very presence of God and his throne in heaven) is not only accorded to Jesus (1.3; 4.14; 5.10; 7.28; 8.1; 9.24; 10.12; 12.2) and to the angelic hosts, but to dead Christians and to the Old Testament faithful of Heb. 11 who are τετελειωμένοι.

They have attained, therefore, a high priestly status with regard to their access to God, based on the mediatorial work and sacrifice of Jesus. Into this cultic sphere the readers gained access, but only through worship and in hope, since their earthly predicament belies any final and complete access into God's heavenly sanctuary. They possess as yet only an incomplete high priestly access, realized in 'hope'.

---

1. We would argue therefore, that the author could just as easily have rendered Heb. 12.22 as, 'but you have drawn near to the heavenly holy of holies'. He was restricted from doing so on the basis of his *Vorlage*, and the desire to maintain the parallel between Mt Sinai and Mt Zion.

Chapter 4

ΕΙΣΕΡΧΕΣΘΑΙ AND HEBREWS

We now proceed to an investigation of the term εἰσέρχεσθαι (and εἰσιέναι) which occurs occasionally in Heb. to designate a cultic activity in the Old Testament ritual, or in connection with Jesus Christ the high priest (Heb. 9.6, 7, 25; 9.11-12; 9.24; 6.19-20), and which in the LXX occurs frequently in cultic contexts.

1. Εἰσέρχεσθαι *in the* LXX

The Hebrew *bô'* possesses a multitude of meanings.[1] However, in the pertinent cultic occurrences, *bô'*, rendered most often in the LXX by εἰσέρχεσθαι, εἰσπορεύεσθαι, and εἰσιέναι,[2] is used to describe the priestly approach to the altar, the cultic entrance into the first tent or tent of meeting, and the high priest's entering into the holy of holies on the annual Day of Atonement.

The description of the priest 'going' to the altar or 'coming' into the court with an offering occurs infrequently in the Old Testament.[3] We have already seen in our discussion of προσέρχεσθαι that 'to draw near' is more prevalent where the context refers to the cultic procedures involving the altar.

Much more frequent is the characterization of the priest who, in his cultic office, enters into the tent of meeting.[4] That *bô'* remains distinct

---

1. See E. Jenni, *'bô'*, *THAT*, 1.264-69; H.D. Preuss, *'bô'*, *TDOT*, 2.20-25; J. Schneider, 'εἰσέρχομαι', *TDNT*, 2.676-78.
2. For specific passages refer to BAG, p. 231. There see the words εἴσειμι and εἰσέρχομαι.
3. Pss. 43.4(42.4[LXX]); 66.13(65.13[LXX]); 96.8(95.8[LXX]); Ezek. 44.27. Cf. Lev. 16.3.
4. Exod. 28.29, 30, 35, 43; 30.20, 21(LXX only); 33.8, 9; 34.34, 35; 40.32, 35; Lev. 9.23; 10.9; 16.3, 23; Num. 4.3, 5, 19, 20, 23, 30, 35, 39, 43, 47; 7.89; 8.15, 22, 24; 16.43; 25.8; 2 Chron. 23.6, 19; 26.16-17; 27.2; 29.16; 30.8; Hos. 9.4; Ezek. 42.14; 44.3, 9, 17, 21, 27; 46.9. At Exod. 20.21, the LXX renders *niggaš* by

## 4. Εἰσέρχεσθαι and Hebrews

from *qārêb* and *niggaš* is apparent both by the object following the verbs, and by the occasional juxtaposition of the verbs in the LXX.[1] The utilization of both εἰσπορεύεσθαι and προσπορεύεσθαι suggests that they are not used appositionally (e.g. as a hendiadys) when they appear together, but, rather, that they express two distinct functions of the cultic ritual.

Another distinction from the use of 'to draw near' is that the 'προσέρχεσθαι into the tent' was specifically for the presenting of offerings at either the table of shewbread or the altar of incense.[2] Only twice, however, is '"to enter" into the tent' associated with the offering at the table of shewbread (Ezek. 44.16; Hos. 9.4), and once at the altar of incense (2 Chron. 26.16-17). Far more conspicuous are the occurrences where the purpose for the entering does not appear to be a sacrificial offering: for instance, to speak to God (Exod. 34.35; Num. 7.89), to take down the curtain (Num. 4.5), to remove priestly garments (Lev. 16.23), or to do custodial service at the tent (Num. 4.3; 8.15, 22, 24; 2 Chron. 29.16).

Most cultically relevant appear to be the occurrences where the blood is 'brought' or 'taken' into the tent in accordance with the sin offering ritual (Lev. 4.5-7, 16-19; 9.23; 10.18; 16.17) in order to effect atonement.[3] The manipulation and sprinkling of blood are integral elements in the purification ritual, although they are seldom characterized by the verb 'to offer' (*hqryb*),[4] but more frequently by 'to bring' (*hby'*) and 'to take' (*lqḥ*). But we shall see that the verbs 'to bring' and 'to take' are subsumed under the whole sacrificial procedure seen as 'offering'.[5] Therefore, whereas the 'drawing near'

---

εἰσέρχεσθαι rather than by προσέρχεσθαι, the only such translation in the Old Testament, according to Hatch and Redpath, *A Concordance*.

1. Exod. 28.43; 30.20; 40.32; Lev. 10.9. See above in Chapter 3, section 1.
2. Cf. above, Chapter 3, section 1.
3. εἰσφέρειν describes the means by which atonement is effected at Lev. 4.5, 16, 20. That the priest is absent from the list of persons who bring the sin offering (4.1-5, 13), signifies that the priest and the Israelite are subject to the same procedures. See Milgrom, 'Studies in the Temple Scroll', p. 506 n. 21.
4. Lev. 1.5; 7.33; Ezek. 44.7, 15.
5. For instance, see M. Noth, *Leviticus: A Commentary* (OTL; rev. edn; Philadelphia: Westminster, 1977), pp. 39, 121-22. Thus we believe that Stott ('The Conception', p. 64) puts too much emphasis on the placement of the occurrences of 'offer', 'take', and 'bring' in Lev. 16. The shortcomings of Stott's argument are also noted by N.H. Young ('The Gospel According to Hebrews 9', *NTS* 27 [1981], pp. 198-210), and W.E. Brooks ('The Perpetuity of Christ's Sacrifice in the Epistle

into the tent referred to the presentation of specific bread or incense offerings, 'to enter' into the tent refers to the priestly effecting of atonement by 'bringing' (or 'offering') the blood before the second curtain.[1]

It is to be noted, however, that although *qārêb, niggaš*, and *bô'* all describe common priestly activity in the vicinity of the altar and within the tent, they restrict the common priest's ministry to that activity outside the holy of holies, the second tent.

The uniqueness of εἰσπορεύεσθαι (*bô'*) in the cultic context is seen in its application to the role of the high priest on the Day of Atonement (Lev. 16). Thus, the high priest (Aaron) alone 'enters' into the holy of holies once a year (Lev. 16.2, 17, 23).[2] The high priest enters to make atonement 'for himself and for his house and for all the assembly of Israel' (16.17b, 34)[3] by 'taking' (λαμβάνειν) or 'bringing' (εἰσφέρειν) blood into the holy of holies and into contact with the mercy seat (Lev. 16.12, 14, 15) as was specified already at Lev. 4.5, 16. That this use of blood is a characterization of an offering is seen clearly in Lev. 1.5 and Lev. 7.33 (also Ezek. 44.7, 15), where blood is 'offered'.[4] The high priestly access to this direct presence of God within the holy of holies is indeed unique, for in the Old Testa-

---

to the Hebrews', *JBL* 89 [1970], pp. 205-14). Stott states that 'in the account in Leviticus the word "offer" (*hqryb*) is used only before the death of the bullock and the goat. It is not used of the act of the High Priest in taking the blood into the Most Holy Place, where two other words with no special meanings are used, "take" (*lqḥ*) and "bring" (*hby'*)'. However, insofar as the 'bringing' is an element in the 'offering' it clearly has no meaning apart from its function as part of the whole sacrificial procedure. At Lev. 4.3-4 and at Lev. 16.6, 11, with the use of προσάγειν, the description of the entire sacrificial offering is stated in anticipation of the procedural action that will follow in the subsequent verses. Hence, we are given a description of the imminent activity, proleptically.

1. For cultic uses in Philo and Josephus, refer to Braun, *Hebräer*, p. 255.
2. προσέρχεσθαι at Lev. 16.3 is a reference to the entrance into the first tent.
3. For a good summary of the efficacy of the sin offering with regard to the atonement of sin, see J. Milgrom, 'Sacrifices and Offerings, OT', *IDB Suppl.*, pp. 766-67, and *idem*, 'Day of Atonement', *IDB Suppl.*, pp. 82-83. Also see G.J. Wenham, *The Book of Leviticus* (NICOT; Grand Rapids: Eerdmans, 1979), pp. 88-96. Observe that he is dependent on Milgrom for his exposition here.
4. Noth (*Leviticus*, pp. 121-22) considers the early mention of 'offering' and 'presenting' (16.6, 11) as making a reference to the 'whole sacrificial procedure'. Also see Westcott, *Hebrews*, p. 251.

ment the only other figure who goes into the inner and most holy place is the 'Lord' (Ezek. 41.3-4).[1]

When, therefore, the high priest is concerned at the Day of Atonement, the Old Testament consistently characterizes him as 'entering' (εἰσπορεύεσθαι and synonyms) into the holy of holies, not as 'drawing near' to the mercy seat, although the two phrases would appear to be synonymous. The high priest's function is to 'bring' (or 'offer') the blood that will atone for even presumptuous sins within the *adyton*, the most holy place.[2] This unparalleled access into God's very presence was not available to the other priests either at the altar or within the first tent.

Hence, we shall investigate the significance of εἰσέρχεσθαι in Heb.,[3] on the basis of the Epistle's affinity with matters cultic, and in particular the Day of Atonement paradigm.

## 2. Εἰσέρχεσθαι *in Hebrews*

After our initial look at the cultic usage of εἰσέρχεσθαι (and its synonyms) in the LXX, we are ready to examine the sacerdotal occurrences of εἰσέρχεσθαι in Heb. We first consider the usages which refer to the former old covenant practices, and then those concerning Jesus Christ, the high priest in heaven.

*Heb. 9.6, 7*
Immediately following the discussion of the arrangements within τὸ ἅγιον κοσμικόν (9.1-5) Heb. considers the ritual practice that occurs within the ἅγια and the ἅγια ἁγίων (9.6-10), using present-tense

---

1. The priestly status of Moses is shrouded in obscurity. He appears to be a high priest as seen in his direct access to God within the cloud (where the LXX at Exod. 20.21 renders the Hebrew with εἰσέρχεσθαι and not προσέρχεσθαι), or into the tent of meeting (e.g. Exod. 33.8, 9; 34.35). At Exod. 40.35, the priestly role of Moses is abruptly curtailed by his further inability to enter into the tent—a privilege henceforth reserved for priests.

2. Hence, Milgrom ('Sacrifices and Offerings', pp. 766-67) sees this greatest degree of temple penetration as atoning for the 'transgressions' (i.e. rebellious sins) of the people (Lev. 16.16, 21, 34).

3. We observe that Heb. makes no use of εἰσπορεύεσθαι, but employs instead its synonym, εἰσέρχεσθαι. This argues for the author's reliance on the occurrence of εἰσέρχεσθαι as found at Ps. 94.11 [LXX] and introduced at Heb. 3.1–4.13; he then used this term consistently throughout Heb.

verbs.[1] This does not suggest that the Mosaic ritual is still continuing down to the present time of the Epistle's composition,[2] but rather that the author is employing the desert tabernacle as the 'antitype' of the 'real' (e.g. 9.24).[3] Here Heb. betrays a Hellenistic influence in its use of the present tense to express repeated or customary actions, as well as prohibitions.[4]

The genitive absolute τούτων κατεσκευασμένων refers to the cultic accouterments in 9.2-5 which were described by κατασκευάζειν in 9.2. Thus, the verb κατασκευάζειν (9.2, 6) circumscribes the consideration of the cultic arrangements[5] and introduces a new thought concerning the different priestly services.[6] As has been observed by most scholars, Heb. 9.1-10 evinces a chiastic structure whereby the 'regulations for worship' and the 'earthly sanctuary' in 9.1 are dealt with in reverse order in 9.2-5 and 9.6-10.[7]

The first-mentioned priestly service agrees with the sequence in 9.2, whereby the priests 'enter' into the first tent (or ἅγια) διὰ παντός. This is then contrasted with the description of the service by the high priest on the Day of Atonement within the ἅγια ἁγίων, or second tent (9.3, 7), ἅπαξ τοῦ ἐνιαυτοῦ. This contrast is clearly identified by the 'μὲν . . . δέ' usage in 9.6-7 which further justifies

---

1. W.E. Brooks (p. 213) quotes from A. Vanhoye ('De "aspectu" oblationis Christi secundum Epistolam ad Hebraeos', *Verbum Domini* 37 [1959], p. 34): 'Whenever he (the author) treats the priesthood in general or the liturgy of the Old Testament he uses the repetitious present. Whenever, on the other hand, he treats the priesthood of Christ, he uses the aorist.' See also Stott, 'The Conception', p. 65.
2. This is a viewpoint held by many scholars, for instance: Delitzsch, 2.62; G. Lünemann, *Critical and Exegetical Handbook to the Epistle to the Hebrews* (trans. from the 4th edn of the German by M.J. Evans; Edinburgh: T. & T. Clark, 1882), pp. 319-20; or recently by Strobel, 'Der Brief', p. 171, and Hughes, *A Commentary*, p. 321.

3. For evidence that the Old Testament cultus is no longer operating at the time of the author, see Riggenbach, *Der Brief*, pp. 248-49; Moffatt, *Commentary*, p. 117; Braun, *Hebräer*, p. 255; Rissi, *Die Theologie*, p. 37.
4. This present tense usage is seen, for instance, at Exod. 28.23(LXX). For a full discussion refer to Braun, *Hebräer*, p. 255, and BAG, p. 231 (εἴσειμι).
5. See Riggenbach, *Der Brief*, p. 247; A. Vanhoye, *La structure littéraire de l'Epître aux Hébreux* (Studia Neotestamentica, 1; Paris: de Brouwer, 1963), p. 145; Braun, *Hebräer*, p. 254.
6. See Michel, *Kommentar*, p. 305.
7. See Braun, *Hebräer*, p. 247; Lünemann, p. 319; Vanhoye, *Structure*, pp. 144-45, 150; O. Hofius, 'Das "erste" und das "zweite" Zelt: Ein Beitrag zur Auslegung von Heb. 9.1-10', *ZNW* 61 (1970), p. 271 n. 1; Peterson, p. 132.

## 4. Εἰσέρχεσθαι and Hebrews

the absence of εἰσιέναι from 9.7 since it already appears in 9.6.[1] A similar example of ellipsis occurs at 9.24-25, except that there the verb involved is εἰσέρχεσθαι. Situated as it is within Heb. 9 the occurrence of εἰσιέναι is undoubtedly cultic in meaning. Despite its infrequent use in the LXX, εἰσιέναι does on occasion render *bô'* in its cultic usage (e.g. Exod. 28.29, 31). While εἰσέρχεσθαι is preferred in Heb., elsewhere in the New Testament εἰσιέναι describes the activity of entering into the temple (Acts 3.3; 21.26), and possesses a cultic meaning in the contemporaneous extra-biblical texts, such as Philo, Josephus and Greek literature.[2]

εἰσιέναι in 9.6 describes the functioning of the common priests whose access extends only εἰς τὴν πρώτην σκηνήν, i.e. into the holy place, or *hekal*, as seen already in 9.2.[3] This is in full agreement with our introductory discussion of εἰσέρχεσθαι and its synonyms, where the priests' major functioning role occurred within the holy place.[4] The priests 'enter' in order to ἐπιτελεῖν τὰς λατρείας.[5] As already observed in our discussion of the LXX and εἰσέρχεσθαι, the 'entering' practiced by priests is, typically for the care of the utensils and the incense offering.[6] Among such practices by the priests mentioned in the Old Testament are the daily morning and evening maintenance of sanctuary candles (Exod. 27.20-21; 30.7-9), the daily bringing of the

---

1. So Young, p. 199 n. 11, who sees the 'μὲν . . . δέ' linking 9.6 to 9.7 securely. See Braun, *Hebräer*, p. 254.
2. For a thorough listing of the relevant passages and texts refer to Braun, *Hebräer*, p. 255. Braun further remarks that the absence of the verb in 9.7 could suggest that the omission may be replaced by either εἰσιέναι, εἰσέρχεσθαι (9.12), or even with εἰσπορεύεσθαι (Lev. 16.17, 23).
3. See Braun, *Hebräer*, p. 254, and Hofius, *Der Vorhang*, p. 62. While both see the holy place as related to the 'first tent' in 9.2, they mistakenly relate the 'true tent' in 8.2 with the holy place. This is based on the misunderstanding of the occurrences of ἅγια in Heb., when it occurs with the article (i.e. always designating the holy of holies) and when without (i.e. when it refers to the holy place or the entire sanctuary). For a detailed examination of these precise differences, see Rissi, *Die Theologie*, pp. 35-41.
4. See section 1 of the present chapter, above.
5. The cultic character of ἐπιτελεῖν is seen in the Hellenistic tradition where it is frequently accompanied with a cultically determinative object (e.g. λειτουργίας, θυσίας), especially in Philo, according to Moffatt (*Commentary*, p. 117). For uses in Hellenistic literature refer to Michel, *Kommentar*, p. 305 n. 2; Riggenbach, *Der Brief*, p. 248 n. 89; Windisch, *Hebräerbrief*, p. 76.
6. Braun, *Hebräer*, p. 255.

incense offering at morning and evening (Exod. 30.7-9), and the weekly preparation of the shewbread and the placing of it on the table within the holy place (Lev. 24.5-8).[1]

In contrast to the earthly priests of Heb. 9.6 the high priest (ὁ ἀρχιερεύς) enters εἰς δὲ (μὲν at 9.6) τὴν δευτέραν (cf. τὰ ἅγια at 9.25). This occurs but once a year, making the reference to the Day of Atonement festival (Lev. 16) 'unmistakable'.[2] Access into the 'holy place within the veil' (Lev. 16.2, 3, 16, 17, 20, 23, 27) was granted only to the high priest in order that he might perform specific duties:

> attired not in his violet robe and its accessories, but in vestments of white linen which were reserved for special sacrificial occasions, he entered the holy of holies twice. On the first occasion he carried the blood of the bullock which had been sacrificed as a sin-offering for himself and his household, and sprinkled it on the front of the mercy-seat, which all the time was shrouded in the cloud arising from the incense which burned on the golden altar. Then, when the goat had been slaughtered as a sin-offering for the people at large, he brought its blood too into the holy of holies and sprinkled it on and before the mercy seat.[3]

The contrast portrayed between the simple priests and the high priest is striking. First of all, 'only' (μόνος) the high priest could enter into the holy of holies, whereas a multitude of priests had access to the holy place.[4] Second, the high priest entered only once a year (ἅπαξ τοῦ ἐνιαυτοῦ, e.g. 9.25; 10.3)[5] as prescribed at Lev. 16.2, 34, which contrasts with the continuous and repetitive nature of the priests' entrance at 9.6. It is further to be observed that the prescription of an annual entry did not specify the number of actual entrances the high priest made into the holy of holies on the Day of Atonement, a circumstance which spawned several different accounts of the Day's

---

1. These practices are mentioned in nearly every commentary or pertinent monograph. A partial listing includes: Delitzsch, 2.63-64; Westcott, *Hebrews*, p. 250; Riggenbach, *Der Brief*, p. 248; Windisch, *Hebräerbrief*, p. 76; Michel, *Kommentar*, p. 305; Moffatt, *Commentary*, p. 117; Spicq, *L'Epître*, 2.252; Bruce, *Hebrews*, p. 192; Zimmermann, *Das Bekenntnis*, p. 185; Strobel, 'Der Brief', p. 171; Braun, *Hebräer*, p. 255.
2. Young, p. 199; Brooks, p. 208.
3. See Bruce, *Hebrews*, pp. 193-94.
4. For the use of μόνος in contemporary literature, see Braun, *Hebräer*, p. 255; BAG, pp. 529-30 (μόνος).
5. See Braun, *Hebräer*, p. 255.

events,¹ but which was of no concern to the author of Heb. He was much more preoccupied with the Day's unique access once a year to the holy of holies on the part of the high priest.

The entry of the high priest is further qualified by οὐ χωρὶς αἵματος, ὃ προσφέρει ὑπὲρ ἑαυτοῦ καὶ τῶν τοῦ λαοῦ ἀγνοημάτων. By bearing the blood of slain animals into the holy of holies the high priest's entry was not only safeguarded,² but his 'offering' of the blood by sprinkling within the holy of holies (e.g. Lev. 1.5)³ atoned for himself, his house and the people (Lev. 16.11, 17, 24, 34), and specifically for the people (Lev. 16.16, 19, 21), as seen already in Heb. 5.3 and 7.27.⁴

Under the old covenant the blood atoned for all sins⁵ (e.g. Lev. 16.34; 17.11; *m. Yoma* 6.2), regardless of whether or not they were 'sins of ignorance' (τὰ ἀγνοήματα).⁶ Moffatt makes clear that the choice of τὰ ἀγνοήματα (also at Heb. 5.2) in no way implied that the people were not responsible for their sins, or that they were not sinners.⁷ Thus the view that in Heb. a narrowing of the atoning efficacy of blood occurs, so that it atones only for 'sins of ignorance',⁸ does not appear to be correct. Heb. seems, rather, to set a condition similar to that in *m. Yoma* 5.6; 8.8-9 (e.g. Heb. 10.26), so that

---

1. Hence, there appear to be at least two 'enterings' in the LXX account (Lev. 16.12, 14-17); two in Philo, *Leg. ad G.* 307; four in *m. Yoma* 5.1, 3, 4; 7.4. Such considerations are dealt with by Delitzsch, 2.64; Lünemann, p. 321; Westcott, *Hebrews*, pp. 250-51; Riggenbach, *Der Brief*, p. 248 n. 91; Michel, *Kommentar*, p. 305; Spicq, *L'Epître*, 2.253; Str–B, *Kommentar*, 3.171-72, 741; Attridge, *Hebrews*, p. 239.
2. Bruce, *Hebrews*, p. 194.
3. See Westcott, *Hebrews*, p. 251.
4. See Riggenbach, *Der Brief*, p. 248. Michel (*Kommentar*, p. 305) is careful to note the somewhat blurred distinction between the immolation, atoning ritual, and sacrifice, for he notes, 'Die ganze Opfer- und Sühnhandlung am grossen Versöhnungstag wird also als eine Einheit aufgefasst, bei der die Sühnung der eigenen Schuld sowie der Sünden des Volkes im Mittelpunkt stehen'. This blurring of the meaning of 'offering' will be looked at further when we deal with the texts where the heavenly high priest is portrayed as 'having entered' into the true holy of holies.
5. Buchanan, *To the Hebrews*, p. 144.
6. For an examination of τὸ ἀγνόημα refer to Braun, *Hebräer*, p. 256. Also see Riggenbach, *Der Brief*, p. 248 n. 90; BAG, p. 11 (ἀγνόημα); Michel, *Kommentar*, p. 306; Moffatt, *Commentary*, p. 117; Bultmann, 'ἀγνοέω, ἀγνόημα', *TDNT*, 1.116.
7. Moffatt, *Commentary*, p. 117.
8. See Braun, *Hebräer*, p. 256.

'ἀγνόημα ist nicht eine in ihrer Schwere bestimmbare Sünde, sondern eine durch die Busse sühnbare Sünde'.[1] Central to any atonement by blood is first and foremost a penitent and contrite posture.[2] Thus the use of εἰσιέναι here to describe the entering of the priests and the high priest into their respective tents in order to perform the proper worship ritual finds its background in the language of regulations that are already familiar from the Old Testament.

## Heb. 9.25

The synonymity between εἰσιέναι and εἰσέρχεσθαι is seen in 9.25. Here the author again takes up the consideration of the high priest under the old covenant on the Day of Atonement seen in 9.7[3] within a subordinate clause using the comparative conjunction, ὥσπερ. It serves, therefore, to contrast the work of Christ as high priest (9.24, 25) with the work of the earthly high priest (9.25b), a contrast previously set out in 9.1-10 (e.g. μέν) and 9.11-14 (e.g. δέ). The entering by the high priest into τὰ ἅγια, or the holy of holies (9.7, the second tent), is 'not without blood' (9.7), but ἐν αἵματι ἀλλοτρίῳ, for example. The picture is that of a high priest who takes with him into the holy of holies the blood of the slain beasts (here, 'fremdes Blut').[4] The preposition ἐν is employed in 9.25 with an associative sense, which is based on the corresponding Hebrew inseparable preposition b- rendered 'with' or 'mit' in translation.[5] The high priest enters 'with' blood in order to apply it according to the ritual stipulations in Leviticus 16 (e.g. Heb. 9.13).

---

1. Michel, *Kommentar*, p. 306. Zimmermann (*Das Bekenntnis*, p. 186) supports this view, stating, 'ἀγνόημα ist also nicht eine aus Unwissenheit begangene Sünde, sondern die Verfehlung, die in Verbindung mit der Umkehr am Versöhnungstag gesühnt wird'.
2. We are not concerned here with the question of the efficacy of the sacrificial blood or whether or not it accomplished what it was purported to achieve. Clearly, as we have seen already in our discussion at 10.1 and throughout, no authentic purification was attained, as is evidenced by the repeated necessity for the identical presentations year after year. For those ministering under the old covenant, such practices did in fact accomplish atonement (that is to say 'de jure' atonement, not 'de facto'), as seen clearly in the early chapters of Leviticus.
3. Zimmermann, *Das Bekenntnis*, p. 200.
4. Michel, *Kommentar*, p. 325.
5. BDF, *Grammar*, p. 106, especially paragraph 198; BAG, p. 258 (ἐν); Braun, *Hebräer*, p. 283. Michel (*Kommentar*, p. 325 n. 2) classifies ἐν as followed by an instrumental dative (as at BDF, *Grammar*, pp. 117-18), but his meaning appears to be the same, i.e. 'with'.

The previously considered contrast (μέν... δέ) in 9.6-7 between the priests and the high priest, whereby the common priests entered διὰ παντός while the high priest entered ἅπαξ τοῦ ἐνιαυτοῦ, is evident again at 9.25. However, in 9.25 it contrasts the high priest with Christ's priesthood of an entirely new order. The high priest's ministry is rightly characterized by the term πολλάκις (even though he enters only once a year) when compared to Christ's own high priestly ministry (e.g. ἅπαξ, 9.26, 27, 28).[1] According to 9.25a the negative οὐδέ points to the fact that what Christ did (i.e. his entrance)[2] was not πολλάκις. Thus Heb. uses a negative formulation which is congruent with the meaning of ἅπαξ used with the aorist tense of the verb.

*Heb. 9.11-12*

The section Heb. 9.11-14 'presents a mirror image of the preceding (9.1-10), focusing on the heavenly pole of the basic antithesis'.[3] This is seen by the use of μέν... δέ at 9.1 and 9.11 in order to contrast the superiority of the heavenly presentation of Christ with that of the old covenant high priest.[4] It is further characterized by what is being contrasted. On the Day of Atonement the high priest would enter into the 'earthly sanctuary' (τὸ ἅγιον κοσμικόν), composed of the ἅγια and the ἅγια ἁγίων (9.1-3), but at 9.11 the 'greater and more perfect tent' is the location of Christ's appearing. This σκηνή is understood to be the entire sanctuary, as at 8.2, not simply the holy place or first tent.[5] This understanding accords well with the conception of a

---

1. See Braun, *Hebräer*, p. 283; Michel, *Kommentar*, p. 325; Attridge, *Hebrews*, p. 264. We shall have to discuss the character of Christ's ministry and sacrifice when we look at the use of εἰσέρχεσθαι in relation to his high priesthood. For instance, does the typology between the earthly high priest and the heavenly high priest mean, as 9.12 and 9.25 seem to suggest, that Christ carries blood with him into the holy of holies, as did the high priest?
2. Following οὐδέ, the εἰσῆλθεν from 9.24 is to be taken over. See Riggenbach, *Der Brief*, p. 286.
3. H.W. Attridge, 'The Uses of Antithesis in Hebrews 8–10', in *Christians among Jews and Gentiles: Essays in Honor of Krister Stendahl on His Sixty-fifth Birthday* (ed. G.W.E. Nickelsburg with G.W. MacRae; Philadelphia: Fortress, 1986), p. 6. Also see Hofius, *Der Vorhang*, pp. 66-67.
4. E.g. see Michel, *Kommentar*, p. 309; Hofius, *Der Vorhang*, p. 65; Vanhoye, *Structure*, p. 150; Thompson, *The Beginnings*, p. 105; Braun, *Hebräer*, p. 265.
5. According to Loader (*Sohn*, p. 167) through the words διὰ τῆς μείζονος καὶ τελειοτέρας σκηνῆς οὐ χειροποιήτου, τοῦτ' ἔστιν οὐ ταύτης τῆς κτίσεως (9.11) 'wird deutlich, dass hier primär an den Gegensatz zwischen dem himmlischen

heavenly temple in the Old Testament and in early Jewish apocalyptic where the earthly sanctuary is the copy of the prototype already existing in heaven.[1] At Heb. 8.5 (cf. 9.21; 13.10) Exod. 25.40 is quoted explicitly and the earthly σκηνή erected by Moses is described as ὑπόδειγμα καὶ σκιά of the heavenly τύπος.[2] O. Hofius has further observed that the occurrence of σκηνή and τὰ ἅγια (8.2; 9.11-12) together in Heb. is not without precedent. Contrary to those who view the two terms at 8.2 as separated by an 'explicative' καί,[3] which suggests the synonymity of the terms, a 'Biblizismus' occurs in Leviticus 16. At Lev. 16.20, the holy of holies and the tent of meeting are mentioned together, where they clearly refer to the holy of holies (τὸ ἅγιον) and the entire sanctuary (ἡ σκηνή), respectively. This is found also to be the case at Lev. 16.16, 33.[4] This means that 'unter der σκηνὴ ἀληθινή (8.1) dürfen wir das himmlische Heiligtum in seiner

---

und dem irdischen Tempel gedacht ist, von dem der Vf in 8.2ff. ausführlich gesprochen hat und auf den er in 9.1 bewusst Bezug genommen hat. Als bewusster Gegensatz dazu (vgl 9.1 εἶχε μὲν . . . ἅγιον κοσμικόν; 9.11 Χριστὸς δὲ . . . διὰ τῆς μείζονος . . ; in 9.6 steckt kein Gegensatz zu 9.1) hebt er diese Eigenschaften hervor.' For a listing of proponents and opponents of this position, refer to Loader (*Sohn*, p. 166 n. 19).

The notion that the 'greater and more perfect tent' is to be identified with the Body of Christ (for a bibliography of proponents, see Loader, *Sohn*, p. 166 n. 18) seems totally in error. Also Swetnam, 'Christology', pp. 80-82. First, this view would appear to be contradicted by the words, τοῦτ' ἔστιν οὐ ταύτης τῆς κτίσεως. Second, the author of Heb. does not seem to be intent on obfuscation; rather, he is seeking to elucidate. Thus, where the author is speaking metaphorically or parabolically, he explicitly says so, e.g. 9.9; 11.19. To be added to Loader's listing of opponents is Schröger ('Der Gottesdienst', pp. 165-66).

1. Exod. 25.40; 26.30; 27.8; 2 *Bar.* 4.5; *T. Levi* 5.1-7; Wis. 9.8. See A. Cody, *Heavenly Sanctuary and Liturgy in the Epistle to the Hebrews* (St. Meinrad, IN: Grail, 1960), pp. 14-36. See also Str–B, *Kommentar*, 3.700-704; Bietenhard, pp. 123-26, for Rabbinic examples. Also, L. Goppelt, *Typos: The Typological Interpretation of the Old Testament in the New* (trans. D.H. Madvig; Grand Rapids: Eerdmans, 1982), pp. 166-67.

2. Hofius (*Der Vorhang*, pp. 55-56 n. 48), and Rissi (*Die Theologie*, pp. 37-38) discuss the prominent Hellenistic language used in the contrast. Also see Cody, *Heavenly Sanctuary*, p. 150.

3. See Hofius, *Der Vorhang*, p. 59 n. 68.

4. *Ibid.*, pp. 59-56.

Gesamtheit verstehen und in τὰ ἅγια eine Bezeichnung für das Allerheiligste dieses Heiligtums erblicken'.[1]

That this heavenly sanctuary is οὐ ταύτης τῆς κτίσεως shows that Heb. distinguishes between at least two οὐρανοί, the transitory and the eternal.[2] The heaven that is transitory belongs to the created realm (e.g. 1.10-12; 7.26; 11.12; 12.26).[3] Christ the high priest, however, is elevated 'higher than the heavens' (7.26) which is an ascription given to God in several Psalms (e.g. Pss. 8.2; 56.6[LXX]; 107.6[LXX]; 112.4[LXX]). This suggests that the dwelling place of God is a 'heaven' or 'heavens' distinct from that heaven which is 'created'. Here God resides (Heb. 4.16; 8.1; 12.2), here the heavenly high priest dwells (Heb. 1.3, 13; 10.12; 12.22-24), and here the sanctuary is present (Heb. 4.14; 9.11-12, 24).[4] In rejecting all notions of a vertical ascent to a 'highest heaven', M. Rissi remains true to the typology as practiced by the Old Testament high priest which was a '"horizontale" Bewegung'. Thus Rissi can argue: 'An übereinanderliegende Sphären oder an einen Aufstieg des Christus von der Erde zum Himmel zu denken, liegt diesen Texten vollkommen fern'.[5]

---

1. *Ibid.*, p. 60, and Riggenbach, *Der Brief*, p. 220. This could just as easily apply to our text in 9.11-12; so Hofius, *Der Vorhang*, p. 66.

2. Michel (*Kommentar*, p. 312) notes 'auf alle drei Arten von "Himmel" lässt sich sowohl der Singular (οὐρανός) als auch der Plural (οὐρανοί) anwenden'. Rissi (*Die Theologie*, p. 35) finds no difference in meaning between the singular and plural.

3. Rissi, *Die Theologie*, pp. 35-36.

4. *Ibid.* Lünemann (p. 328); Michel (*Kommentar*, pp. 311-12); and Hofius (*Der Vorhang*, pp. 68-71 [especially p. 71]), all attempt to distinguish a vertical scheme situated above the created heavenly realm, as 'a preliminary stage to the heavenly holy of holies'. This erroneous notion is based on the misunderstanding of what Heb. means when it talks of the heavenly high priest 'going through' the heavens (e.g. 4.14; 7.26; 9.11-12, 24). G.W. MacRae ('Heavenly Temple and Eschatology in the Letter to the Hebrews', *Semeia* 12 [1978], pp. 187-88) goes to the other extreme and finds that any difference in meaning of οὐρανός in Heb. is 'hard to substantiate'.

5. Rissi, *Die Theologie*, p. 39. He notes prior to this: 'An einen besonderen Ort in der Himmelswelt zu denken, z.B. den obersten Himmel, hat keinen Anhalt im Text, der nie verschiedene Himmel in der Gotteswelt unterscheidet. 9.24 entspricht genau 9.11: der himmlische Hohepriester ist durch das Zelt hindurch in das Allerheiligste eingetreten, so wie der irdische Hohepriester durch das irdische Heiligtum hindurchzuschreiten hatte.' On the other hand, P. Ellingworth ('Jesus and the Universe in Hebrews', *EvQ* 58 [1986], pp. 337-50) seeks to show that the author combined horizontal and vertical imagery 'without embarrassment or confusion', although it certainly remains problematical.

Heb. ventures even further than the Old Testament and early Jewish tradition on the heavenly sanctuary, in which it represents the 'Urbild' of the earthly structure. In 9.24 the heavenly sanctuary is characterized by its synonym, ὁ οὐρανὸς αὐτός, that is, as 'heaven itself'.[1] Thus Heb. depicts two horizontally parallel sanctuaries; one, the earthly antitype of the 'true', and the other, the archetype which is in heaven itself. But, with L. Goppelt, we are careful to note that 'there is no metaphysical speculation in this concept'.[2] The only hint of the metaphysical antithesis common in Hellenistic philosophy is in the concept of the sanctuary and cult. Perhaps therefore Heb. has used this antithesis 'as a means for rounding out the picture of Christ as high priest and simply as a practical way of expressing Christ's work as our representative at God's right hand... The major point of comparison is not an earthly sanctuary versus a heavenly one, but the priestly service of the Old Covenant in the past and the priestly service of the New Covenant in the present.'[3]

Already at the outset of Heb. 9.11 the priestly service of the old covenant is contrasted with that of the new. Christ is called the ἀρχιερεὺς τῶν γενομένων ἀγαθῶν,[4] a phrase which looks forward to the mention of the law (specifically, its cultic regulations) which only foreshadows τὰ μέλλοντα ἀγαθά, as at 10.1. With the arrival of the present time (ὁ καιρὸς ὁ ἐνεστηκώς)[5] at 9.9, which is the καιρὸς διορθώσεως (9.10), i.e. the period inaugurated by the advent

---

1. See our discussion of Heb. 9.24 in the following section of this chapter. Also Rissi, *Die Theologie*, pp. 36-41, and in particular, pp. 38-39, for the explanation of ἅγια as the entire sanctuary, based on the content of 9.23. Others concurring are: Riggenbach, *Der Brief*, pp. 258, 285, and Laub, p. 200. Also see Hofius, *Der Vorhang*, p. 50 n. 5, for further bibliography. H. Traub ('οὐρανός', *TDNT*, 5.527) sees 'heaven' at 9.11, in addition to 9.24.
2. Goppelt, p. 167. Also see the 'allegorical' typology in J. Smith, *A Priest for Ever*.
3. Goppelt, p. 167. See also Rissi, *Die Theologie*, pp. 37, 40-41; Attridge (*Hebrews*, p. 248) also sees Heb. as being concerned with the entry of Christ 'into the realm where God is truly worshiped'.
4. ἀγαθά are not 'irdische Schätze oder sittliche Handlungen, sondern eschatologische Gaben von Gott her (Isa. 52.7 = Rom. 10.15)'. As such, '"Gutes" ist Ausdruck für das, was die messianische Zeit vermittelt'. See Michel, *Kommentar*, p. 310.
5. Here in Heb. the present time is the endtime already inaugurated in Christ. This helps to explain the parallel in Heb. 1.2, according to Hofius (*Katapausis*, p. 219 n. 878). Also see Moe (p. 165) where the εἰς at 9.9 is considered to mean 'bis auf', which would be consistent with our understanding.

## 4. Εἰσέρχεσθαι and Hebrews

of Jesus Christ with his new διαθήκη,[1] the good things have already come (9.11). This was something not yet possible (since they were still μέλλειν) under the former order.[2] The accomplishment of 'good things', only foreshadowed in the old, is seen further by the 'concentric symmetry' in 9.11-12 itself.[3] Thus, the 'eschatological redemption' secured by Christ's death and subsequent session in heaven (9.12b)[4] is symmetrical with 9.11a (both verses have aorist participles) which speaks of the 'good things which have come', indicating the parallel and fulfilled character of that performed by Christ.[5]

In accordance with the high priestly Day of Atonement typology, Christ the high priest 'entered' (εἰσέρχεσθαι) διὰ τῆς μείζονος καὶ τελειοτέρας σκηνῆς. Here the expression is not to be taken with παραγενόμενος but with εἰσῆλθεν, as in the διά clauses in 9.12.[6] The 'local' character of the preposition διά, therefore, depicts Christ as walking through or traversing the heavenly sanctuary as he enters into the holy of holies in heaven.[7] Thus the entrance is portrayed as a horizontal movement, paralleling the identical practice of the earthly high priest. In fact, at *m. Yoma* 5.1, the high priest is said to have 'gone "through" the sanctuary until he came to the space between the two curtains'.[8] In light of the consistent use of typology in Heb., there is no need to conceive, at 4.14, 9.11, or 9.24, of a high priest either

---

1. Moffatt, *Commentary*, pp. 118-19.
2. See most major commentaries for a discussion on the textual variants; also Metzger, *A Textual Commentary*, p. 668. See Cody, *Heavenly Sanctuary*, pp. 138-41.
3. Vanhoye, *Structure*, p. 149.
4. See below.
5. So Rissi (*Die Theologie*, p. 80) may comment that in 9.11-14 'der Dienst des alttestamentlichen Hohenpriesters [ist] Typus dessen, was der Christus tut, aber wiederum so, dass jener Dienst überwunden und überboten wird durch den eschatologischen Dienst des Christus'.
6. E.g. see Braun, *Hebräer*, p. 265; Loader, *Sohn*, p. 167. A. Snell (*New and Living Way: An Explanation of the Epistle to the Hebrews* [London: Faith, 1959], p. 111), notes that παραγενόμενος means that 'Christ arrived on the scene of history as High Priest'.
7. For the understanding of διά at 9.11 and 12, see below.
8. Hofius (*Der Vorhang*, pp. 67-68) confirms that 'going through' need not mean that one fully departs one tent, and then enters the next. He comments, 'sondern es kann ebenfalls gebraucht werden, wenn er an diesem Ort bleibt, ihn also nur "durchzieht"'. Hofius cites several references from Acts to support this argument.

attaining to the highest sphere in a graduated realm of heavens,[1] or an ascension by Christ from the earth (i.e. the first tent) through space and into heaven (i.e. the holy of holies).[2] The texts in Heb. which characterize Christ as 'going through' (διά or διέρχεσθαι, e.g. 4.14; 9.11) 'gehören zu der im ganzen Heb. einheitlichen, aus der Tradition der Leser stammenden Vorstellung des Himmels als des vollkommenen Heiligtums'.[3]

Christ, after going through the sanctuary, entered into the holy of holies. The aorist εἰσῆλθεν denotes this event as an unrepeatable occurrence. The superiority of the high priesthood of Christ is based on the fact that he entered into the very presence of God and remained there at God's right hand (1.3; 8.1; 10.12; 2.2). This aorist force is strengthened by the occurrence of ἐφάπαξ (7.27; 9.12; 10.10) which vividly contrasts the inferior earthly priesthood's annual offering, and emphasizes the unrepeatable and incomparable nature of Christ's own priesthood.[4]

Into the very presence of God Christ entered, in a manner parallel, albeit superior, to that approach of the earthly high priests who took with them the 'blood of animals' (7.27; 9.11, 25). He entered διὰ τοῦ ἰδίου αἵματος. Hence Heb. describes Christ's offering in a manner that corresponds to that of the earthly high priest's offering (cf. 9.7, οὐ χωρὶς αἵματος), as would be expected. Thus διά here (ἐν occurs at 9.24) has an 'instrumental' force best rendered 'with' or 'taking' (as in the RSV). Clearly such a translation is to be preferred, if we seek to maintain the thoroughgoing high priestly typology.[5] Any other ren-

---

1. See Hofius, *Der Vorhang*, p. 71.
2. See R. Gyllenberg, 'Die Christologie des Hebräerbriefes', *Zeitschrift für Systematische Theologie* 11 (1934), pp. 662-90, especially pp. 674-75; Käsemann, *The Wandering People*, pp. 223-32. Both of these works, which were highly influential, seem to put an unwarranted emphasis on the 'ascension', something the Epistle itself is silent about. The vertical dimension is not so prominent as these scholars and others suggest. See Loader, *Sohn*, pp. 183-84.
3. Rissi, *Die Theologie*, p. 39.
4. Michel, *Kommentar*, p. 312; Héring, p. 77.
5. The controversy over the meaning of διά in both vv. 11 and 12 was far more animated until Hofius showed that a preposition could be used with objects of the same case and still possess a different meaning. See Hofius, 'Incarnation und Opfertod', pp. 136-37; *idem, Der Vorhang*, p. 67 n. 110. Also see Loader (*Sohn*, pp. 167-68 n. 23) for a thorough review of the various positions and their proponents. Others who render the διά in 9.12 as 'mit' or 'with' include: Goppelt, pp. 166, 168; Laub, pp. 169, 184-85; Barrett, 'The Eschatology', p. 389; Bietenhard, p. 128; Rissi, *Die Theologie*, pp. 40, 80. On the basis of 9.24-25, both Braun

dering besides the instrumental 'with' 'wäre vollig unvorbereitet'.[1] A certain degree of support for this comes from Heb. itself where the figurative 'blood of sprinkling' is with Jesus Christ in heaven (12.24).[2]

The conspicuous disparities that come to light in this presentation of the contrasting earthly, old covenant priesthood and heavenly high priesthood must now be examined.[3] It appears that the author of Heb. places his major emphasis on the death of Christ as the pivotal event.[4] This is done, however, while maintaining the Day of Atonement typology. The Day of Atonement, in accordance with the interests of Heb., is concerned with the first two elements of the sin-offering ritual: the immolation and the taking of blood within the holy of holies. No consideration is given to the presentation and subsequent sending away of the scapegoat which is integral to Leviticus 16. In the contrast portrayed in Heb. the high priest under the old covenant oversaw both portions of the sacrifice, whereas Christ is featured in the dual role of immolated object and bearer of the blood. Thus in light of the practice of sacrifice it appears to be difficult to distinguish qualitatively between the varying procedural acts that comprise the sacrifice.

Even the diminished importance of the immolation of the animal (over against the atoning principle ascribed to the presentation of blood) already present in the Old Testament cultic material takes on a larger significance when considered under the scrutiny of the founda-

---

(*Hebräer*, p. 282) and Zimmermann (*Das Bekenntnis*, p. 200) see Christ before God 'mit' blood.

Hofius's argument, however, is on far shakier ground with respect to 10.19-21. There the second occurrence of διά is absent, yet he presumes it. To my knowledge, however, no such case of the 'inconsistent' use of the preposition exists in the New Testament literature.

1. This is correctly surmised by Loader, *Sohn*, p. 167. He further perceives, rightly, I think, that the antipathy toward this position is based on one's failure to recognize that the presentation is 'bildhaft gemeint' (p. 168).

2. See our discussion above at Heb. 12.18-24.

3. Héring (pp. 76-77) speaks for many when he observes four distinctive features: (1) the heavenly sanctuary is superior and more perfect than the earthly Temple; (2) the offering is of his own blood, not that of animals; (3) the offer of the sacrifice is made only once, once for all; (4) the salvation of the faithful is assured for eternity. Michel (*Kommentar*, p. 312) notes three such features; Hofius (*Der Vorhang*, p. 66) comments on two features and adds another in a footnote.

4. So Rissi (*Die Theologie*, p. 81) may say, 'Für den Verfasser ist der Tod Jesu das eigentliche Heilsereignis', and proceed to cite the references: Heb. 2.9, 14; 7.28; 9.28; 10.10, 12, 14; 12.2f.; 13.12. See Riggenbach, *Der Brief*, p. 287.

tional passage explicating the reason for the blood's efficaciousness, namely Lev. 17.11 (cf. Deut. 12.23): 'For the life of the flesh is in the blood; and I have given it for you upon the altar to make atonement for your souls; for it is the blood that makes atonement, by reason of the life'.[1] This verse presupposes the death of that animal whose blood is offered. Blood not only serves as the atoning substance but also as a constant reminder of a former 'life', prior to the immolation.

We need not be surprised, therefore, when the death of Jesus represents the pivotal circumstance in the typology of Heb. Riggenbach says as much when he writes, 'der Verfasser [findet] das Opfer Christi im Sterben vollzogen'.[2] Thus the entire act of offering (the immolation and the presenting of blood), in the Old Testament as well as in Heb., is best viewed as a 'unitary act' which cannot be readily divided into disparate, sequential actions, with one possessing greater efficacy than the other, save that the presentation of blood obviously depends upon a preceding immolation (i.e. death).[3] Furthermore, the author's affinity for the 'unitary act' is also evidenced in his arrangement of the particularities of Christ's heavenly session after his death. In Heb. the author appears little interested in establishing or asserting any temporally precise sequence of events in heaven, as can be seen in the otherwise seeming contradictions found in 5.9-10, 6.20, and 9.12.

The inescapable conclusion therefore, with regard to the work of Christ the heavenly high priest, is that his achievement is inextricably linked to his earthly life and death.[4] In taking up again the depiction of

---

1. Translation from RSV.
2. Riggenbach (*Der Brief*, p. 286) continues, 'Die Selbstdarstellung Christi vor Gott im Himmel bildet demgegenüber nicht einen Akt von gesonderter Bedeutung; sie bringt nur das Todesopfer zur Vollendung, indem der Erhöhte in und mit seiner Person seine Todesleistung Gott darbringt und dauernd wirksam macht'.
3. This is seen in the use of θυσία in Heb. 5.1; 7.27; 8.3; 9.9, 23, 26; 10.1, 5, 8, 11, 12, 26; 11.4; 13.5, 16. Frequently the term encompasses the entire act of sacrifice, at other times it may refer to a specific event in the sacrifice itself. But conspicuous is the 'unitary act' of sacrifice. According to J. Behm ('θύω', *TDNT*, 3.185), sacrifice was viewed as a general means of personal intercourse between God and humans.
4. E.g. see Rissi, *Die Theologie*, p. 80: 'Das eigenartige Bild hält unaufgebbar fest, dass der Dienst des himmlischen Christus völlig und für immer an seine irdische Geschichte, an seine Hingabe in den Tod, gebunden bleibt, d.h. dass der Verherrlichte nur als der Gekreuzigte erkannt und geglaubt werden kann'. Loader (*Sohn*, pp. 187-89) presents the argument against the position that Christ's atoning sacrifice occurred in heaven.

the Day of Atonement ritual presented in Heb. 9.7 the author illustrates the centrality of Christ's death in the context of the antitype. First, rather than entering with the blood of goats and bulls, Christ the high priest entered διὰ τοῦ ἰδίου αἵματος (9.12). Implicit here is the death which had to precede any such offering of a victim's blood.

Second, Christ entered ἐφάπαξ and this further looks not so much to his offering, as to the sacrifice of himself (7.27; 10.10). Human beings die once and so do not 'enter' continually with the blood of a single offering, as contrasted with the repeated sacrifices of animals. The emphasis on Christ's death is further illustrated by the addition of supporting material inserted after 9.15. Heb. 9.16-17 posits a new covenant based upon a death εἰς ἀπολύτρωσιν τῶν ἐπὶ τῇ πρώτῃ διαθήκῃ παραβάσεων, although this addition does not seem to fit into the cultic presentation.[1]

Third, Christ entered into the heavenly holy of holies (9.12) after securing an eschatological redemption (αἰωνίαν λύτρωσιν εὑράμενος). The aorist participle, εὑράμενος, points to an event antecedent to the action of the indicative verb (εἰσῆλθεν).[2] Thus, despite the fact that most major commentaries point to the coincident (even subsequent) action expressed by the participle, thereby stressing the inseparability of the death from the session in heaven, such an uncharacteristic rendering of the aorist participle is not necessary. We have already seen that the events are conjoined. Accordingly the death of Christ remains the premier event, subsequent to which the arrangement of all other details becomes less significant, though not unimportant.[3] Therefore, as elsewhere in Heb., although the redemption or the atonement for sins appears to have been accomplished at the cross,[4] this ought not lead us to discount altogether (as do, for

---

1. E.g. Loader, *Sohn*, p. 168: 'Es ist wahrscheinlich, dass man die Einmaligkeit des Eintretens von der Einmaligkeit des Sich-opferns ableiten muss, die die Ewigkeit der Erlösung begründet'.
2. See C.F.D. Moule, *An Idiom Book of New Testament Greek* (Cambridge: Cambridge University Press, 1953), p. 110 n. 1; Lünemann, p. 329; Riggenbach, *Der Brief*, p. 262; Hughes, *A Commentary*, pp. 329-30; Peterson, p. 137; Loader, *Sohn*, p. 186; Hagner, *Hebrews*, pp. 119-20; contra Attridge, *Hebrews*, pp. 248-49.
3. Hence the point made above (under 9.6-7, present section) regarding the author's characterization of the entire sacrificial rite as a unitary act is again relevant here.
4. See Heb. 9.15, 24-28; 10.5-10; 13.11-12. Also see Riggenbach, *Der Brief*, p. 286; Bruce, *Hebrews*, p. 200.

instance, Loader and Bruce[1]) the salvific efficacy inherent, as well, in Christ's subsequent entry and presentation of his blood.

In Heb. Christ's sacrificial death is actually inseparable from his later activity. Were this not the case, we would be hard pressed to explain the author's keen interest in the action occurring within the heavenly holy of holies. This has led Young to observe a chiastic correspondence between the old covenant presentation and that of the new, commenting that 'the repeated entrance followed by a repeated blood-sprinkling in the old order is now in the new age a once-for-all sacrifice-cum-sprinkling followed by a once-for-all entrance'.[2] This is correct, provided it is further observed that the heavenly high priest also takes his blood with him into the holy of holies (9.11-12, 24-25; 12.24).

The consistency of this presentation in Heb. is seen in the similar appraisals of redemption and salvation.[3] At 9.11-12 eschatological redemption appears to be the result of the death of Christ and his subsequent entry into the holy of holies. At 5.9 Christ, as the 'source of eschatological salvation', appears to be effective as high priest only after his death and entrance (here, τελειοῦν) into the holy of holies. The interest is primarily in the activity of the high priest in heaven, but this interest is always premised on his preceding death. The intercessory activity of Jesus on earth (5.7-8) continues in heaven (7.25; 9.24; cf. 6.20) where Christ enters with his own blood, symbolizing the perpetually efficacious offering of his life.[4]

Hence in light of the real danger of 'falling away' (6.4; 10.26) in the time when οὔπω ὁρῶμεν αὐτῷ τὰ πάντα ὑποτεταγμένα (2.8a) the 'help in time of need' (4.16; 13.20) appears to be the heavenly high

---

1. Thus Loader overstates his case by ignoring the necessity of the heavenly session guaranteed by the resurrection and ascension, when he comments, 'Das Mitnehmen des Blutes (und gemäss 12.24 das Versprengen im Allerheiligsten) wird am besten bildlich verstanden als die Darstellung einer auf Erden vollbrachten Aufgabe, nämlich: für Sünden zu sterben' (p. 192). The necessity to divide Christ's sacrifice into two phases, as though the cross were not sufficient in itself, is roundly criticized by Bruce (*Hebrews*, pp. 200-201). Michel (*Kommentar*, p. 312) argues that 9.12 'klingt... wie eine selbständige Deutung des Todes Christi'.

2. Young, p. 209. However, Loader (*Sohn*, p. 192) overemphasizes the 'Selbstopfer Jesu' and ignores the importance of his subsequent session.

3. Redemption and salvation are identical terms; so Loader, *Sohn*, p. 45 n. 16; J. Schneider and C. Brown, 'σώζω', *NIDNTT*, 3.220; and implied by Rissi, *Die Theologie*, p. 32; R.H. Smith, pp. 75-76.

4. See Rissi, *Die Theologie*, pp. 95, 99.

## 4. Εἰσέρχεσθαι and Hebrews

priest (cf. 1 Jn 2.1-2).[1] Just as Jesus' blood (his death and entry) secured eternal redemption by effecting the forgiveness of sins, thereby signaling the Messianic age,[2] so he continues as the 'intercessor' for human beings (ὑπὲρ ἡμῶν) as the heavenly mediator. And God hears his prayers because of the perpetual symbol of his death, his blood, which he has taken into the holy of holies with him. Thus, in this present time when the good things have come, when redemption has been secured (9.28a), yet when the actual eschatological 'salvation' is still hidden and 'not yet' (e.g. 9.28b), and both external and internal temptations threaten the church, Christ serves as the source of end-time salvation, staving off the threat of judgment (9.27; 10.30-31) by interceding at God's right hand.[3] Hence Heb. presents a view of salvation ('Heil') 'that is a reality now and that is coming in the future'.[4]

The aorist tense verb εἰσῆλθεν is particularly appropriate, therefore, to describe the action of the heavenly high priest. Christ, the high priest, entered into the heavenly holy of holies, the very presence of God, and he was perfected (5.9) once-for-all, with his own blood, thus securing the eschatological redemption (9.12) and bringing the good things to come (9.11) through his death and entry. Thus εἰσῆλθεν refers to the fact that Christ 'died', and only then was he perfected and designated a high priest after the order of Melchizedek (5.10; 6.20; 7.28). εἰσέρχεσθαι, with reference to Christ in this high priesthood typology, directs our attention to his death, after which he was granted immediate access to God within the holy of holies.

### Heb. 9.24

It is generally agreed that Heb. 9.23-28 returns to the argument left off at 9.11-14 by again considering the contrasting earthly and

---

1. On the problem of ἐντυγχάνειν, see the discussion in Peterson, pp. 114-16, and Hughes, *A Commentary*, pp. 349-54.
2. Michel, *Kommentar*, pp. 312-13.
3. Goppelt, p. 169; Rissi, *Die Theologie*, pp. 81, 95, 127; R.H. Smith, p. 109; Lünemann, p. 210. J. Schneider and C. Brown ('σώζω', *NIDNTT*, 3.220) suggest that at his first coming, Jesus laid the foundation for the 'future saving' activity of God by his atoning sacrifice.
4. Goppelt, p. 167.

heavenly spheres.[1] The relationship between 9.24-28 and 9.11-14 is seen from the inclusio formed by the two sections around 9.15-22.[2] In this sense 9.23 serves as a transitional verse which reintroduces the context of the heavenly realm and yet which continues to rely on the material content of what immediately precedes it in 9.21-22 (e.g. οὖν, 9.23). The ritual purification of the tent and its appurtenances, described in 9.21-22, leads directly to the consideration of the earthly things as 'copies' (τὰ ὑποδείγματα) of a heavenly original (8.2, 5; 9.11, 12),[3] and from there the discussion proceeds immediately to a consideration of Christ who 'entered' εἰς αὐτὸν τὸν οὐρανόν (9.24) in the performance of his 'better sacrifice'.

In keeping with our understanding of an earthly sanctuary and its heavenly counterpart,[4] the heavenly sanctuary being referred to here as 'heaven itself' (9.24), Heb. 9.23a expresses this parallelism by referring to the copies of the things which are in (the) heaven(s), i.e. the heavenly sanctuary.[5] Thus, the 'copies of the things in heaven' are the earthly sanctuary and its accouterments, already introduced at 9.1-10, 21, which require purification by 'these' (τούτοις) rites (9.21-22).[6] Contrasting with the material purification (cf. μὲν . . . δέ) is that cleansing performed by 'better sacrifices', the blood of Christ (e.g. 9.14, 26; 10.10, 12; 13.12), on αὐτὰ τὰ ἐπουράνια.[7]

---

1. Riggenbach, *Der Brief*, p. 281; Michel, *Kommentar*, p. 323; Attridge, 'The Uses', pp. 7-8 and *Hebrews*, p. 260.
2. See especially Vanhoye, *Structure*, p. 157. Also Buchanan, *To the Hebrews*, p. 156. Zimmermann (*Das Bekenntnis*, pp. 198, 199) observes parallels in the same material, but finds 9.25b paralleling 9.7, that is, outside of 9.11-14; e.g. 9.24 = 9.11, 12 and 9.28 = 9.14.
3. Braun, *Hebräer*, p. 280; Strobel, 'Der Brief', p. 185; Hagner, *Hebrews*, p. 127.
4. See above in our discussion of 9.11-12.
5. The occurrence of both singular and plural forms of ὁ οὐρανός has led to countless attempts at their reconciliation. Hofius (*Der Vorhang*, pp. 67-71) identifies the singular οὐρανός with God's residence in heaven, or other vertical scheme, which he derives from *T. Levi*. Also see Lünemann, p. 304. However, see Rissi, *Die Theologie*, pp. 35-36, for a convincing view that the singular and plural are, in fact, used interchangeably.
6. Riggenbach, *Der Brief*, p. 282.
7. Most commentaries consider the apparently incongruous use of the plural in 9.23b. This is thought by most to be a 'generic plural' which corresponds to or was accommodated to the plural, 'these rites' (9.23a). So Hughes, *A Commentary*, p. 379. The context to follow as well as the mention of 'better' sacrifices, alludes to the blood of Christ, e.g. 8.3. See Michel, *Kommentar*, p. 323.

## 4. Εἰσέρχεσθαι *and Hebrews*

A general consensus regarding the precise meaning of τὰ ἐπουράνια has proved elusive in the history of investigation,[1] primarily because 'our author has not expressed himself with his usual felicity, and hence the contortions of commentators at this point'.[2] Authorial style aside, Heb. is not nearly so obscure as the number of explanations would seem to suggest. The 'things' requiring a 'better sacrifice', the blood of Christ, are made explicit in Heb. The blood of Christ serves to purify the συνείδησις (9.14; 10.2, 22) of the worshiper, or the worshiper κατὰ συνείδησιν (9.9).[3] It is precisely this 'inner spiritual condition' of the worshiper that has a direct access to heaven, i.e. this is the 'heavenly' thing, since it is 'perfected' and has direct access to God.

Therefore, as we saw previously, προσέρχεσθαι identifies the spiritual, inner, κατὰ συνείδησιν, access to heaven on the part of the Christian community still residing in the world.[4] This access, available because of a purified conscience, already designates the earthly people of God as 'heavenly things'.[5] Hence the interior realities—the heart, mind, and conscience—whereby the worshiper enters into God's

---

1. For a review of proposed positions, see Michel, *Kommentar*, pp. 323-34; Hughes, *A Commentary*, pp. 379-82; or Braun, *Hebräer*, p. 281. Many have argued for a parallel with the earthly sanctuary in 9.23a (e.g. Braun, *Hebräer*, p. 281; Delitzsch, 2.124-26; Westcott, *Hebrews*, p. 271; Windisch, *Hebräerbrief*, p. 85; Spicq, *L'Epître*, 2.266-67), thereby including the heavenly sanctuary and its accouterments. However, this never overcomes the obstacle of explaining why such heavenly things need to be purified in the first place. Bietenhard (p. 130 n. 1) notes that there is actually very little known about Satan's presence in the heavenly temple. He suggests that the nearest allusion may be Job 15.15, where it is stated, 'Die Himmel sind nicht rein in seinen Augen'. Hence, without the work of Christ, there is no true purity in either earth or heaven. But this again avoids a direct addressing of the reason why heaven must be cleansed. Young (p. 206), Hagner (*Hebrews*, p. 12) and Lincoln D. Hurst ('Eschatology and "Platonism" in the Epistle to the Hebrews', in *Society of Biblical Literature 1984 Seminar Papers*, 23 [ed. K. Richards; Chico, CA: Scholars Press, 1984], pp. 65-67) appear to be arguing to transform what are apparently 'spatial' characteristics into 'temporal' categories. 'Heavenly' is thus a reference to the new order, whereby it is seen in Heb. that such new realities require a final, ultimate sacrifice. However, this ignores the fact that elsewhere in Heb., ἐπουράνιος refers to things found in heaven itself (e.g. 8.5; 9.23; 12.22).
2. Montefiore, p. 160.
3. At 9.9, the RSV improperly makes the 'conscience' the object, when the actual object should be 'worshipers', followed by the prepositional phrase.
4. See Chapter 3; also Wilson, p. 165.
5. Rissi, *Die Theologie*, p. 81.

direct presence have been made 'heavenly' by these 'better sacrifices'.[1] Thus W. Loader may write that 'τὰ ἐπουράνια refers to those people who are "called" (3.1; 9.15) who belong to heaven'.[2]

This would appear to include those spirits who are now in heaven worshiping God the Judge and Christ the mediator (12.22-24), since their presence there has resulted from the death of Christ (9.15; 11.40). But just how their status differs from that of those still on earth must be considered after the examination of εἰσέρχεσθαι.

Christ's entrance was once-for-all: εἰσῆλθεν is an aorist indicative verb. In a manner corresponding to 9.11 Christ did not enter the sanctuary made by hands, the antitype of the true (9.2, 5, 11-12), that is the earthly one, but into the heavenly sanctuary, which is here called αὐτὸς ὁ οὐράνος. That the anarthrous ἅγια does not refer to the holy of holies but to the entire sanctuary is made evident in several ways.[3]

First, the parallelism with 9.11 shows that the σκηνή there corresponds to the ἅγια in 9.24. As we observed in 9.11-12 the σκηνή refers to the entire sanctuary comprising both the first and second tents.[4]

Second, the reference in 9.23 to the ὑπόδειγμα is to the sanctuary and its accouterments, in their entirety, not to the holy of holies. Thus 'die himmlischen Dinge stehen hier im Gegensatz zu ihren Abbildern auf Erden und bezeichnen das ganze Zeltheiligtum samt allen gottesdienstlichen Geräten darin'.[5]

Third, the ἅγια is further described appositionally in 9.24 as αὐτὸς ὁ οὐρανός. This ἅγια parallels the earthly arrangement since the αὐτός does not describe a sphere or realm of different heavens, but one heaven,[6] because Heb. never differentiates between several distinct heavens in God's domain.[7] Heaven as a sanctuary corresponding to the earthly copy, of course, is composed of both the holy place and the

---

1. See, Attridge, 'The Uses', p. 8; Montefiore, p. 160; Bruce, *Hebrews*, pp. 218-19; Cody, *Heavenly Sanctuary*, p. 190; Schierse, *Verheissung*, p. 48; Attridge, *Hebrews*, p. 292.
2. Loader, *Sohn*, pp. 169-70.
3. Heb. consistently applies τὰ ἅγια to the holy of holies. See Rissi, *Die Theologie*, pp. 38-39; Hofius, *Der Vorhang*, pp. 56-58, although only Rissi correctly observes the lack of the article in 9.24.
4. See above in our discussion of 9.11-12. Also see Wilson, pp. 150-51.
5. Rissi, *Die Theologie*, p. 38; J. Thompson, *The Beginnings*, p. 106.
6. Riggenbach, *Der Brief*, pp. 284-85.
7. Rissi, *Die Theologie*, p 39.

## 4. Εἰσέρχεσθαι and Hebrews

holy of holies.¹ Thus, as seen in 9.11-12, the entry of Christ through the sanctuary refers to his approach and subsequent entry into (εἰς) the holy of holies in heaven.

The single entry of Christ into the direct presence of God is characterized by the seemingly peculiar adverb νῦν. Here the term does not refer to an event first occurring at the time of the Epistle's sending to the readers. Rather this νῦν describes the present time from the moment of the heavenly high priest's session with God. Thus ὁ καιρὸς ὁ ἐνεστηκώς of 9.9 has its parallel in νῦν. With this entry a new age has begun and will continue until Christ comes again (1.6; 9.28).² This 'now' is already the time of salvation (5.9; 9.12, 15).

That Christ entered through the sanctuary and into the holy of holies is seen by the fact that he did so 'now to appear before God'. He entered into the direct presence of God, whereas the earthly high priest only entered into the humanly constructed facsimile of the heavenly, and therefore not into God's actual presence. Furthermore, this new age is marked by Christ's heavenly high priestly activity, characterized by his standing with his blood before God (9.11-12, 24; 12.24).³ This appearing (ἐμφανίζειν) before God is further clarified

---

1. Among those who view the correspondence between the ἄγια and 'heaven' are: Riggenbach (*Der Brief*, pp. 284-85), Michel (*Kommentar*, p. 323), Kuss ('Der Brief', pp. 125-26), Braun (*Hebräer*, p. 282), Hughes (*A Commentary*, pp. 379, 382-83), Traub ('οὐρανός', *TDNT*, 5.527-28), Montefiore (p. 160) J. Thompson (*The Beginnings*, p. 106) and Rissi (*Die Theologie*, p. 39). Hofius (*Der Vorhang*, pp. 70-71), Lünemann (p. 304) and Young (p. 209), are among those who relate heaven to the 'holy of holies'.

2. For this understanding of νῦν, see Michel, *Kommentar*, p. 325; Windisch, *Hebräerbrief*, p. 85; Zimmermann, *Das Bekenntnis*, p. 199; Braun, *Hebräer*, p. 282; Rissi, *Die Theologie*, p. 74. To the contrary, see A. Seeberg, *Der Brief an die Hebräer* (Evangelisch-Theologische Bibliothek; Leipzig: Quelle & Meyer, 1912), p. 108.

3. Because Christ stands before God with his blood in the heavenly holy of holies, we see that he is constantly bearing a reminder of his death ὑπὲρ ἡμῶν. The death of this earthly high priest is inseparable from his subsequent session in the presence of God, as it is both of these elements together that constitute salvation. See our considerations above on 9.11-12. So Cody (*Heavenly Sanctuary*, p. 172) writes that 'the passion and death of Jesus are, in the place of God, necessary for our salvation. Without that stage of the work there would be no entrance into the sanctuary, no achievement of salvation. But that initial, earthly stage of the heavenly liturgy is incomplete, and it receives its perfection and its efficacy in the same way that Christ's priesthood receives its crown of perfection and efficacy: by proceeding on to its term in the sanctuary, where the blood of aspersion, shed on Calvary, is now "speaking better than Abel's" (12.24).'

by the frequent ὑπὲρ ἡμῶν.[1] The context of Heb. makes clear that this appearing on the people's behalf is for the purpose of interceding (6.20; 7.25; cf. Rom. 8.34), although Heb. nowhere explicitly explains the meaning of the 'intercession' performed by the high priest in heaven.[2]

However, in light of the passages in Hebrews where the endangerment of the readership appears imminent (e.g. 6.4-8; 10.26-31) and in view of the fact that the threat of losing the gift already received is a real possibility, Christ's high priestly intercessory role appears to be as one who knows our 'weakness' (4.15).[3] Further, we have seen that already in his earthly life Jesus was a high priest whose offerings (προσφέρειν) while yet on earth were prayers of intercession (5.7-10; cf. Lk. 22.31-32) and we may therefore expect that this same heavenly high priest would continue to intercede before God.[4]

Concerning the period before Christ's 'second' coming, when salvation is available but not yet fully realized and the threat of falling away remains, Grässer is quite correct to write that 'das Eintreten Christi für die Glaubenden die Vergebung gelegentlicher gegen-

---

Thus, as we have seen above, the blood within the holy of holies is not being literally sprinkled, but rather compares typologically to the blood that was sprinkled under the old covenant. This blood borne into the sanctuary by Christ, however, is of a new order—it creates 'forgiveness'—whereas the blood of others was impotent to do so, and the shed blood of Abel cried out for revenge. For instance, see Rissi, *Die Theologie*, p. 81.

1. BAG, p. 257 (ἐμφανίζω). Riggenbach (*Der Brief*, p. 285 n. 72) observes that the probable Old Testament sense is found in Ps. 42.3 (41.3[LXX]). Michel (*Kommentar*, p. 324) allows the meaning of ἐμφανίζειν to refer to entry into the holy of holies, but at p. 325, admits that the addition of ὑπὲρ ἡμῶν adds a 'special and decisive meaning' to the appearing before God.

2. Montefiore (p. 161) remarks that this is counsel on 'our behalf', that is, he is pleading on our behalf. But he further admits that the meaning of this pleading is not known. Others arguing for the 'intercession' of Christ in 9.24 include: R.H. Fuller, 'The Letter to the Hebrews', in *Hebrews–James–1 and 2 Peter–Jude–Revelation* (Proclamation Commentaries; ed. G. Krodel; Philadelphia: Fortress, 1977), p. 16; Loader, *Sohn*, pp. 150, 170; Hagner, *Hebrews*, p. 128; Hughes, *A Commentary*, pp. 382-83 (see, pp. 349-54 for a thorough examination of intercession in Heb.). Braun (*Hebräer*, pp. 282-83) observes that 'zugunsten', e.g. 2.9, is a formulation of the 'Fürbitte' (7.25).

3. Rissi, *Die Theologie*, p. 114.

4. See the discussion above in Chapter 2, section 1. Also, Rissi, *Die Theologie*, pp. 57, 69.

wärtiger Sünden bewirkt'.[1] Further, because Christ stands as mediator when we draw near through prayer, we are able to receive help in times of need (4.16), since Christ constantly holds forth his blood (e.g. 12.24)—the vivid reminder of his death for the human race—before the presence of God.[2] The entry of the high priest before God is therefore inextricably linked with his preceding death, with the actual entry itself referring to his subsequent session before God.[3]

The importance of Christ's death in this presentation is further elucidated by Heb. 9.25-26. It is generally agreed that the εἰσῆλθεν in 9.24 carries over into 9.25 as evidenced by the parallelism between the negative οὐ and its connective οὐδέ.[4] Christ entered in order that he might be with God forever. The actual contrast in 9.25-26 therefore appears to be presented by the careful employment of πολλάκις in 9.25, 26, and ἅπαξ at 9.26, 27, 28. These 'Lieblingsworte' of the author argue convincingly that the achievement of

---

1. Grässer, *Der Glaube*, p. 161. To the contrary, see Loader (*Sohn*, p. 142), who argues that 'die Hilfe für die Versuchten [besteht] darin, dass Jesus für sie bittet. Er bittet nicht um Vergebung für sie, nachdem sie den Versuchungen erlegen sind, sondern um Hilfe für sie, damit sie diesen widerstehen und das Leiden durchstehen können (2.18; 4.15-16; 7.25). Das Thema der Hilfe beschäftigt den Vf auch nach dem paränetischen Abschnitt 3.7–4.13. Hier wird nochmals auf die jetzige Stellung Jesu als Hoherpriester hingewiesen (4.14) und auf seine Fähigkeit, uns in unserer Versuchung zu helfen (4.15). Wie wir ist auch er versucht worden; allerdings gab er nicht nach. Darum werden die Leser ermutigt, vor Gott zu treten, um von ihm Hilfe zu bekommen (4.16). Jesus selbst wird zwar in 4.16 nicht erwähnt, aber seine Tätigkeit als Fürsprecher steht zweifellos im Hintergrund.'

2. See our discussion above of Heb. 4.16. Also see Zimmermann, *Das Bekenntnis*, p. 200.

3. Cody (*Heavenly Sanctuary*, pp. 171) and Spicq (*L'Epître*, 2.136-37), among others, distinguish a three-stage development in the saving activity of Christ: suffering and death, the glorification of Christ (resurrection and ascension), and the establishment of Christ as the source of salvation (session before God). However, this seems to be based on a vertical understanding of the heavens, through which Christ is said to have passed upwards. Thus Cody (*Heavenly Sanctuary*, pp. 175-76) is at a loss to explain the apparent inconsistencies in Heb. 1.3; 8.1; 12.2, where the intervening 'mysteries' between the death and the session before God are absent. So Cody (*Heavenly Sanctuary*, p. 176) inadvertently arrives at the correct statement when he observes that the session is that which perfects the priesthood of Christ, although he misunderstands the spatial arrangement in Heb. It would be far more logical, in light of the two-stage development, to see the resurrection, ascension, and session as one and the same divine activity.

4. E.g. see Westcott, *Hebrews*, p. 273; Riggenbach, *Der Brief*, pp. 385-86; Michel, *Kommentar*, p. 325; Braun, *Hebräer*, p. 283.

Christ requires no repetition.¹ So, whereas the contrasting clauses in 9.25 would appear to argue that προσφέρειν ἑαυτοῦ is hinting at the earthly high priest's presentation of 'strange' blood within the holy of holies, as we have seen, the indivisible character of Christ's death and self-presentation with the blood in the holy of holies permits Heb. to conceive of προσφέρειν as the unitary act encompassing both his earthly sacrifice and his heavenly performance. So O. Michel writes, 'Der Zusammenhang lässt erkennen, dass für den Heb. das Opfer Christi hier auf Erden und seine Vollendung durch den Gang ins Allerheiligste als eine einzige Handlung erscheint'.²

That προσφέρειν makes reference to the death of Christ (9.14, 26-28; 10.14), which is not to be repeated continuously (contrary to the κατ' ἐνιαυτόν offering under the old convenant), is further indicated by the causal conjunction in 9.26a followed by a parallel (πολλάκις) παθεῖν which describes his death. Similarly, at Heb. 13.12 παθεῖν depicts Christ's death outside the gate.³ Thus, the entry of Christ in order to offer himself points back to his death rather than exclusively to his 'entering' with blood (e.g. 9.27-28; 10.14),⁴ because both may be subsumed under the οὐ πολλάκις, which indicates the unique quality of Christ's high priestly sacrifice.

## Heb. 6.19-20

The location of the high priestly entry of Jesus is further clarified at Heb. 6.20, where the aorist εἰσῆλθεν occurs in order to describe the action of Jesus. Jesus 'entered' ὅπου, that is, εἰς τὸ ἐσώτερον τοῦ καταπετάσματος (6.19b) which, as has been seen elsewhere in Heb., describes the once-for-all entry into the holy of holies (9.11, 24-25; 10.20). An Old Testament expression for the entrance of the high priest into the earthly holy of holies is being employed here (Lev. 16.2, 12, 15; Exod. 26.33; cf. Heb. 9.3).⁵ Thus, as in 9.11-12 and

---

1. Delitzsch, 2.129; Westcott, *Hebrews*, p. 273-74; Windisch, *Hebräerbrief*, p. 85; Fiorenza, 'Cultic Language', p. 170; Braun, *Hebräer*, p. 283.
2. Michel, *Kommentar*, p. 325; also, Riggenbach, *Der Brief*, pp. 286-87.
3. Riggenbach, *Der Brief*, p. 287; Windisch, *Hebräerbrief*, p. 85; Moffatt, *Commentary*, p. 132.
4. Young, pp. 208-209.
5. So Michel (*Kommentar*, pp. 253-54) writes, '"Das Innere des Vorhangs" ist eine Umschreibung für das Allerheiligste'. See also Delitzsch, 1.320; Riggenbach, *Der Brief*, 176; Grässer, *Der Glaube*, p. 34 n. 115; Braun, *Hebräer*, p. 191; Rissi, *Die Theologie*, pp. 41-42. For a thorough review of καταπέτασμα, see Braun, *Hebräer*, pp. 191-92.

## 4. Εἰσέρχεσθαι and Hebrews

9.24-25, by the use of εἰσέρχεσθαι the self-sacrifice (i.e. the death) of the high priest Jesus is emphasized.[1] Here again the indivisibility of the earthly Jesus from the heavenly high priest Jesus is maintained, with the recurrence of 'der schlichte Jesusname'.[2]

Heb. 6.20 provides the explanation as to why 'hope' (6.18-19) is able to enter into the holy of holies in heaven. The very same earthly high priest, Jesus (3.1; 4.14), has entered into the heavenly sanctuary 'for us' (ὑπὲρ ἡμῶν).[3] This once-for-all entry 'for us' is also observed at 9.24. Delitzsch is correct to link the ὑπὲρ ἡμῶν to the verb εἰσέρχεσθαι, basing his reasoning on the cultic action of the earthly high priest who 'entered' on behalf of the people (e.g. 5.1-3; 7.28; 8.3; 9.7) and not as their πρόδρομος, although his entry is at the same time an opening of the way for us to be with him.[4]

According to 9.24 and 7.25 the high priest's entry was effected in order to intercede for us but at 6.20 the mention of πρόδρομος further intimates the believer's own subsequent entry and place before God (e.g. Jn 14.2-3).[5] As πρόδρομος, Jesus is the precursor of the believers,[6] the first in a series to follow after him, since he has opened up the way behind the curtain (10.19-22) which had been in place εἰς

---

1. E.g. see Hofius, *Der Vorhang*, p. 88.
2. Michel, *Kommentar*, p. 254.
3. According to Delitzsch (1.321) Heb. 6.20 helps to explain how hope, which is inside the holy of holies, 'brings to present rest our tempest-driven souls, and enables them to outride the storms of worldly life. It is by our having Jesus there already in, enthroned, and working for us within the veil.' Seeberg (p. 73) observes that at Heb. 6.20 we read, 'wodurch der Christ weiss, dass sein Hoffnungsgut an der Stätte Gottes geborgen ist'. See also, Riggenbach, *Der Brief*, p. 177; Hofius, *Der Vorhang*, p. 88.
4. Delitzsch, 1.321. Also see Lünemann, pp. 256-57. To the contrary, see O. Bauernfeind ('πρόδρομος', *TDNT*, 8.235), who sees ὑπὲρ ἡμῶν linked with πρόδρομος. We need not belabor this cultic comparison, however, because the sense of the sentence is the same when applied to Jesus, whether we understand him as one who 'entered for us' or as 'the forerunner for us'. Thus Rissi (*Die Theologie*, p. 56) is correct to note the intermingling of the application of ὑπὲρ ἡμῶν, when he comments that Jesus Christ became the 'forerunner' and 'captain' of salvation (6.19-20; 12.2; cf. 2.10) for his followers in that he was considered to have been in heaven and walking through the sanctuary.
5. Riggenbach (*Der Brief*, p. 177) notes, 'Dorthin ist nämlich Jesus uns zu gut eingegangen (9.12, 24), nicht nur um priesterliche Intercession zu üben (7.25), sondern um auch uns den Eintritt zu ermöglichen und uns dort eine Stätte zu bereiten (Jn 14.2f.)'.
6. So Bruce, *Hebrews*, p. 131, and also E.K. Simpson, 'The Vocabulary of the Epistle to the Hebrews. II', *EvQ* 18 (1946), p. 187.

τὸν καιρὸν τὸν ἐνεστηκότα (9.9).[1] The various depictions of πρόδρομος elsewhere in literature all appear to encompass what Heb. expresses: Jesus is 'das Anfangsglied einer Reihe'.[2] This precursing by Jesus is seen elsewhere in Heb. when he entered, (1) to obtain pardon for us (9.12), (2) to represent us in the presence of God (9.24), and (3) to open up for us an entrance into heaven (10.19-22).[3] This he did by bringing in with him the sign of the perpetual efficacy of his sacrifice, his blood.

Therefore, just as under the old covenant the high priest represented the people of God in the holy of holies on the Day of Atonement— although he was unable to open up a way for them—Jesus has entered with his blood as a perpetual reminder of his sacrifice as 'forerunner'. He is the first of many who will follow (as in a military procession),[4] since by his entry he has forged a way that is now open behind the καταπέτασμα.[5] As has been seen at 9.12, this Christ event which encompassed not only his death but also his unique entry 'secured eschatological redemption'. This reiterates what was said at 5.9 about Jesus who became the 'source of eschatological salvation', which is the ground for all 'hope' (it is the 'Hoffnungsgut' of our 'hoping'), since final and complete salvation, though assured, is not yet fully consummated.[6]

Further description of Jesus' high priestly ministry is portrayed by his entry κατὰ τὴν τάξιν Μελχισέδεκ ἀρχιερεὺς γενόμενος εἰς τὸν αἰῶνα. When Jesus entered behind the curtain he was the high priest after the order of Melchizedek. This phrase provides a further basis

---

1. Lünemann, p. 256; Hofius, *Der Vorhang*, p. 86, Rissi, *Die Theologie*, pp. 80, 99.
2. Braun, *Hebräer*, p. 192, who gives a thorough review of various meanings of πρόδρομος in the Hellenistic literature. See also Bauernfeind, 'πρόδρομος', *TDNT*, 8.235; Simpson, p. 187; C. Spicq, '"Αγκυρα et Πρόδρομος dans Heb. VI.19-20', *Studia Theologica* 3 (1950), pp. 186-87; and most commentaries. Spicq and Bauernfeind especially point to the nautical terms in Heb. as suggestive of a connection between πρόδρομος, ἄγκυρα, and Ἰησοῦς. See below.
3. So Lünemann, p. 256. Braun (*Hebräer*, pp. 192-93) writes, 'Er ist Vorläufer nicht bloss ἡμῶν, wie [MS] 489 verschreibt, sondern ὑπὲρ ἡμῶν; er stellt einen bisher nicht vorhandenen Weg ins himmlische Heiligtum her (10.20); als Heilsführer (2.10); als Urheber ewigen Heils für die ihm Gehorchenden (5.8f.; Bauernfeind), die sich nun freilich selber bewegen müssen (12.1; 13.13)'.
4. E.g. Bauernfeind, 'πρόδρομος', *TDNT*, 8.235, and Simpson, p. 187.
5. Riggenbach, *Der Brief*, pp. 176-77; R.H. Smith, pp. 86-87.
6. See below, and our consideration of 'hope' in Chapter 3 above (on 7.19).

for the certainty of hope considered at 6.19.[1] The use of the aorist participle γενόμενος corresponds to similar contexts at 5.9-10 and 9.12. This is not, however, to suggest that Jesus became high priest solely upon his 'becoming' and 'designation as' a high priest 'after the order of Melchizedek'. We have already seen that Heb. asserts that Jesus is high priest already in his earthly life.[2] A striking parallel to 6.20 is found at 5.9-10, the conclusion to the section which was interrupted by the stern warning at 5.11–6.20. It appears that 5.11–6.20 concludes on the identical note as that which it interrupted at 5.10, thus leading into the discussion of Melchizedek and Christ in Heb. 7.[3]

Heb. 5.9-10 speaks of Christ who was perfected and who became the αἴτιος σωτηρίας αἰωνίου. As has been seen, this clause makes reference to his coming into the direct presence of God in the heavenly holy of holies. This is further described in 5.10 by προσαγορευθεὶς ὑπὸ τοῦ θεοῦ ἀρχιερεὺς κατὰ τὴν τάξιν Μελχισέδεκ. We observe therefore that at 6.20 Jesus' becoming the high priest according to the order of Melchizedek parallels his designation as such by God at 5.10, i.e. both are included in the verb τελειοῦν. Therefore when Jesus was 'perfected' and became a high priest in heaven, he then entered into the heavenly holy of holies, i.e. he had access to God's direct presence.[4] It is precisely this immediate access that distinguishes Jesus' earthly priesthood from his heavenly one.

We have already established that through the Christ event the readership is living amidst 'the good things that have come' (9.11), i.e. in the time of reformation (9.10). Thus the 'hope' in 6.18 may be described as, in fact, a present object and a subjective confidence to

---

1. Grässer, *Der Glaube*, p. 34.
2. See Chapter 2. Also see Michel (*Kommentar*, p. 254) who states, 'Gerade der geschichtliche Jesus ist der Vorläufer'. See also Riggenbach (*Der Brief*, pp. 62 n. 60, 177 n. 81) who comments, 'Bei der starken Betonung der Worte κατὰ τὴν τάξιν Μελχ. ist es unbegründet aus γενόμενος zu schliessen, Jesus sei mit seiner Erhöhung überhaupt erst Hoherpriester geworden'.
3. E.g. Bauernfeind, 'πρόδρομος', *TDNT*, 8.235. G.W. MacRae (*Hebrews* Collegeville Biblical Commentary [Collegeville, MN: Liturgical Press, 1983], p. 27) observes how characteristic this is of most transitional passages in the Epistle: 'They summarize the theme of hope; reintroduce the next topic, a priest like Melchizedek; and give advance warning of a new topic, which "extends beyond the veil"'.
4. For a brief discussion of the sequential arrangement of these events in Heb., see under the discussion of 9.25 in the present chapter.

which the readers are to hold fast (e.g. 4.14).[1] As was seen in our investigation at Heb. 7.19,[2] 'hope' is an objective reality centered in the Christ event ('Hoffnungsgut') which provides the believer with the 'subjective confidence' or 'hoping' (das Hoffen). Without the objective hope which is based on the Christ event and God's oath (6.18) there could be no subjective 'hope'. Here at 6.18-20 ἐλπίς appears to refer to the subjective 'hoping' grounded in the Christ event and the oath which comprise the cornerstone of 'hope'.[3]

This 'hope' is further characterized by the application of a common Hellenistic metaphor for hope, ἄγκυρα.[4] That to which the anchor was attached could be considered 'sure and steadfast'[5] because the nautical metaphor depicts a 'mooring' impervious to the storms and tempests that threaten the 'anchored' object. Thus the hope of the Christian—which is centered in Christ—is described as a sure and steadfast anchor, since 'der Anker im Allerheiligsten ist auf alle Fälle Bild für die Hoffnung'.[6] Insofar as Jesus entered behind the curtain (6.20) and so remains the grounds for hope, the reason why hope is described as a 'sure and steadfast' anchor of 'our soul' is based on the fact that our hope also 'enters behind the curtain'.[7]

---

1. For instance, see Riggenbach, *Der Brief*, p. 175; also Grässer, *Der Glaube*, pp. 32-33; J. Moffatt, *Commentary*, pp. 88-89. D. Guthrie (*The Letter to the Hebrews: An Introduction and Commentary* [Leicester: Inter-Varsity Press, 1983], p. 153) writes: 'It is both set out as an objective reality to be seized and also as a subjective reality to be personally experienced'. So also Westcott, *Hebrews*, p. 162. Hofius (*Der Vorhang*, pp. 85-87) lists proponents of both positions in his footnotes. He rejects the notion of a 'present' ('schon vorhandene') hope in favor of a 'future' ('in Aussicht gestellte') hope which will be realized only at the entrance into the 'Allerheiligste Gottes'. It appears to us, however, that Hofius overlooks the emphasis the author places on the fact that 'entry' into the holy of holies is already a very real possibility, even before the 'rest'.
2. See Chapter 3 above.
3. Lünemann, p. 255; Riggenbach, *Der Brief*, p. 176; and Rissi, *Die Theologie*, p. 97, who writes: ' "Hoffnung" ist hier nicht als Hoffnungsinhalt gemeint, sondern "das Hoffen" '. To the contrary, see Hofius, *Der Vorhang*, pp. 85-86 and n. 210.
4. Michel, *Kommentar*, p. 253. For a discussion of ἄγκυρα, see most commentaries. Also Spicq, ' "Αγκυρα', pp. 185-86.
5. ' "Sicher und fest" ist ebenfalls eine beliebte hellenistische Verbindung'; so Michel, *Kommentar*, p. 253.
6. Therefore, it makes no real difference whether 'hope' or 'anchor' is that which enters into the holy of holies. See Rissi, *Die Theologie*, p. 98; Hughes, *A Commentary*, pp. 234-36.
7. Thus, we do not go so far as Windisch (p. 59); Käsemann (*The Wandering People*, p. 227 n. 155); and Spicq (' "Αγκυρα', p. 186) who identify the anchor

## 4. Εἰσέρχεσθαι *and Hebrews*    181

Whether the conjunction καί is epexegetical, so that the participle has a causal force as maintained by Hofius,[1] is not necessary for us to resolve here. It suffices to say that the 'entering' is a third attribute of the anchor.[2] The present ψυχή is rendered safe and secure from every storm besetting it because 'hope' connects our 'inner life' irrevocably to the holy of holies, to the very presence of God. Insofar as Christians possess 'hope', they are anchored to the holy of holies with open access to God (4.16; 7.19; 10.19-22).

Therefore, in the 'present time' when, indeed, the good things have come, 'hope' is still described as 'entering' (εἰσερχομένη) into the holy of holies, because it characterizes the 'inner' life's predicament of being tempted constantly to drift away from the hope which is founded on Christ. Thus the present participle of εἰσέρχεσθαι (6.19) occurs here. Christians, neglecting as they do always to maintain the proper view of Christ, are continually having to be called back in order 'to hold fast' to the present 'hope' and to trust in the future it portends (i.e. to express faith). So Westcott is correct to describe hope 'as ever entering afresh into the Divine Presence encouraged by past experience'.[3]

This occurrence of the present participle to describe the believers' continual entering behind the curtain with 'hope' appears to reiterate what was observed by the meaning of προσέρχεσθαι, which itself expressed an inner spiritual access to God grounded in hope (e.g. 7.19). The synonymity is most clearly drawn at Heb. 10.19-22, which introduces the conclusion of this central section in Heb. In light of the believers' freedom to enter into the holy of holies,[4] and in view of the

---

as Christ. Rather, the anchor (or hope) is 'grounded' in the Christ-event. It therefore is intimately linked with Christ, but is not Christ himself. E.g. see Michel (*Kommentar*, p. 254) who writes, 'Jesus ist auch nicht einfach mit der Hoffnung identifiziert, weil dann V. 20 überflüssig wäre'. See Attridge, *Hebrews*, p. 184.

1. Hofius, *Der Vorhang*, p. 87 n. 226.
2. Delitzsch, 1.319.
3. Westcott, *Hebrews*, p. 163. Also see Riggenbach, *Der Brief*, pp. 176-77. This constant need to return to 'hope' is best seen in the paraenetical sections. Rissi (*Die Theologie*, p. 113) comments: 'Zur Hoffnung muss der Leserkreis immer wieder zurückgerufen werden'. See further p. 114, where Rissi writes, 'Das ganze Leben des Glaubens darf und soll Ausdruck der Hoffnung werden in allen Anfechtungen und in der ganzen Hilflosigkeit der Gemeinde Jesus der Welt gegenüber'.
4. Regarding the verbal usage of εἴσοδος, see Braun, *Hebräer*, p. 306.

full discussion (10.19-21 is a terse review of 4.14–10.18)[1] of what comprises the Christian hope, the readers are exhorted to do so at 10.22: προσερχώμεθα.[2] We observe, then, that entrance into the presence of God is through prayer and worship, activities which indicate a cleansed conscience that holds fast to 'hope'.[3]

At 7.19 it is through the 'better hope' that we draw near to God—a clear parallel to the statement at 6.19-20 that we enter into the holy of holies through hope. At 4.16 entry into the holy of holies, characterized as 'drawing near to the throne of grace', is accomplished through prayer, i.e. an inner disposition clinging to 'hope'.[4]

So, to conclude, the author appears to have employed the present tense cultic occurrences of εἰσέρχεσθαι (and εἴσοδος) in a manner equivalent to his usage elsewhere of προσέρχεσθαι (for instance, observe the parallelism at 10.19 and 10.22). Both terms describe the current situation of the readers who may approach God and enjoy his direct presence. The apparent reason for this use of εἰσέρχεσθαι here (rather than προσέρχεσθαι) is the presence of a cultic object grammatically requiring such a verb form. Here it is 'entering into' the inner curtain, and such is also the case at 10.19 where entry is 'into' the holy of holies. That Heb., however, prefers to describe the present situation of believers with προσέρχεσθαι is seen at 4.16; 7.19; 10.1, 22; 11.6; 12.22,[5] although the high priestly context of certain passages (e.g. 6.19; 10.19) has compelled the author occasionally to employ εἰσέρχεσθαι. Thus, we shall see how the author of Heb. is able to apply τελειοῦν to both verbs since they both describe the believer's access into the direct presence of God.[6] προσέρχεσθαι and εἰσέρχεσθαι are synonymous cultic terms which are used interchangeably in Heb. as the object necessitates, although the present

---

1. This same point appears to be echoed by Loader (*Sohn*, p. 47) where he writes of 'the summarizing words of 10.19ff., which follow the long section about the sacrifice of Jesus'. See also the section on Heb. 10.21 in Chapter 3 above.
2. E.g. see Rissi, *Die Theologie*, p. 98.
3. See Chapter 3 above.
4. See our discussion above (Chapter 3, on 7.19).
5. At 10.1, Heb. uses προσέρχεσθαι absolutely in order to describe the entry of the high priest into the holy of holies, rather than the typical εἰσέρχεσθαι which was prevalent immediately prior to this in Heb. 9 and in the LXX for the high priestly entry. As we observed, this high priestly entry at 10.1 depicted the people's entry as well, although vicariously.
6. See Chapter 5 below.

tense of προσέρχεσθαι and the aorist tense of εἰσέρχεσθαι are most prominent in the appropriate cultic contexts.

Therefore the believer's 'hope' is already evidence of 'perfection' and 'salvation'. God is accessible through prayer and worship, evidence of a cleansed conscience, since Christ is there as 'forerunner'. The careful distinction maintained by Heb. differentiates between the present circumstance of the readers, who do not yet see God (12.14), and the future hope of this more complete access which is now at least partially enjoyed by the dead in Christ. Christ has entered into the holy of holies (6.20; 9.11-12, 24-25) and appears before God (cf. 7.25). At 12.22-24 Christ is not alone in the heavenly holy of holies. There are also deceased Christians and the Old Testament heroes of faith in the worshipful assembly.[1] Those dead Christians and heroes of faith have also 'entered' into the presence of God and are also perfected (11.40; 12.23).[2]

But even their vision of God is at best partial, for this is not yet the final and complete 'rest'. God still has not exercised his judicial prerogative (12.23). Heb., in agreement with the Apostle Paul at Rom. 8.24, suggests that salvation already occurs in hope, yet presupposes a full and final salvation in the future based on hope.[3] This will occur when Christ comes a second time for salvation (Heb. 9.28; cf. 1.6). It is clear that entry into heaven is not the final 'rest', for Christ who has entered heaven is not himself at 'rest' yet (according to the definition of 'rest' at 4.10) but labors on (6.20; 7.25; 9.24).

The aorist occurrences of εἰσέρχεσθαι therefore emphasize the necessity of their own deaths before Christians can gather around the throne in heaven, seeing God in part[4] and offering the very same worship of prayer and praise as those who draw near on earth. 'To draw near' and 'to enter', therefore, both describe the situation of Christians before the end of time. Heb. most frequently employs the verbs in a manner that distinguishes between different modes of inner, spiritual human existence (i.e. between those living and those dead),

1. See our discussion of Heb. 12.18-24 in Chapter 3 above.
2. The tradition of a depiction of the dead gathered about the throne in heaven is found in several texts; e.g. *4 Macc.* 17.18; *1 En.* 22.1-14; Rev. 6.9; 7.9-17; 15.2.
3. Rissi (*Die Theologie*, p. 98) considers this similarity between Heb. and Paul.
4. Rissi (*Die Theologie*, p. 98) sees 12.14 applying to the occasion of full communion with God at the end-time. However, tradition and Heb. suggest that already the dead in heaven appear to have sight of God, although not yet in the new πόλις.

but both words still relate to the same stage of perfection and salvation, viz. still awaiting the End.

Chapter 5

ΤΕΛΕΙΟΥΝ AND HEBREWS

The problematic character of τελειοῦν and related terms[1] is evidenced by the multiplicity of meanings ascribed to this central concept in Heb. by the history of interpretation.[2] Towards the elucidation of the meaning and purpose of τελειοῦν David Peterson has provided a most helpful survey of several of the major positions and their proponents during the past century,[3] but his own conclusions in *Hebrews and Perfection* are neither particularly illuminating, clear, nor convincing.[4]

1. τελειοῦν (2.10; 5.9; 7.19, 28, 9.9; 10.1, 14; 11.40; 12.23); τέλειος (5.14; 9.11); τελειότης (6.1); τελειωτής (12.2); and τελείωσις (7.11).
2. O. Michel observed that τελειοῦν was a term central for the Epistle's understanding already in 'Die Lehre von der christlichen Vollkommenheit nach der Anschauung des Hebräerbriefes', *Theologische Studien und Kritiken* 106 (1934–35), p. 333. Rissi (*Die Theologie*, p. 102) can write, 'Sie ist in der Auslegungsgeschichte der am meisten umstrittene Begriff der Heilslehre des Heb.' The diversity of meanings is seen also in Loader, *Sohn*, p. 46.
3. See Peterson, pp. 1-20. The authors and their works explicated include: J. Kögel, 'Der Begriff "τελειοῦν" im Hebräerbrief im Zusammenhang mit dem neutestamentlichen Sprachgebrauch', in Friedrich Giesebrecht, R. Kögel, K. Bornhäuser, K. Müller, C. Stange, M. Schulze, W. Lütgert, and P. Tschackert, *Theologische Studien: Martin Kähler zum 6. Januar 1905* (Leipzig: A. Deichert [Georg Böhme], 1905), pp. 35-68; Michel, 'Die Lehre', pp. 333-35, and *Kommentar*, especially pp. 145-46 and 225-29; Käsemann, *The Wandering People*, pp. 133-44 and 217-23; T. Häring, 'Über einige Grundgedanken des Hebräerbriefs', *Monatsschrift für Pastoraltheologie* 17 (1920–21), pp. 260-76; E. Riggenbach, 'Der Begriff der "τελείωσις" im Hebräerbrief. Ein Beitrag zur Frage nach der Einwirkung der Mysterienreligion auf Sprache und Gedankenwelt des Neuen Testaments', *Neue kirchliche Zeitschrift* 34 (1923), pp. 184-85, and *Der Brief*, especially pp. 48-49; Dibelius, 'Der himmlische Kultus', pp. 160-76; Spicq, *L'Epître*, 2.214-25; B. Rigaux, 'Révélation des mystères et perfection à Qumrân et dans le Nouveau Testament', *NTS* 4 (1958), pp. 237-62; A. Wikgren, 'Patterns of Perfection in the Epistle to the Hebrews', *NTS* 6 (1960), pp. 159-67; L.K. Kumar Dey, *The Intermediary World and Patterns of Perfection in Philo and Hebrews* (SBLDS, 25; Missoula, MT: Scholars Press, 1975). Other important works include: G. Delling,

That Heb. interprets related terms in different ways[1] permits us to dismiss the occurrences of τέλειος (5.14), τελειότης (6.1), and τελειότερος (9.11) from our discussion. None of these occurrences alludes to a cultic context, which appears to be the characteristic usage of τελειοῦν in Heb.[2] At 5.14 and 6.1 τέλειος and τελειότης are used to contrast levels of spiritual maturity among Christians able to handle 'solid food', i.e. the 'mature', 'full-grown', and those other Christians who still require elementary doctrines ('liquid milk') for their spiritual nourishment, i.e. the 'babes', 'infants'.[3] At 9.11 the comparative τελειότερος is employed as a synonym for κρείττων, as observed by Dibelius.[4] Thus the terms have been used outside the cultic sphere of meaning.

We have already had occasion to observe not only the close affinities between προσέρχεσθαι and εἰσέρχεσθαι, but also between these

---

'τέλειος, τελειότης, τελειόω, τελείωσις, τελειωτής', *TDNT*, 8.67-87; Loader, *Sohn*, pp. 39-49; M. Silva, 'Perfection and Eschatology in Hebrews', *WTJ* 39 (1976), pp. 61-71; Moe, especially pp. 165-68; and P.J. du Plessis, *'ΤΕΛΕΙΟΣ': The Idea of Perfection in the New Testament* (Kampen: J.H. Kok, 1959), pp. 206-33. Most recently see Rissi, *Die Theologie*, pp. 79 and 102-103, and his earlier 'Die Menschlichkeit', pp. 32-34; also Swetnam, 'Christology', pp. 75-78. Practically all commentaries deal with these terms in some detail, albeit with varying degrees of clarity and understanding. Further works making reference to τελειοῦν may be found in the subsequent notes.

4. See section 1 below. Most recent commentators rely extensively on Peterson: e.g. Wilson, *Hebrews*, and Attridge, *Hebrews*.

1. Loader, *Sohn*, p. 39 n. 2.

2. Thus Dibelius ('Der himmlische Kultus', p. 167 n. 10) writes: 'Ich sehe im folgenden von den zwei Belegen für τέλειος im Hebräerbrief ab; denn 5.14 sind unter τέλειοι die Gereiften zu verstehen im Zusammenhang des bekannten popularphilosophischen Bildes von Milch und fester Speise; von kultischer Bedeutung ist keine Rede (und ebenso gilt τελειότης 6.1 diesem Reifezustand; es heisst eben nicht τελείωσις!). Der Ausdruck "Das grössere und Vollkommenere Zelt" (9.11) aber bezeichnet nichts Kultisches, sondern nur den Grad der Überlegenheit des himmlischen Heiligtums gegenüber dem irdischen, der 7.19, 22; 8.6; 9.23 durch κρείττων ausgedrückt wird'. Rissi ('Die Menschlichkeit', p. 32 n. 9) concurs. Also see A.A. Hoekema, 'The Perfection of Christ in Hebrews', *Calvin Theological Journal* 9 (1974), p. 31.

3. See Best, p. 285; G. Delling, 'τέλειος', *TDNT* 8.77; Sowers, p. 112; J.Y. Campbell, 'Perfection', *IDB*, 3.730; C. Carlston, 'The Vocabulary of Perfection in Philo and Hebrews', in *Unity and Diversity in New Testament Theology: Essays in Honor of George E. Ladd* (ed. R.A. Guelich; Grand Rapids: Eerdmans, 1978), p. 147.

4. Though not stated explicitly, this is implied by Delling, 'τέλειος', *TDNT*, 8.77. See also Best, p. 285.

## 5. Τελειοῦν *and Hebrews*

terms and τελειοῦν.[1] However, before we undertake any further examination of this relationship, it is best if we briefly investigate some of the most frequently held meanings proposed for τελειοῦν.[2]

### 1. Τελειοῦν *and its Meaning*

*The moral-ethical meaning*

The propensity to equate the use of 'perfection' in Heb. with 'moral perfection' has led many to understand Jesus as having been raised to a higher life (i.e. having been made morally perfect), just as the brothers are made perfect by him (2.11).[3] Although Dibelius rejects the consideration of τελειοῦν as a moral category as moot,[4] already Julius Kögel had maintained a thoroughly non-moral understanding of τελειοῦν, since, according to Heb., Christ was morally pure (perfect) from the beginning (4.15; 7.26; 9.14).[5] 'Der stark paränetisch

---

1. See chapters 3 and 4.
2. Attridge (*Hebrews*, pp. 83-87) provides a succinct overview. Obviously a complete investigation of τελειοῦν is beyond the scope of this story, for such an endeavor is worthy of a book-length work in itself—witness the works of D. Peterson and P.J. du Plessis. We shall be content here to critique some of the prevailing opinions regarding τελειοῦν and then to present our own understanding of the term, whereby a coherence throughout the Epistle is maintained.
3. See Cullmann (*Christology*, p. 93) who too easily equates τελειοῦν with the ἁγιάζειν in 2.11. For a good bibliography of others who argue for this 'moral' meaning, refer to Loader (*Sohn*, p. 39 n. 2). Also see Moe, pp. 166-67; Wikgren, pp. 159-67. Delling ('τελειόω', *TDNT*, 8.82 n. 21) is critical of Wikgren's position. This is clearer in the German original.
4. Dibelius ('Der himmlische Kultus', p. 165) writes, 'Nun ist aber die Vokabel "sittlich-religiös" formal wie sachlich dem Neuen Testament fremd; sie trägt neuzeitlich-humanistische Gedanken in den Text ein, und es wäre die höchste Zeit, sie endgültig aus allen Diskussion über urchristliche Begriffe und Gedanke zu verbannen'.
5. Kögel, 'Der Begriff', pp. 41, 55, 62, 65-66. See Peterson, pp. 2-3, 67, 98, regarding Kögel. Further support for this view comes from: Käsemann, *The Wandering People*, pp. 139-40, 143; Lünemann, p. 123; Schierse, *Verheissung*, p. 154; G. Friedrich, 'Das Lied vom Hohenpriester im Zusammenhang von Heb. 4.14–5.10', *TZ* 18 (1962), pp. 106-107; Silva, p. 62; Laub, p. 73; Loader, *Sohn*, pp. 39-40, 41-42, 44-45; A. Stadelmann, 'Zur Christologie des Hebräerbriefes in der neueren Diskussion', *Theologische Berichte* 2 (1973), p. 177; J.Y. Campbell, 'Perfection', *IDB*, 3.730. Hoekema (p. 31) says 'the word τελειόω when applied to Christ cannot mean that He progressed from sinfulness to sinlessness, since the Book of Hebrews itself clearly rules out that interpretation. From 4.15 we learn that Christ is 'one who in every respect has been tempted as we are, yet without sinning', and in 7.26-27 the author states that Christ is a high priest who is 'holy, blameless,

geformte Satz ἔμαθεν ἀφ' ὧν ἔπαθεν τὴν ὑπακοήν (5.8) bedeutet überhaupt nicht, dass Jesus irgendwann ungehorsam war. Er weiss vielmehr, was die Christen in ihrer Situation zu tragen haben, und kann deshalb für sie Fürbitte leisten.'[1] Thus what Christ experienced was not a development of moral character but a full acquaintance with the entire range of human existence and depravity, i.e. his brothers' very situation.

Just as Heb. 5.8 betrays little evidence of a 'Reifeprozess Jesu', neither do the other occurrences of τελειοῦν in Heb.[2] This is seen in the fact that at 2.10; 5.9, and 7.28, the subject of the action is God, not Christ, as evidenced by the passive verbs or construction. In light of the passive usage, the 'perfection' cannot have been any act of acquisition on Christ's part, but of God acting upon him.[3] Furthermore, Jesus 'has perfected' (τετελείωκεν) the believers (10.14) already in the past with continuing effect into the present, as indicated by the perfect tense verb usage. Thus the moral content of the term is absent at 10.14, particularly since its efficacy occurred independently of any act or action by the believers. This, according to Rissi, 'bestätigt ein Blick auf den christologischen Gebrauch des Wortfelds... (2.10; 5.9; 7.28; 12.2)'.[4] Heb. has no interest in categories of moral development.[5]

*Τελειοῦν as 'consecratory sacerdotal'*[6]

The cultic, consecratory content of τελειοῦν (and τελείωσις) in Heb.[7] was thought, very early, possibly to have been derived from the

unstained, separated from sinners', and who does not need to offer sacrifices for his own sins'. Rissi (*Die Theologie*, p. 102) correctly sees the impossibility of moral development at 10.14 with regard to the readers (so also does Campbell), and rightly parallels this to the interpretation of τελειοῦν for Christ as a non-moral category.

1. Loader, *Sohn*, p. 39. This appears to be a reaffirmation of the position held long before by Kögel. See Kögel, 'Der Begriff', pp. 65-66.
2. Loader, *Sohn*, p. 39 n. 2.
3. Friedrich, 'Das Lied', pp. 106-107; Loader, *Sohn*, p. 45. Since God is the subject, du Plessis (p. 214) favors the 'appointment' rather than any notion of a 'gradual acquisitioning' of the office.
4. Rissi, *Die Theologie*, p. 102. Also see Campbell, 'Perfection', *IDB*, 3.730, on Heb. 10.14.
5. This is also confirmed by the occurrence of τελειοῦν in 11.40, according to Kögel, 'Der Begriff', pp. 55-56.
6. This phrase occurs in du Plessis, p. 214.
7. The literature to this discussion is so voluminous that only the most conspicuous works can here be mentioned. Peterson wrestles with this problem throughout

## 5. Τελειοῦν *and Hebrews*

Mysteries, where similar verbs were used to describe the 'initiation' procedures.[1] However, as observed by Dibelius, the Mysteries rely far more frequently upon τελεῖν, τελέται, or μύειν.[2] Thus the suggested link to mystery terminology seems improbable.[3]

On the other hand, a consecration interpretation based on LXX usage has been far more influential. The apparent derivation of τελειοῦν in Heb. from the 'terminus technicus' τελειοῦν τὰς χεῖρας in the LXX, has been used to establish the absolute use of τελειοῦν as a 'terminus technicus' for 'priestly consecration'. The cultic ritual character of τελειοῦν τὰς χεῖρας is well rehearsed in the literature.[4] In the LXX the Hebrew *millē' . . . 'et yād . . .* which characterizes the practice of 'filling of the hand' that symbolically designates the 'consecration of the priest', is rendered not only by the literal formulae ἐμπίμπλαναι τὰς χεῖρας and πληροῦν τὰς χεῖρας, but frequently by τελειοῦν τὰς χεῖρας.[5] τελειοῦν τὰς χεῖρας is an established 'terminus technicus' in both the LXX and in Hellenistic Judaism.[6] This formulaic

his book, with full referencing in the endnotes. Also see du Plessis, esp. pp. 206-33; Delling, 'τελειόω, τελείωσις, τελειωτής', *TDNT*, 8.79-87; Spicq, *L'Epître*, 2.214-25; Westcott, *Hebrews*, pp. 64-68; Michel, *Kommentar*, pp. 225-29. Loader (*Der Sohn*, p. 40 n. 4) offers a concise, recent bibliography on the matter. See further Loader, *Sohn*, pp. 39-49, and add to his bibliography at p. 40, A. Vanhoye, *Old Testament Priests*, p. 133. Most commentaries deal extensively with this discussion.

1. Häring, 'Über einige Grundgedanken', pp. 260-76, and 'Noch ein Wort zum Begriff "τελειοῦν" im Hebräerbrief', *Neue kirchliche Zeitschrift* 34 (1923), pp. 386-89; Windisch, *Hebräerbrief*, p. 45.
2. Dibelius, 'Der himmlische Kultus', p. 166; Carlston, 'The Vocabulary', p. 134.
3. Such is the conclusion of Riggenbach, 'Der Begriff', pp. 188-90; Dibelius, 'Der himmlische Kultus', p. 166; Moe, p. 168; Loader, *Sohn*, pp. 40, 48; Rissi, *Die Theologie*, p. 79.
4. See Peterson, pp. 26-30; Loader, *Sohn*, pp. 40, 47-48. Also see Delling, 'τελειόω', *TDNT*, 8.80-81.
5. Exod. 29.9, 29, 33, 35; Lev. 8.33; 16.32; Num. 3.3. See Loader, *Sohn*, p. 47 n. 2, for further references. Also see Dibelius, 'Der himmlische Kultus', p. 166; Delling, 'τελειόω', *TDNT*, 8.80-81; Peterson, p. 202 n. 41; and commentaries.
6. This assertion seems beyond dispute by scholars. So Loader, *Sohn*, p. 47; Rissi, 'Die Menschlichkeit', p. 34 n. 12, and *Die Theologie*, p. 79. Peterson (p. 28), however, is careful to insist that in the ritual practice of consecration the filling of the hands was but one aspect of an extended ceremony, albeit the most important act in the ritual. He can write, 'It is my contention that the translators of the LXX had in view this literal "filling of the hands" with sacrifices when they rendered the Hebrew expression τελείους τὰς χεῖρας in the Pentateuch. By using τελειοῦν

usage with τελειοῦν has therefore led many to attribute the identical technical character to the absolute occurrences of τελειοῦν.[1] τελειοῦν and τελείωσις occur several times in the LXX without the object, yet in reference to the consecration of priests: e.g. τελείωσις (Lev. 8.33); κριὸς τελειώσεως (Exod. 29.26; Lev. 8.21).[2]

This ignores, however, the diverse ways and disparate contexts in which τελειοῦν is used in the LXX. There is no single uniform sense in which we may understand τελειοῦν, and particularly no grounds to see it as a specific reference to priestly consecration.[3] Thus the cultic consecratory character of τελειοῦν is not grounded in the word itself, but in the context in which the word is situated. τελειοῦν is rendered as 'consecration' in the texts we are considering precisely because the contexts in which it occurs already revolve round the Old Testament ritual and its practice. However, any consideration of τελειοῦν in non-cultic contexts shows clearly that it cannot be a 'terminus technicus' for 'consecration' in the LXX.[4] Instead, τελειοῦν is best

---

and τελείωσις in such contexts, instead of the more literal alternatives, they imparted a particular nuance. They wished to convey the sense that the high point of the consecration ceremony was the action to "perfect" or "qualify" the man himself to act as priest in offering sacrifices to God. Both τελειοῦν and τελείωσις are used here in a purely formal way.' Thus Peterson in no way denies the technical character of the entire phrase τελειοῦν τὰς χεῖρας, although his claim for a purely 'formal' utilization of τελειοῦν will be looked at below.

1. Du Plessis, p. 213; Silva, p. 61. See Delling ('τελειόω', *TDNT*, 8.81-82) where he notes, 'It is obvious why Heb. no longer has τὰς χεῖρας; the way had been prepared for dropping this, cf. Lev. 21.10', thus asserting τελειοῦν to be a technical term already in the LXX. Our consideration of the absolute τελειοῦν occurs below.

2. Such occurrences in the LXX include: Exod. 29.22, 26, 27, 31, 34; Lev. 7.37; 8.22, 26, 27-28, 29, 33; 21.10. See Loader, *Sohn*, p. 47 n. 2. For further references see Riggenbach, 'Der Begriff', pp. 187-89.

3. This is most ardently argued by Peterson (pp. 23-30), who classifies the usages of τελειοῦν in the LXX as formal, religious, and cultic. Highly critical of attempts to view τελειοῦν as meaning 'consecration', he writes, 'When Dibelius argues that the verb in this context is "only explicable as a technical linguistic usage, which is familiar to the LXX translator and his readers, according to which τελειοῦν means "to consecrate", he is making an *unnecessary and unwarranted conclusion*' (Peterson, pp. 28-29 [my italics]). He is equally critical of Delling's similar position regarding τελειοῦν without an object, though he agrees with Delling's assessment of τελειοῦν τὰς χεῖρας, commenting, 'there is nothing to be said against his (Delling's) final assessment of τελειοῦν τὰς χεῖρας as indicating that the priest is able "to practice the cultus"'; cf. Peterson, p. 204 n. 59.

4. Peterson, pp. 24-25.

5. Τελειοῦν *and Hebrews* 191

considered to have a 'general' or 'formal' sense, i.e. 'to complete', 'to fill', 'to make perfect', 'ans Ziel bringen', with a specific rendering dependent solely upon the context itself.[1]

Since most scholars have not recognized the purely formal character of τελειοῦν in the LXX, articulated by the particular context, they have simply transferred the cultic meaning of 'consecration' from LXX over into Heb. This meaning, however, has not been found to have applicability to all occurrences. Therefore, even the staunchest advocates of 'consecration' have had to elaborate their positions, while clinging to the concept itself. This has resulted in confused and all-encompassing attempts at defending the meaning 'consecration', but these attempts approach or resemble more and more the formal usage of τελειοῦν, without their proponents realizing or at least acknowledging this to be the case.[2]

---

1. This point was made already in 1905 by Kögel ('Der Begriff', p. 39): 'Wenn wir diesen wechselnden Gebrauch beobachten, so können wir daraus schon eine Folgerung ziehen, nämlich die, dass τελειόω ein Allgemeinbegriff ist, ohne einen bestimmten Inhalt. Es ist ein rein formaler Ausdruck, der lediglich äusserlich gilt und nichts Bestimmtes einschliesst, welcher erst sein besonderes, näheres Gepräge erhält durch das Object, das ihm beigefügt wird, resp. durch den Zusammenhang, dem er sich eingliedert. Auf dies beides, auf das Objekt und auf den Kontext, kommt es demnach vor allem an, wollen wir den Sinn erfassen, welchen das Verbum im einzelnen Falle hat, und wollen wir in das Verständnis desselben eindringen'. See Kögel again at p. 59. Peterson (e.g. pp. 23, 46-48, 66, 126) repeatedly emphasizes the importance of the context for our understanding of τελειοῦν. Also see Windisch, *Hebräerbrief*, p. 45 ('Die Entscheidung gibt also immer der Zusammenhang') and Rissi, *Die Theologie*, p. 79.

2. This has led to the peculiarly muddled picture of τελειοῦν in Heb., since scholars are continually having to modify their meaning of 'consecration'. For instance, Moe (pp. 166, 168) eventually settles for an interpretation characterizing τελειοῦν as 'nearing God', rather than 'consecration'. Dibelius ('Der himmlische Kultus', pp. 165-68) seems to understand 'Weihe' as that which creates the condition of 'standing before God'. Delling ('τελειόω', *TDNT*, 8.82-84) although he never veers from his position of Heb.'s dependence on the cultic meaning in the LXX, nevertheless defines this consecration as a 'qualifying' or 'putting someone in the position in which he can come, or stand, before God'. So do Bruce (*Hebrews*, p. 44) and Spicq (*L'Epître*, 2.220). Thus, in actuality, τελειοῦν is seen less as meaning 'consecration', and more as depicting the resultant effect of such consecration; i.e. the 'fact' of consecration itself. The ambiguity of meaning among writers is seen in du Plessis (p. 214) who writes that 'This concept expressed in terms of consecration is constituted by the divine decree and ordinance to an office comparable to, but *immeasurably excelling*, that of an ordinary liturgical functionary' (my italics). The comment by du Plessis is so ambiguous as to render its meaning a circuitous obscuring of what he really wishes to say.

So, for instance, M. Silva writes that 'the cultic note provides the background for the use of the term(s) (i.e. τελειοῦν, τελείωσις), but the eschatological exaltation, of Christ, as *the fulfillment of the promise* [my italics], constitutes their concrete designation'.[1]

As we have already observed,[2] the inability of the Old Testament to fulfill the intended 'goal', which has now been successfully attained under the new covenant, is inextricably linked with the concept of τελειοῦν in Heb.[3] This 'general' or 'formal' characterization of τελειοῦν, understood in its various contexts in Heb., depicts τελειοῦν 'nicht von der Priesterweihe, sondern vom Ziel des Priesterdienstes Jesu, vom Eingang ins himmlische Heiligtum, der so wenig Einsetzung ins Hohepriesteramt bedeutet wie der Eingang des irdischen Hohenpriesters ins irdische Heiligtum'.[4]

That τελειοῦν does not mean 'consecration' may thus be determined from the contexts in which it is located in Heb. Loader in particular has illustrated the non-consecratory meaning of τελειοῦν.[5] Furthermore, the consecratory meaning logically asserts that Jesus was not a high priest until his 'perfection' in the heavenly realm. Our

---

1. Silva, p. 67. Whether or not Silva is correct to link the use of τελειοῦν to the LXX cultic usage is not important here. Rather, we wish to emphasize his understanding that in Heb., the 'concrete designation' has to do with 'fulfillment of the promise', that is, it seems to have a 'formal' usage in Heb. Also see Hagner, *Hebrews*, p. 29.
2. See discussions of τελειοῦν in Chapters 3 and 4 above. Also, see the discussion of 'Τελειοῦν in Heb.' below.
3. Sowers (p. 113) agrees, saying that perfection is 'the bringing to completion in the new covenant of that which was anticipated in the old'. Also see J. van der Ploeg ('L'exégèse de l'Ancien Testament dans l'Epître aux Hébreux', *RB* 54 [1947], p. 189). Rissi ('Die Menschlichkeit', p. 33) considers this superseding of the old covenant by the new: 'In Überbietung des AT ist der Sohn als Hoherpriester durch die Himmel hindurchgeschritten, durch das grössere und vollkommenere Zelt, das nicht mit Händen gemacht ist, und zwar hinter den Vorhang, unmittelbar vor das Angesicht Gottes, wo er mit den Königsrechten nach Ps. 110 ausgestattet wird (4.14; 9.18f.; 6.19f.; 6.24; 1.3, 8, 13; 6.12; 8.1f.; 12.2). Das ist das Ziel seines priesterlichen Weges, den er für die Seinen vorangeht (9.24).' See further Peterson, p. 125; Cockerill, p. 86.
4. Rissi, 'Die Menschlichkeit', p. 34 n. 12. Others who describe τελειοῦν as 'ans Ziel bringen (führen)' include Kögel, 'Der Begriff', p. 39; Lünemann, p. 123; G. Friedrich, 'Das Lied', pp. 106-107; Käsemann, *The Wandering People*, p. 140; Strathmann, 'Der Brief', p. 111; Rissi, *Die Theologie*, p. 79.
5. Loader (*Sohn*, pp. 40-47) systematically refutes all such claims that τελειοῦν describes 'Priesterweihe' by carefully analyzing every occurrence in Heb. See Best, p. 285; Riggenbach, *Der Brief*, p. 48 n. 21.

## 5. Τελειοῦν *and Hebrews*

investigation of the high priestly christology, and of Heb. 2.17 in particular, argues against this notion.[1] From his incarnation onward, Jesus' entire service was that of a high priest,[2] so that his 'designation' as heavenly high priest (e.g. 5.9-10) was simply the divine manifestation and affirmation of his true being.[3] Therefore 'τελείωσις gehört zu den Vorstellungen, die der Verfasser benutzt hat, um die gegenwärtige Stellung Jesu hervorzuheben, aufgrund derer er sein Trostwort über die Tätigkeit Jesu als fürsprechender Hoherpriester entwickelt'.[4]

Precisely what τελειοῦν means in Heb. will be examined in more detail subsequently. It suffices to say at this point that τελειοῦν does not mean 'consecration', because such a meaning is inconsistent with (1) the contexts in which τελειοῦν occurs, and (2) the high priestly role which Jesus already had during his earthly existence.

Here perhaps a brief word should be said about the 'vocational', or 'qualificational', interpretation of τελειοῦν which D. Peterson seeks to defend. Despite his distancing himself from the 'consecrational' meaning of τελειοῦν, his own 'vocational' (i.e. 'qualificational') meaning incorporates the similar position that views Jesus as incrementally or progressively qualifying himself for that which he did not already possess, i.e. the high priesthood.[5] Thus Peterson appears merely to be elaborating on the careful avoidance of the term

---

1. See Chapter 2 above. We suggest that Christ is identified as the 'high priest after the order of Melchizedek' upon his being 'perfected'.
2. Cockerill (p. 183) writes: 'When Christ's death is seen in comparison with the sacrifices of the Day of Atonement—a comparison of which our author makes extensive use, then He must have already been a priest on earth. The Day of Atonement sacrifices enabled the high priest to approach the presence of God in the Holy of Holies'. See Rissi, *Die Theologie*, pp. 52, 62, 69.
3. Michel, *Kommentar*, p. 229. See Rissi, 'Die Menschlichkeit', pp. 33-34; idem, *Die Theologie*, pp. 52, 69.
4. Loader, *Sohn*, p. 47. We should insist on his clarifying Jesus' role as high priest and intercessor in heaven.
5. Peterson (pp. 103, 118 [relying on Michel, *Kommentar*, p. 224]), says that the perfecting of Jesus is 'his proving in temptation, his death as a sacrifice for sins, and his heavenly exaltation'. These developments 'qualified' him to 'save absolutely'. See also Peterson, pp. 70-71, for instance: 'If the perfecting of Christ is his qualification to act as Saviour and high priest of his people, it is clear that our writer envisages a *whole sequence of events* as equipping him to act in this way' (emphasis Peterson's). Also see Peterson, p. 98 and Attridge, 'New Covenant', pp. 94-95.

'consecration' already practiced by G. Delling.[1] However, this presumes that Jesus was not a high priest already on earth, a position we have shown to be in error, since Jesus was already performing 'offerings' in his earthly life (5.7; cf. 5.1-3).[2]

With regard to his consideration of the believers' perfection, Peterson's position is much closer to our own.[3] Although he persists in describing the believers as 'qualified' through Christ's acts (e.g. 10.14), the point in Heb. seems to have very little to do with any description of the qualification of believers and far more to do with the simple fact and stark reality that believers *now* possess access to God,[4] which will be fully actualized only in the future.[5]

*The paideutic meaning of* τελειοῦν
The proposed influence of Hellenistic philosophy (and Philo in particular)[6] on Heb. is in part based on the frequent use of τελειοῦν, and its cognates, to refer to the highest plateau of attainment which is the mystic vision of God.[7] This 'perfection' is acquired through the

---

1. See Delling, 'τελειόω', *TDNT*, 8.81-84, who also avoids speaking of 'consecration', but rather speaks of 'being out in a position to come before God', and 'being qualified to come directly before God'.
2. E.g. see Chapter 2 above. Peterson (p. 175) understands the perfecting of Christ as a 'process' culminating in his being a 'perfect' high priest. This then is the difficulty with the recent positions of both Attridge and Wilson, who rely heavily on Peterson's work. Attridge, Wilson, and Swetnam ('Christology', p. 77) are all reluctant to see Jesus as already a high priest on earth.
3. Peterson, pp. 126-67; Attridge, 'New Covenant', p. 96, is also closer to our view here.
4. So Peterson was correct when he intimated already at p. 32: 'I shall argue from several contexts that the perfecting of believers is to be understood in terms of "drawing near to God"'. However, at p. 166 he notes that 'they are *perfected* as would-be worshipers, those who would draw near to God'. They do, however, already have this access; it is not something solely to be anticipated in the future.
5. Peterson, p. 167. Our own consideration of the eschatological elements in Heb. will appear in our Conclusion. Insofar as Peterson reckons the final state to be 'presence with God in heaven' he conforms with most authors who presume that τελειοῦν and κατάπαυσις speak of the identical final, heavenly state. On this point, we will disagree. Wilson (p. 182) echoes Peterson here.
6. For instance, see Dey, *The Intermediary World*. However, to the contrary, see Williamson, *Philo*, a work Dey ignores.
7. For a listing of such occurrences, see Delling, 'τελειόω', *TDNT*, 8.79-80; Peterson, pp. 30-33; Loader, *Sohn*, p. 48; Carlston, pp. 133-60.

## 5. Τελειοῦν and Hebrews

progress attained by teaching, practice, or discipline.[1] However, this progression to perfection is so much tied to 'above all the ethical'[2] that it would suggest little continuity with Heb. As was seen above, perfection in Heb. has nothing to do with the learning of ethical purity.[3] So C. Carlston rightly emphasizes that 'crucial Philonic emphases are missing: the interest in philosophy, the notion of progress in virtue, the strong stress on the ethical and the sense of "training" or pedagogy'.[4] We need, therefore, to locate our understanding of τελειοῦν outside the paideutic.

### 2. Τελειοῦν in Hebrews

In view of the inadequacy of the above-considered proposals for the meaning of τελειοῦν in satisfying the contexts in which it occurs, we were compelled to recognize the 'general' or 'formal' usage as the most suggestive and applicable to literally every occurrence of τελειοῦν in the Epistle.[5]

In a manner suggesting that the author of Heb. desires to clarify his formal understanding of τελειοῦν for his readers (lest they misunderstand him) parallel concepts are introduced in 2.9 and 2.10, the initial occurrence of τελειοῦν in the Epistle. At 2.10 Jesus' being brought to perfection appears as the direct consequence of his suffering and death.[6] The parallel drawn in 2.9-10 suggests that Jesus' being 'crowned with glory and honor' (2.9) corresponds to his 'being

---

1. E.g. see Dey, pp. 68-74. With regard to Jesus' own education to perfection, refer to Dey, pp. 222-25.
2. Carlston, p. 145. For instance, he writes, 'It is unthinkable to Philo that access to the heavenly realm should be available to any but the worthy.'
3. See our discussion above on 'The moral-ethical meaning of τελειοῦν'.
4. Carlston, p. 148.
5. The 'general' meaning, 'to bring to a particular goal or heavenly destination' (for which Kögel was roundly criticized by Käsemann [*The Wandering People*, p. 140] for no longer maintaining the 'neutral' 'leading to the goal'), has already been seen to apply to several texts (e.g. 10.1; 5.1-10; 7.19; 7.11; 9.9; 7.25) in our previous examination of προσέρχεσθαι. Also see below for a further look at these and other occurrences.
6. W. Michaelis ('πάθημα', *TDNT*, 5.934) notes that the plural παθήματα refers to the 'total process of crucifixion', so that 2.9-10 refers to 'suffering which consists in death'. Thus, the similarity with 5.8-10 is observed, as well as with 7.28. See Rissi, *Die Theologie*, p. 79. This is what we have already seen with the application in Heb. of εἰσέρχεσθαι to Jesus.

brought to perfection' (2.10).[1] The context makes plain that his 'crowning with glory and honor' refers to his entering into the heavenly holy of holies, that is, the place of divine glory to which Jesus was promoted after his death.[2] This is in keeping with the other contexts in Heb. where, after his death on the cross, Christ is described as entering into God's heavenly presence and taking his place at the right hand of God (e.g. 1.3; 8.1; 10.12; 12.2; cf. Rev. 3.21). To consider that God has led Jesus to the goal is therefore to understand his 'perfection' as his 'glorification' or 'entry' into the heavenly holy of holies.[3]

Already at 5.9-10 we have observed the affinity between τελειοῦν and the earthly high priest's act of entering into the holy of holies (5.1-3).[4] However (as seen at 2.9, where Christ's death precedes his 'perfection'), this affinity is also in evidence at 5.9-10, for παθεῖν (5.8) is immediately followed by the passive participles τελειωθείς and προσαγορευθείς. This suggests that the consequence of his death (i.e. suffering) was the simultaneous perfection or entry into God's presence and his designation as ἀρχιερεὺς κατὰ τὴν τάξιν Μελχισέδεκ.[5]

---

1. The parallel character of 2.9 and 10 is recognized by many scholars: Rissi, *Die Theologie*, p. 79; Laub, p. 72; Schierse, *Verheissung*, p. 154; Riggenbach, *Der Brief*, p. 48 n. 21; Lünemann, p. 124; Jeremias, 'Hebräer 5.7-10', p. 321. Loader (*Sohn*, p. 43) sees the parallel for τελειοῦν within 2.10 itself. There εἰς δόξαν ἀγαγόντα parallels τελειοῦν (e.g. Käsemann, *The Wandering People*, p. 144). He is correct insofar as he understands that τελειοῦν means the appearing before God's very presence subsequent to his death.

2. For references to the designation of the place of δόξα as God's domain in heaven in relevant literature, see M. Dean-Otting, *Heavenly Journeys: A Study of the Motif in Hellenistic Jewish Literature* (Judentum und Umwelt, 8; Frankfurt am Main: Peter Lang, 1984), pp. 50-58, 286-88; Kittel, 'δόξα', *TDNT*, 2.242-47; O. Schmitz, 'θρόνος', *TDNT*, 3.160-67.

3. Rissi, *Die Theologie*, pp. 79, 102; Kögel, 'Der Begriff', pp. 56 n. 1, 67-68; Käsemann, *The Wandering People*, p. 144; Michel, *Kommentar*, p. 146; Silva, p. 65.

4. See above Chapter 3, section 2 and Zimmermann, *Die Hohepriester-Christologie*, p. 21. The chiastic structure of 5.1-10 is acknowledged by Delitzsch, 1.225; Michel, *Kommentar*, p. 214 n. 1; Bruce, *Hebrews*, pp. 88-106; Rissi, *Die Theologie*, p. 62.

5. Kögel ('Der Begriff', p. 63) rightly asserts that the participles in 5.9 and 5.10 are bound together and ought not to be thought of as separate events in time. Also see Jeremias, 'Hebräer 5.7-10', p. 321; Michel, *Kommentar*, p. 224; Rissi, 'Die Menschlichkeit', p. 33; Zimmermann, *Die Hohepriester-Christologie*, p. 12 n. 27.

## 5. Τελειοῦν *and Hebrews*

Accordingly, 5.1-10 clarifies precisely when Jesus was a high priest. By its language of intercession and by the parallel with Heb. 5.1-3, 5.7 shows that he was already an acting high priest during his earthly life, and 5.9-10 describes his designation as a high priest after the order of Melchizedek as characterizing his heavenly office. Thus Rissi writes,

> Wir haben hier für den Hohenpriesterbegriff dieselbe Problematik vor uns wie für den Sohnesnamen, der Jesus von Anfang an eignet, und den er doch nach 1.4 zu einem bestimmten Zeitpunkt erst κεκληρονόμηκεν. Verständlich wird dieser scheinbare Widerspruch allerdings, wenn wir προσαγορεύειν nicht als Amtseinsetzung, sondern als die himmlische Proklamation, die öffentliche Enthüllung des geheimen Wesens des Erlösers, dessen, was er schon auf Erden in geheimnisvoller Verhüllung war, verstehen.[1]

Once again at 7.28 we have seen portrayed the characteristic dichotomy between the Old Testament high priest and Jesus the high priest.[2] In fact, the emphatic τετελειωμένον starkly contrasts the weakness of the Old Testament priesthood (7.26-27) with the superiority of the new order.[3] The similarity of 7.28 to 2.10 and 5.9 is seen by the emphasis on perfection that results from Christ's death which is expressed in 7.27: τοῦτο γὰρ ἐποίησεν ἐφάπαξ ἑαυτὸν ἀνενέγκας.

Such being the case, τελειοῦν appears to characterize the final stage of the high priesthood of Jesus Christ: he was designated a high priest κατὰ τὴν τάξιν Μελχισέδεκ when he died and entered into the true holy of holies in heaven, taking his seat at the right hand of God in accordance with Psalm 110. Where Jesus is concerned, τελειοῦν has

---

1. Rissi, 'Die Menschlichkeit', pp. 33-34. Rissi (*Die Theologie*, p. 69) reiterates the same, saying, 'Der Verfasser unterscheidet das Priestertum Jesu auf Erden von demjenigen im Himmel. Hoherpriester war Jesus schon auf Erden, aber erst im Himmel wurde er "der Priester nach der Weise des Melchisedek", von Gott dazu eingesetzt und proklamiert (5.10). Dieses himmlische Amt ist abhängig von seinem irdischen Dienst. Es besteht darum keine Spannung, kein Widerspruch und keine chronologische Aporie zwischen seinem Hohepriestersein und seinem Hohepriesterwerden.' Thus Rissi refutes the claims of Braun: see Chapter 2. Loader (*Sohn*, p. 44) comments that τελειοῦν is descriptive of Jesus' 'Einsetzung in das Priesteramt'. Since Loader goes on to reject the sense of 'consecration' here, he appears to agree with Rissi that the distinctive character of the priestly office to which Jesus attained in heaven was that it was κατὰ τὴν τάξιν Μελχισέδεκ.
2. See Chapter 3, section 2.
3. Cockerill, pp. 179-84. Thus 7.28 proffers a 'concluding contrast which summarizes the argument in Heb. 7'. See also Loader, *Sohn*, p. 44. He notes that τελειοῦν cannot be understood to mean 'consecration' since καθίστημι (5.1; 8.3) speaks of consecration. Thus the implied καθίστημι in 7.28b cannot mean the same thing as τελειοῦν.

exactly the same meaning as εἰσέρχεσθαι in Heb. It denotes being in the direct and unmediated presence of God. The passive constructions serve to qualify the actors involved. τελειοῦν (2.10; 5.9; 7.28) is an act of God, whereas εἰσέρχεσθαι describes the activity of Jesus through which God's perfecting is realized. As far as Jesus is concerned, this is accomplished after his death. However, with reference to individuals (i.e. believers), τελείουσθαι is not contingent upon their deaths, and to that subject we now turn.[1]

τελειοῦν 'designates Christ's attaining to his heavenly office as well as the attaining of the believers to the heavenly cultus (incorporation)'.[2] Thus the cultic contexts in which τελειοῦν occurs in Heb. (7.11, 19; 9.9; 10.1, 14) serve to contrast the old covenant cult and its ritual practice—through which access to God was presumed—with the actual realization of such access only under the new covenant.[3] According to Heb. ritual practice was entirely inadequate to perfect its practitioners. The Old Testament law made nothing perfect (9.9; 10.1). Perfection was unattainable through the levitical priesthood (7.11). The sacrifices offered according to the old covenant arrangement could not perfect the worshiper as far as the conscience was concerned (9.9). Under the old covenant no one, not even the high priest, could enter into the direct, true presence of God. The closest the high priest came was his approach into the 'antitype', the earthly and material holy of holies.

Heb. therefore employs τελειοῦν with reference to the old covenant ritual in order to contrast its inadequacy with the real efficacy of the Christ sacrifice—which ushered in the 'present age' (9.9), the time of the 'good things that have come' (9.11).[4] Using Old Testament sacerdotal material, Heb. contrasts two very different orders of real access, whereby the Old Testament cult appears only as a portent of the final, superior access wrought by Christ for believers.

1. Loader (*Sohn*, p. 45) incorrectly concludes that the 'perfection' of the believers occurs only after their death. This is contradicted several times in Heb. where τελειοῦν describes their present circumstance (e.g. 10.14; 11.40), as we shall see.
2. Johnsson, 'Defilement and Purgation', p. 374. Carlston (pp. 146-47) acknowledges that 'perfection' specifies the 'translation to the heavenly realm' (e.g. 12.23; 2.10; 5.9; 7.28; 10.14; 11.40).
3. This has been discussed in Chapter 3 section 2 above, in the subsections on Heb. 10.1 and 7.19.
4. Rissi (*Die Theologie*, pp. 102-103) appears to agree with this division of the former and the present age (which was 'future' to persons living under the old covenant). For comments on these verses see Loader, *Sohn*, pp. 41-42.

## 5. Τελειοῦν and Hebrews

That this 'perfection' available to believers is a present possibility has already been seen in our look at 10.14.[1] 'Perfection' as applied to individuals does not imply their personal deaths. Rather, Christ's death as past event effects the present 'access' of believers, which explains the use of the perfect verb, τετελείωκεν.[2]

But how, then, is this access of believers explained? As we previously observed in our discussion of προσέρχεσθαι,[3] the drawing near to God, the access they realized was a spiritual approach, through worship and prayer. This is precisely the access to God enjoyed by believers when perfection is spoken of. Therefore Rissi is correct to propose that the 'Unterschied zwischen der Vollendung des Christus und der Seinen beruht darauf, dass seine Vollendung seinen endgültigen Einzug ins himmlische Heiligtum bedeutet, während die Glaubenden noch auf Erden leben und erst im Gebet den Zugang zum Thron als die Hoffenden findet. Ihre Vollendung ist noch auf das innere Leben beschränkt.'[4] How could it be otherwise? For the believers addressed have not yet reached the point of shedding blood, i.e. death (12.4).

This 'inner spiritual access' is seen explicitly in 9.9 and implied at 10.1, 14, where the human conscience is that which is spoken of as being perfected (i.e. attaining access to God).[5] At 9.9 the perfection spoken of is of 'the worshiper according to the conscience or, as far as the conscience is concerned' (κατὰ συνείδησιν τελειῶσαι τὸν λατρεύοντα).[6] Thus the worshiper enters into God's presence through the 'inner self' (ἄνθρωπος). This is the meaning of perfection for believers, and it is also what we saw it meant for the readers to 'draw near to God'. Therefore προσέρχεσθαι and τελειοῦν are equivalents (e.g. as were εἰσέρχεσθαι and τελειοῦν) except that the agent who effects perfection is Jesus, whereas believers realize perfection by 'drawing near'.

---

1. See above, present chapter, section 1, under 'The Moral and Ethical Meaning'. B. Lindars ('The Rhetorical Structure of Hebrews', *NTS* [1989], pp. 393, 398 n. 1) too readily links 'perfection' with 'rest', thereby characterizing 'perfection' as future access.
2. So, for instance, Peterson, pp. 152, 167; Rissi, *Die Theologie*, p. 102.
3. See Chapter 3.
4. Rissi, *Die Theologie*, p. 102
5. Silva, p. 67.
6. Most translations of Heb. 9.9 incorrectly make the 'conscience' the object, when clearly the worshiper is the object who is then further clarified by the κατὰ συνείδησιν.

Perfection for the believers is the present access to God's heavenly sanctuary which they enjoy already, not at some future time when they die. Thus τελειοῦν in Heb. encompasses the distinctive significance we found for προσέρχεσθαι and εἰσέρχεσθαι and relies on the context in order to determine whether it is access during life or after death.

This is consistently carried out even with respect to the dead righteous who are characterized as 'perfected' since the death of Christ (11.40; 12.23).[1] These deceased Christians and Old Testament heroes of faith may be said to have entered into the presence of God, as characterized by their worshipful assembly and their communion with Jesus and the angels.[2]

Thus we may conclude that τελειοῦν serves to describe the 'attaining to the goal', which is the direct presence of God. When used of the living believers it bespeaks a present reality and parallels the Epistle's cultic use of προσέρχεσθαι. When dealing with Jesus Christ and the dead faithful it parallels Heb.'s usage of εἰσέρχεσθαι. In both situations, we have shown that the final goal has not yet been reached—since Christians are still alive, since God is still Judge, since Christ is still at work.

τελειοῦν in Heb., then, does not characterize the final state of 'rest' (κατάπαυσις), but more correctly an antepenultimate and penultimate stage in the chronology of the eschatological age.[3] The importance of the initial consideration of τελειοῦν by the author in 2.9-10 becomes evident. Prior to any discussion of the 'rest' in 3.1–4.13, the author carefully underscored his understanding of τελειοῦν as 'access to God', but only after first firmly establishing that this was by no means the final access, since the first two chapters of Heb. already hold out the expectation of a new world at 1.6, 10-12, 13 and 2.5, 8.

1. See the discussion concluding the examination of Heb. 12.22-24 (Chapter 3, section 2, above). Also refer to Loader, *Sohn*, pp. 42-43, and Rissi, *Die Theologie*, p. 103.
2. See our previous consideration of this above in the concluding remarks on Heb. 6.19-20 (Chapter 4, section 2).
3. The one possible reference to this effect is at Heb. 7.25. See the discussion of Heb. 7.25 in Chapter 3, section 2, above. Yet, interestingly, there alone a synonym for τελειοῦν appears, i.e. σώζειν, which as we have seen elsewhere in Heb. possesses both present and future meanings. Zimmermann (*Das Bekenntnis*, pp. 108-109) sees 7.25 as part of a larger body of traditional material employed by the author which, we argue, could explain this single occurrence of σώζειν as a synonym for τελειοῦν.

CONCLUSION

From our investigation we may conclude that the author of Heb. has made a thoughtful and intentional distinction between the cultic occurrences of προσέρχεσθαι and εἰσέρχεσθαι in his Epistle. Just as the LXX distinguishes the meanings of the verbs when located in a cultic context,[1] Heb. maintains this distinction. In Heb., on the one hand, the cultic προσέρχεσθαι is used with reference to the present readership. εἰσέρχεσθαι, on the other hand, occurs in the aorist tense and points to a past completed event. Both, however, converge in the verb τελειοῦν, which in Heb. consistently means to have access to the heavenly holy of holies, or to be in the presence of God.

The careful distinction maintained in Heb. is, therefore, a matter of life and death. Those living draw near or approach God. They have been granted the access to God which is appropriate to their still tangible, corporeal form of present, earthly existence. They have access to God 'as far as the conscience is concerned' (Heb. 9.9), that is, through prayer and worship (both expressions of the inner ψυχή) they approach the holy of holies. The deceased—the first-born who are enrolled in heaven, the spirits of just men made perfect—who are currently gathered around the throne (Heb. 12.22-24) have 'entered' into the heavenly holy of holies, i.e. into God's very presence (12.23).[2] Heb. further characterizes their present state as 'perfection' (e.g. Christ: 2.10; 5.9; 7.28; others: 11.40; 12.23).

1. See Chapter 2, section 1 (on προσέρχεσθαι in the LXX), and Chapter 3, section 1 (on εἰσέρχεσθαι in the LXX), above.
2. This motif is found elswehere in apocalyptic and concurrent literature, e.g. Rev. 6.9; 7.9-19; 15.2; *4 Macc.* 17.5, 18; 18.23; *1 En.* 22.1-14; 39; 40.5; 61.12; 70.4; 71; 103; *4 Ezra* 2.42-48; 7.28, 88-101; 13.52; 14.9, 49; *Apoc. Ezra* 1.9; *T. Job* 39.12; 52.10; *Asc. Isa.* 9.6-42. Most of these references to deceased persons around the throne or before God speak of a temporary resting place, and anticipate a final stage in the apocalyptic drama that is yet to occur. For a look at relevant literature, see P. Volz, *Die Eschatologie der jüdischen Gemeinde im neutestamentlichen Zeitalter nach den Quellen der rabbinischen, apokalyptischen, und apokryphen Literatur* (Tübingen: Mohr [Paul Siebeck], 1924), pp. 256-72. Also see Wilhelm

This access, entry, or perfection, however, is not the final situation of the faithful. The eschatological dimension in Heb. cannot be ignored. Although the readers and the faithful dead have a present access to God, this is by no means the last word because the judgment has yet to take place (Heb. 6.2; 9.27; 10.27, 30-31; 11.6, 26; 12.23, 29; 13.4); Jesus still works (Heb. 7.25; 9.24; 4.10); and he is to come again for salvation (9.28; 1.6, 13; 2.5; 10.13, 25, 37). Thus, the present 'salvation' accessible through hope, and characterized by τελειοῦν, is to be transcended by a final salvation which will come at the parousia of Christ (Heb. 9.28).

The cultic occurrences of the verbs τελειοῦν, προσέρχεσθαι, and εἰσέρχεσθαι do not therefore indicate the actual presence of the final 'rest'. Rather they anticipate the End of Time that is yet to come.[1] Thus we may assert that to have access to God in the heavenly holy of holies is not the 'rest' (κατάπαυσις) which was mentioned in Heb. 3.1–4.13 and derived from Psalm 95 and Genesis 2. The 'rest' typology employed juxtaposes the inability of the old covenant people of God to enter the 'rest' (i.e. the land) with their antitype, i.e. the present readership, and the prospect of their entry into the 'rest' of God, which, correspondingly, is not yet, although it is hoped for.[2] Precisely because the perfection of believers is a present reality, whereas the 'rest' remains that after which Christians are exhorted to strive (4.11), we may not so facilely equate 'perfection' and 'rest', as is even done by the staunchest advocates of the view that the writer of

---

Boussett, *Die Offenbarung Johannis* (MeyerK, 16; rev. edn; Göttingen: Vandenhoeck & Ruprecht, 1906), pp. 270, 285-87, 393; Hofius, *Katapausis*, p. 97.

1. The μέχρι τέλους (3.6, 14) points to the parousia of Christ. See Hofius, *Katapausis*, pp. 57 and 180 n. 356, and Rissi, *Die Theologie*, p. 15.

2. On the future realization of the 'rest' for the people of God, see Rissi, *Die Theologie*, pp. 13-21, 127-28; R. Schnackenburg, *The Moral Teaching of the New Testament* (Freiburg: Herder, 1965), p. 374; J.Y. Campbell, 'Rest', *IDB*, 4.37-38; Moffatt, *Commentary*, p. 51; Michel, *Kommentar*, p. 185; Lindars, p. 393; D.J. McLeod, 'The Doctrinal Center of the Book of Hebrews', *Bibliotheca Sacra* 146 (1989), p. 300. To the contrary is H.W. Attridge, '"Let us Strive to Enter that Rest." The Logic of Hebrews 4.1-11', *HTR* 73 (1980), pp. 279-88, who rejects this typology by comparing it with the logic of the new and old covenant discussion at Heb. 9–10 (pp. 286-87). It becomes clear that how one interprets a specific typology will determine his or her approach to and understanding of Heb. For Attridge (p. 283) the 'rest' is 'a share in God's "sabbatical" repose'. Attridge ('New Covenant', p. 98) insists that faithful Christians may now enter God's rest. However, a true parallel to the Exodus story would deny any such present rest. 'Perfection' and 'rest' are synonymous for Attridge (*Hebrews*, pp. 126-28).

Heb. held to an eschatological worldview. By situating themselves in an inextricable quagmire of confused reasoning they argue that the 'rest' is entered, but yet will somehow still be entered into.[1] They do not deny the future nature of the 'rest', but they incorporate a present access as well, and this finds absolutely no basis in the text of Heb. itself.[2]

A similar difficulty is encountered by those who wish somehow to combine Hellenistic and apocalyptic strands of expectations, for they too are forced to consider 'rest' as a present, accessible reality, as well as a futuristic 'Jenseits' phenomenon.[3]

---

1. This is the case with Barrett ('The Eschatology', p. 372). There he states that the '"rest", precisely because it is God's, is both present and future; men enter it, and must strive to enter it. This is paradoxical, but it is a paradox which Hebrews shares with all primitive Christian eschatology'. At p. 391, he notes that 'in faith' persons now enter into the rest. Also, Hofius (*Katapausis*, p. 142) based on his misunderstanding of Heb.'s use of the heavenly city in 12.22, states, 'Gottes Volk ist bereits an den Toren der kommenden Stadt angelangt und gehört kraft der göttlichen Verheissung und Berufung nicht mehr dem vergehenden Aeon, sondern der neuen Welt an'. Quoting O. Kuss, he continues, 'Es ist schon die andere Welt, die Welt Gottes, die eschatologische Wirklichkeit, von der die Gemeinde getragen wird, sie steht grundsätzlich schon in dem Raum, zu dem das himmlische Jerusalem gehört'. Since Hofius and Barrett do not see the temporal distinction between τελειοῦν and 'rest', they are forced into untenable explanations for the already–not yet description of the 'rest'. Berthold Klappert (*Die Eschatologie des Hebräerbriefs* [Theologische Existenz heute, 156; München: Chr. Kaiser, 1969], pp. 54-58) although avoiding the use of 'rest' gives evidence of this same misunderstanding. G. von Rad ('"There Remains Still a Rest for the People of God": An Investigation of a Biblical Conception', in *The Problem of the Hexateuch and other Essays* (trans. E.W. Trueman Dicken; Edinburgh: Oliver & Boyd, 1966], p. 99) suggests that the 'rest' is only attained 'after this life'. While this is true, it ignores the fact that death itself is not the primary component that determines the enjoyment of the 'rest'. Essential is, rather, the 'parousia' when everything will be shaken, etc. (12.26-28). Also see H.A. Lombard, 'Κατάπαυσις' in the Letter to the Hebrews', *Neot* 5 (1971), pp. 67-69.

2. This is seen at Heb. 4.3, where εἰσερχώμεθα is future in its force, or at least anticipating something which will be realized. See for instance Moffatt, *Commentary*, p. 51; Buchanan, *To the Hebrews*, p. 71; Rissi, *Die Theologie*, p. 18 n. 43. Wilson (p. 82) concedes this possibility. Contra, cf. Attridge, *Hebrews*, p. 126. Precisely how Attridge reconciles 4.3 with 4.11 is not considered.

3. For instance, see the recent contribution by E. Grässer, 'Das wandernde Gottesvolk: Zum Basismotiv des Hebräerbriefes', *ZNW* 77 (1986), pp. 160-79; N. Walter, '"Hellenistische Eschatologie" im Neuen Testament', in *Glaube und Eschatologie: Festschrift für Werner Georg Kümmel zum 80. Geburtstag* (ed. E. Grässer and O. Merk; Tübingen: Mohr [Paul Siebeck], 1985), pp. 351-55; J.R. Sharp, "Philonism and the Eschatology of Hebrews: Another Look', *East Asia Jour-*

However, for the author of Heb., the 'rest' is anticipated as the establishment of a renewed earth.[1] This is suggested in Heb. by the future expectation of a 'city' (e.g. 13.14; 11.10, 13-16; 12.28; cf. Gal. 4.26; Rev. 3.12; 21.2) which corresponds to the 'rest'.[2]

Since therefore the 'rest' is yet future, awaiting the parousia, while the access to God (characterized by 'perfection', 'entry', and 'approach') is a present activity, we may conclude that the present access takes place while still awaiting the End of Time. These verbs in Heb. may describe different stages of human existence (i.e. in life and after death), but they refer to the same larger stage of salvation.[3] Oscar Cullmann's distinction holds true for Heb.: 'The Kingdom of Christ is not yet the Kingdom of God'.[4]

Until the End—when all shall fully be in God's presence, when full salvation now known only partially (e.g. 1.14) by hope shall be enjoyed, when even those living shall see the Lord (12.14)—the readers are characterized as 'priests', as indicated by the cultic verbs describing their priestly access to God and by the sacral activity still attributed to them: sacrifices of praise and acceptable worship (Heb.

---

nal of Theology 2 (1984), pp. 292-94; Thompson, *The Beginnings*, p. 99; Dey, *The Intermediary World*, p. 232; MacRae, 'Heavenly Temple and Eschatology', pp. 179-99. Also see the early work instrumental for this approach: Käsemann, *The Wandering People*, p. 54. Refer to Buchanan, *To the Hebrews*, pp. 71-74, for a critique of persons espousing this view or variations of it.

1. Scholars are in general agreement that κατάπαυσις is a spatial reality, as advocated already quite early by Käsemann, *The Wandering People*, p. 41. This is also the common understanding in apocalyptic and rabbinical works. See the texts cited in Hofius, *Katapausis*, pp. 60-67; Braun, *Hebräer*, p. 92 Rissi, *Die Theologie*, p. 44 n. 25; Str–B, *Kommentar*, 3.573. Attridge ('New Covenant', p. 97) rejects the eschatological view, however, in favor of a 'transcendent place or state into which God himself entered after his labor of creation'. He overlooks the fact that Christians are not at 'rest' from their labors as God 'rested' from his in Gen. 2.21.

2. Although Hofius supports a 'Diesseits' eschatology, it is strange that he considers the 'rest' to be the holy of holies in heaven (e.g. *Katapausis*, p. 58), since: (1) the city itself appears to be the future goal for which the people of God strive, and (2) the heavenly holy of holies is already accessible before the 'Day' (10.25).

3. See our concluding remarks under the discussion of Heb. 6.19-20 in Chapter 4, section 2, above.

4. O. Cullmann, *Christ and Time: The Primitive Christian Conception of Time and History* (trans. F. Filson; Philadelphia: Westminster, 1950), pp. 240-41. Swetnam, 'Christology', pp. 92-93, recognizes that the present Christian approach to God will end with entrance into the definitive Rest of God.

12.28; 13.15).¹ The expression of gratitude and thanksgiving is to occupy their entire existence (13.21).

Have we thus been led too far afield from our original investigation into the priesthood in Chapter 1? To the contrary, we have served to clarify the matter. All of the priesthoods we have examined placed their major emphases upon the continued importance of mediatorial and sacrificially atoning works, either material or spiritual, by the priests. Heb., on the other hand, presents a picture of a present priesthood devoid of any sacrificially atoning responsibility because of the unique, once-for-all sacrifice offered by Christ himself that bears no repeating (7.27; 9.12, 26; 10.2, 10). To be sure, believers are exhorted to service, even sacrifice,² but reconciliation with God and access to his heavenly throne do not depend on such activities.³ Christian activity is therefore a response to the invitation of Christ's past and present priesthood. Such activity describes a proleptic priesthood. Believers are already enjoying access to God and offering sacrifices of praise, worship, and thanksgiving since the end-time days are here (e.g. 1.2; 9.26), and all the while they are anticipating the eschatological future when full and direct access will be enjoyed.⁴ What the old covenant priesthood ignorantly presumed itself to achieve and accomplish, i.e. access to God, is realized only by priests under the new covenant establishment in Christ.

We observe, therefore, that the author employs a similar logical method of interpretation to that which he utilizes elsewhere in Heb.

---

1. See for instance Bruce, *Hebrews*, pp. 405-406; H. Koester, '"Outside the Camp": Hebrews 13.9-14', *HTR* 55 (1962), pp. 299-303; F.V. Filson, *'Yesterday': A Study of Hebrews in the Light of Chapter 13* (Studies in Biblical Theology, 2.4; London: SCM, 1967), pp. 80-81. Attridge (*Hebrews*, p. 288) contends that there is no developed notion of the priesthood of believers in Heb. We believe we have shown otherwise.

2. Heb. 12.28; 13.15. See Michel, *Kommentar*, pp. 522-24.

3. For Moe (p. 163), this explains why the readers are never referred to explicitly as 'priests'. This term is reserved exclusively for Christ himself, since he alone has the special function of 'mediator'. The readers' priestly attribute consists of their 'access' to the holy of holies. Also see Fiorenza, 'Cultic Language', pp. 176-77. Fiorenza notes that 'no further atoning sacrifice and cult is necessary. Christian worship, therefore, is no longer dependent upon cultic institutions and persons, but is actualized in everyday life' (p. 177). Also see E.A. Schick, 'Priestly Pilgrims: Mission Outside the Camp in Hebrews', *Currents in Theology and Mission* 16 (1989), p. 375.

4. Fiorenza (*Priester*, p. 420) characterizes a similar scenario in the Revelation of John.

For instance, in Heb. 3.1–4.13 (especially 4.6-10) the original promise of 'rest' which was spoken again later by David in Ps. 95.7-11 illustrates the fact that the 'rest' had not been fulfilled in the Exodus generation, because otherwise the promise would not have been repeated by David. Similarly, with regard to the priesthood of belivers, the promise to the people of God at Sinai (Exod. 19.6)—that they would be priests—was obviously not accomplished because it was repeated at a later time by Isaiah (Isa. 61.6). For Heb. it is only under the new covenant that what was promised of old to the fathers has been brought to fruition in its readership: 'You shall be to me a kingdom of priests and a holy nation'.[1]

Finally, our investigation gives further support for M. Rissi's contention that the readers of the Epistle embraced a realized eschatology, rife with problems, which resulted from a charismatic movement that utterly transformed their theology and that had ramifications for their common life (Heb. 2.4; 6.4).[2] Already, before the initial occurrence of τελειοῦν at 2.10, the author of Heb. has established the apocalyptic framework within which Heb. is operating (1.6, 10-12, 13; 2.5, 8). Thus Heb. skillfully argues that the 'perfection' which Christians purportedly enjoy cannot, in fact, be the end of the matter. Their 'perfection' is not the κατάπαυσις. The latter is still to come, with dire consequences for those who ignore its claims (e.g. 3.1–4.13; 5.11–6.20; 10.15-39; 11–13). Until the 'rest' comes, Christian labor still has its place as the expression of praise, thanksgiving, and worship of God (4.10; 13.13, 21).[3] This is the only service 'priests' need render to God and to the 'source of our salvation'.

---

1. Observe the reference to the conclusion of the old covenant in Exod. 24.1-8 at Heb. 9.18-21 in the context of which the superiority of the new covenant is emphasized. See Vanhoye, *Old Testament Priests*, pp. 245-46.

2. E.g. see Rissi, *Die Theologie*, pp. 15-16, 21-23, 23-25, 56-59. Obviously, there are innumerable hypotheses (see Attridge, *Hebrews*, pp. 10-13). Our proposal, however, that acknowledges the eschatological interest of the author, the distinction between 'perfection' and 'rest', and the emphasis on the earthly death of Christ, would support this particular hypothesis. A.C. Thiselton ('Realized Eschatology at Corinth', *NTS* 24 [1978], pp. 510-26) and P.H. Towner ('Gnosis and Realized Eschatology in Ephesus [of the Pastoral Epistles] and the Corinthian Enthusiasm', *JSNT* 31 [1987], pp. 95-124) draw out some interesting parallels for Heb., although their works involve different circles of readers.

3. We are disputing, then, Peterson's assertion that there was no 'special polemic against a form of perfectionism being expounded to or by the readers'. See Peterson,

The present priestly character of the readership is expressed both through the applied cultic terminology in Heb. and through its sacerdotal contexts. Both serve to identify the readers as priests already during their earthly existence. The reason for this priestly status is not found in their performance of any sort of atoning ritual service, but solely in their uninhibited access to God, made possible by the past and present priestly service rendered by Christ himself. In Heb. it is precisely this access to God, extended to earthly believers, which characterizes all Christians as 'proleptic priests'. Their priesthood is 'proleptic' and 'penultimate', because their entry into God's very presence is achieved only in the Holy Spirit. Only when the End comes will a priesthood characterized by the believers' absolute and unending access to God be revealed.

p. 187. Rather, we have seen that the readers are duly admonished that access to God ('perfection') will be superseded by the κατάπαυσις.

# BIBLIOGRAPHY

Abba, R., 'Priests and Levites', *Interpreter's Dictionary of the Bible* (New York: Abingdon, 1962), 3.876-89.
Alt, A., *Die Ursprünge des israelitischen Rechts* (Berichte über die Verhandlungen der Sächsischen Akademie der Wissenschaften zu Leipzig, Philologisch-historische Klasse, 86; Leipzig: S. Hirzel, 1934).
*Apuleius; The Golden Ass, being the Metamorphoses of Lucius Apuleius* (trans. W. Adlington; rev. S. Gaselee; Loeb Classical Library; London: Heinemann, 1922).
*Apuleius of Madauros: The Isis-Book (Metamorphoses, Book IX)* (ed. J. Gwyn Griffiths; Etudes préliminaires aux religions orientales dans l'Empire Romain, 39; Leiden: Brill, 1975).
Arndt, W.F. and F.W. Gingrich, *A Greek–English Lexicon of the New Testament and Other Early Christian Literature: A Translation and Adaptation of Walter Bauer's Griechisch Wörterbuch zu den Schriften des Neuen Testaments und der übrigen urchristlichen Literatur* (4th rev. edn, 1952; Chicago: University of Chicago Press, 1957).
Attridge, H.W., *The Epistle to the Hebrews* (Hermeneia Commentary; Philadelphia: Fortress, 1989).
—'Heard because of His Reverence', *Journal of Biblical Literature* 98 (1973), pp. 90-93.
—' "Let Us Strive to Enter That Rest." The Logic of Hebrews 4.1-11', *Harvard Theological Review* 73 (1980), pp. 279-88.
—'New Covenant Christology in an Early Christian Homily', *Quarterly Review* 8 (1988), pp. 89-108.
—'The Uses of Antithesis in Hebrews 8–10', *Christians among Jews and Gentiles: Essays in Honor of Krister Stendahl on his Sixty-fifth Birthday* (ed. G.W.E. Nickelsburg and G.W. MacRae; Philadelphia: Fortress, 1986).
—*The Babylonian Talmud* (ed. I. Epstein; 6 vols.; London: Soncino, 1935–48).
Balz, H. and G. Schneider (eds.), *Exegetisches Wörterbuch zum Neuen Testament* (Stuttgart: W. Kohlhammer, 1980–83).
Barrett, C.K., 'The Eschatology of the Epistle to the Hebrews', *The Background of the New Testament and its Eschatology: Essays in Honour of Charles Harold Dodd* (ed. W.D. Davies and D. Daube; Cambridge: Cambridge University Press, 1954).
Barth, M., *Die Taufe—ein Sakrament?: Ein exegetischer Beitrag zum Gespräch über die kirchliche Taufe* (Zollikon-Zürich: Evangelischer Verlag, 1951).
Baudissin, W.G., *Die Geschichte des alttestamentlichen Priesterthums* (Leipzig: S. Hirzel, 1889).
—'Priests and Levites', *A Dictionary of the Bible: Dealing with its Language, Literature and Contents including the Biblical Theology* (ed. J. Hastings and J.A. Selbie; New York: Charles Scribner's Sons, 1899–1904), 4.667-97.
Baumgarten, J.M., 'Sacrifice and Worship among the Jewish Sectarians of the Dead Sea (Qumran) Scrolls', *Harvard Theological Review* 46 (1953), pp. 141-59.
Best, E., 'Spiritual Sacrifice: General Priesthood in the New Testament', *Interpretation* 16 (1960), pp. 273-99.
Bianchi, U., *The Greek Mysteries* (Iconography of Religion, 17.3; Leiden: Brill, 1976).

Bietenhard, H., *Die himmlische Welt im Urchristentum und Spätjudentum* (Wissenschaftliche Untersuchungen zum Neuen Testament, 2; Tübingen: Mohr [Paul Siebeck], 1951).
Billerbeck, P., and H. Strack, *Kommentar zum Neuen Testament aus Talmud und Midrasch* (5 vols.; München: C.H. Beck [Oskar Beck], 1922–28).
Blass, F., and A. Debrunner, *A Greek Grammar of the New Testament and Other Early Christian Literature* (trans. and rev. R.W. Funk; 9-10th edn; Chicago: University of Chicago Press, 1961).
Boman, T., 'Der Gebetskampf Jesu', *New Testament Studies* 10 (1964), pp. 261-73.
Bornkamm, G., 'Das Bekenntnis im Hebräerbrief', *Studien zu Antike und Urchristentum: Gesammelte Aufsätze*, II (München: Chr. Kaiser, 1959), pp. 188-203.
—'Lobpreis, Bekenntnis und Opfer', *Apophoreta: Festschrift für Ernst Haenchen zu seinem siebzigsten Geburtstag am 10. Dezember 1964* (ed. W. Eltester and F.H. Kettler; Beiheft zur Zeitschrift für die neutestamentliche Wissenschaft, 30; Berlin: Alfred Töpelmann, 1964), pp. 46-63.
Botterweck, J., H. Ringgren and H.-J. Fabry (eds. vols. 4–5), *Theologisches Wörterbuch des alten Testaments* (5 vols.; Stuttgart: W. Kohlhammer, 1973–86).
Bourke, M., 'The Epistle to the Hebrews', *The Jerome Biblical Commentary* (ed. by R.E. Brown, J.A. Fitzmyer, and R.E. Murphy; foreword by Augustin Cardinal Bea; Englewood Cliffs, NJ: Prentice–Hall, 1968), 2.381-403.
Bousset, W., *Die Offenbarung Johannis* (Kritisch-exegetischer Kommentar über das Neue Testament begründet von Heinrich August Wilhelm Meyer; 16th rev. edn; Göttingen: Vandenhoeck & Ruprecht, 1906).
—*Die Religion des Judentums im späthellenistischen Zeitalter* (Handbuch zum Neuen Testament, 21; 3rd rev. edn; ed. H. Gressmann; Tübingen: Mohr [Paul Siebeck], 1966).
Braun, H., *An die Hebräer* (Handbuch zum Neuen Testament, 14; Tübingen: Mohr [Paul Siebeck], 1984).
—*Qumran und das Neue Testament* (2 vols.; Tübingen: Mohr [Paul Siebeck], 1966).
—'Qumran und das Neue Testament: Ein Bericht über 10 Jahre Forschung (1950–1959)', *Theologische Rundschau* 28 (1962), pp. 97-234.
Brooks, W.E., 'The Perpetuity of Christ's Sacrifice in the Epistle to the Hebrews', *Journal of Biblical Literature* 89 (1970), pp. 205-14.
Brown, C. (ed.), *The New International Dictionary of New Testament Theology* (3 vols.; Exeter: Paternoster, 1975–78).
Brown, F., S.R. Driver, and C.A. Briggs (eds.), *Hebrew and English Lexicon of the Old Testament with an Appendix Containing the Biblical Aramaic* (Oxford: Clarendon, 1952).
Brown, R.E., *The Epistles of John. Translated with Introduction, Notes, and Commentary* (Anchor Bible, 30; Garden City, NY: Doubleday, 1982).
—'The Messianism of Qumran', *Catholic Biblical Quarterly* 19 (1957), pp. 53-82.
Bruce, F.F., *The Epistle to the Hebrews: The English Text with Introduction, Exposition, and Notes* (The New International Commentary on the New Testament; Grand Rapids: Eerdmans, 1964).
Buchanan, G.W., 'The Present State of Scholarship on Hebrews', *Christianity, Judaism and other Greco-Roman Cults: Studies for Morton Smith at Sixty* (ed. J. Neusner; Studies in Judaism in Late Antiquity, 12.1; Leiden: Brill, 1975), pp. 299-330.
—*To the Hebrews: Translation, Comment, and Conclusions* (Anchor Bible, 36; Garden City, NY: Doubleday, 1972).
Burrows, M., *More Light on the Dead Sea Scrolls: New Scrolls and New Interpretations; With Translations of Important Recent Discoveries* (New York: Viking, 1958).

Byrne, B., *'Sons of God'—'Seed of Abraham'*: *A Study of the Idea of the Sonship of God of All Christians in Paul against the Jewish Background* (Analecta Biblica, 83; Rome: Pontifical Biblical Institute, 1979).

Calvin, J., *Commentaries on the Epistle of Paul the Apostle to the Hebrews* (trans. and ed. John Owen; Edinburgh: Calvin Translation Society, 1853; repr. edn, Grand Rapids: Eerdmans, 1948).

Campbell, J.Y., 'Perfection', *Interpreter's Dictionary of the Bible* (New York: Abingdon, 1962), 3.730.

—'Rest', *Interpreter's Dictionary of the Bible* (New York: Abingdon, 1962), 4.37-38.

Carlston, C., 'The Vocabulary of Perfection in Philo and Hebrews', *Unity and Diversity in New Testament Theology: Essays in Honor of George E. Ladd*, pp. 133-60 (ed. R.A. Guelich; Grand Rapids: Eerdmans, 1978).

Carmignac, J., 'L'utilité ou l'inutilité des sacrifices sanglants dans la "Règle de la Communauté" de Qumrân', *Revue Biblique* 63 (1956), pp. 524-32.

Casey, J.M., 'Christian Assembly in Hebrews: A Fantasy Island?', *Theology Digest* 30 (1982), pp. 323-35.

Chamberlin, J.V., 'Toward a Qumran Soteriology', *Novum Testamentum* 3 (1959), pp. 305-13.

Charles, R.H. (ed.), *The Apocrypha and Pseudepigrapha of the Old Testament in English, with Introductions and Critical and Explanatory Notes to the Several Books* (2 vols.; Oxford: Clarendon, 1913).

Charlesworth, J.H. (ed.), *The Old Testament Pseudepigrapha* (2 vols.; Garden City, NY: Doubleday, 1983, 1985).

—'Odes of Solomon', *The Old Testament Pseudepigrapha* (ed. J.H. Charlesworth; Garden City, NY: Doubleday, 1985), 2.725-71.

Cockerill, G.L., 'The Melchizedek Christology in Heb. 7.1-28' (ThD dissertation, Union Theological Seminary in Virginia, 1976).

Cody, A., *Heavenly Sanctuary and Liturgy in the Epistle to the Hebrews: The Achievement of Salvation in the Epistle's Perspective* (St Meinrad, IN: Grail, 1960).

—*A History of Old Testament Priesthood* (Analecta Biblica, 35; Rome: Pontifical Biblical Institute, 1969).

Cross, F.M., *The Ancient Library of Qumran and Modern Biblical Studies* (rev. edn; Garden City, NY: Doubleday, 1958).

—'The Priestly Houses of Early Israel', *Canaanite Myth and Hebrew Epic: Essays in the History of Israel* (Cambridge, MA: Harvard University Press, 1973), pp. 195-215.

Cullmann, O., *Christ and Time: The Primitive Christian Conception of Time and History* (trans. F.V. Filson; Philadelphia: Westminster, 1950).

—*The Christology of the New Testament* (rev. edn: trans. S.C. Guthrie and C.A.M. Hall; Philadelphia: Westminster, 1963).

Cumont, F., *Oriental Religions in Roman Paganism* (London: G. Routledge & Sons, 1911; repr. edn, New York: Dover, 1956).

Dahl, N.A., 'A New and Living Way: The Approach to God according to Hebrews 10.19-25', *Interpretation* 5 (1951), pp. 401-12.

Daly, R.J., *Christian Sacrifice: The Judaeo-Christian Background before Origen* (Catholic University of America Studies in Christian Antiquity, 18; Washington, DC: Catholic University of America Press, 1978).

Danby, H., *The Mishnah: Translated from the Hebrew with Introduction and Brief Explanatory Notes* (London: Oxford University Press [Geoffrey Cumberlege], 1933).

Davidson, A.B., *The Epistle to the Hebrews: With Introduction and Notes* (Edinburgh: T. & T. Clark, n.d.).

Dean-Otting, M., *Heavenly Journeys: A Study of the Motif in Hellenistic Jewish Literature* (Judentum und Umwelt, 8; Frankfurt am Main: Peter Lang, 1984).

Deissmann, G.A., *Biblical Studies: Contributions Chiefly from Papyri and Inscriptions to the History of the Language, the Literature, and the Religion of Hellenistic Judaism and Primitive Christianity* (2nd edn; trans. A. Grieve; Edinburgh: T. & T. Clark, 1909).

Delitzsch, F., *Commentary on the Epistle to the Hebrews* (trans. T.L. Kingsbury; 2 vols.; Edinburgh: T. & T. Clark, 1871; repr. edn, Minneapolis: Klock & Klock, 1978).

Dey, L.K. Kumar, *The Intermediary World and Patterns of Perfection in Philo and Hebrews* (Society of Biblical Literature Dissertation Series, 25; Missoula, MT: Scholars Press, 1975).

Dibelius, M., 'Der himmlische Kultus nach dem Hebräerbrief', *Botschaft und Geschichte: Gesammelte Studien*. Vol. 2: *Zum Urchristentum und zur hellenistischen Religionsgeschichte* (ed. G. Bornkamm and H. Kraft; Tübingen: Mohr [Paul Siebeck], 1956), pp. 160-76.

Doran, R., 'Pseudo-Hecataeus', *The Old Testament Pseudepigrapha* (ed. J.H. Charlesworth; Garden City, NY: Doubleday, 1985), 2.905-19.

Driver, S.R., *The Book of Exodus* (Cambridge: Cambridge University Press, 1911).

Drummond, J., *Philo Judaeus: or, The Jewish-Alexandrian Philosophy in its Development and Completion* (2 vols.; London: Williams & Norgate, 1888).

Dumbrell, W.J., 'The Spirits of Just Men Made Perfect', *Evangelical Quarterly* 48 (1976), pp. 154-59.

du Plessis, P.J., *'ΤΕΛΕΙΟΣ : The Idea of Perfection in the New Testament* (Kampen: J.H. Kok, 1959).

Dupont-Sommer, A., *The Essene Writings from Qumran* (trans. Geza Vermes; Cleveland: World, 1962; Meridian Books, 1962).

Edwards, J.R., 'The Use of Προσέρχεσθαι in the Gospel of Matthew', *Journal of Biblical Literature* 106 (1987), pp. 65-74.

Eichrodt, W., *Theology of the Old Testament* (2 vols.; trans. J.A. Baker; Philadelphia: Westminster, 1967).

Ellingworth, P., 'Jesus and the Universe in Hebrews', *Evangelical Quarterly* 58 (1986), pp. 337-50.

Engelmann, H., *The Delian Aretalogy of Sarapis: With a Frontispiece and 1 Figure* (Etudes préliminaires aux religions orientales dans l'Empire Romain, 44; Leiden: Brill, 1975).

Filson, F.V., *'Yesterday': A Study of Hebrews in the Light of Chapter 13* (Studies in Biblical Theology, 2.4; London: SCM, 1967).

Fiorenza, E.S., 'Cultic Language in Qumran and in the New Testament', *Catholic Biblical Quarterly* 38 (1976), pp. 159-77.

—*Priester für Gott: Studien zum Herrschafts- und Priestermotiv in der Apokalypse* (Neutestamentliche Abhandlungen, 7; Münster: Aschendorff, 1972).

Floor, L., 'The General Priesthood of Believers in the Epistle to the Hebrews', *Neotestamentica* 5 (1971), pp. 72-82.

Flusser, D., Review of *The Temple Scroll* (Hebrew edn), by Y. Yadin, *Numen* 26 (1979), pp. 271-74.

Friedrich, G., 'Das Lied vom Hohenpriester im Zusammenhang von Heb. 4.14–5.10', *Theologische Zeitschrift* 18 (1962), pp. 95-115.

Fuller, R.H., 'The Letter to the Hebrews', *Hebrews, James, 1 and 2 Peter, Jude, Revelation* (ed. G. Krodel; Proclamation Commentaries; Philadelphia: Fortress, 1977), pp. 1-27.

Gärtner, B., *The Temple and the Community in Qumran and the New Testament: A Comparative Study in the Temple Symbolism of the Qumran Texts and the New Testament* (Society for New Testament Studies Monograph Series, 1; Cambridge: Cambridge University Press, 1965).

Gaster, T.H. (ed. and trans.), *The Dead Sea Scriptures: In English Translation with Introduction and Notes* (Garden City, NY: Doubleday, 1956).

Glombitza, O., 'Erwägungen zum kunstvollen Ansatz der Paränese im Brief an die Hebräer—x,19-25', *Novum Testamentum* 9 (1967), pp. 132-50.
Goodenough, E.R., *By Light, Light: The Mystic Gospel of Hellenistic Judaism* (New Haven: Yale University Press, 1935).
Goppelt, L., *ΤΥΠΟΣ: The Typological Interpretation of the Old Testament in the New* (trans. D.H. Madvig; Grand Rapids: Eerdmans, 1978).
Gowie, A.E., 'Shadow and Substance', *Expository Times* 28 (1916–17), pp. 397-99.
Grässer, E., *Der Glaube im Hebräerbrief* (Marburger Theologische Studien, 2; Marburg: N.G. Elwert, 1965).
—'Der Hebräerbrief 1938–1963', *Theologische Rundschau* 30 (1964), pp. 138-236.
—'Das wandernde Gottesvolk: Zum Basismotiv des Hebräerbriefes', *Zeitschrift für die neutestamentliche Wissenschaft* 77 (1986), pp. 160-79.
Grant, R.M., *Gods and the One God* (Library of Early Christianity, 1; Philadelphia: Westminster, 1986).
Gray, G.B., *Sacrifice in the Old Testament: Its Theory and Practice* (Oxford: Clarendon, 1925).
Gunneweg, A.H.J., *Leviten und Priester: Hauptlinien der Traditionsbildung und Geschichte des israelitischen-jüdischen Kultpersonals* (Forschungen zur Religion und Literatur des Alten und Neuen Testaments, 89; Göttingen: Vandenhoeck & Ruprecht, 1965).
Guthrie, D., *The Letter to the Hebrews: An Introduction and Commentary* (Leicester: Inter-Varsity Press, 1983).
Gyllenberg, R., 'Die Christologie des Hebräerbriefes', *Zeitschrift für Systematische Theologie* 11 (1934), pp. 662-90.
Häring, T., 'Noch ein Wort zum Begriff "τελειοῦν" im Hebräerbrief', *Neue kirchliche Zeitschrift* 34 (1923), pp. 386-89.
—'Über einige Grundgedanken des Hebräerbriefs', *Monatschrift für Pastoraltheologie* 17 (1920–21), pp. 260-76.
Hagner, D.A., *Hebrews* (Good News Commentaries; San Francisco: Harper & Row, 1983).
Hahn, F., *Christologische Hoheitstitel: Ihre Geschichte im frühen Christentum* (Forschungen zur Religion und Literatur des Alten und Neuen Testaments, 83; Göttingen: Vandenhoeck & Ruprecht, 1963).
Haran, M., 'Priests and Priesthood', *Encyclopedia Judaica* (New York: Macmillan, 1972), 13.1069-76.
Harris, R., and A. Mingana (eds.), *The Odes and Psalms of Solomon* (2 vols.; Manchester: Manchester University Press, 1920).
Hatch, E., and Redpath, H.A. (eds.), *A Concordance to the Septuagint and the Other Greek Versions of the Old Testament (Including the Apocryphal Books)* (3 vols.; Oxford: Clarendon, 1897–1906; repr. edn, Grand Rapids: Baker, 1983).
Héring, J., *The Epistle to the Hebrews* (trans. A.W. Heathcote and P.J. Allcock; London: Epworth, 1970).
Hoekma, A.A., 'The Perfection of Christ in Hebrews', *Calvin Theological Journal* 9 (1974), pp. 31-37.
Hofius, O., 'Das "erste" und das "zweite" Zelt: Ein Beitrag zur Auslegung von Heb. 9.1-10', *Zeitschrift für die neutestamentliche Wissenschaft* 61 (1970), pp. 271-77.
—'Inkarnation und Opfertod Jesu nach Heb. 10.19f.', *Der Ruf Jesu und die Antwort der Gemeinde: Festschrift für Joachim Jeremias* (ed. E. Lohse; Göttingen: Vandenhoeck & Ruprecht, 1970), pp. 132-41.
—*Katapausis: Die Vorstellung vom endzeitlichen Ruheort im Hebräerbrief* (Wissenschaftliche Untersuchungen zum Neuen Testament, 11; Tübingen: Mohr [Paul Siebeck], 1970).

# Bibliography 213

—*Der Vorhang vor dem Thron Gottes: Eine exegetisch-religionsgeschichtliche Untersuchung zu Hebräer 6.19f. und 10.19f.* (Wissenschaftliche Untersuchungen zum Neuen Testament, 14; Tübingen: Mohr [Paul Siebeck], 1972).

Horbury, W., 'The Aaronic Priesthood in the Epistle to the Hebrews', *Journal for the Study of the New Testament* 19 (1983), pp. 43-71.

Hughes, P.E., *A Commentary on the Epistle to the Hebrews* (Grand Rapids: Eerdmans, 1977).

Hurst, L.D., 'Eschatology and "Platonism" in the Epistle to the Hebrews', *Society of Biblical Literature 1984 Seminar Papers*, 23 (ed. K.H. Richards; Chico, CA: Scholars Press, 1984), pp. 41-74.

Jenni, E. with C. Westermann (ed.), *Theologisches Handwörterbuch zum Alten Testament* (2 vols.; München: Chr. Kaiser, 1971–76).

Jeremias, J., 'Hebräer 5.7-10', *ABBA: Studien zur neutestamentlichen Theologie und Zeitgeschichte* (Göttingen: Vandenhoeck & Ruprecht, 1966), pp. 319-23.

—'Hebräer 10.20: τοῦτ' ἔστιν τῆς σαρκὸς αὐτοῦ', *Zeitschrift für die neutestamentliche Wissenschaft* 62 (1971), p. 131.

—*Jerusalem in the Time of Jesus: An Investigation into Economic and Social Conditions during the New Testament Period* (Philadelphia: Fortress, 1969).

Jewett, R., *Letter to Pilgrims: A Commentary on the Epistle to the Hebrews* (New York: Pilgrim, 1981).

Johnsson, W.G., 'Defilement and Purgation in the Book of Hebrews' (PhD dissertation, Vanderbilt University, 1973).

*Josephus* (trans. H.St.-J. Thackery; Loeb Classical Library; 9 vols.; London: Heinemann, 1926–65).

Käsemann, E., *The Wandering People of God: An Investigation of the Letter to the Hebrews* (trans. R.A. Harrisville and I.L. Sandberg; Minneapolis: Augsburg, 1984).

Kee, H.C., 'Testaments of the Twelve Partriarchs', *The Old Testament Pseudepigrapha* (ed. J.H. Charlesworth; Garden City, NY: Doubleday, 1985), 1.775-828.

Kittel, R., and P. Kahle (eds.), *Biblica Hebraica* (7th edn. rev. A. Alt and O. Eissfeldt; Stuttgart: Württembergische Bibelanstalt, 1951).

Klappert, B., *Die Eschatologie des Hebräerbriefs* (Theologische Existenz heute, 156; München: Chr. Kaiser, 1969).

Klinzing, G., *Die Umdeutung des Kultus in der Qumrangemeinde und im Neuen Testament* (Studien zur Umwelt des Neuen Testaments, 7; Göttingen: Vandenhoeck & Ruprecht, 1971).

Kögel, J., 'Der Begriff "τελειοῦν" im Hebräerbrief im Zusammenhang mit dem neutestamentlichen Sprachgebrauch', in F. Giesebrecht, R. Kögel, K. Bornhäuser, K. Müller, C. Stange, M. Schulze, W. Lütgert, P. Tschackert, *Theologische Studien: Martin Kähler zum 6. Januar 1905* (Leipzig: A. Deichert [Georg Böhme], 1905), pp. 35-68.

Koester, H., *Introduction to the New Testament* (2 vols.; Philadelphia: Fortress, 1982).

—' "Outside the Camp": Hebrews 13.9-14', *Harvard Theological Review* 55 (1962), pp. 299-315.

Kraus, H.-J., *Worship in Israel: A Cultic History of the Old Testament* (trans. G. Buswell; Richmond, VA: John Knox, 1966).

Kuhn, H.-W., *Enderwartung und gegenwärtiges Heil: Untersuchungen zu den Gemeindeliedern von Qumran mit einem Anhang über Eschatologie und Gegenwart in der Verkündigung Jesu* (Studien zur Umwelt des Neuen Testaments, 4; Göttingen: Vandenhoeck & Ruprecht, 1966).

Kuhn, K.G. (ed.), in association with A.-M. Denis, R. Deichgräber, W. Eiss, G. Jeremias, and H.-W. Kuhn, *Konkordanz zu den Qumrantexten* (Göttingen: Vandenhoeck & Ruprecht, 1960). Supplemented by K.G. Kuhn (ed.), assisted by U. Müller, W.

Schmücher, and H. Stegemann, 'Nachträge zur *Konkordanz zu den Qumrantexten*', *Revue de Qumran* 4 (1963), pp. 163-234.

—'Qumran', *Die Religion in Geschichte und Gegenwart* (3rd edn; Tübingen: Mohr, 1957–62), 5.745-54.

—'The Two Messiahs of Aaron and Israel', *The Scrolls and the New Testament* (ed. K. Stendahl; New York: Harper & Row, 1957), pp. 54-64.

Kuss, O., 'Der Brief an die Hebräer', *Der Brief an die Hebräer und die katholischen Briefe* (ed. O. Kuss and J. Michl; Das Neue Testament, 8; Regensburg: Friedrich Pustet, 1953), pp. 11-127.

—'Der theologische Grundgedanke des Hebräerbriefes. Zur Deutung des Todes Jesu im Neuen Testament', *Auslegung und Verkündigung*, Vol. I: *Aufsätze zur Exegese des Neuen Testamentes* (Regensburg: Friedrich Pustet, 1963), pp. 281-328.

LaSor, W.S., 'Dead Sea Scrolls', *International Standard Bible Encyclopedia* (ed. G.W. Bromiley; Grand Rapids: Eerdmans, 1979), 1.883-97.

Laub, F., *Bekenntnis und Auslegung: Die paränetische Funktion der Christologie im Hebräerbrief* (Biblische Untersuchungen, 15; Regensburg: Friedrich Pustet, 1980).

Laubach, F., *Der Brief an die Hebräer* (Wuppertaler Studienbibel; Wuppertal: R. Brockhaus, 1967).

Lenski, R.C.H., *The Interpretation of the Epistle to the Hebrews and of the Epistle of James* (Columbus, OH: Wartburg, 1946).

Lescow, T., 'Jesus in Gethsemane bei Lukas und im Hebräerbrief', *Zeitschrift für die neutestamentliche Wissenschaft* 58 (1967), pp. 215-39.

Levine, B.A., 'The Temple Scroll: Aspects of its Historical Provenance and Literary Character', *Bulletin of the American Schools of Oriental Research* 232 (1978), pp. 5-23.

Liddell, H.G., and R. Scott (comps.), *A Greek–English Lexicon* (9th edn, rev. H.S. Jones and R. McKenzie; Oxford: Clarendon, 1953).

Lindars, B., 'The Rhetorical Structure of Hebrews', *New Testament Studies* 35 (1989), pp. 382-406.

Loader, W.R.G., *Sohn und Hoherpriester: Eine traditionsgeschichtliche Untersuchung zur Christologie des Hebräerbriefes* (Wissenschaftliche Monographien zum Alten und Neuen Testament, 53; Neukirchen-Vluyn: Neukirchener Verlag, 1981).

Lohse, E., *The New Testament Environment* (trans. J.E. Steely; Nashville: Abingdon, 1976).

Lombard, H.A., 'Κατάπαυσις in the Letter to the Hebrews', *Neotestamentica* 5 (1971), pp. 60-71.

Luck, U., 'Himmlisches und irdisches Geschehen im Hebräerbrief: Ein Beitrag zum Problem des "historischen Jesus" im Urchristentum', *Novum Testamentum* 6 (1963), pp. 192-215.

Lünemann, G., *Critical and Exegetical Handbook to the Epistle to the Hebrews* (trans. M.J. Evans; Edinburgh: T. & T. Clark, 1882).

McCready, W.O., 'The Sectarian Status of Qumran: The Temple Scroll', *Revue de Qumran* 11 (1983), pp. 183-91.

McCullough, J.C. 'Some Recent Developments in Research on the Epistle to the Hebrews', *Irish Biblical Studies* 2 (1980), pp. 141-65.

—'Some Recent Developments in Research on the Epistle to the Hebrews: II', *Irish Biblical Studies* 3 (1981), pp. 28-45.

McNamara, M., *Palestinian Judaism and the New Testament* (Good News Studies, 4; Wilmington, DE: Michael Glazier, 1983).

MacLeod, D.J., 'The Doctrinal Center of the Book of Hebrews', *Bibliotheca Sacra* 146 (1989), pp. 291-300.

MacRae, G.W., 'Heavenly Temple and Eschatology in the Letter to the Hebrews', *Semeia* 12 (1978), pp. 179-99.

# Bibliography 215

—*Hebrews* (Collegeville Biblical Commentary, 10; Collegeville, MN: Liturgical Press, 1983).
Maier, J., *The Temple Scroll: An Introduction, Translation and Commentary* (JSOT Supplements, 34; Sheffield: JSOT, 1985).
—*Die Texte vom Toten Meer* (2 vols.; München: Ernst Reinhardt, 1960).
Maurer, C., '"Erhört wegen der Gottesfurcht." Heb. 5.7', *Neues Testament und Geschichte: Historisches Geschehen und Deutung im Neuen Testament, Oscar Cullmann zum 70. Geburtstag* (ed. H. Baltensweiler and B. Reicke; Zürich: Theologischer Verlag, 1972), pp. 275-84.
Melbourne, B.L., 'An Examination of the Historical-Jesus Motif in the Epistle to the Hebrews', *Andrews University Seminary Studies* 26 (1988), pp. 281-97.
Metzger, B.M., *A Textual Commentary on the Greek New Testament: A Companion Volume to the United Bible Societies Greek New Testament* (3rd corrected edn; New York: United Bible Societies, 1975).
Michel, O., *Der Brief an die Hebräer* (Kritisch-exegetischer Kommentar über das Neue Testament, 13; Göttingen: Vandenhoeck & Ruprecht, 1984).
—'Die Lehre von der christlichen Vollkommenheit nach der Anschauung des Hebräerbriefes', *Theologische Studien und Kritiken* 106 (1934–35), pp. 333-55.
Milgrom, J., 'Atonement in the OT', *Interpreter's Dictionary of the Bible, Supplementary Volume* (Nashville: Abingdon, 1976), pp. 78-82.
—'Atonement, Day of', *Interpreter's Dictionary of the Bible, Supplementary Volume* (Nashville: Abingdon, 1976), pp. 82-83.
—'Further Studies in the Temple Scroll', *Jewish Quarterly Review* 71 (1980), pp. 1-17.
—'Further Studies in the Temple Scroll (cont.)', *Jewish Quarterly Review* 71 (1980), pp. 89-106.
—'Sacrifices and Offerings, Old Testament', *Interpreter's Dictionary of the Bible: Supplementary Volume* (Nashville: Abingdon, 1976), pp. 763-71.
—'Studies in the Temple Scroll', *Journal of Biblical Literature* 97 (1978), pp. 501-23.
—'The Temple Scroll', *Biblical Archaeologist* 41 (1978), pp. 105-20.
Milik, J.T., *Ten Years of Discovery in the Wilderness of Judaea* (trans. J. Strugnell; Studies in Biblical Theology, 26; London: SCM, 1959).
Moe, O., 'Der Gedanke des allgemeinen Priestertums im Hebräerbrief', *Theologische Zeitschrift* 5 (1949), pp. 161-69.
Moffatt, J., *Grace in the New Testament* (New York: Long & Smith, 1932).
—*A Critical and Exegetical Commentary on the Epistle to the Hebrews* (International Critical Commentary; New York: Charles Scribner's Sons, 1924).
Montefiore, H., *A Commentary on the Epistle to the Hebrews* (Black's New Testament Commentaries; London: A. & C. Black, 1964).
Moore, G.F., *Judaism: In the First Centuries of the Christian Era, The Age of the Tannaim* (3 vols.; Cambridge, MA: Harvard University Press, 1927–30).
Moule, C.F.D., *An Idiom Book of New Testament Greek* (Cambridge: Cambridge University Press, 1953).
Moulton, J.H., *A Grammar of New Testament Greek* (Edinburgh: T. & T. Clark, 1908–76; Vol. 4: *Style*, by N. Turner, 1976).
Moulton, W.F., and A.S. Geden (eds.), *A Concordance to the Greek Testament according to the Texts of Westcott and Hort, Tischendorf and the English Revisers* (5th edn rev. H.K. Moulton; Edinburgh: T. & T. Clark, 1978).
Müller, K.-H., Review of *Enderwartung und gegenwärtiges Heil*, by H.-W. Kuhn, *Biblische Zeitschrift* 12 (1968), pp. 303-306.
Nauck, W., 'Blut Christi', *Die Religion in Geschichte und Gegenwart* (3rd edn; Tübingen: Mohr, 1957–62), 1.1329-30.

—'Zum Aufbau des Hebräerbriefes', *Judentum, Urchristentum, Kirche: Festschrift für Joachim Jeremias* (ed. W. Eltester; Beihefte zur Zeitschrift für die neutestamentliche Wissenschaft, 26; Berlin: Alfred Töpelmann, 1960), pp. 199-206.

Newsom, C., *Songs of the Sabbath Sacrifice: A Critical Edition* (Harvard Semitic Studies, 27; Atlanta: Scholars Press, 1985).

Niditch, S., 'Ezekiel 40–48 in a Visionary Context', *Catholic Biblical Quarterly* 48 (1986), pp. 208-24.

Nilsson, M. P., *Geschichte der griechischen Religion* (2 vols.; Handbuch der Altertumswissenschaft, 5.2; München: C.H. Beck, 1941–50).

—*Greek Popular Religion* (New York: Columbia University Press, 1940).

—*A History of Greek Religion* (trans. F.J. Fielden; Oxford: Clarendon, 1925).

Nock, A.D., *Conversion: The Old and the New in Religion from Alexander the Great to Augustine of Hippo* (Oxford: Clarendon, 1933).

—'Eunuchs in Ancient Religion', *Arthur Darby Nock: Essays on Religion and the Ancient World* (ed. Z. Stewart; Oxford: Clarendon, 1972), I.7-15.

—'The Genius of Mithraism', *Arthur Darby Nock: Essays on Religion and the Ancient World* (ed. Z. Stewart; Oxford: Clarendon, 1972), I.452-58.

Noth, M., *Leviticus: A Commentary* (Old Testament Library; rev. edn; Philadelphia: Westminster, 1977).

—'Office and Vocation in the Old Testament', *The Laws in the Pentateuch and Other Studies* (trans. D.R. Ap-Thomas; Edinburgh: Oliver & Boyd, 1966), pp. 229-48.

*Novum Testamentum Graece* (ed. K. Aland, M. Black, C.M. Martini, B.M. Metzger and A. Wikgren; Stuttgart: Deutsche Bibelstiftung, 1979).

Parsons, M.C., 'Son and High Priest: A Study in the Christology of Hebrews', *Evangelical Quarterly* 60 (1988), pp. 195-215.

Pedersen, J., *Israel: Its Life and Culture* (London: Geoffrey Cumberlege, Oxford University Press, 1926–40).

Peterson, David, *Hebrews and Perfection: An Examination of the Concept of Perfection in the 'Epistle to the Hebrews'* (Society for New Testament Studies Monograph Series, 47; Cambridge: Cambridge University Press, 1982).

*Philo* (trans. and ed. F.H. Colson, G.H. Whitaker, and Ralph Marcus; Loeb Classical Library; 10 vols., plus 2 suppl. vols.; London: Heinemann, 1929–53).

*Philonis Alexandrini Opera quae supersunt* (ed. L. Cohn, P. Wendland, S. Reiter, and H. Leisegang; 7 vols.; Berlin: Walter de Gruyter, 1896–1930; repr. edn, Berlin: Walter de Gruyter, 1962–63).

Ploeg, J. van der, 'L'exégèse de l'Ancien Testament dans l'épître aux Hébreux', *Revue Biblique* 54 (1947), pp. 187-228.

*Plutarch's Moralia* (trans. and ed. F.C. Babbit, W.C. Helmbold, P.H. De Lacy, B. Einarson, P.A. Clement, H.B. Hoffleit, E.L. Minar, Jr, F.H. Sandbach, H.N. Fowler, and L. Pearson; Loeb Classical Library; 16 vols.; London: Heinemann, 1927–76).

*Prudentius* (trans. H.J. Thompson; Loeb Classical Library; 2 vols.; Cambridge, MA: Harvard University Press, 1949–53).

Rad, G. von, *Old Testament Theology* (trans. D.M.G. Stalker; 2 vols.; New York: Harper & Row, 1962–65).

—' "There Remains Still a Rest for the People of God": An Investigation of a Biblical Conception', *The Problem of the Hexateuch and Other Essays* (trans. E.W. Trueman Dicken; Introduction by N.W. Porteous; Edinburgh: Oliver & Boyd, 1966), pp. 94-102.

Rahlfs, A. (ed.), *Septuaginta* (2 vols.; Stuttgart: Deutsche Bibelgesellschaft, 1979).

Riessler, P., *Altjüdisches Schrifttum ausserhalb der Bibel* (Augsburg: Dr Benno Filser, 1928).

Rigaux, B., 'Révélation des mystères et perfection à Qumrân et dans le Nouveau Testament', *New Testament Studies* 4 (1958), pp. 237-62.

Riggenbach, E., 'Der Begriff der τελείωσις im Hebräerbrief. Ein Beitrag zur Frage nach der Einwirkung der Mysterienreligion auf Sprache und Gedankenwelt des Neuen Testaments', *Neue kirchliche Zeitschrift* 34 (1923), pp. 184-95.

—*Der Brief an die Hebräer* (Kommentar zum Neuen Testament, 14; 2nd and 3rd edn; Leipzig: A. Deichert [Dr Werner Scholl], 1922).

Rissi, M., 'Die Menschlichkeit Jesu nach Heb. 5.7 und 8', *Theologische Zeitschrift* 11 (1955), pp. 28-45.

—*Die Theologie des Hebräerbriefs: Ihre Verankerung in der Situation des Verfassers und seiner Leser* (Wissenschaftliche Untersuchungen zum Neuen Testament, 41; Tübingen: Mohr [Paul Siebeck], 1987).

Robinson, R.B., 'The Levites in the Pre-Monarchic Period', *Studia Biblica et Theologica* 8 (1978), pp. 3-24.

Robinson, S.E., 'Testament of Adam', *The Old Testament Pseudepigrapha* (ed. J.H. Charlesworth; Garden City, NY: Doubleday, 1985), I.989-95.

Robinson, T.H., *The Epistle to the Hebrews* (The Moffatt New Testament Commentary; London: Hodder & Stoughton, 1933).

Sabourin, L., *Priesthood: A Comparative Study* (Studies in the History of Religions [Supplements to *Numen*], 25; Leiden: Brill, 1973).

Sanders, J.A., 'Cave 11 Surprises and the Question of Canon', *New Directions in Biblical Archaeology* (ed. D.N. Freedman and J.C. Greenfield; Garden City, NY: Doubleday, 1969), pp. 101-16.

—'Text and Canon: Old Testament and New', *Mélanges Dominique Barthélemy: Etudes bibliques offertes a l'occasion de son 60ᵉ anniversaire* (ed. P. Casetti, O. Keel, and A. Schenker; Orbis Biblicus et Orientalis, 38; Fribourg: Editions Universitaires, 1981), pp. 373-94.

Sandmel, S., *Philo of Alexandria: An Introduction* (New York: Oxford University Press, 1979).

Schick, E.A., 'Priestly Pilgrims: Mission Outside the Camp in Hebrews', *Currents in Theology and Mission* 16 (1989), pp. 372-76.

Schierse, F.J., *Verheissung und Heilsvollendung: Zur theologischen Grundfrage des Hebräerbriefes* (Münchener Theologische Studien, 9; München: Karl Zink, 1955).

Schille, G., 'Erwägungen zur Hohepriesterlehre des Hebräerbriefes', *Zeitschrift für die neutestamentliche Wissenschaft* 48 (1955), pp. 81-109.

Schnackenburg, R., *The Moral Teaching of the New Testament* (Freiburg: Herder, 1965).

Schröger, F., 'Der Gottesdienst der Hebräerbriefgemeinde', *Münchener Theologische Zeitschrift* 19 (1968), pp. 161-81.

—*Der Verfasser des Hebräerbriefes als Schriftausleger* (Biblische Untersuchungen, 4; Regensburg: Friedrich Pustet, 1968).

Schubert, K., 'Zwei Messiasse aus dem Regelbuch vom Chirbet Qumran', *Judaica* 11 (1955), pp. 216-35.

Schürer, E., *The History of the Jewish People in the Age of Jesus Christ (175 B.C.–A.D. 135* (rev. ed. G. Vermes, F. Millar, M. Goodman; Edinburgh: T. & T. Clark, 1987).

Seeberg, A., *Der Brief an die Hebräer* (Evangelisch-theologische Bibliothek; Leipzig: Quelle & Meyer, 1912).

Sharp, J.R., 'Philonism and the Eschatology of Hebrews: Another Look', *East Asia Journal of Theology* 2 (1984), pp. 289-98.

Silberman, L.H., 'The Two "Messiahs" of the Manual of Discipline', *Vetus Testamentum* 5 (1955), pp. 77-82.

Silva, M., 'Perfection and Eschatology in Hebrews', *Westminster Theological Journal* 39 (1976), pp. 61-71.

Smith, J., *A Priest for Ever: A Study of Typology and Eschatology in Hebrews* (London: Sheed & Ward, 1969).
Smith, R.H., *Hebrews* (Augsburg Commentary on the New Testament; Minneapolis: Augsburg, 1984).
Snell, A., *New and Living Way: An Explanation of the Epistle to the Hebrews* (London: Faith, 1959).
Sowers, S.G., *The Hermeneutics of Philo and Hebrews: A Comparison of the Interpretation of the Old Testament in Philo Judaeus and the Epistle to the Hebrews* (Basel Studies of Theology, 1; Richmond, VA: John Knox, 1965)
Spicq, C., '"Αγκυρα et Πρόδρομος dans Héb. VI. 19-20', *Studia Theologica* 3 (1950), pp. 185-87.
—*L'Epître aux Hébreux* (2 vols.; Paris: Libraire Lecoffre, Gabalda, 1952).
—'La panégyrie de Héb. XII, 22', *Studia Theologica* 6 (1953), pp. 30-38.
Stadelmann, A., 'Zur Christologie des Hebräerbriefes in der neueren Diskussion', *Theologische Berichte* 2 (1973), pp. 135-221.
Stambaugh, J.E., 'The Functions of Roman Temples', *Aufstieg und Niedergang der römischen Welt: Geschichte und Kultur Roms im Spiegel der neueren Forschung*, II.16 (ed. W. Haase; Berlin: de Gruyter, 1978), pp. 554-608.
Stott, W., 'The Conception of "Offering" in the Epistle to the Hebrews', *New Testament Studies* 9 (1962), pp. 62-67.
Strack, H.L., *Introduction to the Talmud and Midrash* (New York: Jewish Publication Society of America, 1931: repr. edn, New York: Atheneum, 1969).
Strathmann, H., 'Der Brief an die Hebräer', in J. Jeremias and H. Strathmann, *Die Briefe am Timotheus und Titus; Der Brief an die Hebräer* (Das Neue Testament Deutsch, 9; 9th edn; Göttingen: Vandenhoeck & Ruprecht, 1967), pp. 69-158.
Strobel, A., 'Der Brief an die Hebräer', *Die Briefe an Timotheus und Titus; Der Brief an die Hebräer*, by J.J. and A. Strobel (Das Neue Testament Deutsch, 9; Göttingen: Vandenhoeck & Ruprecht, 1975), pp. 79-255.
—'Die Psalmengrundlage der Gethsemane-Parallele Heb. 5.7ff.', *Zeitschrift für die neutestamentliche Wissenschaft* 45 (1954), pp. 252-66.
Swetnam, J., 'Christology and the Eucharist in the Epistle to the Hebrews', *Biblica* 70 (1989), pp. 185-97.
—*Jesus and Isaac: A Study of the Epistle to the Hebrews in the Light of the Aqedah* (Analecta Biblica, 94; Rome: Biblical Institute, 1981).
Teicher, J.L., 'Priests and Sacrifices in the Dead Sea Scrolls', *Journal of Jewish Studies* 5 (1954), pp. 93-99.
Theissen, G., *Untersuchungen zum Hebräerbrief* (Studien zum Neuen Testament, 2; Gütersloh: Gütersloher Verlagshaus [Mohn], 1969).
Thiselton, A.C., 'Realized Eschatology at Corinth', *New Testament Studies* 24 (1978), pp. 510-26.
Thompson, J.W., *The Beginnings of Christian Philosophy: The Epistle to the Hebrews* (The Catholic Biblical Quarterly Monograph Series, 13; Washington, DC: The Catholic Biblical Association of America, 1982).
Thüsing, W., '"Lasst uns hinzutreten..." (Heb. 10.22)', *Biblische Zeitschrift* NF 9 (1965), pp. 1-17.
Thyen, H., *Der Stil der jüdisch-hellenistischen Homilie* (Forschungen zur Religion und Literatur des Alten und Neuen Testaments, 47; Göttingen: Vandenhoeck & Ruprecht, 1955).
Towner, P.H., 'Gnosis and Realized Eschatology in Ephesus (of the Pastoral Epistles) and the Corinthian Enthusiasm', *Journal for the Study of the New Testament* 31 (1987), pp. 95-124.

Turner, N., *Style*, vol. 4 of J.H. Moulton, *A Grammar of New Testament Greek* (Edinburgh: T. & T. Clark, 1908–76 [1976]).
Unnik, W.C. van, 'The Christian's Freedom of Speech in the New Testament', *Bulletin of the John Rylands Library* 44 (1962), pp. 466-88.
Vanhoye, A., 'De "aspectu" oblationis Christi secundum Epistolam ad Hebraeos', *Verbum Domini* 37 (1959), pp. 32-39.
—*Old Testament Priests and the New Priest: According to the New Testament* (trans. J.B. Orchard; Studies in Scripture; Petersham, MA: St Bede's, 1986).
—*La structure littéraire de l'Epître aux Hébreux* (Studia Neotestamentica, 1; Paris: Desclée de Brouwer, 1963).
Vaux, R. de, *Ancient Israel* (2 vols.; New York: McGraw–Hill, 1965).
Volz, P., *Die Eschatologie der jüdischen Gemeinde im neutestamentlichen Zeitalter nach den Quellen der rabbinischen, apokalyptischen, und apokryphen Literatur* (Tübingen: Mohr [Paul Siebeck], 1934).
Wacholder, B.Z., *The Dawn of Qumran: The Sectarian Torah and the Teacher of Righteousness* (Monographs of the Hebrew Union College, 8; Cincinnati: Hebrew Union College Press, 1983).
Walter, N., ' "Hellenistische Eschatologie" im Neuen Testament', *Glaube und Eschatologie: Festschrift für Werner Georg Kümmel zum 80. Geburtstag* (ed. E. Grässer and O. Merk; Tübingen: Mohr [Paul Siebeck], 1985), pp. 335-56.
Weiss, B., *A Commentary on the New Testament* (trans. G.H. Schodde and E. Wilson; 4 vols.; New York: Funk & Wagnalls, 1906).
Wellhausen, J., *Prolegomena to the History of Ancient Israel: with a reprint of the article Israel from the Encyclopaedia Britannica* (trans. J. Sutherland Black and A. Menzies; Edinburgh: A. & C. Black, 1985).
Wenham, G.J., *The Book of Leviticus* (The New International Commentary on the Old Testament, 3; Grand Rapids: Eerdmans, 1979).
Wenschkewitz, H., 'Die Spiritualisierung der Kultusbegriffe Tempel, Priester und Opfer im Neuen Testament', *ΑΓΓΕΛΟΣ: Archiv für neutestamentliche Zeitgeschichte und Kulturkunde* 4 (1932), pp. 70-232.
Westcott, B.F., *The Epistle to the Hebrews* (2nd edn; London: Macmillan, 1902; repr. edn; Grand Rapids: Eerdmans, 1950).
Wikgren, A., 'Patterns of Perfection in the Epistle to the Hebrews', *New Testament Studies* 6 (1960), pp. 159-67.
Williamson, R., 'The Eucharist and the Epistle to the Hebrews', *New Testament Studies* 21 (1975), pp. 300-12.
—*Philo and the Epistle to the Hebrews* (Arbeiten zur Literatur und Geschichte des hellenistischen Judentums, 4; Leiden: Brill, 1970).
Wilson, R.McL., *Hebrews* (New Century Bible Commentary; Grand Rapids: Eerdmans, 1987).
Windisch, H., *Der Hebräerbrief* (Handbuch zum Neuen Testament, 14; 2nd rev. edn; Tübingen: Mohr [Paul Siebeck], 1931).
Wolfson, H.A., *Philo: Foundations of Religious Philosophy in Judaism, Christianity, and Islam* (2 vols.; Cambridge, MA: Harvard University Press, 1947).
Yadin, Y., *The Message of the Scrolls* (London: Weidenfeld & Nicolson, 1957).
—'The Temple Scroll', *Biblical Archaeologist* 30 (1967), pp. 135-39.
—*The Temple Scroll* (3 vols.; Jerusalem: Israel Exploration Society, 1983).
—'The Temple Scroll, the Longest and Most Recently Discovered Dead Sea Scroll', *Biblical Archaeology Review* 10 (1984), pp. 32-49.
Young, N.H., 'The Gospel According to Hebrews 9', *New Testament Studies* 27 (1981), pp. 198-210.

Zimmermann, H., *Das Bekenntnis der Hoffnung: Tradition und Redaktion im Hebräerbrief* (Bonner Biblische Beiträge, 47; Köln: Peter Hanstein, 1977).

—*Die Hohepriester-christologie des Hebräerbriefes* (Vorträge beim Antritt des Rektorats und zur Eröffnung des Studienjahres 1963/64 der Philosophisch-Theologischen Akademie zu Paderborn gehalten am 22. Oktober 1963; Paderborn: Ferdinand Schöningh, 1964).

# INDEXES

## INDEX OF BIBLICAL REFERENCES

### OLD TESTAMENT

| Genesis | | 19.6 | 11, 63, | 28.30 | 150 |
|---|---|---|---|---|---|
| 2 | 202 | | 206 | 28.35 | 150 |
| 2.21 | 204 | 19.9-25 | 138 | 28.36 | 15 |
| 5.21-22 | 25 | 19.10-12 | 139 | 28.38 | 16 |
| 5.22-24 | 132 | 19.12 | 140 | 28.41 | 15, 16, |
| 5.22 | 133, 134 | 19.14-15 | 139 | | 22 |
| 5.24 | 133-35 | 19.21-22 | 118 | 28.42 | 52, 92 |
| 6.9 | 133 | 19.21 | 139 | 28.43 | 16, 91, |
| 17.1 | 134 | 19.22 | 92, 101, | | 92, 150, |
| 18.23 | 118 | | 118, 139 | | 151 |
| 22.31 | 15 | 19.25 | 139 | 29.1 | 15 |
| 22.54 | 15 | 20.18-21 | 138 | 29.4-9 | 21 |
| 24.40 | 134 | 20.21 | 139, 150 | 29.4 | 22, 129 |
| 39.4 | 133 | 21.8 | 133 | 29.7 | 16 |
| 34 | 27 | 20.24 | 23 | 29.9 | 15, 189 |
| 46.1 | 15 | 21.15 | 15 | 29.21 | 16, 129 |
| 48.15 | 134 | 22.29-30 | 14 | 29.22 | 190 |
| 49 | 27 | 22.8 | 94 | 29.26 | 190 |
| | | 24.1-8 | 206 | 29.27 | 190 |
| Exodus | | 24.2 | 94, 118 | 29.29 | 15, 189 |
| 2.1 | 14, 17 | 24.3-8 | 20 | 29.31 | 190 |
| 3.5 | 94, 118 | 24.6-8 | 129 | 29.33 | 189 |
| 6.19-25 | 14 | 24.6 | 17 | 29.34 | 16, 190 |
| 12 | 69 | 25.40 | 97, 160 | 29.35 | 15, 189 |
| 12.48-49 | 135 | 26.30 | 160 | 29.36 | 23 |
| 13.2 | 14 | 26.33 | 176 | 29.37 | 16, 23 |
| 16.9 | 92, 94, | 27.1 | 20 | 29.44 | 15 |
| | 100, 101 | 27.8 | 160 | 30.7-10 | 20 |
| 17.8-16 | 21 | 27.20-21 | 155 | 30.7-9 | 155, 156 |
| 18.13-26 | 19 | 28 | 22 | 30.10 | 16, 23 |
| 18.15 | 17 | 28.1 | 14, 15 | 30.17-21 | 16 |
| 18.19 | 17 | 28.2 | 16 | 30.20 | 91, 92, |
| 19.5 | 92 | 28.23 | 154 | | 150, 151 |
| | | 28.29 | 150, 155 | 30.21 | 150 |

| | | | | | |
|---|---|---|---|---|---|
| 30.30 | 22, 129 | 4.16 | 21, 151, | 10.4-5 | 93 |
| 30.35 | 16 | | 152 | 10.7 | 22 |
| 32.25-29 | 15, 27 | 4.17 | 129 | 10.8-11 | 16 |
| 32.26-29 | 17 | 4.20 | 20, 151 | 10.9 | 91, 92, |
| 33.7-11 | 17 | 4.26 | 20 | | 150, 151 |
| 33.7 | 17 | 4.29 | 20 | 10.10-11 | 18 |
| 33.8 | 150, 153 | 4.31 | 20 | 10.12-20 | 52 |
| 33.9 | 150, 153 | 4.33 | 20 | 10.18-19 | 23 |
| 33.11 | 17 | 4.35 | 20 | 10.18 | 151 |
| 34.19-20 | 14 | 5.6 | 20 | 11.13-14 | 17 |
| 34.32 | 101 | 5.8 | 20 | 11.15 | 17 |
| 34.34 | 150 | 5.9 | 129 | 16 | 20, 22, |
| 34.35 | 150, 151, | 5.10 | 20 | | 23, 33, |
| | 153 | 5.13 | 20 | | 34, 65, |
| 36.1 | 92 | 5.16 | 20 | | 84, 98, |
| 36.3 | 92 | 5.18 | 20 | | 158, |
| 36.4 | 92 | 6.5-6 | 23 | | 160, 165 |
| 36.6 | 92 | 6.7 | 20 | 16.1 | 93, 94 |
| 39 | 22 | 7.33 | 151, 152 | 16.2 | 94, 152, |
| 40.12-15 | 16 | 7.35-36 | 22 | | 156, 176 |
| 40.12 | 22 | 7.37 | 190 | 16.3 | 150, |
| 40.13 | 15 | 8 | 15 | | 152, 156 |
| 40.15 | 15, 22 | 8.6 | 16, 22, | 16.4 | 22, 52, |
| 40.30-32 | 129 | | 129 | | 129 |
| 40.31-32 | 16 | 8.11 | 129 | 16.6 | 86, 198 |
| 40.32 | 91, 92, | 8.12 | 16 | 16.7-10 | 98 |
| | 150, 151 | 8.14 | 17 | 16.11-14 | 98 |
| 40.35 | 150, 153 | 8.15 | 23 | 16.11 | 86, 101, |
| | | 8.18 | 17 | | 152, 157 |
| *Leviticus* | | 8.21 | 190 | 16.12 | 152, |
| 1–7 | 20 | 8.22 | 190 | | 157, 176 |
| 1.5 | 20, 151, | 8.23 | 129 | 16.14-17 | 157 |
| | 152, 157 | 8.24 | 129 | 16.14 | 129, 152 |
| 1.14-15 | 20 | 8.26 | 190 | 16.15-16 | 98 |
| 2.9 | 91 | 8.27-28 | 190 | 16.15 | 101, |
| 3.2 | 20 | 8.29 | 190 | | 129, |
| 3.8 | 20 | 8.30 | 16, 129 | | 152, 176 |
| 3.13 | 20 | 8.33 | 15, 189, | 16.16 | 22, 156, |
| 4.1-5 | 151 | | 190 | | 157, 160 |
| 4.3-4 | 152 | 9.5 | 92, 94, | 16.17 | 67, 86, |
| 4.3 | 21 | | 100, 101 | | 151, 152, |
| 4.5-7 | 151 | 9.7-8 | 91, 100, | | 155-57 |
| 4.5 | 15, 21, | | 123 | 16.19 | 86, 101, |
| | 151, 152 | 9.22-24 | 21 | | 157 |
| 4.6 | 129 | 9.23 | 150, 151 | 16.20-22 | 98, 99 |
| 4.13 | 151 | 10.1-3 | 93 | 16.20 | 156, 160 |
| 4.14 | 20 | 10.3 | 92, 93, | 16.21 | 157 |
| 4.16-19 | 151 | | 118 | | |

# Index of Biblical References

| | | | | | |
|---|---|---|---|---|---|
| 16.23 | 150-52, 155, 156 | 4.4 | 16 | 25.8 | 150 |
| | | 4.5-15 | 16 | 27.21 | 18 |
| 16.24 | 157 | 4.5 | 150, 151 | 35.25 | 21 |
| 16.27 | 156 | 4.15 | 16 | 35.28 | 21 |
| 16.32 | 189 | 4.19-20 | 93 | 35.32 | 21 |
| 16.33 | 160 | 4.19 | 92-94, 150 | |  |
| 16.34 | 98, 129, 152, 156, 157 | | | *Deuteronomy* | |
| | | 4.20 | 150 | 4.11-12 | 138, 139 |
| | | 4.22-23 | 16 | 4.11 | 92, 94, 118, 139 |
| 17.11 | 20, 166 | 4.23 | 150 | | |
| 19.33 | 135 | 4.30 | 150 | 4.12 | 139 |
| 20.24 | 52 | 4.35 | 150 | 4.29 | 137 |
| 20.26 | 52 | 4.39 | 150 | 5.22-27 | 138 |
| 21.3 | 118 | 4.43 | 150 | 5.22 | 139 |
| 21.6 | 15 | 4.47 | 150 | 5.27 | 94, 139 |
| 21.7 | 16 | 5.12-31 | 65 | 9.19 | 138 |
| 21.10-15 | 22 | 6.22-27 | 21 | 10.8 | 15-17, 21, 52, 53 |
| 21.10 | 21, 190 | 7.89 | 150, 151 | | |
| 21.16-24 | 14 | 8.5-7 | 15 | | |
| 21.17-24 | 100, 123 | 8.6-7 | 129 | 12–26 | 60 |
| 21.17-22 | 42 | 8.7 | 16 | 17.8-9 | 18, 65 |
| 21.7 | 93, 101 | 8.11 | 16 | 17.12 | 16 |
| 21.18 | 91, 92, 101 | 8.14 | 52 | 17.17 | 53 |
| | | 8.15 | 150, 151 | 18.1 | 52 |
| 21.21 | 91, 93, 118 | 8.19 | 94 | 18.2 | 16 |
| | | 8.22 | 150, 151 | 18.5 | 16, 20, 53 |
| 21.23 | 91-94, 118 | 8.24 | 150, 151 | | |
| | | 9.14 | 135 | 20.2-7 | 34 |
| 22.1-33 | 52 | 10.1 | 21 | 18.7 | 16, 20, 53, 63 |
| 22.3 | 91, 92, 100, 123 | 10.2 | 21 | | |
| | | 10.3-10 | 101 | 21.5 | 16, 18, 20, 21, 91 |
| 23.26-32 | 98 | 10.10 | 21 | | |
| 26.13 | 109 | 12.6-8 | 17 | | |
| | | 15.32-36 | 65 | 27.9 | 18 |
| *Numbers* | | 16.5 | 94 | 27.12 | 20 |
| 1.50-52 | 16 | 16.9 | 15 | 27.14-16 | 18 |
| 1.51 | 94 | 16.19 | 52 | 27.18 | 18 |
| 3.3 | 15, 22, 189 | 16.40 | 93 | 31.9 | 16, 18 |
| | | 16.43 | 150 | 31.10-11 | 18 |
| 3.38 | 94 | 17.5 | 20 | 31.25-26 | 16 |
| 3.9 | 16 | 18.3 | 91, 92 | 31.30 | 146 |
| 3.11-13 | 14 | 18.4 | 100 | 33.8-10 | 17 |
| 3.21-26 | 16 | 18.7 | 91 | 33.8 | 17, 18 |
| 3.31 | 16 | 18.11 | 52 | 33.10 | 17, 19 |
| 3.32 | 16 | 19 | 17 | | |
| 3.38 | 16 | 19.3 | 129 | *Joshua* | |
| 3.41 | 14 | 19.9 | 148 | 3.3 | 16 |
| 4.3 | 150, 151 | 19.19 | 129 | 3.4 | 94 |

| | | | | | |
|---|---|---|---|---|---|
| 3.14 | 16 | 15.24-29 | 16 | 26.13-14 | 53 |
| 4.10-14 | 16 | 20.26 | 22 | 29.5 | 15 |
| 6.20-28 | 15 | | | | |
| 8.33 | 16 | *1 Kings* | | *2 Chronicles* | |
| | | 1.9 | 15 | 3.49 | 21 |
| *Judges* | | 2.26-27 | 16 | 5.4-5 | 16 |
| 6.25-26 | 19 | 2.35 | 16 | 5.14 | 19 |
| 13.16-23 | 19 | 3.4 | 19 | 5.15 | 21 |
| 17–18 | 14 | 3.15 | 19 | 7.16 | 21 |
| 17 | 16 | 4.1 | 16 | 13.9 | 15, 91 |
| 17.5 | 15, 22 | 8.5 | | 13.14 | 21 |
| 17.10 | 22 | 8.53 | 52 | 17.8-9 | 19 |
| 17.12 | 15, 22 | 8.62-64 | 19 | 19.8 | 19 |
| 18 | 17 | 9.25 | 19 | 23.6 | 150 |
| 18.4 | 22 | 12.31 | 16 | 23.19 | 150 |
| 18.19 | 22 | 13.33 | 15 | 24.20-22 | 27 |
| 18.30 | 14, 16, 22 | 14.5 | 18 | 26.16-18 | 20 |
| | | 18.30-38 | 15 | 26.16-17 | 150, 151 |
| 19–20 | 27 | 22.5-28 | 18 | 27.2 | 150 |
| 20.2 | 146 | 22.10 | 105 | 28.11 | 60 |
| | | 22.19 | 105 | 29.11 | 53 |
| *1 Samuel* | | | | 29.16 | 19, 150, 151 |
| 1–2 | 14, 16 | *2 Kings* | | | |
| 1.3 | 14, 19 | 3.11 | 18 | 29.21 | 19 |
| 1.4 | 19 | 8.7-13 | 18 | 29.26-28 | 21 |
| 1.21 | 19 | 16.12-15 | 19 | 29.31 | 15, 91 |
| 2.19 | 19 | 19.15 | 104 | 30.8 | 150 |
| 2.25 | 21 | 19.16 | 27 | 30.16 | |
| 2.27 | 14 | 22.11-20 | 18 | 30.17 | 20 |
| 2.36 | 21 | | | 35.3 | 19 |
| 4.4 | 14, 104 | *1 Chronicles* | | 35.11 | 19 |
| 4.11 | 14 | 6.7-13 | 14 | 35.16 | 16 |
| 4.17 | 14 | 6.18-23 | 14 | | |
| 6.14-15 | 15 | 6.33-38 | 14 | *Ezra* | |
| 7.1 | 15, 16 | 12.27-28 | 29 | 2.63 | 18 |
| 13.9-10 | 19 | 13.25-32 | 16 | 3.10 | 21 |
| 14.41-42 | 18 | 15.2 | 16 | 6.21 | 52 |
| 15.2 | 21 | 16.4 | 16 | 9.1 | 52 |
| 23.9-12 | 18 | 16.6 | 21 | 9.6-15 | 21, 25 |
| 24.25 | 19 | 16.41 | 16 | 10.11 | 52 |
| 30.7-8 | 18 | 23.13 | 15, 20, 21, 52 | | |
| | | | | *Nehemiah* | |
| *2 Samuel* | | 24.3 | 14, 16 | 3.1 | 21 |
| 6.2 | 104 | 24.5 | 53 | 3.20 | 21 |
| 6.7-13 | 14 | 24.7 | 53 | 7.65 | 18 |
| 6.13 | 19 | 24.31 | 53 | 8.7 | 19 |
| 6.17-18 | 19 | 25.8 | 53 | 8.9 | 19 |
| 15.2-4 | 14 | 25.9 | 53 | 9.2 | 52 |

# Index of Biblical References

| | | | | | |
|---|---|---|---|---|---|
| 9.3-31 | 132 | 51.19 | 57, 58 | *Proverbs* | |
| 10.29 | 52 | 56.1 | 112 | 15.8 | 57, 58 |
| 12.35 | 21 | 56.6 LXX | 161 | 15.18 | 58 |
| 12.41 | 21 | 56.13 | 134 | | |
| 13.28 | 21 | 56.14 | 58 | *Ecclesiastes* | |
| | | 57.1 | 112 | 4.17 | 118 |
| *Job* | | 59.11 | 112 | | |
| 15.15 | 171 | 66.13 | 150 | *Isaiah* | |
| 22.23-27 | 109 | 68.33 | 137 | 1.11-17 | 21 |
| 22.26-27 | 109, 110 | 69.1 | 112 | 2.3 | 18 |
| 26.9 | 105 | 69.31 | 58 | 6 | 104 |
| 27.9-10 | 109, 110 | 70.12 | 112 | 6.1-13 | 105, 147 |
| | | 78 | 132 | 7–9 | 47 |
| *Psalms* | | 80.1 | 105 | 29.13 | 92, 118 |
| 3.8 | 21 | 86.3 | 112 | 52.7 | 162 |
| 6.2 | 112 | 86.16 | 112 | 53.12 | 86 |
| 8.2 | 161 | 89.6 | 145 | 56.1 | 57 |
| 9.4 | 147 | 89.14 | 147 | 58.2 | 92, 118 |
| 9.7 | 147 | 93.2 | 147 | 61.6 | 11, 16, |
| 9.13 | 112 | 94.11 | 153 | | 206 |
| 11.4-7 | 147 | 95 | 202 | 66.1-2 | 147 |
| 11.4 | 105 | 95.7-11 | 103, 206 | 66.1 | 105 |
| 16.33 | 18 | 96.8 | 150 | | |
| 19.2 | 112 | 97.2 | 147 | *Jeremiah* | |
| 19.15 | 58 | 103.19 | 105, 147 | 3.17 | 105, 141 |
| 21.19 | 112 | 103.21 | 145 | 7.16 | 94, 107 |
| 25.7 | 112 | 105 | 132 | 14.12 | 147 |
| 26.3 | 134 | 106 | 132 | 14.21 | 105 |
| 30.10 | 112 | 107.6 LXX | 161 | 17.12-13 | 105 |
| 31.9 | 112 | 107.12 | 112 | 29.13 | 21 |
| 31.9 LXX | 94 | 109.26 | 112 | 31.21-22 | 16 |
| 33.5 | 137 | 110 | 83, 192 | 33.18 (MT) | 19 |
| 34.2 | 112 | 110.1 | 84 | 42.1-6 | 107 |
| 34.5 | 107 | 110.4 | 84, 99, | | |
| 35.14 | 134 | | 113, 119, | *Ezekiel* | |
| 37.22 | 112 | | 121 | 1.26 | 105 |
| 40.10 | 58 | 112.4 LXX | 161 | 7.26 | 18 |
| 40.17 | 58 | 116.9 | 134 | 10.1 | 105 |
| 41.4 | 112 | 119.88 | 112 | 20 | 132 |
| 41.10 | 112 | 119.108 | 58 | 22.26 | 18 |
| 42.3 | 174 | 119.149 | 112 | 32.29 | 15 |
| 43.4 | 150 | 119.159 | 112 | 36.25 | 13 |
| 44.26 | 112 | 123.3 | 112 | 40–48 | 611 |
| 45.6-7 | 106, 147 | 135 | 132 | 40.40 | 16 |
| 47.8 | 147 | 136 | 132 | 40.46 | 91, 118 |
| 51.1 | 112 | 141.2 | 58 | 41.3-4 | 153 |
| 51.7 | 148 | 148.2 | 145 | 42.13 | 91, 118 |
| 51.17 | 58 | 148.14 | 92, 118 | 42.14 | 150 |

| | | | | | |
|---|---|---|---|---|---|
| 43.7 | 105 | 7.10 | 146 | *Zephaniah* | |
| 43.19 | 91, 118 | | | 3.2 | 94, 118 |
| 43.26 | 15 | *Hosea* | | | |
| 44.3 | 150 | 2.11 | 146 | *Haggai* | |
| 44.7 | 151, 152 | 2.19-20 | 57 | 1.1 | 21 |
| 44.8 | 91 | 4.6-9 | 21 | 1.12 | 21 |
| 44.9 | 42, 150 | 5.6 | 21 | 1.14 | 21 |
| 44.11 | 20, 53 | 6.6 | 21, 57 | 2.15 | 118 |
| 44.13 | 91, 118 | 9.4 | 150, 151 | 2.2 | 21 |
| 44.15 | 16, 51, 151, 152 | 12.7 | 118 | 2.4 | 21 |
| | | 14.3 | 57, 58 | 2.11-13 | 18 |
| 44.16 | 16, 92, 93, 151 | *Amos* | | *Zechariah* | |
| 44.17 | 52 | 5.21 | 146 | 3.1 | 21 |
| 44.21 | 150 | | | 3.2 | 22 |
| 44.23 | 18 | *Joel* | | 3.8 | 21 |
| 44.27 | 150 | 1.9 | 16 | 6.11 | 21 |
| 44.29 | 52 | 1.13 | 16 | 6.13 | 22 |
| 45.4 | 118 | 2.17 | 16 | 7.3 | 18 |
| 45.14 | 91 | | | | |
| 46.9 | 150 | *Micah* | | *Malachi* | |
| 46.11 | 146 | 3.11 | 18 | 2.7-9 | 18 |
| | | 4.2 | 18 | | |
| *Daniel* | | 6.6-8 | 21, 57 | | |
| 3.38 LXX | 57 | | | | |

NEW TESTAMENT

| | | | | | |
|---|---|---|---|---|---|
| *Matthew* | | 21.26 | 155 | 1.3 | 84, 86, 88, 106, 141, 149, 161, 164, 175, 192, 196 |
| 26.36-46 | 87 | | | | |
| | | *Romans* | | | |
| *Mark* | | 8.27 | 85 | | |
| 7.9 | 114 | 8.29 | 146 | | |
| 14.32-42 | 87 | 8.34 | 84, 85, 174 | | |
| | | | | 1.4 | 89, 116 |
| *Luke* | | 10.15 | 162 | 1.6 | 107, 145, 146, 173, 183, 200, 202, 206 |
| 10.20 | 140 | 12.1-2 | 135 | | |
| 13.11 | 120 | 14.18 | 135 | | |
| 22.31-32 | 174 | | | | |
| 22.39-46 | 87 | *Galatians* | | 1.8 | 100, 106, 121, 192 |
| | | 3.19 | 148 | | |
| *John* | | 4.26 | 141, 204 | 1.10-12 | 161, 200, 206 |
| 14.2-3 | 177 | | | | |
| | | *Ephesians* | | 1.13 | 84, 106, 141, 161, 192, 200, 202, 206 |
| *Acts* | | 1.20 | 84 | | |
| 3.3 | 155 | 1.1-3 | 120 | | |
| 7 | 132 | 1.2 | 162, 205 | | |
| 15.17 | 137 | | | | |

# Index of Biblical References

| | | | | | | | |
|---|---|---|---|---|---|---|---|
| 1.14 | 122, 145, 204 | 4.3 | 132, 203 | 5.2 | 85, 157 | | |
| 1.20 | 84 | 4.6-10 | 206 | 5.3 | 101, 133, 157 | | |
| 2.3 | 122 | 4.10 | 183, 206 | 5.5-10 | 104 | | |
| 2.4 | 206 | 4.11 | 202, 203 | 5.5 | 89 | | |
| 2.5 | 200, 202, 206 | 4.14–10.39 | 103 | 5.6 | 83, 100, 121 | | |
| | | 4.14–10.18 | 125, 127, 182 | 5.7-10 | 88, 174 | | |
| 2.8 | 168, 200, 206 | 4.14–5.10 | 108 | 5.7-8 | 87 | | |
| 2.9-10 | 88, 195, 200 | 4.14-16 | 88, 103, 125 | 5.7 | 86, 87, 108, 112, 126, 133, 194, 197 | | |
| 2.9 | 86, 165, 174, 195, 196 | 4.14-15 | 104, 113 | | | | |
| | | 4.14 | 82, 84, 85, 105–107, 111, 128, 149, 161, 163, 164, 175, 177, 180, 192 | 5.8-10 | 195 | | |
| 2.10-18 | 90, 146 | | | 5.8-9 | 178 | | |
| 2.10 | 84, 122, 177, 185, 188, 195–98, 201, 206 | | | 5.8 | 188, 196 | | |
| | | | | 5.9 | 84, 103, 188, 196–98 | | |
| | | | | 5.9-10 | 166, 179, 193, 196, 197 | | |
| 2.11 | 89, 187 | 4.15-16 | 175 | | | | |
| 2.12 | 89 | 4.15 | 85, 87, 88, 174, 175, 187 | 5.9 | 121-23, 168, 169, 173, 178, 185, 188, 198, 201 | | |
| 2.13 | 89 | | | | | | |
| 2.14-15 | 89 | | | | | | |
| 2.14 | 89, 165 | 4.16 | 91, 101, 103, 104, 106, 108–12, 117–19, 122, 123, 125–28, 135, 136, 140, 141, 144, 145, 161, 168, 175, 181, 182 | | | | |
| 2.16 | 89 | | | | | | |
| 2.17-18 | 103, 104, 117, 122 | | | 5.10 | 122, 149, 169, 179, 196, 197 | | |
| 2.17 | 82-89, 119, 126, 193 | | | 5.11–6.20 | 179, 206 | | |
| 2.18 | 85, 89, 112, 175 | | | 5.14 | 185, 186 | | |
| 3.1–4.16 | 125 | | | 6.1 | 135, 185, 186 | | |
| 3.1–4.13 | 103, 200, 202, 206 | | | 6.2–10.18 | 125 | | |
| 3.1 | 82, 85, 117, 128, 172, 177 | 5.1-10 | 86, 87, 103, 104, 117, 126, 195-97 | 6.2 | 202 | | |
| | | | | 6.4-8 | 174 | | |
| | | | | 6.4 | 168, 206 | | |
| | | | | 6.5 | 97 | | |
| 3.6 | 110, 117, 202 | | | 6.7 | 100 | | |
| | | 5.1-4 | 104 | 6.9 | 122 | | |
| 3.7–4.13 | 175 | 5.1-3 | 87, 103, 126, 177, 194, 196, 197 | 6.11 | 117, 119 | | |
| 3.8 | 87 | | | 6.12 | 89, 192 | | |
| 3.12 | 128, 134, 137 | | | 6.13-15 | 89, 90, 117 | | |
| 3.13 | 98 | 5.1 | 86, 101, 133, 166, 197 | 6.18-20 | 102, 180 | | |
| 3.14 | 117, 202 | | | 6.18-19 | 177 | | |
| 4.1 | 137 | | | | | | |

| | | | | | | |
|---|---|---|---|---|---|---|
| 6.18 | 97, 117, 179, 180 | | 82, 185, 186, 195, 198 | 8.1-12 8.1-2 | 88 104, 106, 192 |
| 6.19-20 | 84, 90, 98, 117, 126, 136, 143, 150, 176-84, 192, 200, 204 | 7.20-22 7.21 7.22 7.23-25 | 113 83, 100, 113, 121 85, 116, 119, 120, 124, 186 113, 124 | 8.1 8.2-4 8.2 | 84, 106, 141, 149, 160, 161, 164, 175, 196 160 84, 106, |
| 6.19 | 100, 176, 179, 181, 182 | 7.23-24 7.23 | 115, 119, 120 120, 123, | 8.3 | 155, 159, 160, 170 101, 119, |
| 6.20 | 85, 100, 117, 121, 130, 166, 168, 169, 174, 176, 177, 179, 180, 183 | 7.24 7.25 | 124 83, 100, 113, 121, 122 85, 91, 101, 106, 108, 112, | 8.4 8.5 | 133, 166, 170, 177, 197 133 97, 102, 118, 160, 170, 171 |
| 6.24 7.1–10.18 | 192 95, 96, 98 | | 115, 116, 118-24, 127, 139, | 8.6 8.8 | 116, 148, 186 96 |
| 7.1-28 7.3 | 118, 123 99, 100, 121 | | 141, 144, 148, 168, 174, 175, | 9–10 9 9.1-10 | 88, 202 95 154, 158, |
| 7.5 7.9 7.11-25 7.11-12 7.11 | 96 101 113 113 83, 113-15, 119, 140, 185, 195, 198 | 7.26-28 7.26-27 7.26 7.27-28 7.27 | 177, 183, 195, 200 88, 119 187, 197 161, 187 86, 101, 102, 115 86, 98, | 9.1-5 9.1-3 9.1 9.2-5 9.2 | 170 153 159 95, 118, 159, 160 154 154, 155, 172 |
| 7.12 7.14 7.15 7.16 7.17 | 113 86 83 96, 114 83, 100, 113, 121 | 7.28 | 120, 124, 133, 157, 164, 166, 167, 197, 205 84, 100, | 9.3 9.5 9.6-15 9.6-10 9.6-7 | 154, 176 104, 172 126 153, 154 154, 159, 167 |
| 7.18-19 7.18 7.19 | 102, 113, 114, 140 113 91, 102, 113-19, 123, 124, 126, 127, 143, 180- | 8–9 8.1–10.18 | 121, 122, 149, 165, 169, 177, 185, 188, 195, 197, 198, 201 96 88 | 9.6 9.7 | 150, 153-56, 160 98, 101, 120, 124, 133, 150, 153-55, 158, 164, |

# Index of Biblical References

| | | | | | | | |
|---|---|---|---|---|---|---|---|
| | | 167, 170, 177 | 9.15 | 147, 148, 167, 172, 173 | 9.27 | 159, 169, 175, 202 |
| 9.8-10 | 140 | | | | 9.28 | 85, 86, 122, 133, 143, 159, 165, 169, 170, 173, 175, 183, 202 |
| 9.9 | 102, 103, 115, 129, 133, 160, 162, 166, 171, 173, 178, 185, 195, 198, 199, 201 | | 9.16-17 | 167 | | |
| | | | 9.18-22 | 129, 130, 148 | | |
| | | | 9.18-21 | 206 | | |
| | | | 9.18-19 | 192 | | |
| | | | 9.18 | 119 | | |
| | | | 9.19-21 | 129 | 10.1-18 | 95, 96 |
| | | | 9.19 | 96 | 10.1-4 | 126, 129 |
| 9.10 | 162, 179 | | 9.21-22 | 170 | 10.1-3 | 120 |
| 9.11-14 | 88, 158, 159, 163, 169, 170 | | 9.21 | 160, 170 | 10.1 | 87, 91, 95, 96, 98-102, 105, 114, 115, 118, 120, 121, 123, 124, 127, 133, 140, 144, 158, 162, 166, 182, 185, 195, 198, 199 |
| | | | 9.22 | 86, 96, 116 | | |
| 9.11-12 | 84, 104, 150, 159-61, 163, 168, 172, 173, 176, 183 | | 9.23-28 | 169 | | |
| | | | 9.23 | 86, 116, 148, 162, 166, 170-72, 186 | | |
| | | | 9.24-28 | 167, 170 | | |
| 9.11 | 95, 97, 159, 160, 162-64, 169, 170, 172, 176, 179, 185, 186, 198 | | 9.24-25 | 155, 168, 176, 177, 183 | | |
| | | | 9.24 | 84, 85, 130, 141, 148-50, 154, 158, 159, 161-64, 168-78, 183, 192 | 10.2-3 | 98 |
| | | | | | 10.2 | 96, 101, 115, 118, 130, 133, 171, 205 |
| 9.12 | 86, 123, 130, 155, 159, 163, 166, 167, 169, 170, 173, 177, 178, 205 | | | | 10.3-4 | 98 |
| | | | | | 10.3 | 96, 156 |
| | | | 9.25-28 | 126 | 10.4 | 98, 120, 124 |
| | | | 9.25-26 | 175 | | |
| | | | 9.25 | 98, 100, 130, 133, 150, 156, 158, 159, 164, 170, 175, 176, 179 | 10.5-10 | 167 |
| 9.13-14 | 90 | | | | 10.5 | 166 |
| 9.13 | 129, 130, 148, 158 | | | | 10.8 | 96, 133, 166 |
| 9.14 | 86, 108, 115, 123, 126, 130, 131, 133, 148, 170, 171, 176, 187 | | | | 10.10 | 86, 90, 96, 126, 165, 167, 170, 205 |
| | | | 9.26-28 | 176 | | |
| | | | 9.26 | 86, 100, 113, 159, 166, 170, 175, 176, 205 | 10.11 | 96, 98, 100, 101, 120, 124, 129, 133, 166 |
| 9.15-22 | 170 | | | | | |
| | | | 9.27-28 | 96, 176 | | |

| | | | | | | |
|---|---|---|---|---|---|---|
| 10.12 | 84, 86, 96, 99, 100, 106, 121, 133, 141, 149, 161, 164-66, 170, 196 | 10.26 | 157, 166, 168 | | | 177, 185, 188, 192, 196 |
| | | 10.27 | 202 | | | |
| | | 10.29 | 90 | 12.3-17 | 144 |
| | | 10.30-31 | 169, 202 | 12.4 | 199 |
| | | 10.32-39 | 103, 144 | 12.7 | 133 |
| | | 10.34 | 116 | 12.10-17 | 144 |
| | | 10.35 | 109, 136 | 12.10 | 144 |
| 10.13 | 202 | 10.37-39 | 85 | 12.11 | 144 |
| 10.14 | 90, 96, 99, 100, 121-22, 126, 147, 165, 176, 185, 188, 198, 199 | 10.37 | 143, 202 | 12.12-17 | 137 |
| | | 11–13 | 206 | 12.14-17 | 144 |
| | | 11.1 | 97, 131-33, 135, 136 | 12.14 | 183, 204 |
| | | | | 12.18-24 | 91, 123, 183 |
| | | 11.2 | 131 | 12.18-21 | 137-41, 143, 148 |
| | | 11.3 | 131 | | |
| 10.15-39 | 206 | 11.4 | 131, 133, 166 | 12.18 | 101, 138, 139, 149 |
| 10.18 | 95, 126 | | | | |
| 10.19-39 | 119 | 11.5-6 | 133 | 12.19 | 137 |
| 10.19-25 | 103, 125, 128, 135, 145 | 11.5 | 131, 135 | 12.22-29 | 107 |
| | | 11.6 | 91, 101, 123, 127, 131-37, 140, 144, 182, 202 | 12.22-24 | 107, 137, 138, 140, 142-45, 148, 161, 172, 183, 200, 201 |
| 10.19-22 | 177, 178, 181 | | | | |
| 10.19-21 | 104, 111, 125-27, 165, 182 | | | | |
| | | 11.7-9 | 131 | | |
| | | 11.10 | 142, 204 | 12.22 | 101, 106, 107, 127, 138, 141, 144, 145, 148, 171, 182 |
| 10.19-20 | 84, 88 | 11.11-12 | 131 | | |
| 10.19 | 86, 109, 110, 124, 126, 129, 182 | 11.12 | 89, 161 | | |
| | | 11.13-16 | 131, 136, 142, 204 | | |
| | | 11.17-25 | 131 | | |
| 10.20 | 87, 88, 176, 178 | 11.19 | 160 | 12.23 | 183, 185, 198, 200-202 |
| | | 11.26 | 136, 202 | | |
| 10.21 | 83, 127 | 11.27-31 | 131 | | |
| 10.22-25 | 144 | 11.27 | 133 | 12.24 | 84-86, 130, 137, 145, 147, 165, 168, 173, 175 |
| 10.22 | 91, 101, 109, 115, 117, 125-31, 134-37, 140, 141, 148, 171, 182 | 11.32-38 | 131 | | |
| | | 11.39-40 | 147 | | |
| | | 11.40 | 147, 172, 183, 185, 188, 198, 200, 201 | | |
| | | | | 12.25-29 | 85, 137, 138, 143, 144 |
| | | 12.1 | 125, 178 | | |
| 10.23 | 82, 128 | 12.2-3 | 165 | 12.26-28 | 203 |
| 10.25 | 85, 128, 202, 204 | 12.2 | 84-86, 88, 106, 141, 161, 164, 175, | 12.26 | 161 |
| | | | | 12.28 | 108, 123, 135, 204, 205 |
| 10.26-31 | 174 | | | | |

# Index of Biblical References

| | | | | | |
|---|---|---|---|---|---|
| 12.29 | 202 | *Philippians* | | *2 John* | |
| 13.1-21 | 144 | 4.3 | 146 | 3 | 112 |
| 13.4 | 202 | | | | |
| 13.5 | 166 | *Colossians* | | *Jude* | |
| 13.8 | 100, 121 | 3.1 | 84 | 14 | 146 |
| 13.9 | 115 | | | | |
| 13.10-16 | 107 | *1 Timothy* | | *Revelation* | |
| 13.10 | 102, 118, 160 | 1.2 | 112 | 3.5 | 146 |
| | | | | 3.12 | 141, 204 |
| 13.11-12 | 167 | *2 Timothy* | | 3.21 | 106, 196 |
| 13.12 | 86, 90, 165,170, 176 | 1.2 | 112 | 4–5 | 47 |
| | | | | 5.11-12 | 141, 145 |
| | | *Titus* | | 5.11 | 146 |
| 13.13 | 178, 206 | 1.4 | 112 | 6.9 | 183, 201 |
| 13.14 | 97, 142, 204 | 3.9 | 115 | 7.9-19 | 201 |
| | | | | 7.9-17 | 183 |
| 13.15 | 100, 124, 205 | *1 Peter* | | 13.8 | 146 |
| | | 1.2 | 148 | 15.2 | 183 |
| 13.16 | 108, 123, 134, 166 | 3.22 | 84 | 17.8 | 146 |
| | | | | 20.4 | 146 |
| 13.18 | 115 | *1 John* | | 20.15 | 146 |
| 13.20 | 86, 148, 168 | 2.1-2 | 169 | 21.1-4 | 141 |
| | | 2.1 | 85 | 21.2 | 204 |
| 13.21 | 100, 124, 134, 206 | 3.12 | 111 | 21.22 | 142 |
| | | 4.17 | 111 | 22.1 | 106 |
| | | 5.14 | 111 | 22.3 | 106 |

## APOCRYPHA

| | | | | | |
|---|---|---|---|---|---|
| *1 Esdras* | | 9.46 | 25 | 5.5 | 42 |
| 1.18 | 24 | 9.48 | 26 | 9.8 | 160 |
| 5.46 | 24 | 9.49 | 26 | 10 | 132 |
| 5.48-49 | 24 | | | | |
| 5.50-53 | 24 | *Tobit* | | *Sirach* | |
| 5.59 | 24 | 1.6 | 24 | 1.28 | 136 |
| 7.9 | 24 | 13.10-16 | 141 | 1.30 | 128 |
| 8.3 | 26 | | | 2.1 | 138 |
| 8.7 | 26 | *Judith* | | 2.9 | 112 |
| 8.8 | 26 | 4.6 | 27 | 4.15 | 136 |
| 8.9 | 26 | 4.14 | 24 | 7.29-31 | 24 |
| 8.46 | 24 | 4.15 | 24, 25 | 35.1 | 58 |
| 8.58 | 24 | 8.27 | 92 | 44–50 | 132 |
| 8.74-90 | 25 | 11.3 | 24 | 44.16 | 132, 134 |
| 9.16 | 26 | 15.9-10 | 25 | 45.6-22 | 24 |
| 9.39 | 26 | | | 45.17 | 26 |
| 9.40 | 26 | *Wisdom of Solomon* | | 45.23-26 | 24 |
| 9.42 | 26 | 4.10 | 132 | 45.26 | 26 |

| | | | | | |
|---|---|---|---|---|---|
| 49.14 | 132 | 2.54 | 24 | 14.44 | 24 |
| 50.1-24 | 24 | 2.66 | 27 | 14.47 | 24, 28 |
| 50.12 | 24 | 3.1 | 27 | 15.1 | 28 |
| | | 3.49 | 24 | | |
| Prayer of | | 3.51 | 24 | 2 Maccabees | |
| Azariah | | 4.36-61 | 24 | 1.18-36 | 24 |
| 2 | 25 | 4.42-51 | 27 | 1.21 | 24 |
| | | 5.67 | 27 | 1.23 | 24, 25 |
| 1 Maccabees | | 7.33 | 24 | 1.30 | 24 |
| 1.46 | 24 | 7.36 | 24, 25 | 3.15 | 24, 25 |
| 2.1-48 | 27 | 10.42 | 24 | 4.14 | 24 |
| 2.1 | 27 | 14.29 | 27 | 14.31 | 24 |
| 2.6 | 27 | 14.41 | 24, 28 | 14.34 | 24, 25 |
| 2.52-60 | 132 | 14.42 | 24 | 15.31 | 24 |

PSEUDEPIGRAPHA

| | | | | | |
|---|---|---|---|---|---|
| Apocalypse of Abraham | | 71 | 201 | 14.9 | 201 |
| 17–18 | 47 | 71.8 | 146 | 14.49 | 201 |
| | | 71.13 | 146 | | |
| Apocalypse of Ezra | | 90.26-39 | 141 | Joseph and Aseneth | |
| 1.9 | 201 | 103 | 201 | 27.6 | 27 |
| | | 104.1-5 | 109 | | |
| Ascension of Isaiah | | 104.6 | 42 | Jubilees | |
| 9.6-42 | 201 | | | 4.23-26 | |
| | | 2 Enoch | | 10.17 | 132 |
| 2 Baruch | | 20.21 | 47 | 21.7-18 | 24 |
| 4.2-7 | 141 | 55.2 | 141 | 30.18-20 | 24, 27 |
| 4.5 | 160 | 69–71 | 24, 28 | 31.12-17 | 26, 28 |
| | | 70.14 | 281 | 31.14 | 24 |
| 1 Enoch | | 70.16-19 | 25 | 31.16 | 24, 52 |
| 1.9 | 146 | 70.21 | 25 | 31.17 | 27 |
| 14.22 | 146 | 71.18-23 | 28 | 32.2 | 25 |
| 22.1-14 | 183, 201 | 71.18 | 25 | 32.3-9 | 24 |
| 39–40 | 47 | 71.30-31 | 25 | 45.16 | 26 |
| 39 | 201 | | | | |
| 39.4-8 | 42 | 4 Ezra | | Epistle of Aristeas | |
| 40.5 | 201 | 2.42-48 | 201 | 87 | 24 |
| 47.2-4 | 109, 111 | 7.26 | 141 | 92–93 | 24 |
| 48.8 | 109 | 7.28 | 201 | 95 | 24 |
| 51.5 | 109 | 7.87 | 109 | 96–99 | 24 |
| 60.1 | 146 | 7.88-101 | 201 | | |
| 61.1-13 | 109 | 7.98-101 | 107 | 3 Maccabees | |
| 61.12 | 201 | 8.52 | 141 | 1.11 | 24, 98 |
| 62.3-5 | | 10.27 | 141 | 1.16 | 24, 25 |
| 63.1-12 | 109 | 10.54 | 141 | 2.1-20 | 24, 25 |
| 69.26 | 109 | 13.36 | 141 | 6.1 | 25 |
| 70.4 | 201 | 13.52 | 201 | 6.4-8 | 132 |

# Index of Biblical References

| | | | | | |
|---|---|---|---|---|---|
| 7.13 | 25, 27 | 15.1 | 112 | *T. Levi* | |
| 7.16 | 121 | | | 3.8 | 47 |
| | | *Sibylline Oracles* | | 4.2 | 24 |
| *4 Maccabees* | | 3.787 | 141 | 4.3 | 26 |
| 4.19 | 24, 25 | 5.250-51 | 141 | 4.5 | 26 |
| 5.35 | 26 | | | 5.1-7 | 160 |
| 17.5 | 201 | *T. Adam* | | 5.2 | 24 |
| 17.18 | 105, 183, 201 | 1.7 | 27 | 5.3 | 27 |
| | | 1.12 | 24, 25 | 8 | 52 |
| 18.11-19 | 132 | 2.10 | 27 | 8.1-19 | 24 |
| 18.23 | 201 | | | 9.6 | 24, 26 |
| | | *T. Dan* | | 9.7 | 24 |
| *Lives of the Prophets* | | 5.12 | 141 | 13.2 | 26 |
| 22.2 | 27 | | | 13.9 | 26 |
| 23.1-2 | 27 | *T. Isaac* | | 14.4 | 26 |
| | | 4.8 | 42 | 14.5-8 | 24 |
| *Odes of Solomon* | | 4.32-42 | 24, 25 | 14.6 | 26 |
| 20.1-10 | 24, 28 | | | 17.1-11 | 24 |
| | | *T. Job* | | 18 | 24 |
| *Ps.-Hecataeus* | | 39.12 | 201 | 18.1-14 | 26 |
| 187-88 | 24 | 52.10 | 201 | | |
| 187 | 24 | | | *T. Moses* | |
| 199 | 24 | *T. Judah* | | 7.1-10 | 24 |
| | | 21 | 52 | 10.2 | 24, 27 |
| *Psalms of Solomon* | | 21.2-5 | 48 | | |
| 2.3 | 24 | 21.2 | 28 | *T. Solomon* | |
| 8.33-34 | 112 | 21.4 | 28 | 6.4 | 24 |
| 9.16 | 112 | | | | |

## QUMRAN

| | | | | | |
|---|---|---|---|---|---|
| *1QapGen* | | 11.10-14 | 42, 53 | 18.28 | 53, 55 |
| 21.20 | 44 | 11.10 | 56 | | |
| 21.1-4 | 44 | 11.11 | 53 | *1QpHab* | |
| | | 11.12 | 56 | 2.5-6 | 39 |
| *1QH* | | 11.13 | 53, 56 | 8.8-13 | 36 |
| 1.36 | 58 | 11.14 | 56 | 9.4-5 | 36 |
| 2.14 | 51 | 12.3-11 | 58 | 9.6 | 39 |
| 3.19-36 | 39 | 12.4 | 58 | 11.12-15 | 36 |
| 3.21 | 53, 56 | 12.7 | 58 | 12.1-10 | 40 |
| 3.22 | 56 | 12.22-24 | 53 | 12.7-9 | 36 |
| 3.23 | 56 | 12.23 | 54, 55 | | |
| 4.21 | 53 | 14.14 | 55 | *1QM* | |
| 6.25-34 | 57 | 15.24 | 54 | 2.1-6 | 47, 57 |
| 7.30-31 | 53 | 16.7 | 54 | 2.1-3 | 48 |
| 7.30 | 55, 56 | 16.12 | 56 | 2.1 | 46 |
| 8.1 | 51 | 16.13 | 53 | 2.3 | 49 |
| 11.6 | 58 | 18.10 | 53 | 2.5-6 | 44 |

| | | | | | | |
|---|---|---|---|---|---|---|
| 3.2 | 51 | 5.1-3 | 44 | 10.14 | 58 | |
| 4.10 | 51 | 5.2-4 | 44 | 10.21 | 58 | |
| 7.3 | 52 | 5.2-3 | 53 | 10.22 | 57, 58 | |
| 7.9-13 | 46 | 5.3 | 57 | 10.23 | 58 | |
| 7.10-13 | 46 | 5.6 | 40, 58 | 10.26–11.1 | 57 | |
| 7.11 | 47, 49 | 5.10 | 52 | 11.8 | 42 | |
| 8.8-14 | 62 | 5.13 | 52 | 12.18-23 | 45 | |
| 9.1-9 | 46 | 5.14-20 | 53 | | | |
| 10.2-5 | 45 | 5.14-17 | 52 | *1QSa* | | |
| 12.14 | 55 | 6.2-8 | 45 | 1 | 39 | |
| 13.1–14.16 | 45 | 6.3-5 | 44 | 1.2-3 | 54 | |
| 13.1-3 | 46 | 6.8-9 | 44 | 1.4 | 52 | |
| 14.2-5 | 46 | 6.16-17 | 52 | 1.9 | 53 | |
| 14.7 | 58 | 6.16 | 55 | 1.12 | 55 | |
| 15.4-15 | 46 | 6.17 | 53 | 1.15-16 | 41 | |
| 15.4 | 46 | 6.19 | 53, 55 | 1.16 | 40 | |
| 15.6-11 | 45 | 6.22 | 53, 55 | 1.20 | 53 | |
| 16.11-13 | 46 | 6.25 | 53 | 1.23 | 40 | |
| 16.13 | 46 | 7.6 | 53 | 1.28 | 58 | |
| 17.10-15 | 47 | 7.21 | 55 | 2.1 | 45 | |
| 18.3-6 | 47 | 8.1-10 | 40, 57 | 2.3-10 | 52 | |
| 18.5 | 46 | 8.1 | 44 | 2.5-6 | 39 | |
| 19.9-13 | 47 | 8.2-4 | 57 | 2.11-16 | 48 | |
| 19.11 | 55 | 8.3-4 | 58 | 2.11-12 | 45 | |
| | | 8.6 | 40, 54, 58 | 2.13 | 40, 41 | |
| *1QpHab* | | | | 2.18-21 | 48 | |
| 2.8-9 | 45 | 8.8 | 48 | 2.19 | 45 | |
| | | 8.10 | 54, 58 | 2.20 | 45 | |
| *1QS* | | 8.18 | 55 | 3.25-26 | 42 | |
| 1.1-2 | 137 | 8.23 | 53 | 4.24-26 | 42 | |
| 1.7 | 55 | 9.2 | 58 | 9.6 | 39 | |
| 1.12 | 53 | 9.3-6 | 57 | | | |
| 1.18–2.25 | 45 | 9.3-5 | 45, 54, 57 | *1QSb* | | |
| 1.24 | 57 | | | 3.1-5 | 38 | |
| 2.7-9 | 42 | 9.4-5 | 43, 58 | 3.1-3 | 57 | |
| 2.19-21 | 40 | 9.5-7 | 40, 58 | 4.25 | 42 | |
| 2.19 | 39 | 9.5 | 44, 58 | | | |
| 2.20 | 45 | 9.6 | 40 | *1Q* | | |
| 2.26–3.12 | 57 | 9.7-9 | 53 | 22.3.11–4.3 | 44 | |
| 3.2 | 53 | 9.7 | 40 | 24.5-8 | 44 | |
| 3.4-12 | 58 | 9.9 | 58 | | | |
| 3.4-11 | 52 | 9.10-11 | 48 | *4QDib Ham* | | |
| 3.20 | 51 | 9.11 | 40 | 4.9-11 | 57 | |
| 3.22 | 51 | 9.14 | 51 | | | |
| 4.20-22 | 38 | 9.15 | 55 | *4QFlor* | | |
| 4.22 | 58 | 9.26 | 58 | 1 | 44 | |
| 4.25 | 40 | 10 | 58 | 1.2 | 49 | |
| 5.1-7 | 57 | 10.6-8 | 58 | 1.3-4 | 42 | |

# Index of Biblical References

| | | | | | |
|---|---|---|---|---|---|
| 1.3 | 49, 55 | 32.12 | 62 | 6.11–7.6 | 38, 53 |
| 1.4 | 42 | 34.13 | 62 | 6.12–7.6 | 36 |
| 1.5-7 | 38 | 35.1-9 | 62 | 6.12 | 55 |
| 1.6-7 | 57, 58 | 35.4-9 | 63 | 6.14-16 | 53 |
| 1.6 | | 36.1–38.11 | 62 | 6.14 | 39 |
| 1.10 | 61 | 45.7–48 | 63 | 7.7-9 | 52 |
| 2.2-3 | 61 | 57.1-3 | 62 | 9.14-16 | 43 |
| | | 57.11-15 | 62 | 9.22 | 47 |
| 4QM$^a$ | | 58.18-21 | 62 | 10.5-6 | 45 |
| 5 | 58 | 59 | 60 | 10.5 | 40, 44 |
| | | 60.10-11 | 62 | 10.6-7 | 42 |
| 4QpPs 37 | | 60.14 | 63 | 11.17–12.2 | 43, 57 |
| 2.10-13 | 47 | 61.8 | 62 | 11.20-22 | 45, 47 |
| 3.11 | 49 | 61.15–62.16 | 62 | 11.22 | 55 |
| | | 63.3-4 | 62 | 12.22–14.12 | 44 |
| 4QSb | | | | 12.23 | 48 |
| 4.25 | 49 | CD | | 13.3-4 | 45 |
| | | 1.7 | 40 | 13.7-13 | 44 |
| 4Q Shir Shabb | | 1.10 | 137 | 14.3-6 | 40, 45 |
| | 43, 51 | 2.11 | 51 | 14.19 | 48 |
| | | 3.1 | 48 | 15.7 | 39 |
| 4QTestim | | 3.18–4.4 | 41 | 15.10 | 39 |
| 18 | 44 | 3.21–4.4 | 50, 51, 57 | 15.15-17 | 42 |
| | | | | 16.13-19 | 57 |
| 11QT | | 4.2 | 55 | 16.13-16 | 43 |
| 13.8-30 | 62 | 4.3 | 51 | 19.2-5 | 52 |
| 19.10 | 61 | 4.4 | 51 | 19.10 | 48 |
| 22.4 | 63 | 4.18-19 | 36 | 20.1 | 48 |
| 25.14 | 62 | 5.6-15 | 53 | 20.2 | 55 |
| 26.7 | 62 | 5.6 | 36 | 20.28 | 55 |
| 26.9 | 62 | 5.18 | 40 | | |
| 29.8-10 | 61 | 6.10 | 39 | | |

## MISHNAH

| | | | | | |
|---|---|---|---|---|---|
| Ab. | | 4.6 | 33 | Ḥul. | |
| 5.5 | 34 | 5.4 | 33 | 1.6 | 32 |
| | | | | 10.1-4 | 33 |
| 'Arak. | | Beṣ. | | | |
| 8.5-7 | 33 | 1.6 | 33 | Kel. | |
| | | | | 1.6-9 | 32 |
| Bek. | | Bikk. | | | |
| 7.1-7 | 32 | 3.2 | 35 | Ket. | |
| | | 3.12 | 33 | 1.5 | 34 |
| Ber. | | | | 13.1-2 | 34 |
| 1.1 | 33 | Ḥal. | | | |
| 4.5 | 33 | 4.11 | 33 | Kidd. | |
| | | | | 4.4 | 32 |

| | | | | | | |
|---|---|---|---|---|---|---|
| 4.5 | 31 | Sanh. | | Ter. | |
| 4.6 | 32 | 1.5 | 34 | 8.1 | 31 |
| | | | | | |
| Meg. | | Šeq. | | Yeb. | |
| 4.3-10 | 33 | 5.2 | 33 | 7.6 | 34 |
| | | 7.6 | 31 | 9.1 | 32 |
| Mid. | | | | 11.7 | 33 |
| 1.1 | 33 | Soṭ. | | | |
| 4.5 | 32 | 3.7 | 33 | Yom. | |
| 4.7 | 32 | 7.2 | 34 | 1.1-8 | 32 |
| 5.4 | 31 | 7.7 | 33 | 1.2 | 32 |
| | | 7.8 | 33 | 1.8 | 31 |
| Naz. | | 8.1 | 34 | 2.3-5 | 31 |
| 7.1 | 31 | | | 3.3 | 129 |
| | | Suk. | | 3.8 | 33 |
| Ned. | | 5.6-8 | 34 | 3.9 | 32 |
| 11.3 | 33 | | | 4.1 | 32 |
| | | Taʿan. | | 4.2 | 33 |
| Neg. | | 4.2 | 33 | 5.1 | 32, 33, |
| 14.10 | 32 | | | | 157, 163 |
| | | Tam. | | 5.3 | 157 |
| Par. | | 1.1 | 33 | 5.4 | 157 |
| 3.5 | 32 | 3.1 | 31 | 5.5 | 31 |
| 3.9 | 32 | 4.3 | 31 | 5.6 | 157 |
| | | 5.1 | 33 | 6.2 | 33, 157 |
| Pes. | | 7.2 | 33 | 7.1 | 33 |
| 1.6 | 31 | 7.3 | 32, 34 | 7.4 | 157 |
| | | | | 8.8-9 | 157 |
| Roš Haš. | | Tem. | | 8.8 | 35 |
| 1.7 | 34 | 3.4 | 31 | | |

BABYLONIAN TALMUD

| | | | | | |
|---|---|---|---|---|---|
| ʿAbod. Zar. | | Meg. | | Taʿan. | |
| 32 | 34 | 31b | 35 | 27b | 35 |
| | | | | | |
| B. Bat. | | Sanh. | | Yom. | |
| 38a | 34 | 59a | 34 | 16a | 30 |
| | | | | 19a | 33 |
| Hag. | | Soṭ. | | 52b | 32 |
| 12b | 141 | 39a | 33 | | |
| | | 39b | 33 | | |
| Kidd. | | 40a | 33 | | |
| 23b | 33 | | | | |

# Index of Biblical References

## MIDRASH

| Lev. R. | | Sifre Num. | |
|---|---|---|---|
| 7.3 | 35 | 6.23 | 33 |

## PHILO

| Abr. | | Gig. | | Prov. | |
|---|---|---|---|---|---|
| 198 | 65 | 52 | 65, 67, 98 | 2.64 | 70 |
| Agr. | | | | Quaest. in Ex. | |
| 94 | 121, 123 | Jos. | | 1.4-5 | 68 |
| | | 28 | 64 | 1.8 | 69 |
| Cher. | | | | 1.10 | 67, 68 |
| 91 | 146 | Leg. ad G. | | 1.12 | 67 |
| 92 | 146 | 234 | 65 | 1.15 | 69 |
| 99–100 | 170 | 306 | 98 | 1.19 | 64 |
| | | 307–308 | 67 | 2.51-106 | 67 |
| Conf. Ling. | | 307 | 65, 157 | 2.52 | 64 |
| 55 | 136 | | | 107-24 | 67 |
| | | Leg. All. | | | |
| Cong. | | 3.9 | 118 | Quis Rer. Div. Her. | |
| 89 | 65 | 3.9b | 97 | 5-29 | 109 |
| 103 | 65 | 3.135 | 65 | 21 | 111 |
| 105 | 65 | | | 82-85 | 65 |
| 106 | 69 | Migr. Abr. | | 82-83 | 66, 69 |
| | | 2 | 121, 123 | 84 | 65, 67 |
| Dec. | | 25 | 69 | 174 | 65 |
| 44 | 137 | 124 | 123 | 192 | 69 |
| 159–60 | 68 | 174 | 67 | 303 | 66 |
| 159 | 65 | | | 20-21 | 70 |
| | | Mut. Nom. | | | |
| Deus imm. | | 13 | 136 | Quod Deus | |
| 161 | 118 | | | 8 | 70 |
| | | Op. Mun. | | 132-35 | 60 |
| Ebr. | | 13 | 64 | | |
| 2 | 65 | 34 | 64 | Quod Omn. | |
| 72 | 123 | 130 | 64 | 75 | 43 |
| 111 | 123 | 144 | 136 | | |
| 126 | 65 | | | Sacr. | |
| 129 | 65 | Plant. | | 63 | 69 |
| 136 | 65, 98 | 64 | 136 | | |
| | | 97 | 136 | Som. | |
| Fug. | | 108 | 70 | 1.81-84 | 66 |
| 41 | 136 | 126-29 | 70 | 1.86 | 123 |
| 93 | 65 | 126 | 70 | 1.125 | 65 |
| 108 | 67 | | | 1.206 | 64 |
| 110 | 67 | Praem. | | 1.215 | 67 |
| | | 56 | 65 | 2.74 | 65 |

| | | | | | | |
|---|---|---|---|---|---|---|
| 2.189 | 67 | 1.191 | 70 | *Vit. Cont.* | | |
| 2.231 | 67 | 1.200 | 64 | 82 | 65 | |
| | | 1.205 | 66 | | | |
| *Spec. Leg.* | | 1.243 | 66 | *Vit. Mos.* | | |
| 1.66-298 | 64 | 1.252 | 123 | 1.214 | 65 | |
| 1.66-75 | 67 | 1.257-58 | 70 | 2.24 | 70 | |
| 1.72 | 65, 98 | 1.272 | 70 | 2.71-108 | 67 | |
| 1.82 | 65 | 1.287 | 70 | 2.107-108 | 70 | |
| 1.84-97 | 67 | 2.39-222 | 64-64 | 2.109-35 | 67 | |
| 1.96-97 | 67 | 2.147 | 69 | 2.131 | 67 | |
| 1.96 | 65 | 2.163-64 | 69 | 2.138 | 65 | |
| 1.98 | 65 | 2.163 | 68 | 2.141 | 65 | |
| 1.113 | 65 | 2.17b | 146 | 2.145-46 | 68 | |
| 1.122 | 65 | 2.2-4 | 146 | 2.150-53 | 65 | |
| 1.125 | 65 | 3.5b-60 | 65 | 2.174 | 65 | |
| 1.131 | 65 | 3.207 | 64 | 2.224-25 | 68 | |
| 1.151 | 65 | 4.190 | 65 | 2.224 | 65 | |
| 1.168-256 | 65 | | | | | |

JOSEPHUS

| | | | | | |
|---|---|---|---|---|---|
| *Ant.* | | 13.151 | 52 | *War* | |
| 1.85 | 132 | 13.158 | 52 | 2.123 | 52 |
| 2.52 | 109 | 13.1-2 | 24 | 2.137 | 52 |
| 2.131 | 109 | 18.1-5 | 43 | 2.8.5 | 42 |
| 5.38 | 109 | 63.1-5 | 24 | 5.229 | 52 |
| 11.196 | 115 | | | | |

OTHER ANCIENT AUTHORS

| | | | | | |
|---|---|---|---|---|---|
| *1 Clement* | | 11.23 | 77, 78 | *Homeric Hymn* | |
| 62.2 | 133 | 11.25 | 80 | *to Demeter* | |
| | | | | 480-82 | 72 |
| Apuleius | | Hippolytus | | | |
| *Golden Ass* | 75 | *Ref. Omn. Haer.* | | Prudentius | |
| | | 5.8.39 | 80 | *Peristephenon* | |
| *Metamorphoses* | | | | 10.1011-50 | 78 |
| 11.8-16 | 76 | | | | |
| 11.23-30 | 79 | | | | |

## INDEX OF AUTHORS

Abba, R. 14
Allcock, P.J. 100
Alt, A. 19
Ap-Thomas, D.R. 14
Arndt, W.F. 87, 121, 124, 156-58, 174
Attridge, H.W. 12, 83, 87, 88, 98, 108, 111, 114, 119, 121, 125, 128, 140, 146, 148, 157, 159, 162, 167, 170-72, 181, 186, 187, 193, 194, 202-206

Baker, J.W. 14
Baltensweiler, H. 87
Balz, H. 96
Barrett, C.K. 139, 141, 142, 164, 203
Barth, M. 130, 131
Baudissin, W.G. 13, 17, 22
Bauer, W. 121, 124, 156-58, 174
Bauernfiend, O. 177-79
Baumgarten, J.M. 45
Bengel, J.A. 138
Best, E. 9, 118, 186, 192
Beyer, H.W. 25
Bianchi, U. 71-73, 80
Bietenhard, H. 88, 141, 160, 164, 171
Billerbeck, P. 29, 32, 33, 106, 141, 146, 157, 160, 204
Black, J. Sutherland 13
Blass, F. 96, 131, 140, 158
Blendinger, C. 106
Boman, T. 87
Bornhäuser, K. 185
Bornkamm, G. 25, 78, 86, 128, 130
Botterweck, G. 94
Bourke, M. 116, 117
Bousset, W. 66, 68, 201, 202
Braun, H. 82, 83, 87, 88, 96, *et passim*

Bromiley, G.W. 14, 40
Brooks, W.E. 151, 154, 208
Brown, C. 25, 168, 169
Brown, R.E. 39, 46, 47, 111, 116
Bruce, F.F. 88, 97, 98, 100, 103, 106, 113-15, 120, 124, 147, 156, 157, 167, 168, 172, 177, 191, 196, 205
Buchannan, G.W. 89, 105, 110, 114, 121, 125, 157, 170, 203, 204
Büchsel, F. 112
Bultmann, R. 112, 117, 157
Burrows, M. 38, 39, 44, 45, 48, 51
Byrne, B. 23

Calvin, J. 130, 131
Campbell, J.Y. 186-88, 202
Carlston, C. 186, 189, 194, 195, 198
Carmignac, J. 38
Casey, J.M. 138, 140, 143
Chamberlin, J.V. 39
Charlesworth, J.H. 23, 24, 26-28
Cockerill, G.L. 88, 91, 100, 102, 114, 116, 122-24, 192, 193, 197
Cody, A. 13-15, 17, 19, 20, 22, 23, 26, 160, 172, 173, 175
Colson, F.H. 65
Conzelmann, H. 112
Cross, F.M. 29, 36, 37, 43, 45, 46
Cullmann, O. 87, 187, 204
Cumont, F. 72, 74-77, 80

Dahl, N.A. 107, 108, 110, 123, 127
Daly, R.J. 37, 48, 50, 51, 57, 58, 65, 67-69
Danby, H. 30, 35
Daube, D. 139
Davidson, A.B. 86

Davies, W.D. 139
Dean-Otting, M. 196
Debrunner, A. 96, 140, 158
Delitzsch, F. 96-101, 103, 105-109,
  111, 114-17, 120, 123, 129, 130,
  132, 133, 135, 138, 139, 145, 154,
  156, 157, 171, 176, 177, 181
Delling, G. 87, 121, 147, 185, 186,
  189-91, 194
Dey, L.K. Kumar 185, 194, 204
Dibelius, M. 86, 88, 95, 102, 185-87,
  189-91
Dickens, E.W. Trueman 203
Dodd, C.H. 139
Doran, R. 26
Driver, S.R. 92
Drummond, J. 70
Du Plessis, P.J. 186-91
Dumbrell, W.J. 139, 142, 145, 147
Dupont-Sommer, A. 44, 51

Edwards, J.R. 95
Eichrodt, W. 14, 17, 20, 104
Ellingworth, P. 161
Eltester, W. 25, 103
Engelmann, H. 75
Evans, M.J. 154

Fabry, H.-J. 94
Filson, F.V. 204, 205
Fiorenza, E.S. 36, 39, 41, 176, 205
Fitzmyer, J.A. 116
Floor, L. 9, 118
Flusser, D. 60
Fohrer, G. 122, 123
Förster, W. 122, 123, 133-35
Freedman, D.N. 36
Friedrich, G, 14, 47, 187, 188, 192
Fuller, R.H. 174
Funk, R.W. 96, 140, 158

Gärtner, B. 36-38, 40-51, 57, 58, 61
Gaster, T.H. 25
Giesebrecht, F. 185
Gingrich, F.W. 87, 121, 124, 156-58,
  174
Glombitza, O. 125
Goodenough, E.R. 69

Goodman, M. 64
Goppelt, L. 160, 162, 164, 169
Gowie, A.E. 97
Grässer, E. 9, 110, 125, 136, 175, 176,
  179, 180, 203
Gray, G.B. 14, 15, 17
Green, D.E. 94
Greenfield, J.C. 36
Greeven, H. 136
Gressmann, H. 66
Grieve, A. 114
Griffiths, J.G. 75
Grundmann, W. 97
Guelich, R. 186
Gunneweg, A.H.J. 14
Gutbrod, W. 96
Guthrie, D. 180
Guthrie, S.C. 87
Gyllenberg, R. 164

Haase, W. 74
Hagner, D.A. 105, 121, 135, 167, 170,
  171, 174
Hahn, F. 82
Hall, C.A.M. 87
Haran, M. 14, 17
Häring, T. 185, 189
Harris, R. 28
Harrisville, R.A. 10
Hastings, J. 13
Hatch, E. 23, 94, 151
Hauck, F. 95
Heathcote, A.W. 100
Héring, J. 100, 106, 120, 130, 145, 165
Hoekema, A.A. 186, 187
Hofius, O. 10, 88, 103, 104, 122, 142-
  44, 147, 154, 155, 159-65, 170,
  173, 177, 178, 180, 181, 202-204
Horbury, W. 142
Howard, W. 99
Hübner, H. 96, 102
Hughes, P.E. 121, 154, 167, 169-71,
  174, 180
Hunzinger, C.-H. 129
Hurst, L.D. 171

Jenni, E. 94, 150

## Index of Authors

Jeremias, J. 31-34, 87, 88, 103, 111, 126, 196
Jewett, R. 92, 119, 127, 128, 144
Johnsson, W.G. 95, 99, 137, 140, 142, 144, 145, 198

Kähler, M. 185
Käsemann, E. 10, 83, 102, 107, 109, 112, 135, 137, 138, 143, 147, 164, 181, 185, 187, 192, 195, 196, 204
Kettler, F.H. 25
Kingsbury, T.L. 96
Kittel, R. 14, 97, 196
Klappert, B. 203
Kleinknecht, H. 97
Klinzing, G. 38-59, 63
Koester, H. 71, 79, 80, 205
Kögel, J. 185, 187, 188, 191, 192, 195, 196
Kraft, H. 86
Kraus, H.-J. 14, 18
Krodel, G. 174
Kuhn, H.-W. 38, 42, 56
Kuhn, K.G. 46, 48, 53, 55
Kühlewein, J. 94
Kümmel, W.G. 203
Kuss, O. 82, 101, 109, 111, 120, 144, 145, 173, 203

Ladd, G.E. 186
LaSor, W.S. 40
Laub, F. 131, 162, 164, 187, 196
Laubach, F. 89
Lenski, R.C.H. 120
Leskow, T. 87
Levine, B.A. 36, 59, 60, 63
Lindars, B. 199, 202
Link, H.-G. 25
Loader, W.R.G. 82, 83, 159, 160, 163-68, 172, 174, 175, 182, 185-90, 192-94, 196-98, 200
Lohse, E. 72, 76, 78, 88
Lombard, H.A. 203
Luck, U. 83
Lünemann, G. 154, 157, 161, 167, 169, 170, 173, 177, 178, 180, 187, 192,1 96
Lütgert, W. 185

Maier, J. 36, 42, 48-50, 55, 59-63
Marcus, R. 65
Maurer, C. 87, 88, 98
McCullough, J.C. 9, 125
MacLeod, D.J. 202
McNamara, M. 63
MacRae, G.W. 159, 161, 179, 204
Melbourne, B.L. 86
Menzies, A. 13
Merk, O. 203
Metzger, B.M. 100, 163
Michaelis, W. 195
Michel, O. 83, 84, 86, 95, *et passim*
Milgrom, J. 20, 52, 59-63, 151
Milik, J.T. 52
Millar, F. 64
Mingana, A. 28
Moe, O. 102, 118, 124, 127, 162, 186, 187, 189, 191, 205
Moffatt, J. 86, 95, 97-99, 107-109, 111, 113, 115-17, 120, 124, 125, 128, 136, 154-57, 163, 180, 202, 203
Montefiore, H. 97, 99, 107, 120, 127, 171-74
Moore, G.F. 31, 33, 35
Moule, C.F.D. 167
Moulton, J.H. 99
Müller, K. 185
Müller, K.-H. 38
Murphy, R.E. 116

Nauck, W. 103, 125, 127
Newsom, C. 36, 37, 42, 43, 47, 50-52
Nickelsburg, G.W.E. 159
Niditch, S. 61
Nilsson, M.P. 72-81
Nock, A.D. 72, 74, 77, 78, 80
Noth, M. 14, 16, 151, 152

Owen, J. 130

Parsons, M.C. 87
Pedersen, J. 13, 15
Peterson, D. 91, 95-100, *et passim*
Ploeg, J. van der 192
Preisker, H. 95
Preuss, H.D. 94, 150
Pridik, K.-H. 96

Rad, G. von 54, 105, 203
Redpath, H.A. 23, 94, 151
Reicke, B. 87
Richards, K.H. 171
Riessler, P. 23
Rigaux, B. 185
Riggenbach, E. 83, 96-100, *et passim*
Ringgren, H. 94
Rissi, M. 83, 84, 86-89, *et passim*
Robinson, R.B. 27
Robinson, S.E. 27
Robinson, T.H. 120

Sabourin, L. 13, 15, 36, 37, 41, 45, 48, 50, 51
Sandberg, I.L. 10
Sanders, E.P. 29
Sanders, J.A. 36
Sandmel, S. 64, 67, 70
Sasse, H. 100
Schenk, G. 14, 17, 33, 34, 66, 67, 69, 83
Schick, E.A. 205
Schierse, F.J. 103, 107-10, 122, 137, 142, 144, 172, 187, 196
Schille, G. 83
Schlier, H. 109, 110
Schmidt, K.L. 95
Schmitz, O. 104-106, 147, 196
Schnackenburg, R. 202
Schneider, C. 93
Schneider, G. 96
Schneider, J. 92, 94, 100, 123, 150, 168, 169
Schodde, G.H. 127
Schröger, F. 107, 120, 127, 140, 160
Schubert, K. 47
Schultz, S. 95, 97
Schultze, M. 185
Schürer, E. 64, 66
Selbie, J.A. 13
Seeberg, A. 173, 177
Seesemann, H. 145, 146
Selbie, J.A. 13
Sharp, J.R. 203
Silberman, L.H. 39
Silva, M. 186, 187, 190, 192, 196, 199
Simpson, E.K. 177; 178

Smith, J. 87, 148, 162
Smith, M. 125
Smith, R.H. 96, 99, 103, 105, 114, 130, 138, 168, 169, 178
Snell, A. 163
Sowers, S.G. 66, 67, 192
Spicq, C. 9, 10, 97, 98, 106, 107, 110, 115, 119, 120, 123, 125, 126, 145-47, 156, 157, 171, 175, 178, 180, 181, 185, 189, 191
Stadelmann, A. 187
Stalker, D.M.G. 54
Stambaugh, J.E. 74, 76, 80
Stange, C. 185
Sowers, S. 64, 186
Stendahl, K. 159
Stewart, Z. 72, 75
Stott, W. 93, 151, 152, 154
Strack, H. 29, 30, 32, 33, 106, 141, 146, 157, 160, 204
Strathmann, H. 102, 118, 120, 129, 192
Strobel, J.J. 88, 111, 120, 154, 156, 170
Swetnam, J. 89, 92, 95, 160, 136, 194, 204

Teicher, J.L. 45
Temporini, H. 74
Theissen, G. 100, 131, 143, 144
Thiselton, A.C. 206
Thompson, H.J. 78
Thompson, J.W. 121, 141, 143, 159, 173, 204
Thüsing, W. 101, 123, 125, 127, 137
Thyen, H. 131, 132
Towner, P.H. 206
Traub, H. 162, 173
Tschackert, P. 185
Turner, N. 99

Unnik, W.C. van 110

Vanhoye, A. 21, 154, 159, 163, 170, 189, 207
Vaux, R. de 13, 15, 17, 19-23
Vermes, G. 44, 46, 64
Volz, P. 201

# Index of Authors

Wacholder, B.Z. 59, 60
Walter, N. 203
Weiss, B. 127
Weiss, K. 87, 99
Wellhausen, J. 13
Wenham, G.J. 152
Wenschkewitz, H. 26
Westcott, B.F. 87, 96-101, 104, 105, 107, 111, 114, 115, 119, 123, 126-29, 138, 139, 145-48, 152, 156, 157, 170, 175, 176, 180, 181, 187, 189
Westermann, C. 94
Whitaker, G.H. 65
Wikgren, A. 185, 187

Williamson, R. 10, 66-70, 127, 146, 194
Willis, J.T. 94
Wilson, E. 120, 127
Wilson, R.McL. 88, 143, 144, 186, 194, 203
Windisch, H. 83, 95-100, *et passim*
Wolfson, H.A. 70

Yadin, Y. 36, 46, 48, 59-62
Young, N.H. 151, 155, 156, 168, 171

Zimmerli, W. 112
Zimmermann, H. 82, 83, 95, 98, 100, 119, 121, 122, 156, 165, 170, 173, 175, 196, 200

JOURNAL FOR THE STUDY OF THE NEW TESTAMENT

Supplement Series

1   THE BARREN TEMPLE AND THE WITHERED TREE
    William R. Telford
2   STUDIA BIBLICA 1978
    II. PAPERS ON THE GOSPELS
    Edited by E.A. Livingstone
3   STUDIA BIBLICA 1978
    III. PAPERS ON PAUL AND OTHER NEW TESTAMENT AUTHORS
    Edited by E.A. Livingstone
4   FOLLOWING JESUS
    DISCIPLESHIP IN MARK'S GOSPEL
    Ernest Best
5   THE PEOPLE OF GOD
    Markus Barth
6   PERSECUTION AND MARTYRDOM IN THE THEOLOGY OF PAUL
    John S. Pobee
7   SYNOPTIC STUDIES
    THE AMPLEFORTH CONFERENCE 1982 AND 1983
    Edited by C.M. Tuckett
8   JESUS ON THE MOUNTAIN
    A STUDY IN MATTHEAN THEOLOGY
    Terence L. Donaldson
9   THE HYMNS OF LUKE'S INFANCY NARRATIVES
    THEIR ORIGIN, MEANING AND SIGNIFICANCE
    Stephen Farris
10  CHRIST THE END OF THE LAW
    ROMANS 10.4 IN PAULINE PERSPECTIVE
    Robert Badenas
12  THE LETTERS TO THE SEVEN CHURCHES OF ASIA IN THEIR LOCAL
    SETTING
    Colin J. Hemer
13  JESUS AND THE LAWS OF PURITY
    TRADITION HISTORY AND LEGAL HISTORY IN MARK 7
    Roger P. Booth
14  THE PASSION ACCORDING TO LUKE
    THE SPECIAL MATERIAL OF LUKE 22
    Marion L. Soards
15  HOSTILITY TO WEALTH IN THE SYNOPTIC GOSPELS
    T.E. Schmidt
16  MATTHEW'S COMMUNITY
    THE EVIDENCE OF HIS SPECIAL SAYINGS MATERIAL
    S.H. Brooks

17  THE PARADOX OF THE CROSS IN THE THOUGHT OF ST PAUL
    A.T. Hanson
18  HIDDEN WISDOM AND THE EASY YOKE
    WISDOM, TORAH AND DISCIPLESHIP IN MATTHEW 11.25–30
    C. Deutsch
19  JESUS AND GOD IN PAUL'S ESCHATOLOGY
    L.J. Kreitzer
20  LUKE: A NEW PARADIGM
    M.D. Goulder
21  THE DEPARTURE OF JESUS IN LUKE–ACTS
    THE ASCENSION NARRATIVES IN CONTEXT
    M.C. PARSONS
22  THE DEFEAT OF DEATH
    APOCALYPTIC ESCHATOLOGY IN 1 CORINTHIANS 15 AND ROMANS 5
    M.C. De Boer
23  PAUL THE LETTER-WRITER
    AND THE SECOND LETTER TO TIMOTHY
    M. Prior
24  APOCALYPTIC AND THE NEW TESTAMENT
    ESSAYS IN HONOR OF J. LOUIS MARTYN
    Edited by J. Marcus & M.L. Soards
25  THE UNDERSTANDING SCRIBE
    MATTHEW AND THE APOCALYPTIC IDEAL
    D.E. Orton
26  WATCHWORDS
    MARK 13 IN MARKAN ESCHATOLOGY
    T. Geddert
27  THE DISCIPLES ACCORDING TO MARK
    MARKAN REDACTION IN CURRENT DEBATE
    C.C. Black
28  THE NOBLE DEATH
    GRAECO-ROMAN MARTYROLOGY AND
    PAUL'S CONCEPT OF SALVATION
    D. Seeley
29  ABRAHAM IN GALATIANS
    EPISTOLARY AND RHETORICAL CONTEXTS
    G.W. Hansen
30  EARLY CHRISTIAN RHETORIC AND 2 THESSALONIANS
    F.W. Hughes
31  THE STRUCTURE OF MATTHEW'S GOSPEL
    A STUDY IN LITERARY DESIGN
    D.R. Bauer
32  PETER AND THE BELOVED DISCIPLE
    FIGURES FOR A COMMUNITY IN CRISIS
    K.B. Quast

33  MARK'S AUDIENCE
    THE LITERARY AND SOCIAL SETTING OF MARK 4.11–12
    M.A. Beavis
34  THE GOAL OF OUR INSTRUCTION
    THE STRUCTURE OF THEOLOGY AND ETHICS IN THE PASTORAL
    EPISTLES
    P.H. Towner
35  THE PROVERBS OF JESUS
    ISSUES OF HISTORY AND RHETORIC
    A.P. Winton
36  THE STORY OF CHRIST IN THE ETHICS OF PAUL
    AN ANALYSIS OF THE FUNCTION OF THE HYMNIC MATERIAL
    IN THE PAULINE CORPUS
    S.E. Fowl
37  PAUL AND JESUS
    COLLECTED ESSAYS
    A.J.M. Wedderburn
38  MATTHEW'S MISSIONARY DISCOURSE
    A LITERARY CRITICAL ANALYSIS
    D.J. Weaver
39  FAITH AND OBEDIENCE IN ROMANS
    A STUDY IN ROMANS 1–4
    G.N. Davies
40  IDENTIFYING PAUL'S OPPONENTS
    THE QUESTION OF METHOD IN 2 CORINTHIANS
    J.L. Sumney
41  HUMAN AGENTS OF COSMIC POWER IN HELLENISTIC
    JUDAISM AND THE SYNOPTIC TRADITION
    M.E. Mills
42  MATTHEW'S INCLUSIVE STORY
    A STUDY IN THE NARRATIVE RHETORIC OF THE FIRST GOSPEL
    D.B. Howell
43  JESUS, PAUL AND TORAH
    COLLECTED ESSAYS
    H. Räisänen
44  THE NEW COVENANT IN HEBREWS
    S. Lehne
45  THE RHETORIC OF ROMANS
    ARGUMENTATIVE CONSTRAINT AND STRATEGY AND PAUL'S
    'DIALOGUE WITH JUDAISM'
    N. Elliot
46  THE LAST SHALL BE FIRST
    THE RHETORIC OF REVERSAL IN LUKE
    J.O. York

47  JAMES AND THE 'Q' SAYINGS OF JESUS
    Patrick J. Hartin
48  TEMPLUM AMICITIAE:
    ESSAYS ON THE SECOND TEMPLE PRESENTED TO ERNST BAMMEL
    Edited by W. Horbury
49  PROLEPTIC PRIESTS
    AN INVESTIGATION OF THE PRIESTHOOD IN HEBREWS
    J.M. Scholer
50  PERSUASIVE ARTISTRY
    STUDIES IN NEW TESTAMENT RHETORIC
    IN HONOR OF GEORGE A. KENNEDY
    Edited by Duane F. Watson
51  THE AGENCY OF THE APOSTLE
    A DRAMATISTIC ANALYSIS OF PAUL'S RESPONSES TO CONFLICT IN
    2 CORINTHIANS
    Jeffrey A. Crafton
52  REFLECTIONS OF GLORY
    PAUL'S POLEMICAL USE OF THE MOSES–DOXA TRADITION IN
    2 CORINTHIANS 3.1-18
    Linda L. Belleville
53  REVELATION AND REDEMPTION AT COLOSSAE
    Thomas J. Sappington
54  THE DEVELOPMENT OF EARLY CHRISTIAN PNEUMATOLOGY
    WITH SPECIAL REFERENCE TO LUKE–ACTS
    Robert P. Menzies
55  THE PURPOSE OF ROMANS
    A COMPARATIVE LETTER INVESTIGATION
    L. Ann Jervis
56  THE SON OF THE MAN IN THE GOSPEL OF JOHN
    Delbert Burkett
57  ESCHATOLOGY AND THE COVENANT
    A COMPARISON OF 4 EZRA AND ROMANS 1-11
    Bruce W. Longenecker
58  'NONE BUT THE SINNERS'
    RELIGIOUS CATEGORIES IN THE GOSPEL OF LUKE
    David A. Neale